EMMA
and
JOSEPH
Their Divine Mission

OTHER BOOKS AND BOOKS ON CASSETTE BY GRACIA N. JONES:

*Priceless Gifts: Celebrating the Holidays
with Joseph and Emma Smith*

At the dedication of the Kirtland Temple, the Prophet Joseph Smith prayed:
*Oh Lord, remember thy servant Joseph Smith, Jun.,
and all his afflictions and persecutions . . .
that he hath sincerely striven to do thy will.*

*Have mercy, O Lord, upon his wife and children,
that they may be exalted in thy presence,
and preserved by thy fostering hand.*

*Have mercy upon all their immediate connections,
that their prejudices may be broken up and swept away as with a flood;
that they may be converted and redeemed with Israel,
and know that thou art God.*
(Doctrine and Covenants 109:68-70)
I dedicate this book to the purpose of this precious prayer.

Cover painting *Ye Shall Be a Comfort* © Liz Lemon Swindle, Repartee & Foundation Arts

Published by Covenant Communications, Inc.
American Fork, Utah

Printed in the United States of America
First Printing: August 1999

06 05 04 03 02 01 00   10 9 8 7 6 5 4

ISBN 1-57734-529-0

Library of Congress Cataloging-in-Publication Data
Jones, Gracia N.
  Emma and Joseph : their divine mission / Gracia N. Jones
      p.   cm.
  Includes bibliographical references.
  ISBN 1-57734-529-0
  1. Smith, Emma Hale. 2. Smith, Joseph, 1805-1844. 3. Mormons--United
  States Biography.   I. Title.
BX8695.S515J66 1999
289.3' 092'2--dc21
[B]   99-26715
                                                              CIP

EMMA and JOSEPH

Their Divine Mission

GRACIA N. JONES

Covenant Communications, Inc.

ACKNOWLEDGMENTS

Many people have contributed greatly to this book. There are too many to name them all individually. First, I wish to thank all those who shared documents, insights, and perceptions with me. You know who you are.

Much of the material in this book appeared in my first book, *Emma's Glory and Sacrifice: A Testimony,* published by Homestead Publishing and Distribution, Hurricane, Utah, 1987. My love and everlasting appreciation go to Janice and Van DeMille. Van is a descendant of Joseph Knight Senior, and as true a friend to Joseph's descendants as his ancestor was to the Prophet. Janice did the major work of preparing *Emma's Glory and Sacrifice* for publication. Her sacrifice will never be forgotten by our family. I also appreciate Jules Kreyling for all he did in printing that first book.

Equally important is the contribution made by Michael and Darcy Kennedy. Michael is the president of our Joseph Smith, Jr., Family Organization, which in large measure inspired the original effort to tell this story for our family.

I appreciate the keepers of historical documents housed in the following archives: The Reorganized Church of Latter Day Saints, in Independence, Mo.; The Church of Jesus Christ of Latter-day Saints, in Salt Lake City, Utah; and Special Collections in the Harold B. Lee Library, Brigham Young University, in Provo, Utah. I am so grateful for the friendly assistance I received in all of these locations.

I appreciate my husband, C. Ivor Jones. He has endured a lot to make it possible for me to write: eating late meals or fast-food instead of home cooked, staying home to work while I travel for research, and putting up with me burning the midnight oil so I can meet publishing deadlines. He also has driven hundreds of miles with me while I meet and interview people to gather data. His good nature, patience, and tact make friends for him wherever he goes. Often, when he has attended conferences and firesides with me, he has been called upon to bear his testimony. His powerful testimony of the gospel has inspired many.

In a special way, I appreciate our family—our children and grandchildren—who give us constant encouragement and support. It is for them, and their children and grandchildren, this story needs to be told.

I appreciate my good friend Buddy Youngreen, who tutored me in my early attempts to discover the testimony of my great-great-grandparents. His encouragement has been a constant support and has kept me going when discouragement threatened. He taught me that every story has a human side that cannot be taken out of context of its time and place without distorting the truth. This has been invaluable in my nearly forty years of sifting facts and fables concerning Emma and Joseph Smith.

I appreciate Valerie Holladay, and the staff at Covenant Communications, without whose expert services this book could not have been produced. My sincere thanks to Valerie for the inspired and knowledgeable editing she has done on this book.

Most of all, I am thankful for Emma and Joseph Smith—for the lives they lived and the service they rendered to mankind—and all those who have walked in their footsteps to further the work they began.

In most cases, the original spelling and punctuation have been retained to give a flavor for the times and the individual quoted. Some corrections have been made where it was felt necessary to clarify the information given.

For any errors in detail or perception in this book, I take full responsibility.

Alexander Hale Smith family, about 1898. Back row: Don Alvin, Coral (author's grandmother), Joseph George, Emma Belle, Arthur Marion. Front row: Vida Elizabeth, Alexander Hale Smith, Elizabeth Kendall Smith, Frederick Alexander. Not pictured: Ina Inez and Eva Grace. Family photograph.

PREFACE

Although it seems I always knew our family had a distant relationship to a man named Joseph Smith, in my branch of the family it was never discussed. As a youngster, I was admonished not to reveal this relationship. No explanation was given. It would be years before I would discover that this admonition was born of fear, not shame.

Generations of our family had endured persecution, including my own mother, who was born in Southern Iowa. In childhood, she had endured ridicule from young classmates at school who taunted her about being related to "Joe Smith." She had no information with which to combat this ridicule. Her mother, Coral Smith Horner, the youngest daughter of Alexander Hale Smith, the third of Joseph and Emma's four sons, did not teach her children the doctrine, nor educate them in the religious tradition in which she had been reared, that is, The Reorganized Church of Jesus Christ of Latter Day Saints (RLDS). Whether she did not know the doctrine or just did not know how to discuss it, still she held her grandfather's memory in reverence and conveyed to her children a respect for him, if not adherence to religious dogmas. Apparently she did not know the full story of her grandfather's vision. She told her children only that her grandfather had "seen an angel."

When the family left Iowa for the West, in the early 1930s, eventually settling in northwestern Montana, they were effectively cut off from all Latter Day Saint influence. Subsequent research has revealed that nearly every branch of Joseph and Emma's descendants share the same ambivalence my mother did—generally not rejecting the belief that Joseph Smith experienced something remarkable, but definitely determined to keep the relationship a closely held family secret.

At that time, in 1955, as far as I have been able to determine, there were no direct descendants of Joseph and Emma in the LDS Church.

My first encounter with the story of Joseph Smith's vision came when I began babysitting for the Lederer family, who happened to be members of The Church of Jesus Christ of Latter-day Saints (LDS). The mother of the family, Dee, began telling me about Joseph Smith, whom she called "a prophet." My understanding of religious terms was limited, and I was puzzled by this information. Of course, I eventually revealed to her that Joseph Smith was the name of my great-great-grandfather. With awe, this woman realized, as I did not, what a remarkable encounter this was.

When Dee discovered that I knew nothing about the Restoration, or the history of the Church, or even of Joseph Smith himself, she began to tell me of the amazing things that had come to pass through the efforts of my ancestor. Naturally, I was astonished. I immediately challenged my mother, asking, "Why has the family kept this a secret for so long?" Mother had no answers to give. She and my father had no background knowledge, only a vague uneasiness concerning the subject of Mormonism. In fact, I had never heard the word "Mormon" spoken in my home until I began babysitting for Dee Lederer. At that time, my mother urged me not to tell her of my relationship. "She'll think you should be a Mormon," my mother told me.

My desire to learn more about the subject brought great consternation to our household. Soon after I began asking questions, my parents' Protestant friends enjoined them not to let me have anything to do with those "Mormons"!

However, my parents were tolerant, open-minded people, always encouraging their children to learn about everything. While they wanted to protect me from hurt, they also wanted to be true to their idea that it is good to learn of all things; they had an innate abhorrence for any kind of prejudice or bigotry. So they allowed me to take the lessons from the missionaries, with the admonition that I was not to "get involved" with the religion (which is about like being told you can go swimming, but don't go near the water!). Later on, when I expressed a desire to be baptized, my father refused, saying, "Not under my roof."

While his refusal was very distressful to me, I understood that my father was not expressing antipathy towards the Mormons. It was just that he was concerned that I was too young to know my own mind.

However, I had had a remarkable experience of my own, which fueled my persistence. It occurred when I first met the missionaries.

Dee Lederer informed the missionaries in the area of my relationship to Joseph Smith. These two young men, Elder James Waldron and Elder Dean Richins, were serving full-time missions for the Church in Montana. They were eager to present me with a copy of the Book of Mormon. Dee invited me to her home, saying, "The missionaries want to give you a gift." Naturally, I was curious and interested. I could not imagine what they wanted to give me.

When I walked into the room, one young man handed me a small black book. He said. "This is the Book of Mormon. It was translated by the gift and power of God, by your great-great-grandfather, and it is true!"

As my hands closed around the book, a tremendous thrill went through my entire being. It seemed as if there was a light inside me, and in my mind I distinctly heard the words, "It's true! It's really true!"

This sensation filled every particle of my soul. I KNEW it was true.

Taking the book home, I found myself consumed with interest, curiosity, and excitement. As I read, my mind was enlightened to understand what I was reading—a sacred record of the Lord's prophets who ministered among a people led by the hand of the Lord out of Jerusalem, and across the ocean to the Americas, six hundred years before the birth of Christ. The record told of events spanning many centuries of the doings of these people, their building of a great civilization, their wars, and eventual destruction through their rejection of the laws of God, which had been given to them through their prophets. I felt it was a remarkable book, and I was delighted with it.

However, when my parents found out what I was reading, they were not delighted; they were worried. They would not listen to the missionaries, and they would not read the Book of Mormon. Nevertheless, they were cordial to those young men, and they allowed me to take the missionary discussions, in order to satisfy my curiosity.

Of course, having the burning testimony of the Spirit, once I understood the importance of the Church and the need for baptism, I wanted very much to be baptized. When my father refused his permission, I had to wait until my eighteenth birthday. After I left home, I was baptized a member of the LDS Church on 17 March

1956. I was the first descendant to join the Church and stay, in over a hundred years. With the passing of the years since, a few members of my immediate family have joined the Church, including my mother, a sister, and several cousins. My children and grandchildren are members. The posterity of the Prophet Joseph and Emma are scattered worldwide. Members of the Smith family who have been baptized into the LDS Church number more than 100. Many have received their temple endowments, and many have served, or are currently serving, full-time missions.

During all the years since my baptism, I have diligently sought for information with which to bring my finite mind to the degree of knowledge to match the magnificent witness I experienced the day I received my first copy of the Book of Mormon. With all I have studied, with all I have discovered, I have identified the source from which the burning testimony came. Without a doubt, I know this witness came by the power of the Holy Ghost.

With the passing of the years, I have often been asked to share my testimony. It has been easy because it is so very strong within me. But it has not been easy to understand what happened to our family—how we came to be lost from the Church. Over time, I have come to understand that process—how after Joseph and Hyrum's martyrdom in 1844, Emma, with her five young children, remained in Illinois, as Brigham Young led the bulk of the Church membership on the long westward trek to settle at last in the Salt Lake Valley.

Because Emma did not go west, a tradition developed and was passed down among Church members in Utah, causing many to have mixed feelings toward her. Some defend her, others view her as an apostate.

After I joined the Church, I received some strange reactions from people when I told them I was from Emma's lineage. Some people didn't believe me because they thought she didn't have any living children. Others expressed their great esteem for the Prophet, but then dismissed Emma with comments like, "Poor Emma. What will become of her?" Some declared that because she rejected the truth, after all she suffered during Joseph's lifetime, Joseph would surely have to go to hell to get her.

I hardly knew how to deal with these mixed attitudes. Not having been raised with any knowledge about either Joseph or Emma, I was in the dark, often swept along with vague feelings of confusion and doubt. I was frequently asked to explain family matters of which I knew nothing.

With my curiosity stimulated by the conflict and mystery surrounding Emma, I was motivated to write because of my growing recognition of her enormous contribution to the success of Joseph Smith's mission and the marvelous events of his life which I learned when I was a young woman.

Thus began my great pilgrimage to uncover the past. It has been a labor of love, a sacred journey, undertaken to discover for myself what there is to know regarding the incredible experiences of this remarkable couple. The Prophet's vision of the Father and the Son is well known. His work of restoration of scriptures, doctrines, and ordinances, and establishing the church organization are documented fact, but what of Emma? What did she believe about the Restoration and her husband's prophetic calling?

My first effort to write about Emma was published in 1987, under the title *Emma's Glory and Sacrifice: A Testimony.* This book is now out of print. Next came an article in the *Ensign,* in August 1992. This article, "My Great-Great-Grandmother Emma Hale Smith" contains a thorough documentation of significant events in her life and is the most accurate in terms of dates available in the Church today. The material in this present book, *Emma and Joseph: Their Divine Mission,* encompasses all the material of my first book, but I have expanded, revised, and corrected the text, bringing to this new work an added dimension born of more mature observation as well as further research. In this book, I have added a good deal more detail and many more personal insights. It is my fond hope that all who read this book will experience what I have in writing it.

While this book is historical in nature, it is by no means a comprehensive history. Rather it is a very personal look at the life and experiences of Joseph Smith, the founder of The Church of Jesus Christ of Latter-day Saints, and his wife, Emma Hale Smith Bidamon. It is the product of many years of research and many long hours of pondering over every document and story I could find about my great-great-grandparents. The research process was a thrilling experience which has brought me great inspiration and an incredible personal witness of the truth regarding the restoration of the gospel, which came through the Prophet Joseph Smith. And even more, I obtained a deeper understanding of Emma's role in these events. My appreciation for her sacrifices and contributions overflowed.

One of the most important things my research has taught me is that Church history is not a linear chronology, from New York, to Ohio, to Missouri, to Illinois. Instead, it is like a hub of a wheel, with spokes going out from the center—rolling along as events transpired, so that the center of the wheel was always located where the Prophet Joseph was situated, whether that was in a cabin, a farmhouse, a covered wagon, a filthy jailhouse, or a temple. Events in New York and Ohio overlap, events in Ohio and Missouri overlap, with events in Illinois overlapping them all, to some extent.

The events in the early stages of the Restoration also overlap present-day events. As the spokes of the wheel extend worldwide, every mission, district, stake, ward, and branch, no matter where it is located on this globe, draws upon the events described within this book. The Prophet Joseph Smith and his wife, Emma, are at the very heart of the story of the Restoration. The glorious fruit of their divine mission is available to every person who comes in contact with the restored gospel.

In writing about the activities of my ancestors, I believe I offer a unique view of the history of the Church. For it is a very personal history, one devoted to the unfolding of the spiritual and temporal experiences with which Joseph and Emma were involved.

Although I have many people to thank for their encouragement, information, and insights, I alone am responsible for the conclusions drawn herein. There is no official sanction given to this material just because of who I am. I am as liable as anyone to make mistakes. While I have a tremendous respect—yes, I will say devotion—to my ancestors, I cannot claim much family-inherited information about them. The family is largely devoid of any previously undisclosed valid facts. A few family members possess artifacts, which they treasure without comprehending why; they are often uncommonly emotional about them. Many are steeped in vague presumptions and unnamed fears of even discussing Joseph Smith's work. In this generation, all people, in and out of the family, are dependent, as I am, upon documentary research and spiritual direction for any knowledge we gain about Joseph and Emma.

What I have written herein is drawn from extensive study of documents, but in some instances, my insights rest upon feelings inspired during moments when the veil seemed very thin. From such brief, but profound, moments, I have conclusively recognized one great overshadowing truth—none of the historical characters discussed in these pages is actually "dead and gone." All are as alive as you and I, yet in another realm.

This I know: Emma is not a sepia-toned picture on a wall, Joseph is not a stern, dark-suited man with high collar and cravat. Though their bones lie in Nauvoo, under a granite tomb, their beings are vitally alive in the present. Even now, they are actively engaged on the other side of the veil, doing the work they loved in life. In the presence of the great Mediator, even the Lord Jesus Christ, differences and conflicts have long since been resolved by those who served sincerely, though imperfectly, during their lifetime. We must never forget that they made the sacrifice and they laid the foundation.

Emma and Joseph: Their Divine Mission is the testimony of one of the Prophet Joseph and Emma's descendants who has come to know and love them and the great work they performed. I hope those who read this book will do the same.

G. N. J.

TABLE OF CONTENTS

Emma Hale Smith in her riding habit.
Watercolor by Sutcliffe Maudsley 1842. Courtesy of Buddy Youngreen.

CHAPTER 1

Preparation for a Sacred Mission

June 1844

With trembling hands, Emma caressed the cold, still face of her dead husband. In lantern-lit shadows, the aspect of her anguished countenance struck pity into the heart of every onlooker. The Mansion House on Water Street, in Nauvoo, Illinois, seemed to reverberate with her cries of agony and bewilderment, mingled with the sobbing lamentations of her children.[1] Those nearby strained to hear her muffled words. As her entire life had been since she married Joseph Smith, her mourning was a public event.

1826

Emma Hale first came to the notice of Joseph Smith when he went with his friend Joseph Knight, Sr., to the Hale home. The Hales lived near Harmony, not far from the Susquehanna River, which wends its way through the green rolling hills of northern Pennsylvania. In later years Joseph would speak of Emma as "the wife of my youth and the choice of my heart."[2] In the following account, as described by Joseph Knight, Sr., it would seem that she may also have been chosen by revelation.

While boarding with the Knight family and working in their grist mill, Joseph confided that he had been given a divine commission, by an angelic messenger, to bring forth an ancient record engraved on golden plates. The Knights were vitally interested in the things Joseph shared with them of his visits with the angel during the previous three years, although it is not known exactly how much Joseph may have revealed to them. It was apparently sufficient that they looked forward with anticipation to the time when the record would actually be brought forth. Father Knight related that Joseph said he had asked the angel, "When can I have [the gold plates]?" The answer was the following year on 22 September "if you bring the right person with you." Joseph said, "Who is the right Person?" The answer was "your oldest Brother [Alvin]."3

Father Knight continued:

> But before September Came his oldest Brother died. Then he was disappointed and did not [k]now what to do. But the 22nd day of September next he went to the place and the personage appeared and told him he could not have it now. But the 22nd day of September next he might have the Book if he brought with him the right person. Joseph says, "who is the right person?" The answer was "you will know." Father Knight said Joseph told him that by revelation he "found it was Emma Hale, Daughter of Old Mr. Hale of Pensylvany," a girl that he had seen Before, for he had [been] down there before with me . . . I furnished him with a horse and Cutter to go and see his girl Down to Mr. Hales."4

With encouragement and help from the Knights, Joseph proceeded to court Emma Hale, but when he asked her father for her hand in marriage, Isaac Hale rejected his proposal. Isaac did not approve of Joseph's occupation as a laborer. He considered Joseph to be poorly educated and not a suitable mate for his daughter.5 Mr. Hale was undoubtedly dubious about the prospects of his daughter finding happiness and security with a man who believed himself to have been called of God as a latter-day prophet.

Family tradition among their descendants carries a brightly romantic impression of the relationship that developed between the charismatic young Joseph—handsome, fair-haired, with blue eyes and baby pink coloring—and the tall, slender girl with olive skin, dark brown hair, and snapping brown eyes.

Many years later she told her grown children, "I had no intention of marrying when I left home; but during my visit at Mr.

Stowells, your father visited me there. My folks were bitterly opposed to him . . . [But] being importuned by your father, aided by Mr. Stowell, and preferring to marry him than any one I knew, I consented."[6] They were married 18 January 1827, by Squire Tarbill, at his home in South Bainbridge, New York. Joseph was twenty-one. Emma was twenty-two.

To this day, we might wonder what made Emma prefer Joseph above all other young men she might have known and what made him prefer her. No doubt he would have been impressed by her native intelligence. A fun-loving person himself, he almost certainly would have been attracted by her quick wit and sense of humor.[7] In addition, her culinary skill must surely have been noticed by Joseph when he boarded at the Hale home. Finally, her deep religious convictions would have undoubtedly made a profound impression on him.

Whatever attraction drew them together, it was sufficient to hold them through unrelenting persecution, trials, and privations, committed to each other and to their sacred mission, from the day of their marriage, until the day seventeen and a half years later, when on 27 June 1844, Joseph was felled by assassins' bullets.

Born of Choice Lineage

Emma and Joseph shared a common heritage, being descendants of no less than seven passengers on the historic ship *Mayflower*.[8]

John Fiske, in his *Beginnings of New England*, reported that the Plymouth settlers were ". . . drawn from the sturdiest part of English stock. In all history there has been no other instance of colonization so exclusively effected by picked and chosen men."[9] William Stoughton, in his election sermon of 1668, said, "God sifted a whole nation that he might send choice grain over into the wilderness."[10] The compelling motive for these pilgrims coming was to gain freedom of worship for themselves according to their own interpretation of the teachings of the Bible.

Edward Johnson, in his *Wonder-Working Providence of Zion's Savior in New England*, said, "The Lord Christ intends to achieve greater matter by this little handful than the world is aware of."[11]

Although they probably never knew it, both Joseph Smith and Emma Hale could have traced their lineage back to a common ancestor, John Howland, whose life was miraculously spared during the stormy Atlantic crossing of the *Mayflower* in 1620.

In Bradford's *History of Plymouth Plantation 1606-1646*, the story of this dramatic event is recorded in charming old English. The spelling is retained here to give the reader a feeling for the language of the time. Some explanations have been added to clarify meaning.

> In sundrie of thee stormes the winds were so fierce and ye seas so high as they could not beare a knote of sale, but were forced to hull for diverce days togither. And in one of them, as they thus lay at hull in a mighty storme, a lustie young man (called John Howland), coming upon some occasion above ye grattings, was, with a seele of ye shippe, throwne into ye sea; but it pleased God [that] he caught hold of ye tope-saile hallards which hung over-board, and rane out at length; yet he held his hould (though he was sundrie fadomes under water) till he was hald up by ye rope to ye water, and then with a boat hooke and other means got into ye shipe again and his life was saved; and though he was something ill with it, yet he lived many years after, and became a profitable member of both church and commonewealth.[12]

In fact, John Howland married Elizabeth Tilley, one of the few survivors of the first terrible winter in Plymouth Colony. One cannot help marveling at the twist of destiny that brought these pilgrims through their ordeals to produce two separate family lines, which converge eight generations later, bringing these very distant cousins, Joseph Smith and Emma Hale, together as contemporaries and key participants in one of the most significant events to take place in the history of the world—the restoration of the gospel of Jesus Christ.

Who Is Emma Hale?

Born 10 July 1804, in Harmony, Pennsylvania, Emma was the seventh child and third daughter in a family of nine children (five boys and four girls), born to Isaac and Elizabeth Lewis Hale. Her mother was a sister of a respected Methodist minister. Her father, a well-established farmer and a skilled hunter, was also a veteran of the Revolutionary War.[13]

The Hales, by their industry, enjoyed many cultural and social advantages. Emma was well educated for a girl of her day, and was also a skilled horsewoman. She was well accomplished in the womanly arts of spinning, weaving, and sewing. She was fond of her brothers and sisters, and throughout her tempestuous life she tried to maintain contact with them. She and her father had enjoyed an especially close bond since she was a little girl. According to Michael Bartlett Morse, husband to Emma's sister, Tryal, Isaac overheard six-year-old Emma praying for him and was so moved by her childish faith, that he forsook deism and embraced Christianity.[14] The family were faithful worshipers in the Methodist congregation in Harmony through Emma's growing-up years.

Emma's family never understood her devotion to Joseph Smith and the religious movement he founded. Through her marriage to him and her loyalty to his mission, she became an outcast from her family circle.

Who Is Joseph Smith?

Joseph Smith was born to Joseph and Lucy Mack Smith, on 23 December 1805, in Sharon, Vermont. His parents lived for a time on a farm near Sharon, then moved to several areas before settling in Norwich, Vermont, where they obtained a farm for themselves, and strove to make a living from it. Three years in a row the weather was so cold they could not harvest a crop, so they were forced to look for a better location. In 1816, when Joseph was ten years old, his father moved the family to the small town of Palmyra, in upstate New York. Eventually he purchased land and built a log house in the nearby community of Farmington, which later became Manchester.

The Smiths were soon caught up in the religious revivals that were sweeping through the area at that time. They frequently attended camp meetings where they made a little extra money selling refreshments among the thousands of people who gathered for the revival meetings. After listening to sermons given by various traveling preachers of Baptist, Methodist, or Presbyterian persuasion, the family was caught up in the question of which religion they should join. Joseph Sr. held himself aloof from all churches, but Mother Lucy, Sophronia, and Hyrum joined the Presbyterian Church.[15] Fourteen-year-old Joseph sincerely wanted to know which of all the contending denominations was right and which he should join in order to receive salvation and forgiveness for his sins.

One day, in the spring of 1820, while reading in the Bible, Joseph came across the words, "If any of you lack wisdom, let him ask of God, that giveth to all men liberally and upbraideth not; and it shall be given him. But let him ask in faith, nothing wavering."[16] The words struck deep into his heart, and he concluded that he would do as the scripture advised.

Early one morning, intent upon finding out the truth, he set out across the meadow behind the log cabin and headed for the wood lot. There, making sure he was alone, he knelt, in a grove of trees, to offer up a heartfelt prayer to God. As soon as he began to pray, a terrible darkness came over him. He felt as though he were being smothered—crushed by some invisible power. In horror and despair, he called upon God for deliverance. Suddenly, he saw a brilliant light descending out of heaven. He said it was so bright he wondered that the leaves on the trees were not consumed. In the shaft of light he saw two personages. One of them spoke to him, calling him by name. Then, indicating the other personage, he said, "Joseph, this is my Beloved Son, hear ye him."[17]

Later, Joseph would refer to this experience as his "first vision"— the first of many face-to-face communications he would have with heavenly beings, including his Heavenly Father, his Savior, Jesus Christ, and many prophets and apostles of old, who would tutor him in his awesome responsibility of laying the foundation for the dispensation of the fullness of times.

In this first vision he was told not to join any of the religious groups. The Lord said, "They draw near to me with their lips, but their hearts are far from me, they teach for doctrines the commandments of men, having a form of godliness, but they deny the power thereof."[18] Joseph was told to wait and he would be given further instruction. He left the grove satisfied, as he had been assured that his sins were forgiven, and in due time the Lord would have a work for him to do.

Joseph told his family of his experience, and they believed him. He also told a minister with whom he had become well acquainted. This minister was enraged and told Joseph his vision came from the devil—that God did not talk to mortals in these latter days. Soon Joseph and his family became subjects of ridicule and furious efforts to persuade Joseph to denounce his claim. His response reveals his sincere conviction that what he had seen was real.

> I had beheld a vision. I have thought since, that I felt much like Paul, when he made his defense before King Agrippa, and related the account of the vision he had when he saw a light, and heard a voice; but still there were but few who believed him; some said he was dishonest, others said he was mad; and he was ridiculed and reviled. But all this did not destroy the reality of his vision. . . . So it was with me. I had actually seen a light, and in the midst of that light I saw two Personages, and they did in reality speak to me; and though I was hated and persecuted for saying that I had seen a vision, yet it was true; and while they were persecuting me, reviling me, and speaking all manner of evil against me falsely for so saying, I was led to say in my heart: Why persecute me for telling the truth? I have actually seen a vision; and who am I that I can withstand God, or why does the world think to make me deny what I have actually seen? For I had seen a vision; I knew it, and I knew that God knew it, and I could not deny it, neither dared I do it; at least I knew that by so doing I would offend God, and come under condemnation.
>
> I had now got my mind satisfied so far as the sectarian world was concerned—that it was not my duty to join with any of them, but to continue as I was until further directed. I had found the testimony of James to be true—that a man who lacked wisdom might ask of God, and obtain, and not be upbraided.[19]

Over the next three years, Joseph worked on his father's farm, and as a laborer wherever he could to help earn a living for the family. On the night of 21 September 1823, Joseph retired to his bed in the loft he shared with his younger brothers, determined in his heart that he would pray to know what the Lord might expect of him. He said he fully expected to receive a vision, as he previously had, and so he prayed, anticipating an answer. He was not disappointed.

As he prayed, a shaft of light suddenly came into the room, and there stood a glorious personage, an angel, who introduced himself as Moroni. He told Joseph he had lived ages ago upon the American continent, and was now resurrected, and had been sent from God to give him the information he was seeking. Moroni told Joseph God had a work for him to do; and that Joseph's name "should be had for good and evil among all nations, kindred and tongues, or that it should be both good and evil spoken of among all people."[20]

Joseph learned that centuries ago, Moroni had been charged to complete a sacred record which had been engraved on gold plates by his father, Mormon. Moroni told Joseph this record contained "an account of the former inhabitants of this continent, and the source from whence they sprang. . . . That the fulness of the everlasting Gospel was contained in it, as delivered by the Savior to the ancient inhabitants."[21] Moroni had been commanded to hide the record in the earth until the time came for it to come forth. Moroni said Joseph was chosen to translate and publish this record to the world. Moroni went on to quote many prophecies by Old Testament prophets concerning a prophet to come forth in the latter days to re-establish the gospel on the earth, and he indicated that these things were about to take place.[22] Joseph was to be that prophet.

The vision was repeated two times, and before Moroni left him the last time, he told Joseph to relate this experience to his father. When morning came, Joseph feared that his father would not believe him so he ignored the angel's directive and attempted to work in the field. He felt ill and started back to the house, but fell to the ground. There, Moroni came to him a fourth time, telling him he must tell his father. He also showed him in vision the place where the record was buried.[23]

Now the seventeen-year-old boy went to his father. Father Smith listened to his son's amazing experience, then urged him to go and do as the angel directed. Joseph went to a place near the top of a large, bare hill a few miles from the Smith farm. He recognized the place as the one he had seen in vision. Moroni met him there, showing him the golden plates and the Urim and Thummim (an instrument to be used for translating the record), but forbade Joseph to take the plates at that time.[24] Everything was returned to the stone box buried in the ground and hidden under a large flat stone. Joseph was admonished to return to that place on the same date a year from that time. This pattern was followed each year thereafter for the next four years, during which time the young prophet was given much instruction concerning his future work. Each year he went, expecting to receive the plates, but he did not obtain them until the fall of 1827.

After Joseph and Emma married, in January 1827, the young couple lived with Joseph's parents in their new house just down the road from the old log cabin where his brother Hyrum, and his lovely bride, Jerusha Barden, lived. Joseph and Emma had been married just eight months when the time finally came for him to obtain the record.

A Prophet of God

By her marriage to Joseph, Emma had unwittingly become the wife of the man God had chosen to head the dispensation of the fullness of times. No record has been found to reveal what Emma's feelings were concerning Joseph's prophetic gifts at the time of their marriage. However, the record does show—by her constancy through trial—Emma's steadfast conviction that he was a prophet of God.

The Bible dictionary defines a prophet as a *forthteller* as much as a *foreteller*. During the earthly career of Joseph Smith, there were moments of inspiration regarding the future, but his greatest energy went toward defining doctrine, restoring ordinances and lost scripture, adding many thousands of words to the cannon of inspired religious writings. There is every indication that Emma shared Joseph's values, and believed, as he did, that it was his lot to lay the foundation of the kingdom described by the prophet Daniel.[25]

History records the fulfillment of the promise made by the angel Moroni to the boy prophet, that his name would be had for good and evil through all nations and people of the world. John Taylor, a devoted friend, who would live to carry on the work after Joseph was gone, left this profound testimony:

Joseph Smith, the Prophet and Seer of the Lord, has done more, save Jesus only, for the salvation of men in this world, than any other man that ever lived in it. In the short space of twenty years, he has brought forth the Book of Mormon, which he translated by the gift and power of God, and has been the means of publishing it on two continents; has sent the fulness of the everlasting gospel, which it contained, to the four quarters of the earth; has brought forth the revelations and commandments which compose this book of Doctrine and Covenants, and many other wise documents and instructions for the benefit of the children of men; gathered many thousands of the Latter-day Saints, founded a great city, and left a fame and name that cannot be slain. He lived great, and he died great in the eyes of God and his people; and like most of the Lord's anointed in ancient times, has sealed his mission and his works with his own blood. . . .[26]

A Divine Mission

In 1842, after enduring years of persecution, privation and tribulation, Joseph had matured in his calling as a prophet while his wife, Emma, was acknowledged as the "Elect Lady"—president of the Female Relief Society. The *Times and Seasons*, a church newspaper, carried an editorial that painted a vivid picture of his prophetic mission, concerning both the future of the work in which they were engaged and the reaction of future generations to it.

The blessings of the Most High will rest upon our tabernacles, and our name will be handed down to future ages; our children will rise up and call us blessed; and generations yet unborn will dwell with peculiar delight upon the scenes that we have passed through, the privations that we have endured; the untiring zeal that we have manifested; the insurmountable difficulties that we have overcome in laying the foundation of a work that brought about the glory and blessings which they will realize; a work that God and angels have contemplated with delight, for generations past; that fired the souls of the ancient patriarchs and prophets—a work that is destined to bring about the destruction of the powers of darkness, the renovation of the earth, the glory of God, and the salvation of the human family.[27]

At the time this editorial was written, Joseph and Emma had come a long way in laying the foundation of this great kingdom. In view of all they had accomplished, it seemed that they had every reason to hope for a long life and a prosperous future for themselves and the Church; yet, even then, Joseph was hinting to close associates that his work was nearing its completion, and Emma was wielding a fiercely loyal pen in his defense. Within two years, Joseph would be dead.

Just as the political and social rulers in Christ's day sought to purge their society of Christians, so did nineteenth-century Americans defy their own constitutional laws to attempt to rid themselves of a religious society they called "Mormons," a name they intended to be derogatory.[28]

As the flames of persecution singed the Saints' farms and homes, these driven and persecuted people took up their cross and blazed a trail across the winter prairie. Thousands of Mormons known to themselves and God as "Latter-day Saints" went by covered wagon, on horseback and on foot with handcarts; they danced and sang by campfires, left their fine possessions along the trail, and wept beside shallow graves. As the Saints left Nauvoo, they bid a last farewell to their prophet's widow—for Emma would not go west.

Emma lived her life in the American Midwest and died more than a century ago, a few months short of her seventy-fifth birthday. All her life, Emma confined herself to her immediate family, a close circle of friends, and church duties. She seldom made public addresses. She never traveled beyond the confines of the United States. She boasted little in terms of this world's riches. Living for an unpopular ideal, Emma pursued her own path, leaving a unique legacy to her posterity.

Although generally unacknowledged as the wife of an assassinated candidate for the United States presidency, Emma stands in a particularly defined place in the history of the world beside Mary Todd Lincoln, Ida Saxon McKinley, Ethel and Jacqueline Kennedy, and Coretta King, whose husbands also met violent deaths in the political arena of the United States.

As the wife of the prophet chosen by God to lead the dispensation of the fullness of times, Emma's divine mission must be measured in the context of her husband's life and mission. As his companion, she mounted the steps of fame. With him she shared a transcendent mission. She holds a singular position in world and religious history, standing beside other women in the scriptures—wives of prophets, who played supportive but unheralded roles and suffered much as Emma did.

From the beginning, Emma was an active participant, assisting Joseph in his mission. Bearing her burdens with unusual good nature, she was Joseph's most stalwart advocate. Lucy Mack Smith paid her high tribute:

> I have never seen a woman in my life who would endure every species of fatigue and hardship, from month to month, and from year to year, with that unflinching courage, zeal, and patience, which [Emma] has ever done; for I know that which she has had to endure—she has been tossed upon the ocean of uncertainty—she has breasted the storms of persecution, and [been] buffeted [by] the rage of men and devils, which would have borne down almost any other woman. It may be, that many may have to encounter the same—I pray God, that this may not be the case; but, should it be, may they have grace given them according to their day, even as has been the case with her.[29]

Such praise from her mother-in-law, who knew her over the course of many years and spent her last four years in Emma's care, sets an exemplary tone for us, as we begin our study of the divine mission of Emma and her husband, the Prophet Joseph Smith.

Notes

1. E. Cecil McGavin, *Nauvoo the Beautiful* (Salt Lake City: Bookcraft, 1972), p. 145-46.

2. Joseph Smith, *History of the Church of Jesus Christ of Latter-day Saints*, ed. B. H. Roberts 7 vols. (Salt Lake City: Deseret Book, 1974), vol. 5:107. Hereafter this reference will be cited as *HC*.

3. In William Hartley, *They Are My Friends* (Provo, Utah: Grandin Book,1986), pp. 8-21. Quoted from the writings of Joseph Knight, Sr. Some spelling has been corrected for clarity.

4. Ibid., p. 21.

5. Donna Hill, *Joseph Smith the First Mormon* (Garden City, New York: Doubleday & Company, Inc., 1977), p. 62.

6. Emma Hale Smith Bidamon, *Emma Smith's Last Testimony*, February 1879,

Reorganized Church of Jesus Christ of Latter Day Saints (RLDS) Archives, Independence, Mo. See Author's Note at the end of this book.

7. Buddy Youngreen, *Reflections of Emma, Joseph Smith's Wife* (Orem, Utah: Grandin Book, 1982), p. 69. This book contains the journal entries of Mary Audentia Smith Anderson, Joseph and Emma's granddaughter, who interviewed four other grandchildren. In this entry Emma Smith McCallum reports that Emma had a sense of humor or "she would not have made it." She said Emma was "jolly."

8. Anderson, Mary Audentia Smith, *Ancestry and Posterity of Joseph Smith and Emma Hale* (Independence, Mo.: Herald Publishing House, 1929). For information on Samuel Fuller, see pp. 239-44; for Edward Tilley and wife, Ann and their daughter Elizabeth Tilley, see pp. 471-73; for John Howland, who married Elizabeth Tilley, see pp. 461-68.

There was a possible eighth ancestor of Joseph Smith on the Mayflower. Anderson notes that William Duty, ancestor to Joseph Smith's grandmother, Mary Duty (Smith) may be a descendant of Edward Doty, who was on the ship (p. 117).

The *World Book Encyclopedia* (vol. 15, p. 518) expands our appreciation for our ancestors who were on the Mayflower. "One hundred two Pilgrims sailed from England on the Mayflower. It was a rough passage, taking 65 days. After leaving England in September, they arrived in Provincetown harbor, November 21, [1620] landing in Plymouth harbor on December 26. (November 10th according to the calendar then in use). During the ocean crossing, one died and a baby was born. Four more died and one was born in Provincetown harbor. Ninety-nine Pilgrims landed at Plymouth to build a settlement. During the first winter, almost half of the Pilgrims died of sickness, from lack of food and shelter from the bitterly cold weather." Elizabeth Tilley's parents both died that winter.

9. John Fiske, *The Beginnings of New England of the Puritan Theocracy in Its Relation to Civil and Religious Liberty* (Boston and New York: Houghton, Mifflin & Co.; Cambridge: The Rivertree Press, 1889).

10. William Stoughton was pastor of the Old South Church in Boston. The pastor traditionally presented a sermon on Election Day, and this quote comes from Stoughton's sermon in 1668. Microfiche copies are found in the Harold B. Lee Library, Brigham Young University, Provo, Utah.

11. Edward Johnson, "Wonder-Working Providence of Sion's Savior in New England,"in *Original Narratives of Early American History*, ed. J. Franklin Jameson (New York: Charles Scribner's Sons, 1910).

12. William Bradford, *History of Plymouth Plantation* 1606-1646, ed. W. T. Davis (Charles Scribner's Sons, 1946), p. 63.

13. Anderson, *Ancestry and Posterity of Joseph Smith and Emma Hale*, p. 300. Concerning Isaac Hale's Revolutionary War service, Anderson says, "In 1780, at the age of seventeen, Isaac Hale gave Revolutionary service, marching under Colonel Ebenezer Allen's command, to Castleton, to prevent Sir John Johnson's threatened raids from Canada down into the Mohawk Valley (Vermont Revolutionary Rolls, pp. 208, 209)."

Anderson also includes a brief story of Emma's parents and quotes Emily C. Blackman's *History of Susquehanna County*, Pennsylvania (pp. 102-104):

> [Isaac Hale] married Elizabeth Lewis, sister of Nathaniel Lewis who married about the same time, Sarah Cole. . . . These two men "with their wives . . . a yoke of steers and a cart on which to carry all their baggage, came the distance of about two hundred and twenty miles from Wells, Rutland County, Vermont, to Willingborough, Luzerne County, Pennsylvania. At that time it was known on the court records as Tioga Township. . . . In the summer of 1793 Isaac Hale was one of the viewers of the first roads laid out in Willingborough. He was a great hunter and made his living by procuring game. . . . His wife was for fifty years a consistent member of the Methodist Church. A lady . . . who knew her well, says: "I never visited her but I thought I had learned something useful." Her death occurred in 1842, in her seventy-fifth year.
>
> Isaac Hale was a man of forethought and generosity. He would kill the elk up the Starucca, in the fall when it was the fattest; make troughs of birch or maple to hold it when cut up; carry salt on his back, salt the meat, cover it with bark held down with heavy stones, and then leave it until the snow came, when he could easily bring it down. The fruit of his labor was sometimes exchanged for assistance on his farm, but perhaps as often, found its way, unheralded, to the tables of others, when the occupants of the house were out of sight, and to them the gift seemed almost miraculous.
>
> For many years there stood at Mr. Hale's door a stump mortar and heavy wooden pestle, worked by a spring pole, and his boys were obliged to leave work an hour or two before dark, to grind out meal enough for mush for their supper. The handmill afterward took the place of the mortar and pestle, and could grind half a bushel in a day, —a great Improvement. (Anderson, pp. 301-302)

Isaac died 11 January 1839. Records of deeds for transfer in Susquehanna County, Pennsylvania, from Isaac Hale include one conveying, in 1830, thirteen acres of land in Harmony to Joseph Smith, Jr. Joseph later sold this land. His will is found in Anderson, *Ancestry and Posterity of Joseph Smith and Emma Hale*, pp. 302-304.

Isaac's will left the bulk of his estate to his eldest son, Alva, with instructions for bequests to each of his sons, his wife to be cared for all her days, and (quoting the will) "that the place on which I have so long tarried, may be kept as a sort of home for any of my dear children who may be unfortunate, and need a helping hand at their father's old residence—having confidence that my said son Alva, will be disposed to do right in all such cases, and should he be able after paying his brothers as stated above and it will not endanger his freehold, to pay his sisters such sums as would be right and proper" (Anderson, *Ancestry and Posterity of Joseph Smith and Emma Hale*, pp. 300- 304).

From this brief quote we observe that Isaac did not cut Emma out of his will entirely, but indicated that should she ever desire to return, there would be a place for her in the old home at Harmony. Emma's mother died 16 February 1842. Both Isaac and Elizabeth are buried in the McKune Cemetery, and Isaac's grave was marked with an official marker by the Montrose Chapter, Daughters of the American Revolution, Montrose, Pennsylvania. The grave of Emma and Joseph's first baby is marked by a simple stone in the same cemetery.

14. Anderson, *Ancestry and Posterity of Joseph Smith and Emma Hale*, p. 305. Emma's sister, Tryal, born 21 November 1806, married Bartlett Morse, a teacher of a class in the Methodist Episcopal Church at Harmony, Pennsylvania. They moved to Illinois in 1859, settling on a farm near Amboy. On 3 June 1860, Tryal was killed when a severe wind destroyed their home. A large sliver of wood was driven through her chest; her daughter, Emma, was also injured and died as well. Morse was also severely injured, but survived. His memory is the source of Emma's father's conversion through her prayer although this has been argued by others in the family.

15. Lucy Mack Smith, *History of the Prophet Joseph Smith by His Mother*, ed. Preston Nibley (Salt Lake City: Bookcraft, 1958), p. 69. Nearly every detail used in this chapter can be found in Lucy's book. It is essential reading for any student interested in learning about Joseph and Emma Smith.

Since Lucy Mack Smith is the source for a great deal of information in this book, it is important to understand the nature of sources cited herein. There are currently three published versions of Lucy's history. Each contains substantial editorial differences, and all are taken from the original source manuscript which is known as her Preliminary Manuscript.

During the winter after the martyrdom of her sons, Lucy found herself answering endless questions about the origin of the Restoration and the events with which she was most familiar regarding the progress of Smith family and the growth of the Church from 1830 on. Lucy was encouraged by Brigham Young and the Council of the Twelve to write her history. In early 1845, she began working on this project, with Martha Jane Knowlton Coray writing for her.

Her original manuscript was a very personal, frank expression of her family's and her own experiences. There are two main sources for subsequent collections published under Lucy Mack Smith's name. One is a notebook of about 64 pages, which contained jottings she made. The second is the Preliminary Manuscript, which was 210 pages on foolscap paper, handwritten by Martha Jane Knowlton Coray. Both are currently located in the LDS Archives in Salt Lake City, Utah.

Once Lucy was seriously engaged in this work with Martha Coray, it became obvious that it would be a worthwhile project but a lengthy one. After the

Preliminary Manuscript was done, Martha's husband, Howard, worked to revise the manuscript. Howard's revision attempted to round out places Lucy had not covered and served to fill in historical gaps. His version contains some material that was not in the Preliminary Manuscript; likewise, some information in the Preliminary Manuscript was not included in the revision. The resulting revision was a more formal document, but had lost much of the personal flavor of Mother Smith's own language and style.

Two handwritten copies of the revision were made by the Corays. One was given to Mother Smith, the other to the Church, which took their copy west.

In September 1852, when Orson Pratt was on his way to England on a mission, he stopped to visit Isaac Sheen, and discovered that Sheen had Mother Smith's copy of her Preliminary Manuscript (with Howard's revisions). Sheen had obtained it, by means unknown, from William Smith, brother of the prophet. Orson paid for the revision and took it with him to England, where he published the material in 1853, without permission from the Church leadership.

On checking details in the published version, George Albert Smith, then Church historian, felt uncomfortable that he had been unable to verify absolutely all the statements in the text—and observed that in her old age, Mother Smith may have been somewhat forgetful of exact dates, places, etc. In 1865, Brigham Young issued a recall of this book. Everyone agreed that it was important to make Mother Smith's history available to Church members, but in the great concern to verify its accuracy, the process bogged down the progress of such a publication. Attempts at verification went on for years.

In 1901, a revision was published in a series in the *Improvement Era*, with a preface by Joseph F. Smith. In 1945, Preston Nibley, then assistant historian to The Church of Jesus Christ of Latter-day Saints, published a new edited version.

Some references used in *Emma and Joseph: Their Divine Mission* are taken from Lucy Mack Smith, *History of Joseph Smith by His Mother*, with notes and comments by Preston Nibley (Salt Lake City: Bookcraft, 1958).

In 1912, the Reorganized Church published, through their own printing office, an exact reprint of the version published in 1853, in England, by Orson Pratt. The title of this book is *Biographical Sketches of Joseph Smith the Prophet and His Progenitors for Many Generations*, by Lucy Smith, Mother of the Prophet (Herald Publishing House, Lamoni, Iowa, 1912). The version used in this work was then reprinted by Herald House, in1969, with comments and explanations by Heman C. Smith, RLDS Historian, which were not in the 1853 edition.

The Preliminary Manuscript and Lucy's notebook were discovered in the LDS Archives in the 1960s. When they surfaced, they became the subject of intense interest by historians and scholars. One of the foremost of these was Richard L. Anderson, who provided the author of this book with information concerning certain events, from the Preliminary Manuscript.

In 1996, Scot Facer Proctor and Maurine Jensen Proctor edited a new publication of this material, *The Revised and Enhanced History of Joseph Smith by His*

Mother (Salt Lake City: Bookcraft, 1996). This book presents the background summarized here to help people understand the various references to Lucy Mack Smith within the text of *Emma and Joseph: Their Divine Mission.* I have drawn extensively upon Lucy Mack Smith's story in all its forms in order to obtain documentation for the events related herein. The Proctors' wonderful book restores the personal characteristics of Lucy's expression and style. It broadens our view of the Prophet's mother and her unique perceptions of the events which she lived personally through the tumultuous founding of the Latter-day Saint religion.

I would encourage every individual and every family who loves the story of the restoration of the gospel to obtain Mother Smith's history and read it. It is indeed a strong testimony building tool.

16. The Holy Bible (King James Version), James 1:5.

17. Pearl of Great Price, Joseph Smith—History 1:17.

18. Ibid., 1:19.

19. Ibid., 1:24-26

20. Ibid., 1:33.

21. Ibid., 1:34.

22. Ibid., 1:36-41. See also Isaiah 11 and 29; Joel 2:28-32; Malachi 3 and 4.

23. Ibid., 1:48.-49

24. Ibid., 1:53-54.

25. See Daniel 2:44-45. A careful reading of Daniel's writings, particularly verses 28 through 45, reveals the prophetic expectation upon which this idea is based; see also Doctrine and Covenants 135:3.

26. Doctrine and Covenants 135:3.

27. *Times and Seasons*, 3:775-76 (2 May 1842).

28. Joseph Smith, Jr., *HC*, 5:399-400. Regarding the word "Mormon," Joseph Smith explained: "It has been stated that this word was derived from the Greek word, mormo. This is not the case. There is no Greek or Latin upon the plates from which I, through the grace of the Lord, translated the Book of Mormon. Let the language of the book speak for itself. . . ." He explains that the writers of the book said they wrote in characters, known among them as Reformed Egyptian, and that "none other people knoweth our language." The word Mormon, Joseph said, "means literally, more good."

29. Lucy Mack Smith, *History of Joseph Smith by His Mother*, ed. Preston Nibley (Salt Lake City: Bookcraft, 1958), pp. 190-91. See also Scot Facer Proctor and Maurine Jensen, *The Revised and Enhanced History of Joseph Smith by His Mother* (Salt Lake City: Bookcraft, 1996), pp. 248-49.

This is believed to be a copy of the Anthon transcript containing characters copied from the gold plates, which Martin Harris took to Professor Anthon at Columbia University. Printed in the *Supplement to Saints Herald* (Lamoni, Iowa), September 1909, p. 29. Courtesy of RLDS Archives.

CHAPTER 2

A Marvel and a Wonder

"I was an active participant in the scenes that transpired. . . ."
(Emma Smith)

Emma's active participation with Joseph in the divine mission he
was called to fulfill—that is, the latter-day restoration of the gospel of
Jesus Christ—began when she went with Joseph to the hill to retrieve
the golden plates.

Mother Smith wrote in her history that she stayed up late the
night of 21 September 1827, having a great deal of work to do. She
had a houseful of company, with Joseph Knight, Sr., and Josiah
Stowell arriving on the 20 September, ostensibly to buy wheat.[1] Both
of these men were aware of Joseph's annual meetings with the Angel
Moroni. Undoubtedly they timed their visit hoping to be present
when Joseph brought home the record. On the night of 21
September, the visitors, and most of the family, except Mother Lucy,
had retired. It was after midnight when Joseph came to ask if she had
a chest with a lock and key. Realizing he must need it to hold the
record, she became alarmed because she did not have one. Joseph
soothed her fears and assured her that all would be well.[2]

Lucy recalled, "Joseph's wife passed through the room with her
bonnet and riding dress, [and] in a few minutes they left together,
taking Mr. Knight's horse and wagon. . . ."[3]

Joseph and Emma drove to the hill. Joseph had been directed to
bring the "right person" with him, and he knew that right person was
Emma. Here she was beside him. He must have had every expectation

that now was the time for him to receive the record and begin his labors. What must this drive have been like? Did they talk? Did they wonder? All records are silent on this subject. However, we do know, from Emma's own account, that she did not go up on the hill with him. In the predawn darkness, Emma waited at the foot of the hill that would later be called Cumorah. Joseph ascended to the place, near the top, where he received the sacred record from the Angel Moroni and accepted the responsibility of protecting, translating, and publishing it. This moment symbolically foreshadowed Emma's life as the wife of a prophet. As her husband's divine mission unfolded, Joseph often scaled the heights, while Emma waited—somewhere.

Emma waited from midnight until dawn, faithfully guarding Mr. Knight's horse and wagon. She saw no angel. But she saw the sun rise on a new day before Joseph came back, carrying a heavy burden wrapped in his coat. On the way home she waited again while Joseph took the bundle and hid it in the woods. Then they drove on home.

Mother Lucy, realizing what may be transpiring for her son, could not sleep the remainder of the night. She spent the entire pre-dawn hours praying fervently that nothing would go wrong.

By breakfast time, Emma and Joseph had not returned. When Father Smith was ready to eat, he called for Joseph to come eat with him. Lucy, not wanting to call attention to Joseph and Emma's absence from the house, told her husband to let the young couple have their breakfast together later. The meal was served without further incident, but later on, Mr. Knight became concerned about his missing wagon. Lucy asked Joseph's younger brother, William, to go look for them. However, before William left, Joseph and Emma arrived.

Joseph said nothing about what he had been doing. Seeing that he was empty-handed, his mother became so nervous she had to leave the room. She was fearful that by some failure to comply with God's commandments, Joseph may have been denied the record yet again. Noticing her discomfiture, Joseph followed her. He told her, "Do not be uneasy, mother, all is right—see here, I have got a key."[4]

Lucy said, "I took the article of which he spoke into my hands, and upon examination, found that it consisted of two smooth three-cornered diamonds set in glass, and the glasses were set in silver bows, which were connected with each other in much the same way as old-fashioned spectacles. He took them again and left me, but said nothing respecting the record."[5]

This instrument, which Lucy later learned was called a Urim and Thummim, was to be used in helping Joseph keep the record safe and to translate the engravings. It was carried on his person, in a sort of breastplate, which was worn under his shirt.

Later, Joseph asked his mother if she knew where he could get a chest. She suggested the name of someone who could build one, but since they had no money in the house, it was uncertain when they could afford to get one made.

Protecting the Record Involves Family and Friends

A few days later, Joseph went to work digging a well at Macedon to obtain the money he needed for the chest. Apparently Joseph had said very little about the trip to the hill, and it appears that Emma kept it to herself as well. But his family members seem to have been aware that he had received the plates. Lucy assumed he had hidden them. Some people in the neighborhood, who had heard of Joseph's vision, or of his expectation that he would receive some kind of ancient record, were waiting and watching, hoping to get hold of the treasure, if there was any. While Joseph was at Macedon his father happened to be at a neighbor's house, where he overheard a conversation to the effect that a number of men were gathering to look for the hiding place of the "treasure" Joseph was rumored to have found buried in the hill.

Father Smith hurried home, very much concerned about the safety of the plates. He asked Emma "if she knew whether Joseph had taken the plates from their place of deposit, or if she was able to tell where they were. . . . She said she could not tell where they were or whether they were removed from their place."[6]

From Lucy's report of Emma's response, it is unclear whether Emma did not know where the plates were hidden, or whether she could not tell anyone. One thing is clear—she expressed faith that they would be all right. She did not know if Joseph had moved them, but she supposed that if the Lord had wanted him to, he might have.[7]

To soothe her father-in-law's worry, and perhaps because she wanted to be with Joseph, Emma said if she had a horse she would ride to where he was working and let him know of the danger. William caught a stray horse that had been about the place and brought it to Emma. According to the custom of the day, she put a willow withe (a flexible branch) around the animal's neck to show its status as a stray. She then rode to Macedon, which was only a few miles away.

Joseph was very surprised to see her. When she told him the situation, he consulted the Urim and Thummim, which he was wearing on his person. He told Emma that the plates were safe. However, he borrowed a horse from his employer and rode home with his wife.

At home, he calmed his father's fears. After hearing what his father had overheard, Joseph realized the plates might not be safe in the woods with people actively hunting for them. Therefore, he decided to bring them home. He sent his eleven-year-old brother, Don Carlos, to Hyrum and Jerusha's home, not far away, to ask Hyrum to please come at once. When Hyrum arrived, Joseph asked him to get a chest with a key and have it there by the time he (Joseph) returned from getting the plates from their hiding place, which was about three miles away. More than likely, Hyrum suggested using an old box that their deceased elder brother, Alvin, had used for his drafting tools. Hyrum agreed to bring the box whenever it was needed, and he went back to his house.

Joseph left immediately. As he was returning with the plates wrapped in his linen frock coat, he was attacked three different times. These individuals had been watching to see if he had a treasure, with the intention of taking it away from him.[8] Fighting off each attack, even striking the third attacker with the heavy object he carried and spraining his thumb in the process, Joseph broke free and ran through the woods, jumping over logs and dodging around trees, until he reached his own yard.

When he arrived, he was out of breath. Lucy recalls that he was gasping as he threw himself down by the fence. He asked his mother to send Don Carlos to get his father and the others, and ask them to see if they could find the men who had pursued him.

Father Smith, Mr. Knight, and Mr. Stowell searched the woods and returned without finding the attackers. Don Carlos was then sent again to ask Hyrum to come and bring the chest at once.

It wasn't long before Hyrum arrived with the chest. Joseph locked the record inside and hid it in the house. When everything was quiet, everyone gathered around in the kitchen to hear Joseph tell what had happened. After a few minutes he told his father he couldn't talk any more; he had a painfully sprained thumb, and he needed his father to put it back in place for him.

Joseph's mother gives very few other details of what happened that day. Yet, she paints a vivid picture of the essentials. The gold plates were brought into her house, still wrapped in Joseph's cloak. He locked them in Alvin's old chest. Although visitors and family members gathered to hear about the flight, and everyone knew he had brought in something heavy, Joseph did not uncover the plates or show them to anyone at that time. However, from this day on, Joseph's family became guardians of the ancient Nephite record. His wife, mother, his sisters (Katharine, Sophronia, and Lucy), and his brothers (William and Don Carlos) would all play a major part in its safekeeping. Their lives would be affected adversely from then on because of it. Although none of these family members would ever set eyes upon the plates, all would indicate by word and action, to their dying day, that they believed Joseph brought home the ancient record from which he later translated the Book of Mormon. Three members of his family, Joseph Sr., Hyrum, and Samuel would later see and handle the plates, becoming witnesses to the actual existence of the plates.

Apparently, Josiah Stowell also played a little-known part in the events of that day. Stowell's testimony is found in a letter written to the prophet in 1843 by Martha L. Campbell, on behalf of Stowell: "He says he never staggered at the foundation [of] the work for he knew to[o] much concerning it if I understood him right he was the person that took the plates from your hands the morning you brought them in, and he observed 'blessed is he that seeth and says he has seen and believed. . . .'"[9]

Though Stowell did not see the unwrapped plates, he must have been present when Joseph staggered in the yard. Whatever he saw, it was enough to make a lasting impression upon him, and he believed.

Once it was suspected that the Smith family had some kind of treasure, a certain element of the community made life miserable for the Smiths. Various attempts were made to search for the plates. On one occasion, Lucy watched ruffians turn her house topsy-turvy, looking for them, while she prayed they would not find them hidden under a loose stone on the hearth in front of the fireplace. Not satisfied with harassing the Smiths in this way, some used any pretext to heckle the family. On one occasion, some men came demanding payment for a debt of Hyrum's. It was not even Hyrum's house they came to, but Lucy's. William, who was fourteen and large for his age, came home to find a mob in the house. He picked up a hand spike (a six-foot-long oak staff about four inches in diameter) and raced up the stairs. When he encountered the invaders, he swung the spike with all his power, driving them down the stairs and out the door. He was so enraged that even after they had all left in terror, he continued to swing the stick around and around his head.

Another story comes from Joseph's little sister, Katharine, who recalled to her grandchildren one occasion when someone attempted to get the plates. Fearing that his pursuers would follow him into the house, Joseph thrust a bundle through the window and said for her to hide it quickly. She and her sister, Sophronia, put it under their corn husk mattress and got on the bed, pretending to be asleep. The mob searched the house, but seeing the girls apparently sleeping, did not disturb them.[10]

Contemplating this story, one is struck with the peculiar circumstance Joseph must have faced. He had the gold plates. But where could he find a place of privacy to look them over, not to mention attempt to decipher the characters inscribed upon them? Perhaps he took them into the woods, hoping to study them and was discovered by those who were watching for just such an opportunity. Handing them through the window to his sisters could have been his only choice. Katharine's recounting of her experience gives us an intimate look at the involvement the family had in helping Joseph at this difficult time.

Due to the strenuous efforts of such ruffians to get the record away from Joseph, he and Emma decided to leave Palmyra. Emma's father consented to their going to Harmony. In December 1827, Emma's brother, Alva, made the 155-mile journey from Harmony, to move their belongings in his wagon. Just before they left, a neighbor and friend, Martin Harris, gave Joseph fifty dollars, for which Joseph offered to sign a note. Alva agreed to cosign. Harris told them he wanted to give the money to further the work of the Lord. They accepted the money as a gift and went on their way. They made the four-day trip with the plates hidden in a barrel of beans. Not long after leaving, they were stopped by some men who searched their belongings, but no one dug deep into the bean barrel. At Harmony they moved into a small house, actually an old shed formerly used for tanning hides, across the road from Emma's parents.

Joseph Sr. and Polly Knight Aid the Work

Once settled, they were eager to begin translation of the record. Emma served as scribe for Joseph, although her time was limited because of her household work. Her brother, Alva, also assisted for a time. They had very little money and were undoubtedly too proud to ask Emma's parents for assistance. In desperation, Joseph took Emma and went to Colesville to see the Knights, whom he felt he could ask for help. Mr. Knight wanted to oblige, but his wife, Polly, and others in the Knight family were opposed to giving financial assistance to the strange project. He did give them a little money to buy paper. A short time later, he told his wife that he wanted to go and see Joseph. She asked why he wanted to go so soon. He replied, "Come go and see." So they went together. After Polly talked with Joseph, she changed her attitude.[11]

Martin Harris Seeks Verification

In February 1828, Martin Harris came to their house. Joseph copied some of the characters from the plates for Martin to take to New York to be examined and verified. Martin took them to a Professor Anthon, who "was celebrated for his literary attainments."[12]

According to Martin, Professor Anthon verified the characters as being "Egyptian, Caldaic, Assyric, and Arabic." Martin said Anthon gave him a certificate verifying that "they were true characters."[13] Then, as Martin was about to leave, Anthon asked how they had been obtained. When told that an angel of God had revealed them, the professor asked for the certificate back and destroyed it. He is quoted as having said there is no such thing as ministering angels; if Martin would bring the plates to him, he would translate them. Martin told him he could not bring them because part of them was sealed. Anthon reportedly replied, "I cannot read a sealed book."[14] Later, Anthon denied Martin's story, although he did say a farmer named Harris had visited with him.[15] Whatever the facts may be, Martin was satisfied that the record was authentic, and he felt Anthon had fulfilled prophecy. Harris' wife, however, ridiculed the idea. When Martin went back to Harmony, his wife insisted on going with him. She was determined to see the plates for herself.

Emma's encounter with Mrs. Harris on this occasion was far from pleasant. As soon as she arrived, Mrs. Harris informed Joseph that her object in coming was to see the plates. She declared she would not leave until she had done so and immediately began to ransack the house. When she did not find the plates inside, she searched outdoors. About two in the afternoon she came in, very disgruntled. She warmed herself a bit, then asked Emma if there were any snakes in the area. Emma replied there were not. The woman claimed that while she was walking in the woods, a tremendous black snake stuck his head up in front of her and hissed at her. Thereafter, Mrs. Harris went around the neighborhood telling the story that she had almost found the hiding place, but the snake had scared her and she had run back to the house.

While there is no indication of where the plates actually were at this time, Joseph's mother recalls that during the two weeks she stayed, Mrs. Harris "did all that lay in her power to injure Joseph in the estimation of his neighbors—telling them that he was a grand imposter. She insisted that by his specious intentions, he had seduced her husband into the belief that he [Joseph Smith] was some great one, merely through a design on her husband's property."[16]

Finally, Martin took his wife home to Palmyra. Although she did all she could to persuade Martin not to return to help Joseph, Martin did return and served as Joseph's scribe through the spring. By June, he and Joseph had managed to produce a manuscript of 116 pages.

During this time Emma was awaiting the birth of her first baby. As the time for the baby's delivery approached, Martin made plans to return to Palmyra. Before he left, he begged Joseph to allow him to take the manuscript with him so he could prove to his wife that the work in which he was engaged was valid.

When Joseph enquired of the Lord through the Urim and Thummim whether or not Martin could take the manuscript, he was told not to let the manuscript go. Martin, however, urged him to ask again. Again Joseph was told not to allow it. Martin persisted, saying that unless he could show his wife some proof of what he was doing, she would prevent his returning to help finish the work. In addition, Martin had promised to provide the money for publishing the book. Fearing he would lose Martin's help and support, Joseph asked the Lord a third time. This time he was told that Martin could take the manuscript if he took strict care not to show it outside his own immediate family. Martin promised and left for Palmyra on 14 June 1828, taking the manuscript with him.

Double Tragedy and a Reprieve

The day following Martin's departure, Emma gave birth to a baby boy, who lived but a short time. He was buried near their house. Today, in the cemetery, there is a headstone inscribed "Infant Son of Emma and Joseph Smith."

For several weeks Emma hovered between life and death. Joseph was beside himself with worry. To add to his concerns, Martin did not return when he had said he would. Alarmed about what might have happened to Martin and the manuscript, Joseph left Emma in the care of her mother and went to Palmyra.

As soon as he arrived at his parents' home, he sent for Martin. After a long delay, Martin came slowly toward the Smith home, dreading the necessity of telling Joseph that the manuscript had been lost. No amount of searching or asking anyone in his family had served to find it. When Joseph learned of the loss, he was devastated. His mother described how he wept and paced the floor, and no one could comfort him. In fact, the entire family was in the same state of mind, as "sobs and moans, and the most bitter lamentations filled the house."[17] Joseph agonized at the thought of having to acknowledge to the Lord that through his disobedience the manuscript was gone. He also feared to tell Emma. Along with the loss of their firstborn child, his distress over the lost manuscript was multiplied by the fact that he feared the news would be too much for Emma in her weakened condition, and she might die. Joseph departed for home with a heavy heart.

We have no information as to how Emma took the loss. In her record, Joseph's mother was preoccupied with the story of her son's terrible ordeal and does not mention Emma's reaction to the news. Her baby's death must have been a cutting grief for the young mother as well as the baby's grandmother. The loss of the manuscript, however, eclipsed all else, providing yet another example of how Emma's personal circumstances and feelings were so often trivialized by the events surrounding their mission to re-establish the true and correct church of Jesus Christ on earth.

Joseph must have been very reluctant to approach the Lord to confess the loss. Lucy related that Joseph received a severe chastening from the Angel Moroni, who took back the plates and the Urim and Thummim. Although it was some time before they were returned to him, everyone was greatly relieved to learn that Joseph was still called to the work. When the plates were returned to him, he was told not to retranslate the lost portion, for if he did, those who had stolen it might alter the text and use it to discredit the book.

Joseph was also given a set of smaller plates covering that same period of Nephite history, though it was not identical to the text that had been lost. When he translated these new plates, he learned that the man who had prepared the smaller plates said, in the engraved text, that he did not know why he was commanded to make them, but he supposed it was "for a wise purpose."[18] From this experience, Joseph came to understand that all things are known to the Lord. This may have also been comforting evidence to Emma of divine direction over the work.

Throughout the rest of the year of 1828, Joseph did little if any translating. He labored on the farm he had purchased from his father-in-law, and Emma is quoted as saying, "they [the plates] lay in a box under our bed for months but I never felt at liberty to look at them."[19]

So peaceful were their circumstances that winter, they were completely without fear.

In February 1829, when Joseph's parents visited them in Harmony, Lucy noticed "a red morocco trunk" on Emma's bureau. She said Joseph told her it contained the plates and the Urim and Thummim.

In the spring, they made a new friend.

A Friend in Deed

On 5 April 1829, a young school teacher, Oliver Cowdery, came to see Joseph and Emma. Oliver had been boarding with Joseph's parents during the previous school term. From them he had learned of Joseph's amazing experiences and the ancient record now in Joseph's possession. He was curious and interested. He had come to offer his help with the translation.

Two days after Oliver's arrival, they began translating. Records indicate that Joseph dictated and Oliver wrote "almost without cessation" for several weeks. However, they were not able to keep up that pace because they ran out of provisions. Joseph and Oliver left Emma at home alone while they went to find work in order to earn money so they could continue their task. They stopped at Joseph Knight's place to see if he had work, or if he could give them some provisions, but he was away from home. Mr. Knight recalled: "When I came home my folks told me what Joseph wanted. . . . I Bought a Barrel of Mackerel and some lined paper for writing and . . . I Bought some nine or ten Bushels of grain and five or six Bushels taters [potatoes] and a pound of tea, and I went Down to see him and they ware in want."[20]

Joseph and Oliver were gone when he got there, but Emma was home. She wept with gratitude for the things he brought. Mr. Knight continued, "[Joseph and Oliver] returned home and found me there with the provisions, and they ware glad for they ware out."[21]

Joseph Knight, Sr., was a constant benefactor to them. More than once, just when provisions were badly needed, "Father" Knight came with food, fuel, and paper. Due to his generous help, and to the fact that what they were doing was not yet generally known in Harmony, Joseph and Oliver were able to go quietly about their business of translating without hindrance. There was no question of Joseph stopping again to farm. He had begun his work and he had learned to trust in God.

The translation progressed well. Joseph dictated hour after hour, day after day. One day he and Oliver came upon a reference to baptism. Realizing that there were many confusing methods of baptism, they retired to the woods to inquire of the Lord concerning this principle.

Baptism and the Restoration of the Aaronic Priesthood

The two young men knelt in the quiet woods not far from the Susquehanna River, praying fervently. Suddenly, to their great joy and amazement, a glorious being appeared before them. Introducing himself as "a fellow servant," he said his name was John the Baptist. He laid his hands upon their heads and ordained them saying, "Upon you my fellow servants, in the name of the Messiah, I confer the Priesthood of Aaron, which holds the keys of the ministering of angels and of the gospel of repentance, and of baptism by immersion for the remission of sins."22

With this ordination, they received the authority to baptize. John then instructed them to baptize one another, which they did. Afterward, they returned to the house marveling over this wonderful experience.

Although not a party to the actual restoration of the priesthood, or to the baptisms, Emma was probably the first to know of it from Joseph and Oliver.

A Restoration, Not a Reformation

At first Joseph and Oliver felt they must keep this event secret because of the hostility by the clergy in that day toward the whole idea of revelation. The revelations these two men had received during their ordination to the priesthood brought them to a greater understanding of the mission which lay before them. Joseph now understood they were to establish a *restoration,* not just a reformation. They were to lay the foundation for building latter-day Zion—to establish the Lord's church and make available to all the earth once again the ordinances and principles of salvation.

As their understanding increased, they began to share their new experiences with close friends and relatives. When Joseph's brother Samuel, who was twenty-one years old, came to visit, they told him of the things which had occurred. A very strong-minded young man, he was reluctant to believe. Joseph and Oliver reasoned with him, calling his attention to scriptures in the Bible. They also showed him the manuscript, which was nearly finished. After many questions and much discussion, Samuel went into the woods to pray. He obtained his own answer from the Lord, which caused him to rejoice exceedingly.[23]

On 25 May 1829, Samuel was baptized by Oliver Cowdery, then he returned home to tell his family about the new developments. In a few days Emma's household was bulging with company. Hyrum came to inquire about the things Samuel had told him. Father Knight also came to find out what was happening. It is interesting to note how Joseph's two brothers responded to these new events. Perhaps Samuel, having obtained a testimony for himself, paved the way for Hyrum to believe immediately. Both Hyrum and Father Knight, who had been watching the progress from the beginning, each responded with the question, "What does the Lord want me to do?"

Joseph inquired of the Lord what was required of these two men, and he received a revelation for each of them. They were told, "Now behold, a marvelous work is about to come forth among the children of men."[24] Hyrum was urged to wait until he had received God's word before he went out to proclaim it, and Father Knight was promised he would be called to help build up Zion.

Restoration of the Melchizedek Priesthood

Some time after 15 May 1829, Joseph and Oliver received another manifestation. They were ordained to the Melchizedek priesthood, under the hands of the resurrected apostles, Peter, James, and John. This event, like the ordination of the original apostles, conferred upon Joseph and Oliver a sacred and holy calling, which authorized them to establish the ordinances of the gospel of Jesus Christ, just as Peter, James, and John had been authorized anciently by the Savior before he ascended into heaven.[25] Now the full significance of their calling, and the divine mission before them, began to dawn upon Joseph and Oliver, with Emma sharing in the wonder of each unfolding event.

Gradually, news of the restoration of the priesthood spread. Joseph and the others must have known more persecution would follow them telling anyone, but as they became more dedicated in the work, they could not fail to share it. More than likely, Emma told her mother and sisters, and Joseph and Oliver shared their experience with their families. Emma's family appeared satisfied and promised to protect them against any unlawful treatment.[26]

Rumors of these spiritual experiences spread rapidly. When some local ministers became aware, they were infuriated. Once again, the Smiths' peace was threatened. Only the influence of Emma's family had protected them from severe persecution. Curiosity seekers and critics came, distracting them from the work. Joseph described how one man visited Mr. Hale, "telling falsehoods of a shameful nature against me, which turned the old gentleman and his family against us, that they would no longer promise us protection nor believe our doctrines."[27]

Oliver wrote to a friend, Peter Whitmer, Sr., in Fayette, New York, asking if they might go there to finish the translation.

In the remnants of the original Book of Mormon manuscript, handwriting examples indicate that while Oliver wrote the bulk of the text, there were a few others, including Emma, who had served as scribe during the translation process. More than likely, the lost 116 pages contained the bulk of Emma's transcription work.

Move to Fayette, N.Y. —Three Witnesses Chosen

In June 1829, Peter Whitmer's son, David, brought a two-horse wagon to help move the Smiths to Fayette. Emma did not go with them immediately, but followed later.[28]

This time, the plates were not entrusted to mortal transport, but were carried by heavenly means. At the Whitmers' home, Oliver, Joseph, and Emma were given free board and room. They also had the assistance of the Whitmer brothers, David and John, to transcribe, when needed. In a very short time, the translation was completed.

Up to this time, no one but Joseph had seen the golden plates, uncovered. Now, as the work of translation neared completion, it was time to choose witnesses. More than two thousand years earlier, Moroni, the same angel who had given Joseph the plates, had written:

> And now I, Moroni, have written the words which were
> commanded me. . . . And behold, ye may be privileged that ye
> may show the plates unto those who shall assist to bring forth

this work; and unto three shall they be shown by the power of God, wherefore they shall know of a surety that these things are true. And in the mouth of three witnesses shall these things be established; and the testimony of three, and this work, in the which shall be shown forth the power of God and also his word, of which the Father and the Son, and the Holy Ghost bear record—and all this shall stand as a testimony against the world at the last day.[29]

Joseph was instructed to choose three men who would receive a convincing visual proof that he had the gold plates as well as a spiritual confirmation that the work they were doing was under divine direction. Word was sent to Joseph Smith at Manchester to come to Fayette; Martin Harris was invited to go along with the Smiths. Lucy said she and Joseph still cared about Martin although he had caused them so much trouble. They also felt sorry for him.

Quite a crowd assembled at the Whitmer home, including, "the Whitmer family, the Prophet and his wife and Oliver Cowdery. . . . the Prophet's father and mother and Martin Harris." The usual morning family service was held at the Whitmer residence, namely, scripture reading, singing, and prayer.[30]

Joseph must have knelt to offer the prayer, for Lucy notes: "As soon as Joseph rose from his knees, he approached Martin Harris and said, with a solemnity that thrills through my veins to this day, 'Martin Harris, you have got to humble yourself before your God this day, that you may obtain a forgiveness of your sins. If you do, it is the will of God that you should look upon the plates in company with Oliver Cowdery and David Whitmer.'"[31]

While Joseph and the three prospective witnesses retired to the woods, the rest of the people waited in the Whitmers' home. Sometime between three and four in the afternoon, Joseph returned to the house. He found his parents and Sister Whitmer sitting in one of the bedrooms, visiting.

Joseph threw himself down beside his mother and exclaimed, "Father, Mother, you do not know how happy I am; the Lord has now caused the plates to be shown to three more besides myself. They have seen an angel, who has testified to them, and they will have to bear witness to the truth of what I have said, for now they know for themselves that I do not go about to deceive the people, and I feel as if I was relieved of a burden which was almost too heavy for me to bear, and it rejoices my soul that I am not any longer to be entirely alone in the world."[32]

Joseph had just finished this happy exclamation when Martin Harris came into the room. Lucy says he was ". . . almost overcome with joy, and testified boldly to what he had both seen and heard."[33] Soon Oliver and David entered, expressing their joy and amazement as well.

These three, along with Joseph, had had an all consuming experience. At first the three men had prayed without success. Then Martin, realizing he was the cause of the failure, had withdrawn and begun praying with all his might. As soon as he had gone, Oliver and David received the testimony for which they prayed. The angel came and stood before them, showing them the gold plates, and they heard a voice from heaven declaring to them that they must testify to this truth. After this, Joseph went to find Martin, who was struggling with his lack of faith. When the two of them prayed together, the witness was given, and Martin saw and heard the same things the others had. He cried, "'Tis enough! 'Tis enough; mine eyes have beheld; mine eyes have beheld!" Then jumping up, he shouted, "'Hosanna,' blessing God and otherwise rejoicing exceedingly."[34]

Although Lucy does not mention Emma's presence in the room when Joseph told his parents what had happened, she must have known when he and the others came into the house. The log house was so small that it is unlikely these events could have occurred without her knowing, especially since it would have been of certain importance to her to watch for her husband's return from the woods with the witnesses.

In any case, Emma was personally acquainted with these men and no doubt heard their experiences from their own lips. She would also have seen the printed testimony in the Book of Mormon when it was published.

Testimony of the Three Witnesses

BE IT KNOWN unto all nations, kindreds, tongues, and people, unto whom this work shall come: That we, through the grace of God the Father, and our Lord Jesus Christ, have seen the plates which contain this record, which is a record of the people of Nephi, and also of the Lamanites, their brethren, and also of the people of Jared, who came from the tower of which hath been spoken. And we also know that they have been translated by the gift and power of God, for his voice hath declared it unto us; wherefore we know of a surety that the work is true. And we also testify that we have seen the engravings which are upon the plates; and they have been shown unto us by the power of God, and not of man. And we declare with words of soberness, that an angel of God came down from heaven, and he brought and laid before our eyes, that we beheld and saw the plates, and the engravings thereon; and we know that it is by the grace of God the Father, and our Lord Jesus Christ, that we beheld and bear record that these things are true. And it is marvelous in our eyes. Nevertheless, the voice of the Lord commanded us that we should bear record of it; wherefore, to be obedient unto the commandments of God, we bear testimony of these things. And we know that if we are faithful in Christ, we shall rid our garments of the blood of all men, and be found spotless before the judgment-seat of Christ, and shall dwell with him eternally in the heavens. And the honor be to the Father, and to the Son, and to the Holy Ghost, which is one God. Amen.

Oliver Cowdery
David Whitmer
Martin Harris [35]

Eight Witnesses

Shortly after the meeting in Fayette, Joseph and Emma went to Palmyra to make arrangements to have the Book of Mormon printed. At this time eight more people were chosen to stand as witnesses: Christian Whitmer, Jacob Whitmer, Peter Whitmer, Jr., John Whitmer, Hiram Page (who was married to Peter Whitmer's daughter) two of the Prophet's brothers, Hyrum and Samuel Smith, and his father, Joseph Smith, Sr.

These eight men testified that they saw and handled the plates. They did not receive angelic testimony, but were shown the plates by Joseph. They testified that Joseph did have the engraven plates; they hefted them and examined the pages which Joseph had translated.

They said the plates had the "appearance of gold . . . and we saw the engravings thereon."[36] Their testimony was also placed in the front of the book.

According to Lucy, the eight witnesses viewed the plates in the woods, somewhere near the Smith home, in Manchester Township, New York, prior to Joseph's obtaining the copyright for the Book of Mormon. The copyright was obtained in Palmyra on 11 June 1829.[37]

Lucy explains that after the eight men had returned to the house, "the angel made his appearance to Joseph, at which time Joseph delivered up the plates into the angel's hands."[38]

Joseph made arrangements to pay $3000 for the publication of 5000 copies to be printed by E. B. Grandin Company in Palmyra.[39] Martin Harris guaranteed payment, using part of his land as collateral. Later on, Harris sold his farm to provide the money for the publication of the Book of Mormon.[40]

Now Oliver began the laborious task of copying the entire manuscript.[41] It was delivered to the printer in sections, and was guarded carefully to prevent any mishaps. The printer had to make all divisions in the manuscript, including sentences, paragraphs, and chapters, since the original manuscript had very few punctuation marks. In spite of the enormous amount of work involved, and the many efforts by enemies to stop it, the Book of Mormon came off the press the last week in March 1830. This book was published to stand as a second witness with the Bible—that Jesus is the Christ, the Son of God, the Redeemer of all mankind.

Emma as a Witness

Many years later, when Emma was asked about the coming forth of the Book of Mormon, she told her sons Alexander and Joseph, "I am satisfied that no man could have dictated the writing of the manuscript unless he was inspired; for, when acting as his scribe . . . [Joseph] would dictate to me hour after hour; and when returning after meals, or after interruptions, he would at once begin where he had left off, without either seeing the manuscript or having any portion of it read to him. This was a usual thing for him to do. It would have been improbable that a learned man could do this; and for one so ignorant and unlearned as he was, it was simply impossible."[42]

When asked if she had seen the plates, Emma said she had not, but then gave this interesting description of her own experience with them: "The Plates often lay on the table without any attempt at concealment, wrapped in a small linen tablecloth which I had given him to fold them in. I once felt the plates as they thus lay on the table, tracing their outline and shape. They seemed to be pliable like thick paper, and would rustle with a metallic sound when the edges were moved by the thumb, as one does sometimes thumb the edges of a book."[43]

While Emma never saw an angel or heard a voice from heaven, she is a significant witness to the Book of Mormon. Even though she did not even look upon the ancient record from which the book was translated, yet her testimony concerning the Book of Mormon is that it came forth in her presence and on the foundation of her personal sacrifice. After a lifetime of reflection, just a few months before she died, she said, "My belief is that the Book of Mormon is of divine authenticity. I have not the slightest doubt of it. . . . Though *I was an active participant in the scenes that transpired, and was present during the translation of the plates . . . and had cognizance of things as they transpired*, it is marvelous to me, 'a marvel and a wonder,' as much so as to anyone else."[44]

Notes

1. Scot Facer Proctor and Maurine Jensen, *The Revised and Enhanced History of Joseph Smith by His Mother* (Salt Lake City: Bookcraft, 1996), p. 137. See also *HC*, 1:47 ftnt. See also Lucy Mack Smith, *History of Joseph Smith by His Mother*, ed. Preston Nibley (Salt Lake City: Bookcraft, 1958), p. 102.

2. Proctor and Proctor, *Revised and Enhanced History of Joseph Smith*, p. 137. See also Lucy Smith, *Biographical Sketches of Joseph Smith the Prophet and His Progenitors for Many Generations* (Independence, Mo.: Herald Publishing House, 1969), pp. 113-14 . Hereafter referred to as *Biographical Sketches*.

3. Proctor and Proctor, *Revised and Enhanced History of Joseph Smith*, p. 137. See also *History of Joseph Smith by His Mother*, p. 102, and *Biographical Sketches*, p. 114.

4. Proctor and Proctor, *Revised and Enhanced History of Joseph Smith*, p. 139. See also *History of Joseph Smith By His Mother*, p. 104, and *Biographical Sketches*, p. 116.

5. Proctor and Proctor, *Revised and Enhanced History of Joseph Smith*, p. 139. See also *Biographical Sketches,* p. 116.

6. Proctor and Proctor, *Revised and Enhanced History of Joseph Smith*, p. 141. See also *History of Joseph Smith by His Mother*, p. 106, and *Biographical Sketches,* p. 118.

7. Proctor and Proctor, *Revised and Enhanced History of Joseph Smith*, p. 141. See also *History of Joseph Smith by His Mother*, p. 108.

8. Proctor and Proctor, *Revised and Enhanced History of Joseph Smith*, p. 144. See also *History of Joseph Smith by His Mother*, p. 108.

9. In Larry C. Porter, "The Colesville Branch," found in *A New Light Breaks Forth,* ed. by Lyndon W. Cook and Donald Q. Cannon (Salt Lake City: Hawkes Publishing, 1980), pp. 76-96. This article contains the text of Josiah Stowell's letter, written for Stowell by Martha L. Campbell, to Joseph Smith, Jr., Elmira, Chemung County, New York, dated 19 December 1843. The letter itself is located in LDS Church Archives. Martha L. Campbell was a member of the LDS Church at Elmira, New York, having been baptized at that place on 9 August 1835, under the ministrations of Elder Evan M. Greene and John Young, Jr. Spelling and grammar have been corrected for clarity.

10. Family records in possession of Dorothy Dean, Carthage, Ill. The spelling for Katharine is as she wrote in her life, and as the family indicates she preferred it spelled, although most publications do not spell it that way.

11. William Hartley, *They Are My Friends* (Provo, Utah: Grandin Book, 1986), p. 206.

12. *HC,* 1:20.

13. Ibid.

14. See Isaiah 29:11-12.

15. *HC,* 1:20.

16. Lucy Smith, *Biographical Sketches* p. 122. See also Proctor and Proctor, *Revised and Enhanced History of Joseph Smith*, p. 157.

17. Lucy Smith, *Biographical Sketches*, p. 129; see also Proctor and Proctor, *Revised and Enhanced History of Joseph Smith* p. 166.

18. 1 Nephi 9:2-6; see also Doctrine & Covenants 10.

19. Emma Hale Smith Bidamon, *Emma Smith's Last Testimony*, February 1879, Reorganized Church of Jesus Christ of Latter Day Saints (RLDS) Archives, Independence, Mo. Hereafter cited as *Emma's Last Testimony.*

20. Hartley, *They Are My Friends*, p. 35.

21. Ibid.

22. Doctrine and Covenants 13:1 and *HC,* 1:39.

23. *HC,*1:44.

24. Doctrine & Covenants 4:1; see also Doctrine & Covenants 11:16 and 12:6.

25. *HC,*1:40-43 ftnts.

26. *HC,*1:108.

27. Ibid.

28. Proctor and Proctor, *Revised and Enhanced History of Joseph Smith*, p. 195. See also *History of Joseph Smith by His Mother*, pp. 149-50 ftnt. In the *History of the Church* we read that Joseph Knight came with his wagon to move the family to Fayette and that they arrived in the last week in August. Undoubtedly the latter version is an after-the-fact effort to reconstruct events, giving credit to Joseph Knight instead of David Whitmer. Both the Proctors' and Nibley's version of Lucy Mack Smith's account show that David Whitmer brought the Smiths to Fayette in June. Nibley adds the footnote, "According to David Whitmer it was late in May or early in June, 1829, that he arrived at Waterloo with Joseph and Oliver."

29. Ether 5:1-4; see also 2 Nephi 11:3, 27:14.

30. *HC*, 1:55 ftnt.

31. Lucy Smith, *Biographical Sketches*, p. 164; see also *HC*, 1:55-56 ftnts.

32. *Biographical Sketches*, p. 165. See also *HC*, 1:55-56 and *History of Joseph Smith by His Mother*, p.152.

33. *Biographical Sketches*, p. 165. See also *HC*, 1:56.

34. Ibid.

35. Introduction to the Book of Mormon; see also *HC*, 1:56-58 for original text.

36. Ibid.

37. *HC*, 1:58 ftnt.

38. *History of Joseph Smith by His Mother*, p. 155. See also Proctor and Proctor, *Revised and Enhanced History of Joseph Smith*, p. 203.

39. *HC*, 1:71.

40. See Rhett Stephen James, *The Man Who Knew: The Early Years*, a dramatic biography of Martin Harris (Logan, Utah: Martin Harris Pageant Committee, 1983), p. 162. See also Proctor and Proctor, *Revised and Enhanced History of Joseph Smith*, p. 206 ftnt #7.

41. A significant part of the original Book of Mormon manuscript is still in existence, preserved in the LDS Church Archives in Salt Lake City, Utah. The printer's manuscript, which was prepared by Oliver Cowdery, is also preserved in the archives of the RLDS Church in Independence, Missouri.

42. *Emma's Last Testimony.*

43. Ibid.

44. Ibid.; italics added.

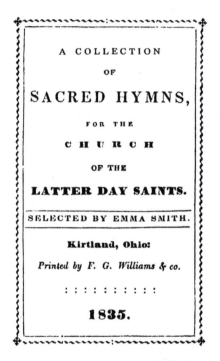

Photocopy of title page of hymn book compiled by Emma (actual size).
A Herald Heritage Reprint, 1973. Courtesy of RLDS Archives.

CHAPTER 3

Founding the Kingdom

"And verily I say unto thee that thou shalt lay aside the things of this world, and seek for the things of a better."
(Doctrine & Covenants 25:10)

As soon as the Book of Mormon was published, it was circulated from hand to hand, and several people believed and asked to be baptized. The time had come for the formal organization of a new church. On Tuesday, 6 April 1830, a fairly large number of people crowded into Peter Whitmer's log home, at Fayette, New York, for that purpose.

The entire Whitmer family, Joseph's parents and brothers and sisters, Joseph and Emma, Oliver Cowdery, Martin Harris, and other friends and relatives were present.

Under the laws of the land, six men were required to officially organize a new church. In an affidavit signed by Joseph Knight, Jr., who kept the records for the event, the six names recorded were Oliver Cowdery, Joseph Smith, Jr., Hyrum Smith, Peter Whitmer, Jr., Samuel H. Smith, and David Whitmer.[1]

Knight's record states that the meeting was opened "by solemn prayer to our Heavenly Father." After the prayer, each of the six brethren was called upon to express his feelings as to whether he believed a church should be organized. They all accepted Joseph and Oliver as their "teachers in the things of the Kingdom of God." The voting was unanimous.[2]

Joseph then laid his hands upon Oliver's head, and ordained him an "Elder" of the Church. Then Oliver ordained Joseph to the same office. The record states, "We then took bread, blessed it, and brake it with them; also wine, blessed it, and drank it with them." Each individual, who had been baptized previously, was blessed in the same manner, "that they might receive the gift of the Holy Ghost, and [be] confirmed . . . members of the Church."[3]

A wonderful outpouring of the Holy Ghost moved some to prophesy, and all to praise the Lord. They "rejoiced exceedingly" that through the grace of God, the blessings of the Holy Ghost were bestowed upon them.[4] They were now members of the church of Jesus Christ, legally organized under the laws of the land, and acknowledged of God.

Joseph's parents, Martin Harris, Porter Rockwell, and others were baptized. Since Emma was not among those who were baptized that day and is not specifically mentioned by name in any of the contemporary accounts of that event, some have assumed that she was not present at the organization of the church. There is no definite proof that Emma was present, but a number of other people known to have been present that day were not listed by name either. As obviously involved and interested in the Restoration as Emma was, it seems unlikely Joseph would have set out to take care of such an important project, leaving her at home. Lucy Mack Smith gives circumstantial evidence that Emma was, in fact, present.[5] After the meeting was completed, Lucy says, "they returned to Harmony." The only "they" to "return to Harmony" are Joseph and Emma. All the others lived elsewhere.

The First Church Conference

Emma stayed at home when Joseph went to Colesville, Broome County, New York, to tell Joseph Knight, Sr., and the rest of his family, about the organization, and invite them to join the Church. The Prophet found the Knight family friendly and hospitable, and spent a great deal of time talking with Father Knight's son Newel.

Throughout the rest of the months of April and May, many meetings were held and many people heard the good news: that Christ's church had been reestablished on the earth and the restoration of the gospel was in progress. During these meetings, the Holy Ghost was manifest and many were convinced of the truthfulness of the Prophet's message.

Newel Knight went to Fayette during the last week in May and was baptized by David Whitmer; the son-in-law of Father Knight, Freeborn DeMille, was also baptized.

The first conference of the Church was held on 9 June 1830, at Fayette. Remarkable manifestations of the Spirit were experienced, and more baptisms were performed. Several men were ordained to the priesthood.[6] The *History of the Church* records Joseph's sentiments:

> Such scenes . . . were calculated to inspire our hearts with joy unspeakable, and fill us with awe and reverence for the Almighty Being, by whose grace we had been called to be instrumental in bringing about, for the children of men, the enjoyment of such glorious blessings as were now at this time poured out upon us. To find ourselves engaged in the very same order of things as observed by the holy Apostles of old; to realize the importance and solemnity of such proceedings; and to witness and feel with our own natural senses, the glorious manifestations of the powers of the Priesthood, the gifts and blessings of the holy Ghost, and the goodness and condescension of a merciful God unto such as obey the everlasting Gospel of our Lord Jesus Christ, combined to create within us sensations of rapturous gratitude, and inspire us with fresh zeal and energy in the cause of truth.[7]

Emma's Baptism

Toward the end of June, Joseph and Emma, accompanied by Oliver Cowdery and John and David Whitmer, traveled from Harmony to Colesville. Though it was only a thirty-mile trip, their journey took them out of Pennsylvania and into New York state. They were made welcome at the home of Polly and Joseph Knight, Sr.

On Saturday, 26 June, the men built a dam across a stream, expecting to have sufficient depth of water for the baptisms they intended to perform the next day, which was the Sabbath. However, a mob gathered during the night and tore down the dam. Since the water was set loose, they could not perform baptisms the next morning, but they decided to have a meeting anyway. Oliver preached and others bore testimony to the truth of the Book of Mormon, the doctrine of repentance, baptism for the remission of sins, and laying on of hands for the gift of the Holy Ghost. After the meeting, some of those who had torn down the dam tried to talk the believers into turning away from this new church and its doctrine. Emily Coburn, the sister of Sally Coburn Knight, was taken away by force by her father and a Reverend Mr. Shearer, who considered himself her pastor.

Early the following morning, 28 June 1830, the dam was quickly repaired. As soon as the water was deep enough, Emma was baptized by Oliver. Nearly all of the Knight family were baptized that day, including Joseph Knight, Sr., his wife, Polly Peck Knight, and their daughter Polly; William Stringham and his wife, Esther Knight Stringham; Joseph Knight, Jr.; Anna Knight DeMille, wife of Freeborn DeMille; Newel K. Knight and his wife, Sally Coburn Knight; Aaron Culver and his wife; Julia Stringham; and Levi Hale.[8]

Mobs Disrupt Baptism and Prevent Confirmation

Even before the baptisms were finished, a mob of about fifty men gathered. The believers retired to the house of Joseph Knight, Sr. Joseph Smith described the mob as "raging with anger, and apparently determined to commit violence upon us. Some asked us questions, others threatened us, so that we thought it wise to leave and go [next] to the house of Newel Knight. There also [the mob] followed us, and it was only by exercise of great prudence on our part, and reliance in our Heavenly Father, that they were kept from laying violent hands upon us; and so long as they chose to stay we were obliged to answer them various unprofitable questions, and bear with insults and threatenings without number."[9]

In addition to breaking up the baptism, the mob vandalized the property of the Knight family. Joseph Knight, Jr., described the scene: "That night our wagons were turned over and wood piled on them, and some sunk in the water, rails were piled against our doors, and chains sunk in the stream and a great deal of mischief done."[10]

On this day, the Prophet's history recalls: "We had appointed a meeting for this evening, for the purpose of attending to the confirmation of those who had been the same morning baptized. The time appointed had arrived and our friends had nearly all collected together, when to my surprise, I was visited by a constable, and arrested by him on a warrant, on the charge of being a disorderly person, of setting the country in an uproar by preaching the Book of Mormon, etc."[11]

With the meeting disrupted in this manner and her husband taken away, Emma and the others who had been baptized, could not be confirmed. While Joseph was taken to South Bainbridge for trial, Emma went to the home of her sister, Elizabeth Wasson, who lived at Colesville.

The land belonging to the Knights was between the town of Colesville, Broome County, and South Bainbridge, Chenango County, so traveling from one town to the other required crossing county lines. This led to Joseph having to face harassment in both counties.

Chenango County Trial

The trial convened on 30 June 1830, in South Bainbridge. During this trial every effort was made to prove something against Joseph's character. His old friend, Joseph Knight, Sr., prevailed upon two of his neighbors, James Davidson and John Reid, to defend him. The two men were well known in the area for their integrity and knowledge of the law. Knight paid the expenses for this defense.

During the trial, Joseph's former employer, Josiah Stowell, was called upon to testify, with the expectation that he would reveal various unsavory aspects of Joseph's character. Mr. Stowell's two daughters were also asked to testify in relation to Joseph's behavior toward them, both in public and private. Mr. Stowell and his daughters gave such fervent support of Joseph, the case was dismissed.[12]

Broome County Trial

No sooner was Joseph freed by the Chenango County authorities, than he was again arrested, this time on a warrant from Broome County. Here many false testimonies were sworn against him. Again, Mr. Knight prevailed upon Mr. Reid and Mr. Davidson to defend him. Many years later in Nauvoo, John Reid made an interesting remark concerning these trials:

> . . . [Joseph Smith] was arrested again, and [sent] on the way to Colesville for another trial. I was again called upon by his friends to defend him against his malignant persecutors, and clear him from the false charges they had preferred against him. I made every reasonable excuse I could, as I was nearly worn down through fatigue and want of sleep; as I had been engaged in law suits for two days, and nearly the whole of two nights. But I saw the persecution was great against him; and here let me say, . . . singular as it may seem, while Mr. Knight was pleading with me to go, a peculiar impression or thought struck my mind, that I must go and defend him, for he was the Lord's anointed. I said I would go, and started with as much faith as the Apostles had when they could remove mountains, accompanied by Father Knight, who was like the old patriarchs that followed the ark of God to the city of David.[13]

Mr. Reid then explained the procedure of the court. Many witnesses were called who swore false testimony, but nothing was proved, so they sent out runners and gathered a company of men from the worst element, to come and swear against Joseph. However, as Mr. Reid reported, "Nothing was proven against him whatever." At two in the morning the court deliberated the evidence for a short time.

Reid continued his narrative:

> . . . We were called in. The court arraigned the prisoner and said, "Mr. Smith, we have had your case under consideration, examined the testimony and find nothing to condemn you, and therefore you are discharged." They then proceeded to reprimand him severely; not because anything derogatory to his character in any shape had been proven against him by the host of witnesses that had testified during the trial, but merely to please those fiends in human shape who were engaged in the unhallowed persecution of an innocent man, sheerly on account of his religious opinions. After they had got through, I arose and said: "This court puts me in mind of a certain trial held before Felix of old, when the enemies of Paul arraigned him before the venerable judge for some alleged crime, and nothing was found in him

worthy of death or of bonds. Yet, to please the Jews, who were his accusers, he was left bound contrary to the law; and this court has served Mr. Smith in the same way, by their unlawful and uncalled for reprimand after his discharge, to please his accusers . . . ."

We got him away that night from the midst of three hundred people without his receiving any injury; but I am well aware that we were assisted by some higher power than man; for to look back on the scene, I cannot tell how we succeeded in getting him away. I take no glory to myself; it was the Lord's work and marvelous to our eyes.[14]

According to Joseph, he was aided by the constable, with whom he had made friends. Once free, he made his way to the Wasson home, where he said, "[I] found my wife waiting with much anxiety the issue of those ungodly proceedings, and in company with her . . . arrived the next day in safety at my own house."[15]

A Revelation for Emma

Joseph made several efforts to go back to Colesville to confirm those who had been baptized, but the roads were watched continually. It became obvious that their enemies were determined to prevent Joseph from making the trip, so he sent Oliver to attend to the confirmations at Colesville. This created a problem because Oliver and Joseph had been working together to organize the revelations for publication. Emma therefore agreed to act as secretary in helping to prepare the material, which made it possible for Oliver to go.

Before Oliver left, Joseph inquired of the Lord on behalf of each of them. The revelations received at that time are found in the Doctrine and Covenants, sections 24 and 25. When viewed together they each become more than either of them alone. The revelation to Emma was given as a comfort, assuring her that she would eventually be confirmed and receive the gift of the Holy Ghost, which would inspire and guide her in her role as wife to the Prophet. This revelation is given here in its entirety because it reveals how the Lord regards his daughters, and this revelation uses Emma to convey, indirectly, significant counsel intended for all.

Hearken unto the voice of the Lord your God, while I speak unto you, Emma Smith, my daughter; for verily I say unto you all those who receive my gospel are sons and daughters in my kingdom.

A revelation I give unto you concerning my will; and if thou art faithful and walk in the paths of virtue before me, I will preserve thy life, and thou shalt receive an inheritance in Zion.

Behold, thy sins are forgiven thee, and thou art an elect lady, whom I have called.

Murmur not because of the things which thou hast not seen, for they are withheld from thee and from the world, which is wisdom in me in a time to come.

And the office of thy calling shall be for a comfort unto my servant, Joseph Smith, Jun., thy husband, in his afflictions, with consoling words, in the spirit of meekness.

And thou shalt be ordained under his hand to expound the scriptures, and to exhort the church, according as it shall be given thee by my Spirit.

For he shall lay his hands upon thee, and thou shalt receive the Holy Ghost, and thy time shall be given to writing, and to learning much.

And thou needest not fear, for thy husband shall support thee in the church; for unto them is his calling that all things might be revealed unto them, whatsoever I will, according to their faith.

And verily I say unto thee that thou shalt lay aside the things of this world, and seek for the things of a better.

And it shall be given thee, also, to make a selection of sacred hymns, as it shall be given thee, which is pleasing unto me, to be had in my church.

For my soul delighteth in the song of the heart; yea, the song of the righteous is a prayer unto me, and it shall be answered with a blessing upon their heads.

Wherefore, lift up thy heart and rejoice, and cleave unto the covenants which thou has made.

Continue in the spirit of meekness and beware of pride. Let thy soul delight in thy husband, and the glory which shall come upon him.

Keep my commandments continually, and a crown of righteousness thou shalt receive. And except thou do this, where I am you cannot come.

And verily, verily, I say unto you, this is my voice unto all. Amen."[16]

A Flurry of Conflict

Oliver went to Colesville, and from there proceeded to the Whitmer home in Fayette. When he told John Whitmer about the project to prepare the revelations for publication, John went to Harmony to assist Joseph in arranging and copying them. While they were engaged in this work, a disturbing letter came from Oliver. He commanded Joseph to erase some words from one of the revelations, claiming that it was "priestcraft."

Because of this disturbing letter, Joseph knew he had to go to Fayette to confront this problem face to face with Oliver and the Whitmers. Leaving Emma at home and taking pains to avoid being seen by his enemies, he went to Fayette. There he found Oliver and the entire Whitmer family caught up in a spirit of false revelation. He spent considerable effort with them and with their son-in-law, Hiram Page, explaining the meaning of the wording in the revelations. Through patient reasoning, he was at last able to overcome the false spirit and proved to them that there was no disharmony with the revelations and the scriptures. He then returned home.[17]

Emma's Confirmation

Early in August, Newel and Sally Knight came to visit. More than a month had passed since Emma and Sally had been baptized, and they were still not confirmed. It was planned that they hold a sacrament meeting at Emma and Joseph's house, and there confirm the ladies.

While Joseph was on his way to buy wine for the sacrament service, he was warned by the Spirit of the Lord not to buy wine locally, because there was a plan to poison them. He was told that they should make their own wine, or use pure water, for the ordinance of the sacrament. It didn't matter what they ate or drank; what mattered was the spirit in which they partook of the bread, which represented the body of the Lord, and the drink, which represented his blood. The ordinance symbolized a renewal of the covenant of baptism, and the prayers used to prepare them to partake of the bread and wine called each one to remember Jesus Christ and keep his commandments.

That evening, they partook of the sacrament and the two women were confirmed. There were five people present for this meeting: John Whitmer, Newel and Sally Knight, Joseph and Emma. Of this evening it was written, "The spirit of the Lord was poured out upon us and we praised the Lord God and rejoiced exceedingly."[18]

A Bitter Parting

When Emma had first married Joseph, her father had barely tolerated him as a son-in-law. Then, for a short time, he extended his protection to them. Now, with all the adverse publicity, Isaac Hale believed the falsehoods and shameful accusations that were leveled against Joseph by a certain man who professed to be a minister of God. Emma's father therefore withdrew his protection from Joseph. The mob spirit that raged in the neighborhood made the situation nearly unbearable.

Once again, Joseph Knight, Sr., came to the rescue. He brought a wagon to move the Smiths to Fayette, New York, where they were again invited to stay with the Peter Whitmer family.

Emma's heart must have broken at her father's bitterness. When she married Joseph, her father had said to him, "You have stolen my daughter. I had rather have followed her to the grave." Now, failing to persuade Emma to stay with them and not go with Joseph, her father's parting words were "No good can ever come of it!"[19]

Emma never saw either of her parents again. This would have constituted one of the most severe sacrifices, for Emma loved her family and longed for their approval. She must have prayed continually thereafter for the time when they would listen and accept the gospel message.[20]

Rejected of Man, Chosen of God

In September, a revelation was given that would clearly mark the path for Joseph as the Prophet of God, and for Emma as his faithful companion. In the presence of six elders of the Church, Joseph dictated the following revelation:

> Listen to the voice of Jesus Christ, your Redeemer, the Great I Am, whose arm of mercy hath atoned for your sins;
>
> Who will gather his people even as a hen gathereth her chickens under her wings, even as many as will hearken to my voice and humble themselves before me, and call upon me in mighty prayer. . . .
>
> Verily, I say unto you that ye are chosen out of the world to declare my gospel with the sound of rejoicing, as with the voice of a trump.
>
> Lift up your hearts and be glad, for I am in your midst, and am your advocate with the Father; and it is His good will to give you the kingdom . . .
>
> . . . And ye are called to bring to pass the gathering of mine elect; for mine elect hear my voice and harden not their hearts. . . .[21]

During the next fourteen years, Emma did, indeed, lay aside the things of this world. She gave up everything and shared the burdens of her prophet husband as he moved forward to lay the foundation of the kingdom of God.

Notes

1. *HC,* 1:76 ftnt.

2. *HC,* 1:77.

3. *HC,* 1:78.

4. Ibid.

5. Richard L. Anderson (manuscript in preparation) has done a comprehensive study of these events and informs me that he feels sure Emma was in Fayette for the organization.

6. *HC,* 1:84

7. *HC,* 1:81-86.

8. *HC,* 1:88. See also *A New Light Breaks Forth,* ed. by Lyndon W. Cook and Donald Q. Cannon (Salt Lake City: Hawkes Publishing, 1980), pp. 83-84.

9. *HC,* 1:87-88.

10. William Hartley, *They Are My Friends* (Provo, Utah: Grandin Book, 1986), p. 53.

11. *HC,* 1:88-89.

12. *HC,* 1:90-93.

13. *HC,* 1:94-95 ftnt. For text of Reid's statement see *Times and Seasons* (17 May 1844), 5:549-52.

14. Ibid.

15. *HC,* 1:96.

16. Doctrine & Covenants 25.

17. *HC,* 1:104-15.

18. *HC,* 1:108.

19. Isaac Hale, Affidavit to Peter Ingersoll, 1833, Brigham Young University Archives. Quoted in memo to author from Richard L. Anderson, 1995.

20. See Doctrine & Covenants 109:68-70.

21. See Doctrine & Covenants 29:1-7.

CHAPTER 4

Prelude to Glory

"Continue in the spirit of meekness and beware of pride. Let thy soul delight in thy husband, and the glory which shall come upon him." (Doctrine & Covenants 25:14)

There is no doubt that Emma put her whole soul into the effort of helping to lay the foundation of the kingdom of God. When she left Pennsylvania, it was for the sake of the gospel and her husband's mission. Her faith in the divinity of his mission caused Emma to turn her back on parents, social position, security, and all things a girl holds dear, to share a beggar's life with her prophet husband, whose entire energy was directed toward fulfilling God's commandment to take the message of the Restoration to the whole world.

Waterloo, New York

After leaving Harmony, Joseph and Emma stayed for a time with the Whitmers. Then they moved to Waterloo, New York, where they set up housekeeping. Emma had her parents send her furniture and her cow. Father and Mother Smith and the rest of their family had already moved to Waterloo while Hyrum and Jerusha were living in Colesville with the Knight family. Everyone worked together to make preparations for the men who were about to leave on missions.[1] The women spun, wove, and sewed to make clothing for the missionaries. Emma worked so hard during this time that she overtaxed her strength and became ill. She was down in bed for several weeks. Her mother-in-law remarked in her history that even as Emma rested, her hands were not idle and she remained cheerful and was able to buoy up everyone else's spirits with her good humor.[2]

In the three years since Joseph and Emma married, the Book of Mormon had been published, the Church had been established, missionaries were being sent into many of the states of America, projected plans included a worldwide missionary effort, and eventually, the building of a city to be called Zion, a place where the pure in heart would dwell. One primary target for missionary work was the western reaches of the country, which were, at that time, along the Missouri River. The brethren felt a special obligation to take the message of the Book of Mormon to the Indian tribes, whom they recognized as descendants of the people of the Book of Mormon.[3]

A young convert, Parley P. Pratt, along with Oliver Cowdery, Peter Whitmer, Jr., and several others, headed west across the state of Ohio. On their way, Parley Pratt stopped to visit with several friends, including Sidney Rigdon, who was preaching for the Campbellite faith at the town of Mentor, near Kirtland, Ohio. Parley Pratt presented his old friend with a Book of Mormon and told him about the organization of the Church. Sidney Rigdon had not heard of the Book of Mormon and was quite surprised at the things Parley told him. He expressed his belief in the Bible as revelation from God, but strongly doubted the Book of Mormon could be what they claimed. The eager missionaries suggested they discuss the subject, but Sidney declined, saying he would read the book and pray about it to determine for himself whether or not it was a revelation from God.[4] He also gave Oliver Cowdery and Parley Pratt permission to address a meeting in his Church. After they concluded their sermons, Sidney Rigdon arose and told the large congregation that they should follow the Apostle's admonition to ". . . prove all things, and hold fast that which is good." He advised them to go home and give the matter consideration, and not turn against it without being thoroughly convinced of its being an imposition, lest they should possibly resist the truth.[5]

Within two weeks, Rigdon had read the Book of Mormon. After prayer and study, he became convinced of the truth of the work. He and about twenty of his congregation were baptized, making a little branch of the Church in Ohio. Among those who heard the message at this time were Frederick Granger Williams and Edward Partridge, two men who would be instrumental in establishing the Church organization, and who would become close friends to Joseph and Emma.

Having had great success in Ohio, the missionaries headed for Missouri to begin their mission to the Indians. Meanwhile, early in December, Sidney Rigdon and Edward Partridge traveled to Fayette to meet the Prophet. After meeting him, Partridge was reassured, and Joseph baptized him in the Seneca River on 11 December 1830.[6]

Emma must have been elated when these well-educated and eminent gentlemen responded to her husband's mission. In spite of continual persecution in New York, thrilling reports of success came from every direction.

Ten months after the Church was organized, Joseph received a revelation on 2 January 1831, commanding him to move the Church to Kirtland, Ohio. The Lord promised in a revelation, "There I will give unto you my law; and there you will be endowed with power from on high."[7]

Move to Ohio

The members of the Church in Colesville and Fayette accepted the command to move to Ohio. Joseph and Emma left with Sidney Rigdon and Edward Partridge in a sleigh provided by Joseph Knight. They arrived in Kirtland, Ohio, on 2 February 1831. Emma was five months pregnant at the time of this trip.

It was snowy and cold when they arrived in front of the Gilbert and Whitney Store in Kirtland. Joseph stepped from the sleigh and assisted Emma. Then he strode into the store, put out his hand, and said, "Newel K. Whitney, thou art the man. . . ." Then he introduced himself as the Prophet Joseph Smith.[8]

Emma and Joseph found a warm welcome in the home of Newel and Elizabeth Whitney. They stayed in the Whitney home for about two weeks and established a friendship that would span many years. Soon a house was built for them at the Morley settlement, a few miles from Kirtland. Joseph's parents and others of his family arrived in March after a long and dangerous journey, by land and water, from

New York State. They lived for a short time with Emma and Joseph before they moved to a farm that Joseph had purchased for them.

While Emma awaited the birth of her baby, she was hostess for many Church meetings in the small house that had been built for them at the Morleys'. There the three witnesses, the eight witnesses, and Joseph often met and related their experiences to visitors. A young girl recalled one occasion when there were not enough chairs to seat everyone. Boards were placed across boxes to make benches. She described the spirit of the meeting, saying that Joseph's face seemed to glow ". . . like he had a searchlight within him . . ." as he bore testimony of his remarkable experiences.[9]

In the Morley settlement, the members of the Church lived in a system patterned after the ancient order of Enoch, holding all things in common. Emma became an integral part of that community. She was treated with great love and tenderness as she anxiously awaited the day when she would hold a baby in her arms.

Thrice Bereaved, Twice Blessed

On 30 April 1831, Emma gave birth to twins.[10] Like her first baby, they only lived a short time. This loss caused sorrow from which Emma was hardly able to recover. While she and Joseph were grieving deeply, they heard of the death of Julia Murdock, who had also given birth to twins. Their father, John Murdock, was beside himself with grief and anxiety. He took the tiny, motherless twins to Emma, and she and Joseph adopted them to raise as their own.[11]

What joy must Emma have felt as her arms embraced two precious babies. At the same time, her joy was no doubt mingled with the sorrow of her loss. The names of Joseph and Julia Murdock Smith are found written in the family Bible. Names are also recorded there for her twins, Thaddeus and Louisa.[12] Although many years later, when interviewed by her sons, she stated that her twins were not named, the names appear to be written in Emma's handwriting.[13] This is just another of the many aspects of Emma's life that have been obscured by conflicting evidence, or are lacking completely.

More Organization for the Church

Within a few weeks of arriving in Ohio, the Prophet received a number of revelations which advanced the organization process and defined the law and doctrine of the Church. Early in February, Edward Partridge was called to serve as bishop to the Church. Joseph received a revelation from the Lord indicating a plan for caring for the poor. It was to be a law of sacrifice and covenant for the Church members and was expected to provide the means for building the Lord's kingdom. It would be called the law of consecration.

Joseph Goes to Missouri—The Law of Consecration

The twins were about a month and a half old when Joseph left for Missouri. He was gone from June 19 until the end of August. Not long after he arrived there, the brethren in Missouri agreed to the law of consecration, and the bishops were given stewardship for administering it. The plan called for the members to voluntarily deed all their property to the Church. They were then given deeds for the portions they needed for necessities, and they gave all surplus produce to the Church.[14] Among the first to embrace this plan were Bishop Partridge, Newel K. Whitney, and Martin Harris, who had already experienced the process of consecration when he gave the money to print the Book of Mormon.

Designation of the Land of Missouri as "Zion"

In July a revelation was given designating the land of Missouri as the gathering place of the Saints and the place for the city of Zion. According to the journal history, Joseph wrote:

> On the second day of August [1831], I assisted the Colesville Branch of the Church to lay the first log, for a house, as a foundation of Zion in Kaw Township, twelve miles west of Independence. The log was carried and placed by twelve men in honor of the twelve tribes of Israel. At the same time, through prayer, the land was consecrated and dedicated by Elder Sidney Rigdon for the gathering of the Saints.[15]

The following day, on 3 August, Joseph "proceeded to dedicate the spot for the temple, a little west of Independence."[16] In the revelations given at this time, members of the Church were told that if they were to obtain the land by purchase, it would prove a blessing. However, if it came to bloodshed—since they were forbidden to shed blood—they would be scourged from city to city, and few would stand to receive an inheritance.[17]

Joseph and Emma's good friends, the Knights and the DeMilles, were among the brethren who assisted in these special occasions. On 7 August, Joseph attended the funeral of Polly Peck Knight. The Prophet stated, "This was the first death in the Church in this land, and I can say, a worthy member sleeps in Jesus till the resurrection."[18]

Before leaving for home, Joseph made arrangements for William W. Phelps to obtain a printing press to be set up in Independence.[19]

When her husband returned to Kirtland on 27 August, after an absence of two and a half months, Emma must have been very glad to see him and show him how much the babies had grown. She may also have exclaimed over the new revelations Joseph had received. Perhaps she trembled at the prospects they implied, and wondered when she, too, would make the thousand-mile trek to Missouri. Or it may be that future possibilities faded from her thoughts as she received the sad news of Polly Knight's death. Surely she would have remembered the many experiences they had shared—watching and listening fearfully while the mob rampaged around Polly's house and wreaked havoc upon the Knights' farm on the day she and Polly were baptized just a little more than a year ago. Emma would probably have been deeply moved by what Newel had said about his mother's faith—that although very ill on the trip from Ohio, she had refused to stop traveling. Newel said "her greatest desire had been to set her feet upon the land of Zion and to have her body interred in that land."[20]

A Healing Miracle

In spite of persecution, the Church was growing rapidly. Although often lonely, Emma must have watched the growth of the Church with eagerness. The blessings of the priesthood were being manifested in many ways. One evening during a meeting held at their house, a miraculous healing occurred. Curious about the Church, the John Johnson family had come to the meeting with friends who were investigating this new religion. During the evening the subject turned to the question of supernatural gifts, such as were conferred in the days of the apostles. During the conversation, someone said:

> "Here is Mrs. Johnson with a lame arm; has God given any power to men now on the earth to cure her?" A few moments later, when the conversation had turned in another direction, Smith rose, and walking across the room, taking Mrs. Johnson by the hand said in a most solemn manner: "Woman, in the name of the Lord Jesus Christ I command thee to be whole" and immediately left the room. The company were awe-stricken at the infinite presumption of the man, and the calm assurance with which he spoke. The sudden mental and moral shock—I know not how better to explain the well-attested fact—electrified the rheumatic arm—Mrs. Johnson at once lifted it up with ease, and on her return home the next day she was able to do her washing without difficulty or pain.[21]

The Johnsons joined the Church. Following this experience, there were other miracles performed quietly by the elders of the Church. Some of the miracles brought converts, some brought skeptics, and some aroused envy among the local doctors and ministers. Also, around this same time, some members were affected by false spirits because they did not understand that the adversary may deceive through false revelation. We have no documents to show what Emma thought about these things. We should not, however, presume she was ignorant of the events, or the problems that arose. She would certainly have been aware that there was so much coming and going in her house, that Joseph had little time to take care of his family and less time to attend to the newly assigned task the Lord had directed him to do—to make a new translation of the Bible.

An Inspired Translation of the Bible

Joseph was directed to translate the Bible in order to clarify those parts that had been lost or changed through the centuries. The Lord told him, "Thou shalt ask, and my scriptures shall be given as I have appointed, and they shall be preserved in safety."[22]

In order to have a quiet place to work, Joseph accepted the invitation to move his family to the John Johnson home in Hiram, Ohio, about thirty miles from Kirtland. They moved in September 1831. Sidney Rigdon, who was now acting as Joseph's scribe, and his wife, Phoebe, set up housekeeping in a small cabin nearby. While Joseph and Sidney worked on the translation of the Bible in an upstairs room of the Johnson farm house, Emma tended her babies and assisted Mrs. Johnson with household duties.

A Heavenly Manifestation

This was a time of great learning and education for the Prophet. The translation was progressing well. He examined several versions of the Bible and said the German translation was very good, but he used the King James version, most probably because it was commonly used. Sidney's skills as a scribe and his knowledge of the Bible and history were extremely valuable to Joseph. On 16 February 1832, Joseph and Sidney had a singular experience of which they noted the following:

> . . . while we were doing the work of translation, which the lord appointed unto us, we came to the 29th verse of the 5th chapter of John, which was given unto us as follows:
> Speaking of the resurrection of the dead, concerning those who shall hear the voice of the Son of Man and shall come forth, they who have done good in the resurrection of the just, they who have done evil in the resurrection of the unjust. . . .
> And while we meditated upon these things, the Lord touched the eyes of our understandings and they were opened, and the glory of the Lord shone round about.
> And we beheld the glory of the Son, on the right hand of the Father, and received of His fulness.[23]

This was Sidney's first experience with revelation. In vision they saw holy angels; they saw many who were sanctified, worshipping before the throne where God and the Savior were sitting. They were also shown the fall of Lucifer, one of the choice sons of God, who rebelled against God and was cast down from heaven to the earth, where he became known as Satan, or the devil, and where he has the power to try and to afflict man. This vision caused Joseph and Sidney to marvel, for they knew it came from God. They later testified: "And now, after the many testimonies which have been given of Him, this is the testimony, last of all, which we give: that He lives! For we saw Him, even on the right hand of God; and we heard the voice bearing record that He is the only Begotten of the Father. That by Him and through Him and of Him, the worlds are and were created, and the inhabitants thereof are begotten sons and daughters unto God. . . ."24

Afterward, Sidney was visibly weak and shaken. When his condition was noted by others, Joseph observed that Sidney was not used to it as he was. Nevertheless, while the Spirit was still upon them, they wrote their testimonies. As she served their meals that day, Emma must have heard them discussing their marvelous experience. Perhaps she and Joseph talked long into the night about the incredible things he had learned in this vision, about the Lord's plan of salvation.

The Johnson family also heard Sidney and Joseph tell about what had occurred, and soon word of the event spread, so that before long friends from Kirtland came to enquire about it. All were encouraged and excited by the new understanding imparted to them concerning the purposes of the gospel.

However, while the members of the Church rejoiced, their enemies plotted their destruction. A little over a month after the vision, a nightmarish event occurred that would bring Emma face to face with the grim reality that her husband's mission would not bring peace, "but a sword."

Mobs, Tar, and Feathers

On 24 March 1832, a mob of angry men broke into the room where Joseph was sleeping. He and Emma had been tending the two eleven-month old babies, who were very sick with measles. Little Joseph Murdock was in bed with Joseph. When the mob came into the room they dragged the Prophet outside. During the confusion, the sick baby was exposed to the cold.

Mobbing was nothing new to Emma, but she had never encountered the depth of hatred exhibited by these men, who showed every intention of doing great bodily harm to Joseph, and had no mercy for her or her innocent children. Unable to protect her husband and terrified, she hid the babies and listened to the noise of the mob screeching obscenities as they dragged Joseph away. The Johnsons heard the noise, but could not help as their door had been barred to keep them in their room. We do not know how they were able to get out; perhaps Emma herself removed the barricade.

Hours later, Emma peered into the darkness, looking for Joseph. At last she saw him staggering toward the house and heard him calling for a blanket. He had been stripped naked and was covered with tar. In the dim light, it looked like he was covered with blood. She was so shocked by the sight she fainted. Tenderly, the Johnsons cared for her as well as Joseph.

After the initial shock, Emma revived, and with the help of the Johnsons, began to remove the tar from Joseph's body. This took most of the night. Some of his hair came out with the tar. His front tooth was broken, and his body was scarred from the severe beating he had received.

The mob had also dragged Sidney from his home, banging his head across the frozen ground as they went. After this horrible treatment, Sidney was not himself for some time. In fact, he never totally regained his full health and stability.[25]

The greatest tragedy for Emma and Joseph came a few days later when little Joseph Murdock died. The child might have died of measles anyway, as many infants did in those days; but Emma undoubtedly felt that exposure to the cold had caused his death. His was the first death in the Church caused by persecution. It would not be the last.

Now four of Emma's precious infants lay in the cold ground; but there was no time for Joseph and Emma to comfort each other. With the persecutors relentlessly pressing their cruel attentions, he was forced to leave Ohio. On 1 April, only three days after they buried the baby, Joseph, Sidney Rigdon, and Newel K. Whitney left for Missouri, leaving Emma and little Julia at the Johnson Farm.

Joseph worried about Emma and Julia. He feared the mob would come back and do them harm. Newel Whitney suggested that Emma go to Kirtland and stay with his wife. Following this advice, Emma took little Julia and traveled to Kirtland, expecting to find refuge with Elizabeth Whitney.[26]

No Room

When Emma and little Julia arrived at the Whitney home, Elizabeth was ill. An aged aunt, who lived with the Whitneys, answered the door. Without consulting Elizabeth, she told Emma she could not stay. Sadly, babe in arms, Emma trudged away—brokenhearted, grieving and alone.[27] She was in the early stages of her third pregnancy. Her husband was far away. She was homeless. She turned to her in-laws for help.

The Smiths' house was extremely crowded so it was impossible for her to remain there for long. Apparently she found lodging with one family and then another during the next three months. Lucy Mack Smith indicates that Emma stayed for a while with the Reynolds Cahoon family and for a time at the home of Dr. Frederick G. Williams. Perhaps she felt most at home with Frederick's wife, Rebecca Williams; Emma and Rebecca had much in common. Rebecca's father had disowned her, forbidding any of her family to communicate with her, because she had joined the Church.

Emma mourned her baby's death and her husband's absence, not knowing for weeks if Joseph was dead or alive. Meanwhile, Joseph did not know that Emma was not staying with Elizabeth Whitney, nor did Elizabeth realize that Emma had been turned away. Therefore, when Elizabeth Whitney wrote to Newel and Joseph did not receive a letter from Emma, he later wrote, chiding her: "Sister Whitney wrote a letter to her husband which was very chearing and being unwell at that time and filled with much anxiety it would have been very consoling to me to have received a few lines from you but as you did not take the trouble I will try to be contented with my lot knowing that God is my friend in him I shall find Comfort I have given my life into his hands I am prepared to go at his Call I desire to be with Christ I count not my life dear to me only to do his will. . . ."[28]

In this letter, he encouraged Emma to give comfort to the others in his family who had lost loved ones, and asked her to give "greetings" from him "to the brethren." He closed without the warmth and tenderness usual in his letters, apparently assuming that Emma had not cared to send a note to him with Elizabeth's. This misunderstanding, along with the loss of her babies and the feeling of not belonging any place, must have caused Emma severe distress. There can be no doubt that Emma would have been deeply stung by the tone of his letter, yet there is no indication of her making any defensive response. In any case, Joseph arrived in Kirtland before a letter could have reached him. In his history, Joseph acknowledged his wife's homeless situation during this time with one stark sentence that says it all. He said he "found Emma most disconsolate."

Joseph's first order of business was to try to arrange for a dwelling for his family. The problem must have been discussed with the Whitneys. When Elizabeth Whitney learned what had happened, she was deeply mortified. She said she would have gladly shared her last morsel of bread with the Prophet and his wife.

A four-room apartment was prepared above the Whitneys' store, which would be "home" to Emma, but just for a while.

The Prophet Sustained in Missouri

Joseph's trip had been unbelievably successful. In Missouri, he had received a unanimous vote of confidence from the brethren. He had established a high council in Zion, and had further defined and refined the Church organization. Edward Partridge was the Church's first presiding bishop, and he now lived in Missouri. Newel Knight was chosen bishop in Kirtland. W. W. Phelps had established a printing press in Independence, one of the first printing presses ever set up west of the Mississippi River. The first edition of the Church newspaper, *The Evening and Morning Star,* was printed in June 1832. It boasted that it was ". . . located twelve miles west of the western limits of the United States, about 120 miles west of any other press in the state."29

Sidney Gilbert was in the process of opening a general store in Missouri. The law of consecration was functioning, with many business ventures in the planning stages. Arrangements had been made for 3,000 copies of the revelations, under the title "Book of Commandments," to be printed on the Church printing press at Independence. Joseph had assigned William W. Phelps, Oliver Cowdery, and John Whitmer to review and prepare the revelations for the press and to print them as soon as possible. He also gave W. W. Phelps and Co. the order to correct and print the hymns that had been selected by Emma.[30]

Left Alone Again

Throughout July and August, Joseph was in Kirtland, working on the translation of the Bible. Emma did not have him at home for long, however. In October, he was off again on the Lord's errand, this time to New York City. He wrote her a wonderfully descriptive letter, expressing his concern and love. Joseph closed his letter with these tender words:

> . . . I feel as if I wanted to say something to comfort you in your peculiar trial and present affliction I hope God will give you strength that you may not faint. I pray God to soften the hearts of those around you to be kind to you and take the burden off your shoulders as much as possible and not afflict you. I feel for you for I know your state and others do not but you must comfort yourself knowing that God is your friend in heaven and that you have one true and living friend on earth. Your Affectionate Husband until death. Joseph Smith.[31]

Joseph's understanding must have comforted her a great deal. Shortly before he arrived home on 6 November 1832, Emma gave birth to their first living child, a son, whom they named Joseph III. How relieved they must have been, and grateful, to have a healthy son.

Brigham Young Meets the Smiths

Two days after the birth of little Joseph, three men came to Kirtland to meet the Prophet. These men would become key players in the work of building the kingdom of God on earth. Their conversions had occurred through something of a domino effect. Samuel Smith had left a copy of the Book of Mormon with the family of John P. Greene. Phineas Young had also received a copy. John Greene's brother-in-law, Brigham Young, Brigham's brother Joseph, and Heber C. Kimball had all read the book, and decided to visit the translator—Joseph Smith.

Brigham wrote of this meeting:

> We proceeded to Kirtland and stopped at John P. Greene's, who had just arrived there with his family. We rested a few minutes, took some refreshment and started to see the Prophet. We went to his father's house and learned that he was in the woods chopping. We immediately repared to the woods, where we found the Prophet, and two or three of his brothers, chopping and hauling wood. Here my joy was full at the privilege of shaking the hand of the Prophet of God, and receiving the sure testimony, by the spirit of prophecy, that he was all that any man could believe him to be as a true Prophet. He was happy to see us and bid us welcome. We soon returned to his house, he accompanying us.[32]

On this occasion, as on many others, the meeting was held in Emma's parlor. When Brigham and Heber met her, Emma was just recovering from the birth of her baby, so undoubtedly her contact with them at this time would have been of limited duration.

Occupied now with a daughter and a son, Emma also welcomed the many other visitors who came to Kirtland to see the Prophet. Although Missouri had been designated as "Zion," and Joseph was sending the Saints to that place as rapidly as they could prepare for the journey, the hub of Church activity was their home in Kirtland.

School of the Prophets Begun in Emma's Home

During the winter of 1833, Joseph made preparations to start a school for the brethren. The school was intended to give the elders of the Church scriptural training as well as language, history, and geography lessons. There was a wonderful spirit of excitement among the Church membership as they began to understand more fully the extent of the restoration that was taking place. It was a time of tremendous learning, a time of study and revelation.

By 2 February 1833, Joseph had completed the review and translation of the New Testament. He intended to have it published in Missouri.[33]

The Word of Wisdom

While the men were in meetings, many of them proceeded to smoke their pipes and chew tobacco. Emma had to clean the room and wash the spittoons after they left, and she made her objections plain to Joseph. This led him to inquire of the Lord. Whether he asked specifically if the use of tobacco was appropriate is not clear. He received the revelation that has become known as "the Word of Wisdom."[34] In this revelation, the Lord indicated that they should use neither tobacco nor strong drink, and were to cease to use "hot drinks"; in addition, they were to use meat sparingly. The substances most commonly used then were tea and coffee, an ale made from barley (similar to beer), and a strong alcoholic liquor. Although not given as a commandment, the Word of Wisdom was strongly urged upon the Saints and constituted nearly as great a sacrifice and change to their way of life as did the law of consecration.[35]

First Presidency Is Organized and Plans Revealed for Temple Building

The first official organization of the First Presidency of the Church occurred on 18 March 1833. Sidney Rigdon and Frederick G. Williams were set apart as counselors to Joseph. The brethren received the ordinance of washing of feet, and enjoyed a spiritual awakening such as they had never known before.[36]

Plans were announced for the building of a complex of temples in Jackson County, Missouri. As the spirit of gathering brought people to Kirtland, some stayed, but others went to Missouri. Emma and Joseph must have shared a buoyant spirit of hope as they contemplated the prospect of eventually moving to Missouri. The time had not come for that, however, as the Lord had directed them to build up Kirtland. In Missouri, news of plans for more and more Mormons to move there, and plans to build a temple, brought immediate hostile reaction from the "old settlers" in Jackson County.

Building a House of the Lord

In spite of the extreme poverty of the early Saints, there was great anticipation and a united effort by the members of the Church to raise the funds for a building in Kirtland. It would be a place to address the people, a school, a place of worship, a place wherein the Lord would reveal the keys of the priesthood. Most of the people viewed it as a meeting house, but the Prophet considered it much more. It was to be a temple.

The place chosen for the building was on the corner of the farm that had been given, under the law of consecration, by Frederick G. Williams. Money was desperately needed in order to construct this building. The Prophet called Joseph Young on a special mission to Canada. He gave him instructions to find and convert one Artimus Millet, who was purported to be a skilled architect and stone mason. Joseph Young was to ask Millet to come to Kirtland and bring a thousand dollars to help build the temple. This mission was successful. Millet accepted the call and joined the Church, leaving his business to be overseen by others. He went to Kirtland and committed his skills to build the Lord's house; he also brought the requested money. Brigham Young later said of him, "He never stopped at a thousand dollars, but gave much more."[37]

Dedication of the temple site in Kirtland took place on 23 July 1833. This event occurred almost simultaneously with a violent attack upon the Saints in Independence, where a mob of two hundred angry men descended upon W. W. Phelps' house. The house was razed, the press was destroyed, and the "type was pied" (or scrambled). The Book of Commandments was on the press at the time. Only a few copies were saved. Bishop Partridge and others were taken out and beaten, tarred, and feathered. Only the meekness of Bishop Partridge and the willingness of John Corrill, John Whitmer, W. W. Phelps, Sidney Gilbert and Isaac Morley, in agreeing to an order to leave the county by 1 January, prevented the total annihilation of the Saints in Jackson County, at that time.[38]

Joseph and Emma's home was the setting for many serious meetings. Joseph and the other Church leaders in Kirtland sent petitions to the governor of Missouri and wrote letters, trying to keep track of the situation of the Missouri Saints. Joseph also had many challenges to cope with in Kirtland. Converts were coming to the city in droves. Most of them were destitute of any means of livelihood, so they looked to the Prophet to give them subsistence. The people in Kirtland were more than willing to help, and every family in Kirtland opened their doors to the needy. Joseph and Emma were no exception. More than once they gave their beds and all their blankets to others, then slept on the floor with nothing but their coats for covers.[39]

Emma must have been beside herself trying to meet all the demands placed upon her as the wife of the Prophet. Joseph would have had little time to discuss household problems with her. He often labored with the others in the quarry, cutting rock for the temple. Added to this was a continual array of lawsuits, instigated against him by individuals who were anxious to discredit him in the eyes of the community because they feared the political influence of so numerous and united a people. The trumped-up charges were usually dismissed quickly by judges who saw through the ruse, but they used up valuable time and resources.

Since the Church press had been destroyed in Independence, it was considered necessary to establish a printing press in Kirtland. A building was framed up not far from the temple, and the firm was called F. G. Williams and Co. Plans were made to publish two newspapers, *The Latter-day Saints' Messenger and Advocate,* and *The Evening and Morning Star.* Joseph asked Oliver to come to Kirtland and conduct the business of publishing these papers.

Joseph's Mission to Canada

On 5 October 1833, Joseph left Emma and the children home in Kirtland, while he went with Sidney Rigdon to upper Canada. While he was gone, work on the temple was suspended, and all the workers put their energy into building the printing office.

It must have been exciting when the Prophet returned on 4 November. He had much to tell Emma about the many new friends they had made and the powerful manner in which the Lord had blessed them on their journey. Perhaps he even described to her the meetings in which he bore his testimony of his first vision and the coming forth of the Book of Mormon, touching the hearts of many and baptizing some.[40]

In turn, Emma would have told Joseph the news from Missouri and that people were spreading a rumor that Zion was to include all of eastern Ohio. Newly arriving members were confused and uncertain as to the plans for gathering.

The same day Joseph arrived home in Kirtland from his successful Canadian mission, Missouri mobs were breaking into the Gilbert and Whitney Store in Independence. They demolished part of the dwelling and arrested Gilbert and other Church leaders on trumped-up charges. Within a few weeks, Joseph would receive a full account of the terrible siege in which one man was killed, several wounded, and women and children driven at gun point. These refugees were forced out into the wintry prairie where they found refuge in hastily erected shelters.

Prior to learning of these events, Joseph could not have known directly of the things the Saints in Missouri were suffering, yet he felt extremely melancholy. On 19 November, he wrote, "My heart is somewhat sorrowful, but I feel to trust in the Lord, the God of Jacob. I have learned in my travels that man is treacherous and selfish, but few excepted. . . ."[41]

At times such as this, Emma may have offered consoling words and given him gentle comfort. Perhaps she reminded him that he had true friends such as Frederick G. Williams. Of him, Joseph wrote: "I have found him ever full of love and brotherly kindness. He is not a man of many words, but is ever winning, because of his constant mind. He shall ever have place in my heart, and is ever entitled to my confidence."[42]

Oliver Cowdery came to Kirtland to give Joseph a firsthand account of the tragic events in Missouri. Elizabeth Cowdery had stayed in Missouri with her parents, Peter and Mary Whitmer. (The Whitmers had settled in Jackson County, near present-day Kansas City, and suffered greatly during the mobbing there. So they moved to Clay County.)

Oliver boarded part of the time with Joseph's parents and part of the time with Emma and Joseph. About two weeks later, Emma made room in her home for Joseph's brother, Don Carlos, who came to live with them.[43] He was to learn the printing trade from Oliver, who was preparing to publish *The Evening and Morning Star*, in Kirtland. Publication had previously taken place in Independence, but when the press had been destroyed, it had ceased.

On 18 December 1833, the Prophet dedicated the new printing establishment. When he retired to his home that evening, he mused in his journal: "Blessed of the Lord is Brother Oliver, nevertheless there are two evils in him that he must needs forsake, or he cannot altogether escape the buffetings of the adversary . . . ."[44]

Joseph then wrote intimate blessings upon each of his family members, his mother, father, and brothers and sisters, closing with this poignant prayer: "And now, O God, let the residue of my father's house ever come up in remembrance before Thee that Thou mayest save them from the hand of the oppressor, and establish their feet upon the Rock of Ages, that they may have place in Thy House, and be saved in Thy kingdom; and let all things be even as I have said, for Christ's sake. Amen."[45]

In all of these musings and blessings, he did not mention Emma by name. She was no doubt so familiar and near to him that perhaps it did not seem necessary.

The Patriarchal Office

The little apartment above the Whitney store in Kirtland was the scene of many profound events, including the School of the Prophets, meetings of the brethren, sacred visions and revelations, and ordinances. The purpose and the organization of the Church were being defined. It became clear that the Church was to be directed under the same order as was outlined by Paul in the New Testament, with apostles, prophets, evangelists, deacons, teachers, and priests. Joseph Smith, Sr., was called to be the evangelist, or presiding patriarch, to the Church.[46] On 18 December 1833, Joseph blessed his father and set him apart to this office. He and his counselors, Sidney Rigdon and Frederick G. Williams, laid their hands on Father Smith's head and ordained him. Oliver Cowdery wrote the blessings as they were given.

A year after this ordination, on 9 December 1834, Father Smith, acting in his office as Church Patriarch, gave blessings to Joseph and Emma.

Patriarchal Blessings

Patriarchal blessings are most sacred and personal to the one receiving them. The Prophet Joseph, as head of the dispensation of the fullness of times, and Emma, as his wife, hold a particularly personal relationship to every soul who embraces the gospel. Because of this, these precious documents do not belong only to their direct descendants; they belong to all.

Joseph's patriarchal blessing gives a glimpse into the place he holds in the eternal scheme of things, as head of the last dispensation. It also sheds some light upon what was being hinted at in the 1830 revelation to Emma, when she was told to rejoice in the "glory" that was to come upon her husband. Although it may seem that Emma is consigned to a reflected glory, the position she holds as wife of the Prophet Joseph Smith is glorious and encompasses great responsibility, both for herself and for her posterity. Both of these blessings define the glorious responsibility of the Prophet and his wife and, especially in the case of Joseph's blessing, transcend mortal expectations. In it we find out a great deal about the biblical Joseph, who was sold into Egypt; we better understand the hopes this Joseph had for the future, knowing that in the latter-days, he would have a namesake who would fulfill a divine mission. Whereas Joseph of old provided grain to save a starving Israel, the latter-day prophet, Joseph would provide sustenance for the soul. Through him the gathering of latter-day Israel would be accomplished, whether from mortal toil or by his sustaining effort from beyond the veil.

The inclusion of these blessings here provides one of the rare occasions for us to read words spoken personally by Joseph Sr.

Joseph's Patriarchal Blessing[47]

Joseph Smith, My son, I lay my hands upon thy head in the name of the Lord Jesus Christ, to confirm upon thee a father's blessing. The Lord thy God has called thee by name out of the heavens. Thou hast heard his voice from on high, from time to time, even in thy youth. The hand of the angel of his presence has been extended toward thee, by which thou hast been lifted up and sustained; yea, the Lord has delivered thee from the hands of thine enemies; and thou hast been made to rejoice in his salvation: thou hast sought to know his ways, and from thy childhood thou hast meditated much upon the great things of his law. Thou hast suffered much in thy youth, and the poverty and afflictions of thy father's family have been a grief to thy soul. Thou hast desired to see them delivered from bondage, for thou hast loved them with a perfect love. Thou hast stood by thy Father, and . . . would have covered his nakedness rather than see him exposed to shame; when the daughters of the gentiles laughed, thy heart has been moved with a just anger to avenge thy kindred. Thou hast been an obedient son and the commands of thy Father, and the reproofs of thy mother, thou has respected and obeyed—for all of these things the Lord my God will bless thee. Thou hast been called, even in thy youth to the great work of the Lord, to do a work in this generation which no other man would do as thyself, in all things according to the will of the Lord. A marvelous work and a wonder has the Lord wrought by thy hand, even that which shall prepare the way for the remnants of his people to come in among the gentiles, with their fullness, as the tribes of Israel are restored. I bless thee with the blessings of thy forefathers, Abraham, Isaac, and Jacob; and even the blessing of thy father Joseph, the son of Jacob. Behold, he looked after his posterity in the last days, when they . . . wept before the Lord. He sought diligently to know from whence the son should come who should bring forth the word of the Lord, by which they might be enlightened, and brought back to the true fold, and his eyes beheld thee, my son: his heart rejoiced and his soul was satisfied, and he said, as my blessings are to extend to the utmost bounds of the everlasting hills; as my father's blessing prevailed above the blessings of his progenitors, and as my branches are to run over the wall, and my seed are to inherit the choice land whereon the Zion of God shall stand in the last days, from among my seed, scattered with the gentiles, shall a choice seer arise, whose bowels shall be as a fountain of truth, whose loins shall be girded with the girdle of righteousness, whose hands shall be lifted with acceptance before the God of Jacob to turn away his anger from his anointed, whose heart shall meditate great wisdom, whose intelligence shall circumscribe and

Emma's Patriarchal Blessing[48]

Emma, my daughter-in-law, thou art blessed of the Lord, for thy faithfulness and truth, thou shalt be blessed with thy husband, and rejoice in the glory which shall come upon him. Thy soul has been afflicted because of the wickedness of men in seeking the destruction of thy companion, and thy whole soul has been drawn out in prayer for his deliverance; rejoice, for the Lord thy God has heard thy supplications. Thou hast grieved for the hardness of the hearts of thy father's house, and thou hast longed for their salvation. The Lord will have respect to thy cries, and by his judgment will cause some of them to see their folly and repent of their sins; but it will be by affliction that they will be saved. Thou shalt see many days, yea, the Lord will spare thee till thou art satisfied, for thou shalt see thy Redeemer. Thy heart shalt rejoice in the great work of the Lord, and no one shall take thy rejoicing from thee. Thou shalt ever remember the great condescension of thy God in permitting thee to accompany my son when the angel delivered the record of the Nephites to his care. Thou hast seen much sorrow because the Lord has taken from thee three of thy children. In this thou art not to be blamed, for he knows thy pure desires to raise up a family, that the name of my son might be blessed. And now, behold, I say unto thee, that thus sayeth the Lord, if thou wilt believe, thou shalt yet be blessed in this thing and thou shalt bring forth other children, to the joy and satisfaction of thy soul, and to the rejoicing of thy friends. Thou shalt be blessed with understanding, and have power to instruct thy sex, teach thy family righteousness, and thy little ones the way of life, and the holy angels shall watch over thee and thou shalt be saved in the kingdom of God, even so. Amen.

Notes

1. Doctrine & Covenants 32.

2. Scot and Maurine Proctor, *The Revised and Enhanced History of Joseph Smith by His Mother* (Salt Lake City: Bookcraft, 1996), pp. 248-49. See also Lucy Smith, *Biographical Sketches of Joseph Smith the Prophet and His Progenitors for Many Generations* (Independence, Mo: Herald Publishing House, 1969), pp. 190-91.

3. *HC,*1:118.

4. *HC,*1:118-23.

5. *HC,*1:124-25.

6. *HC,*1:128-29.

7. Doctrine & Covenants 38:32.

8. *HC,*1:145-46; see also Elizabeth Ann Whitney's account in Hyrum L. Andrus and Helen Mae Andrus, *They Knew the Prophet* (Salt Lake City: Bookcraft, 1974), p. 39

9. In Andrus and Andrus, *They Knew the Prophet*, p. 23.

10. Joseph and Emma Smith's Family Bible. The names of her twins are recorded therein as Thaddeus and Louisa; also the names of Joseph Murdock Smith and Julia Murdock Smith are present. A few weeks before she died, Emma told her sons that her twins were unnamed. However, the names of all four children are recorded in what appears to be her handwriting, in the family Bible. It is not hard to understand that she may have forgotten and to realize that she would not have been looking at the record at the time she was questioned in 1879. Perhaps she wrote the names in the book when the book was new; or perhaps the questions about the babies jogged her memory, and she wrote the names in at that later date. We may never know for sure, but it seems unlikely that someone else would take it upon themselves to give two dead babies names and write them in Joseph and Emma's Bible. Therefore, I have taken these names at face value, assuming they are authentic names.

11. Lucy Smith, *Joseph Smith and His Progenitors*, p. 208.

12. *HC,*1:260; also Joseph and Emma Smith Family Bible. In possession of Buddy Youngreen, Orem, Utah.

13. Emma Hale Smith Bidamon, *Emma Smith's Last Testimony*, February 1879, Reorganized Church of Jesus Christ of Latter Day Saints (RLDS) Archives, Independence, Mo.

14. Doctrine & Covenants 38:34-42; see also Alvin R. Dyer, *The Refiner's Fire* (Salt Lake City, Utah: Deseret Book, 1980), pp. 55-61.

15. *HC,* 1:196-98.

16. Dyer, *The Refiner's Fire*, p. 39.

17. Doctrine & Covenants 63:24-31.

18. *HC,* 1:199.

19. *HC,* 1:217.

20. *HC,* 1:199.

21. *HC,* 1:215 ftnt. (as quoted from *Hayden's History of the Disciples* (a Campbellite work), pp. 250-51).

22. Doctrine & Covenants 42:56.

23. Doctrine & Covenants 76:15-16, 19-20.

24. Doctrine & Covenants 76:22-24.

25. *HC,* 1:260-65; see also Lucy Smith, *Joseph Smith and His Progenitors,* pp. 218-21.

26. *HC,* 1:266.

27. *Exponent,* August-December, 1878-79. LDS Archives, Salt Lake City, Utah.

28. Joseph Smith, Letter to Emma, 6 June 1832. Typescript copy in author's possession. Original in RLDS Archives.

29. *HC,* 1:277.

30. *HC,* 2:273.

31. In Dean C. Jessee, *The Personal Writings of Joseph Smith* (Salt Lake City: Deseret Book, 1984), p. 251. The quote in the text is from a letter from Joseph Smith to Emma, 13 October 1832. Typescript letter in author's possession.

32. Eldon Jay Watson, ed. *Manuscript History of Brigham Young 1801-1844* (Salt Lake City: Smith Secretarial Services, 1968), p. 4.

33. *HC,* 1:324, 341.

34. See Doctrine & Covenants 89.

35. See Doctrine & Covenants 42.

36. *HC,* 1:334.

37. *HC,* 2:205; see also George Francis Millett, *Ancestors and Descendants of Thomas Millett,* (Private printing, 1959), pp. 110-11.

38. *HC,* 1:374-77. The objections of the Jackson County citizens against the Saints were (1) Pretending to claim personal revelations, miracles, tongues, and thereby blaspheming God; (2) Being deluded fanatics; (3) Increasing in numbers daily; (4) Being the very dregs of society; (5) Raising sedition among the slaves; (6) Inviting free Negroes and mulattoes of other states to become Mormons and move to Missouri; (7) Declaring that God has given the state of Missouri to the Saints.

39. Scot and Maurine Proctor, *The Revised and Enhanced History of Joseph Smith by His Mother* (Salt Lake City: Bookcraft, 1996); p. 324; see also *Biographical Sketches,* p. 250.

40. Jessee, *Personal Writings of Joseph Smith,* p. 20. See also *HC,* 1:416-22.

41. *HC,* 1:443.

42. *HC,* 1:444.

43. *HC,* 2:446.

44. *HC,* 1:465.

45. *HC,* 1:467.

46. Joseph Smith, Sr., patriarchal blessing, given by Joseph Smith, Jr., on 18 December 1833. Patriarchal blessings recorded by Oliver Cowdery, Patriarchal Blessing Book #1, LDS Archives. Joseph Jr. gave his father a patriarchal blessing, designating him the Patriarch to the Church. After the death of Joseph Sr., in 1840, Hyrum Smith became Patriarch to the Church. After Hyrum was killed, his brother William Smith was ordained in 1845, but he apostatized and the office was filled by

Joseph Sr.'s brother John Smith. The office later went to Hyrum's son, John. Currently Eldred G. Smith is Patriarch Emeritus. Each stake in the Church now has a patriarch. The work of the evangelist, or patriarch, is to give patriarchal blessings. They are a guideline for a person's life, not a fortune-telling gimmick. They are to give the lineage of the individual, as well as insight into one's particular talents or blessings pertaining to his or her calling in mortality. In some cases, as in Joseph Smith, Jr., the blessing transcends mortal activity, obviously referring to events to come, after the resurrection. (See also *HC,* 1:465-67.)

47. Joseph Smith, Jr., patriarchal blessing, given by Patriarch Joseph Smith, Sr., 9 December 1834, Kirtland, Ohio, Patriarchal Blessing Book #1, LDS Archives. Hereafter referred to as Joseph Smith, Jr., patriarchal blessing.

This blessing contains many passages that are difficult to understand, but when one studies it with an understanding of the symbolic language, it becomes an amazing document that reflects the covenant blessings to leaders in God's righteous army of both earthly and spiritual hosts, who will combine to cleanse the earth for the Savior's second coming, and the *world* will be destroyed. This is not to mean the end of the *earth,* but of the *world.* As Babylon fell in ancient times, the wicked will be destroyed in the last battle, wherein Satan, and those who follow him, will also be destroyed. The important ingredient in this blessing is the scriptural pattern: the righteous will be blessed, the wicked punished. The "wine and oil" are mentioned; these are ingredients in the temple worship enjoyed by the ancient Hebrews and the Jews; the implication here is that the Prophet will be sustained through the ordinances of the temple, which he restored for the benefit of all mankind. G. N. J.

48. Emma Hale Smith, patriarchal blessing, given by Patriarch Joseph Smith, Sr., 9 December 1834, Kirtland, Ohio, Patriarchal Blessing Book #1, LDS Archives.

CHAPTER 5

The Office of Emma's Calling

". . . and the office of thy calling shall be for a comfort
unto my servant Joseph Smith, Jun., thy husband, in his
afflictions. . . ." (Doctrine & Covenants 25:5)

The Lord had made it clear to Emma in the revelation given in
1830, that her primary responsibility was to be a comfort to her
husband. In Kirtland, at last, Emma had her heart's desire. She had
three children and a home to call her own. True, it was only a small
apartment above the store—but important work of the kingdom was
going forward within its walls. It was a place of continual coming and
going as men saw the Prophet on church business.

Recognition of Joseph's position as Prophet stimulated much
loyalty in those who served with him in the councils of the Church.
The Lord was revealing offices and callings of the Church, and the
duties and responsibilities were being clarified by revelation. Emma,
too, was part of the events unfolding daily. She made room to accommodate any need the Prophet might indicate to her. An almost
continuous outpouring of the spirit of revelation was upon them,
with Emma fulfilling her calling as the Prophet's wife. She was loved
and respected for her fine example of charity and goodness, and due
honor was given her.

Joseph was deeply concerned for the welfare of the members who
were being mobbed and plundered in Missouri. In February of 1834,
he traveled throughout the branches of the Church, in New York and
Ohio, calling for volunteers to go to Missouri in the spring, to assist
the besieged Saints who had been driven out of Jackson County.[1]

Many promptly responded, and Emma's duties increased as she housed and fed numerous men who came to help prepare for a rescue mission to Missouri.

One young man who responded to the call was Wilford Woodruff. In April 1834, he arrived in Kirtland and found Joseph and Hyrum target practicing with "a brace of pistols." Joseph invited Wilford to stay at his home, and Wilford recorded, "That night we had a most enjoyable and profitable time in his home. In conversation he smote his hand upon his breast and said, "I would to God I could unbosom my feelings in the house of my friends."[2]

While he was staying with them during this preparation time, Wilford helped Joseph tan a wolf hide. He reported stretching it over the back of a chair in the yard. Undoubtedly, Emma tolerated this use of her furniture and would have prepared good meals and a comfortable place for Wilford to sleep. A close friendship developed between Wilford and both Joseph and Emma.

Everyone was involved in preparing for the rescue trip. The men gathered wagons and teams, firearms and provisions; the women collected clothing, bedding, and food to send to their brethren and sisters in Missouri. The expedition was to leave as soon as the roads were passable in the spring.

On 5 May 1834, Emma said good-bye to Joseph as he led a company of 200 men, with twenty loaded baggage wagons, westward toward Missouri—a journey of about a thousand miles. A few took their wives and children along, but for the most part it was a man's journey. This company became known as "Zion's Camp."[3] According to Heber C. Kimball, who was in the company, they were very solemn, fully conscious that they were risking their lives.

A month later, on 4 June 1834, Joseph wrote to Emma from the east side of the Mississippi River. He detailed the trip as a pleasant experience going into the vast wilderness. He described the scenes of waving grassland and the peacefulness of riding along together with good comrades. Reflectively, he said, "Were it not [that] every now and then our thoughts linger with inexpressible anxiety for our wives and our children, our kindred according to the flesh who are entwined round our hearts, our whole journey would be as a dream. . . . Tell Father Smith and all the family, and brother Oliver to be comforted and look forward to the day when the trials and tribulations of this life will be at an end, and we all enjoy the fruits of our labour if we hold out faithful to the end which I pray may be the happy lot of us all. . . ."4

No doubt Father Smith longed to make the journey, but stayed behind due to his age and health. Oliver Cowdery and Sidney Rigdon had stayed in Kirtland to oversee the few men who remained to work on the temple. Since Oliver's wife was with her parents in Missouri, he may have been understandably disappointed to remain in Kirtland. However, he was in charge of the printing operation for the Church and had to attend to his business.

In the weeks and months to follow, Zion's Camp was to become a testing ground for the brethren of the Church—both those who made the journey and those who remained. It must have also served as a testing ground for Emma, who was left in Kirtland with the responsibility of her children, many aged people, and the entire Church membership looking up to her as an example.

Newspaper Reports

The press made much of the story of the camp. One cannot help wondering what Emma's feelings were if she read the terrifying reports appearing in the Ohio newspapers during the month of July 1834. *The Western Courier* carried this report on 24 July:

> A Mormon Battle,—A letter has been received, by a gentleman in this neighborhood direct from Missouri, stating that a body of well armed Mormons, led on by their great Prophet, Joe Smith, lately attempted to cross the river into Jackson county. A party of citizens of Jackson county opposed their crossing, and a battle ensued, in which, Joe Smith was wounded in the leg, and the Mormons obliged to retreat; that Joe Smith's limb was amputated, but he died three days after the operation.5

The *Chardon Spectator* picked up the following from the St. Louis paper of 13 June:

> The Mormons—the latter-day Saints, as they style them-
> selves, seem to be determined by every means to come and take
> possession of ZION, Jackson County. A company of 300 in
> number, well armed, crossed the Wabash river a few days ago.
> Another is coming from Michigan . . . and a third one has taken
> another direction. It is reported that these Saints of the latter
> days are all well provided with guns and ammunition.[6]

Such exaggerated reports had the effect of inflaming the
Missourians against the Mormons and confusing the general public.
Ironically, the leaders of Zion's Camp were pleased to be viewed as a
formidable force. They were impressed by the respect given them as
they passed through the settlements on their way west. They made a
show of carrying farm tools and claimed to be farmers, but the spirit
of "claiming Zion" pervaded the camp and could not fail to be
noticed by interested observers.

Zion's Camp was not successful in returning the Missouri Saints
to their lands in Jackson County, but they did bring needed support
and supplies to those suffering people. It also served to identify to
Joseph the men who could be trusted, as well as those who could not.

It must have been frightening for Emma, waiting in Kirtland with
no assurance that the reports were false, to read that Joseph had been
wounded and was dead. Although he wrote to her in June, and again
after he arrived in Missouri, she undoubtedly suffered weeks of fear
and anxiety.

Sally's Death

During the summer of 1834, ". . . owing to the exposure of the
previous winter and the hunger and privation," many Missouri Saints
fell victim to "fever and ague," probably malaria. Sally Knight became
very ill. She gave birth to a son at Turnham's Landing in Clay County,
but she and the baby, Eli, both died. Newel Knight said, "Truly she
has fallen a martyr to the gospel of our Lord."[7] Sally was their good
friend. The news of her death must have deeply saddened Emma.

Joseph's Leadership Challenged

Immediately upon returning from Missouri, Joseph faced difficulties within the Church. Some of the men from Zion's Camp were frustrated when Zion was not redeemed as they had expected. One, Sylvester Smith, returned to Kirtland earlier and made accusations against Joseph. In a letter to the high council in Missouri, Joseph wrote:

> I am in Kirtland and found all well on my arrival, as pertaining to health; but our common adversary had taken the advantage of our brother [Sylvester] Smith, and others, who gave a false colloring to almost every transaction from the time we left Kirtland until we returned, and thereby stirred up a great difficulty in the Church against me, accordingly I was met in the face and eyes as soon as I got home with a catalogue [of charges] as black as the author of lies himself and the cry was Tyrant! Pope!! King!!!! Usurper!!!! Abuser of men!!!!! Angel!!!!!! False Prophet!!!!! Prophesying Lies in the name of the Lord and taking consecrated monies!!!!!!!! and every other lie to fill up and complete the catalogue. . . . Such experiences may be necessary to perfect the Church, and render our traducers meet for the devourer and the shaft of the destroying angel. In consequence of having to combat all these, I have not been able to regulate my mind, so as to give you counsel, and the information that you needed: but that God who rules on high, and thunders judgments upon Israel when they transgress, has given me power from the time I was born into the kingdom to stand; and I have succeeded in putting all gainsayers and enemies to flight, unto the present time; and notwithstanding the adversary laid a plan, which was more subtle than all others, as you will see by the next Star, I now swim in good, clean water, with my head out. . . .[8]

The Prophet's Plea for Unity

In this same letter the Prophet told the brethren that they should wait for the excitement to die down. They should take time to lay up provisions so that in two years from the coming September, they might return to Jackson Country and take possession of their homes and lands again. However, he warned them in the name of the Lord, "If the

Church with one united effort perform their duties . . . the work shall be complete—if they do not this in all humility . . . behold there remaineth a scourge for the Church, even that they shall be driven from city to city, and but few shall remain to receive an inheritance. . . ."9

We do not know whether Emma read the Prophet's letter to the Missouri brethren, but most certainly she would have heard the sentiments from his own lips and would have been aware of the difficulties he had to cope with.

Anti-Mormon Literature

We can picture Emma's feelings as she had to stand by and watch Joseph face the crisis brought about through Sylvester's accusations and the Missouri problems. Further accusations came from a man named Philastus Hurlbut[10], who had worked with Eber D. Howe to publish a book containing many affidavits against Joseph's character. They claimed Joseph had plagiarized a manuscript by a man named Spalding in order to write the Book of Mormon. Although there is no resemblance between the two, the accusation has reared its head ever since—despite the fact that it was built upon a foundation of falsehood.

With the publication of the first major anti-Mormon books, Delusions[11] and Mormonism Unveiled, the Angel Moroni's warning—that Joseph's name would be spoken of for both good and evil—was fulfilled on a national scope. Throughout these ordeals, Emma's senses must have been tuned to the least thing she could do to make Joseph's life more comfortable.

It is vital to our understanding of Emma to recognize that as she was tried in the furnace of these times, she came to trust only those whom Joseph trusted. Clearly, she committed her friendship only to those whom she felt proved themselves faithful to him and his best interests.

A Time of Progress

Joseph humbly acknowledged his own imperfections, but stood firm in respect to the revelations he had received. For the most part, he gained support and loyalty from his associates in the Church leadership. As the difficulties were settled, a time of great progress for the Church ensued.

In January 1835, Joseph prepared a series of lectures on theology which became known as the *Lectures on Faith*. They were to be used as a course of study for the brethren in the School of the Prophets, which was still being held in Emma's home above the Whitney Store.[12]

Twelve Apostles Chosen

Further organization for the Church took place on 14 February 1835, at a meeting held for all those who had been with Zion's Camp, along with anyone else who wished to attend. We may assume that Emma was in attendance at this meeting, which was held to allow the Three Witnesses to choose twelve men who would be ordained as Apostles in the Church.

The twelve men chosen and ordained by the laying on of hands were Lyman E. Johnson, Brigham Young, Heber C. Kimball, Orson Hyde, David W. Patten, Luke S. Johnson, William E. McLellin, John F. Boynton, Orson Pratt, William Smith, Thomas P. Marsh, and Parley P. Pratt.[13]

On 5 April 1835, just five years after the Church was organized, Oliver Cowdery delivered a "General Charge to the Twelve." He admonished them to—

> . . . be zealous to save souls. The soul of one man is as precious as the soul of another. You are to bear this message to those who consider themselves wise; and such may persecute you—they may seek your life. The adversary has always sought the life of the servants of God; you are therefore to be prepared at all times to make a sacrifice of your lives, should God require them in the advancement and building up of His cause.[14]

The lengthy charge designated them stewards over the ministry and special witnesses for Christ. When he finished speaking, Oliver took each one by the hand and said, "Do you with full purpose of heart take part in this ministry, to proclaim the Gospel with all diligence, with these your brethren, according to the tenor and intent of the charge you have received?"[15] Each man answered in the affirmative.

The office and calling of the Twelve was to be special witnesses of Christ's name, and "to officiate in the name of the Lord, under the direction of the Presidency of the Church, . . . to build up the church and regulate all the affairs of the same in all nations, first unto the Gentiles and secondly unto the Jews."[16] These apostles were to hold the keys of the ministry, to unlock the door of the Kingdom of Heaven unto all nations, and to ". . . preach [the] gospel unto every creature."[17] To assist them in this work, the Council of Seventy was organized. They were to serve as missionaries under the direction of the Twelve.

Emma's office and calling, to comfort her husband in all his afflictions, took most of her time. With her husband and the officers of the Church rapidly setting up the order of the Church, traveling to Missouri and back, writing letters, meeting strangers, meeting and teaching the newly called missionaries, and overseeing the work on the temple, Emma had the responsibility to somehow maintain an atmosphere of peace and tranquility in her home, which continued to serve as a boarding house, office, and schoolhouse. In addition to her own family, she usually had visitors to cook for, often with scanty provisions. In fact, she frequently shared the last food she had with others who had nothing.

The town was bursting at the seams, with new members of the Church arriving daily, all anxious to meet the Prophet and see for themselves what manner of man he was. In the law of consecration, everything they had was dedicated to the building up of the kingdom of God. As Emma struggled with daily domestic tasks, she must have longed at times for privacy. But her consecration was not grudgingly given.

An Example in Giving

On 25 June 1835, a meeting was held in the partially completed temple, where the need for funds to continue construction on the temple was discussed. Joseph, John Whitmer, W. W. Phelps, and Frederick G. Williams each "subscribed," or contributed, $500.

Oliver Cowdery contributed $750. The money was paid within one hour. A total of $6,232.50 was contributed at that meeting. Church history records, ". . . people were astonished."[18]

Such a large contribution by the Prophet must have required his wife's agreement. There is no indication in any document that Emma ever resented her husband's sacrifice of their personal funds. To the contrary, the few sources that do mention Emma generally refer to her service, her cheerfulness, and her constant support of all that Joseph was doing, in Kirtland, or anyplace else.

Egyptian Artifacts

On 3 July 1835, a man by the name of Michael H. Chandler came to Kirtland, bringing some Egyptian mummies and rolls of papyrus. He had been told that the Prophet could decipher the hieroglyphic characters that were on the papyrus. Joseph gave Chandler the interpretation of some of the characters, and Chandler gave him a certificate indicating that the things the Prophet said coincided exactly with all that he had previously been able to learn respecting the meaning of the writings.

Joseph discovered, to his great joy and wonder, that one of the papyrus rolls contained the writings of Abraham, and another the writings of Joseph of Egypt.[19] Not long afterward, the mummies and papyrus were purchased by some members in Kirtland. Mother Lucy must have contributed to this purchase, since afterward, Joseph always referred to them belonging to her. Joseph, with Oliver and W. W. Phelps as scribes, began to translate the characters, or hieroglyphics.[20]

When people learned about these artifacts, many came to Kirtland to see them and to ask the Prophet about them. If Joseph happened to be away, Emma showed them and explained what she had heard Joseph tell about them. Caroline Crosby brought her brother and another man to view the Egyptian papyrus and later wrote, "We were to see the Prophet but I think he was absent . . . saw Father Smith [Joseph Sr.] and Emma, who showed him the records of Abraham, that were found with the mummies, and explained them. . . ."[21]

During this time, Bishop Edward Partridge and William Phelps, having just arrived from Missouri, went with Joseph to see the artifacts. Bishop Newel K. Whitney and his wife and parents accompanied them. Afterwards, Joseph invited them to dinner. Later Joseph dictated the following description of the evening:

> We were called to supper. While seated at table we indulged in a free interchange of thought, and Bishop Whitney observed to Bishop Partridge that the thought had just occurred to his mind that perhaps in about one year from this time they might be seated together around a table on the land of Zion. My wife observed she hoped it might be the case, that not only they, but the rest of the company present, might be seated around her table on the land of promise.[22]

A Home for Emma

It is not known when Emma and the family moved out of the Whitney Store. Many years later, Emma and Joseph's son, Joseph III wrote: "My earliest recollections . . . begin in Kirtland. I do not remember the erection of the dwelling house which was built for us nor our removal into it from the store building where I was born. . . . The house stood on the west side of the street which runs from the Temple down to the Chagrin River and was not very far from the ford across this little stream."[23]

As the Smith family was in the process of setting up housekeeping, a traveling salesman came by and insisted on setting up a fine stove in the Prophet's new home. He refused payment, saying that it would serve to bring in other sales if the Prophet's wife were using his stove. Little did Emma know that this fine convenience would later become another means of harassment for her husband.

One endearing story told by young Joseph relates how he would watch the other boys fishing in the stream near his home. He wrote: "My mother, to gratify me, procured a little pole and attached a thread thereto, with a bent hook, and away I marched to the creek. I threw my hook without bait into the water and the little fishes gathered to it as it fell. By some strange chance one became fastened to it and was drawn to the shore. In great excitement I dropped the pole and gathered the fish in my hands rushed to the house with it, shouting, "I've got one! I've got one!" [24]

The eventful year of 1835 drew to a close on a high note. Missionaries were spreading the word throughout the United States and Canada. The Book of Mormon was reprinted, the revelations published, and the temple was nearing completion. The Prophet's labors took him more and more from Emma's side, as the world continued to persecute and press in upon her life.

The record shows that through it all, Emma was not found wanting in fulfilling the office of her calling—to wait at home, and be a support and comfort to her husband.

Notes

1. *HC,* 2:40.

2. Matthias F. Cowley, ed., *Wilford Woodruff, History of His Life and Labors* (Salt Lake City: Bookcraft, 1964), p. 39; hereafter cited as *Wilford Woodruff.*

3. *HC,* 2:64; see also Cowley, *Wilford Woodruff,* pp. 183-85, for a list of all who went, including families.

4. Joseph Smith, Letter to Emma, 5 June 1834; see also Dean C. Jessee, *The Personal Writings of Joseph Smith* (Salt Lake City: Deseret Book, 1984), pp. 324-25.

5. *Western Courier* (24 July 1834), quoting a St. Louis paper of June 13. Copies of articles in author's possession.

6. *Chardon Spectator* and *Geauga Gazette* (12 July 1834). Copies of the articles in author's possession.

7. William Hartley, *They Are My Friends* (Provo, Utah: Grandin Book, 1986), p. 102.

8. Dean C. Jessee, *The Personal Writings of Joseph Smith* (Salt Lake City: Deseret Book, 1984), p. 329.

9. Joseph Smith, letter to the high council in Missouri, 1834, quoted in Jessee, *Personal Writings of Joseph Smith,* pp. 330-31. See also Doctrine & Covenants 63:29-31.

10. The name Hurlbut or Hurlburt has been spelled various ways. See Richard L. Anderson, "The Mature Joseph Smith and Treasure Searching," *BYU Studies* (Fall 1984), p. 493.

11. *Delusions,* published in 1832, a reprint of Alexander Campbell's 1831 articles in the *Millennial Harbinger.*

12. *HC,* 2:180.

13. *HC,* 2:187.

14. *HC,* 2:196.

15. *HC,* 2:198.

16. Doctrine & Covenants 107:33.

17. Doctrine & Covenants 18:28

18. *HC,* 2:234.

19. *HC,* 2:236.

20. Traditionally, it has been assumed that these were purchased by Joseph's mother, who kept them after the martyrdom and showed them for a fee.

21. An excerpt from the memoirs of Caroline Crosby, microfilm of holographs in the Historical Department of the LDS Church. Quoted by Kenneth W. Godfrey, Audrey M. Godfrey, and Jill Mulvay Derr, *Women's Voices: An Untold History of the Latter-day Saints 1830-1900* (Salt Lake City: Deseret Book, 1982), p. 52.

22. *HC,* 2:294.

23. Mary Audentia Smith Anderson, ed., *Joseph III and the Restoration* (Independence, Mo: Herald Publishing House, 1952), pp. 11-12.

24. Ibid.

CHAPTER 6

Temple Dedication: A Milestone Preceded and Followed by Great Tribulation

"Holiness To The Lord."
(Inscription on the Kirtland Temple)

Almost everything that happened in Kirtland in 1835 was prerequisite to the great events that would bless the Church once the temple was finished. Just prior to the completion of the building, there was a tremendous outpouring of revelation regarding the organization of the priesthood quorums and offices, and Joseph matured greatly in his office as founder of the Church. He was no longer a boy, yielding to the persecution heaped on him but remaining silent. Now he was a fully qualified leader of a large number of Latter-day Saints. He began to assert himself as an ordained minister in a duly organized church. Nevertheless, county and state officials refused to recognize his right to do so.

A Marriage

Emma was present when on 24 November 1835, Joseph performed the marriage for Newel Knight, who had lived in Kirtland since Sally's death in 1834. The bride was Lydia Goldthwaite, and the marriage took place at Hyrum and Jerusha's home. After prayers, Joseph asked the couple to stand and join hands, then remarked that "marriage was an institution of heaven, instituted in the garden of Eden . . . ." He said, " It [is] necessary it should be solemnized by the authority of the everlasting priesthood," then asked the couple to "covenant to be each other's companion through life, and discharge the duties of husband and wife in every respect." They agreed and he pronounced them man and wife and blessed them.[1] This was the first time Joseph had performed a marriage ceremony.

Kirtland Schools

The Prophet's personal hunger for knowledge, and perhaps his own frustration at lacking the educational skills for so many years of his life, led him to organize classes for all ages. The students studied reading, writing, arithmetic, history, music, and languages. They had an accredited high school with over a hundred students. For the brethren, there was the School of the Prophets, in which they studied the scriptures in depth.

The brethren in Kirtland enjoyed their schooling very much. Throughout the winter of 1835-1836, they were able to attend a Hebrew class taught by Joshua Seixas from Hudson, Ohio. The students in the class were so eager and applied themselves so diligently that Mr. Seixas complimented them, saying he had never taught a class that did so well in Hebrew grammar.[2] Undoubtedly he had never had a class motivated by a prophet of God.

Emma may have married an ignorant plowboy, but she had no cause to be ashamed of Joseph, for in Kirtland he became extremely well-read and self-educated. Joseph was very excited about the Hebrew classes and found great joy in reading the scriptures in the original language. He later studied Greek and German, as well as Latin.[3]

Joseph often spoke on the order of the priesthood. The quorums of seventy, high priests, and elders were designated and organized more fully at this time. The School of the Prophets continued to meet to prepare the brethren for the sacred things they would learn once the temple was completed. A debate school met at the home of William Smith, which led to trouble.

A Family Rift Threatens Unity and Peace

One evening in November 1835, Joseph attended the debate class and was bothered when William behaved in a passionate, unkind manner toward one of the other members of the twelve. When Joseph attempted to give William some instructions regarding the way he was handling the debate, William became angry and physically attacked the Prophet. In fact, he injured Joseph so badly that the Prophet was unable to get around for several days without Emma or someone else helping him.

This incident brought a great deal of sorrow to the entire family and resulted in Joseph inviting his parents to move to his home, rather than stay with William.[4] On top of this family problem, various brethren brought letters to Joseph complaining about the way they were being treated, or the amount of goods they were receiving. (The Church was still living the law of consecration at this time.) The pressure mounted when his problems with William spread through the family, affecting his sisters, Lucy, Katharine, and Sophronia, and their husbands as well. Hyrum came to Joseph to discuss the problem, and they tried to console one another, but each was feeling the depths of sorrow over the rift in the family.

Joseph saw the trouble as a manifestation of the devil's plan to prevent the completion of the temple; to interfere with the spirituality of those nearest and dearest to him, in order to prevent the Lord's spirit from being with them; and to discourage the brethren from coming to the school to prepare to receive the endowment when the temple was finished.

In spite of this, on New Year's Day 1836, Joseph dictated a long discourse of his feelings of both gratitude to God for all the good things that had come during the past year. He also acknowledged the serious anxiety he had for his family and the Church:

> My heart is pained within me, because of the difficulty that exists in my father's family. The devil has made a violent attack on my brother William and also on Calvin Stoddard [Joseph's brother-in-law, who was married to Sophronia], and the powers of darkness seem to lower over their minds, and not only over theirs, but they also cast a gloomy shade over the minds of my brethren and sister, which prevents them from seeing things as they really are; and the powers of earth and hell seem combined to overthrow us and the Church, by causing a division in the family.[5]

And it wasn't only the family. Joseph reflected, "The adversary is bringing into requisition all his subtlety to prevent the Saints from being endowed, by causing a division among the 12, also among the 70, and bickerings and jealousies among the Elders and official members of the Church, and so the leaven of iniquity foments and spreads among the members of the Church."[6]

Joseph was determined that nothing on his part would prevent the settlement of the family difficulties that very day. With this resolve, he went on, "I know that the cloud will burst and Satan's kingdom be laid in ruin with all his black designs, and the saints come forth like gold seven times tried in the fire, being made perfect through sufferings, and temptations, and blessings of heaven and earth multiplied upon our heads which may God grant for Christ's sake Amen —"[7]

Reconciliation

The turning point came later that day, when all the family came to Joseph's house. During the afternoon, Joseph, William, Hyrum, their Uncle John Smith, Father Smith, and Martin Harris met together. After offering a prayer, Father Smith "expressed himself in a very feeling and pathetic manner" and pleaded with them all to resolve the hard feelings. As he was talking, "The spirit of God rested down upon us in might power, and our hearts were melted."[8]

William made a humble apology for his behavior, and Joseph also asked forgiveness for his anger. Then and there, they made a covenant with one another that they would thereafter build one another up and not take offense, nor listen to evil reports about one another.

Emma and Lucy were then called in, along with a scribe so a record would be made of this event. The Smith brothers repeated their covenant to Mother Lucy and Emma. Tears flowed as reconciliation was made. The meeting was then closed with Joseph offering a prayer "and it was truly a jubilee and a time of rejoicing."[9]

Following this reconciliation, the Smith family once again enjoyed a spirit of unity, and this spirit of reconciliation spread through the rest of the Church as well.

Feast for the Poor

Bishop Newel K. Whitney hosted a three-day feast for the poor, beginning on Thursday, 7 January 1836. There was food for all, and the Prophet and his brethren mingled with the people, blessing and comforting them. Although there is no direct reference to Emma's part in this occasion, she would undoubtedly have helped the wives of the bishopric and Church Presidency prepare and serve the food. In addition to feasting, there was singing and much pleasant conversation, which centered around their blessings, and the gathering of the Saints to "Mount Zion" (Missouri). Several received their patriarchal blessings.[10]

Blessing Parties

The organization of the patriarchal office and restoration of the sealing blessings brought great happiness to the members of the Church. According to Caroline Crosby, Joseph attended many "blessing parties," which were held for the purpose of having Father Smith give patriarchal blessings. She wrote of one of these meetings: "It was a general time of rejoicing." The Saints would go to each other's houses and partake of the sacrament; the sick, poor, and afflicted were administered to by the laying on of hands and with powerful prayers. One particular time, Caroline tells of attending a ". . . blessing at Dr. Frederick G. Williams. His eldest daughter had been lately married, and was about to leave for Missouri: he therefore blessed her family previous to their leaving. He laid his hands upon each of their heads, and the scribe wrote [the blessings]. The Prophet Joseph was present, and had a vision of their journey, saw their wagon turn over, but no one was injured. It came to pass even as he said."[11]

Mary Fielding also attended this blessing party. She confirms that Emma was present, saying that Joseph came "with his wife."[12]

Preparations for the Saints to Receive an Endowment

The Lord had promised the Saints that when the temple was completed they would receive an endowment from on high. In preparation for this wonderful blessing, it was essential that the members be reconciled with one another, for disunity drives away the Spirit of the Lord. After the reconciliation in the family, Joseph proceeded to work toward a reconciliation between the brethren in the Church. Whereas there had been a sense of competition and some jealousy, he was able to establish rules of order which they accepted, bringing greater harmony to the quorums.

The Temple: A Milestone in the Church

To say that the Kirtland temple was built by sacrifice and industry is an understatement. Erection of so magnificent a building was an undertaking of unprecedented faith. Joseph, Emma, and many other members of the Church had come to Kirtland destitute. Within the first three years, the foundation for the temple was begun, and by the end of 1835, preparations were under way to finish the building and dedicate it to the Lord.

The men were all engaged in building not only the temple, but a school house, stores, homes, and a printing office. The women all gave unstintingly of their time, preparing meals for the workmen, carding, spinning, weaving, and sewing the tow frocks and britches worn by the men.

In fact, everyone worked on the temple, and every family gave all they could, both in substance and labor. Emma reportedly participated and was a leader among the women in the work of sewing and cooking for the men who were building in Kirtland. Whether she was actually in charge or not, she was certainly involved in the tasks. Many women, such as Vilate Kimball, worked on a "shares" basis. They received wool from the Church, which they washed, carded, spun, and knitted into socks. Vilate could have kept a portion for her own use, but she chose to return it all for the use of the temple workmen.[13] Joseph said of the way the women labored, "Yes, the sisters were the first anciently and they are the first now."[14]

As completion neared, workers toiled feverishly on the finishing touches. From the unique light well in the front foyer to the vaulted ceilings and arched windows, the temple was a tangible symbol of what the Saints had achieved. Inside, the walls were plastered and the woodwork was detailed with intricate, symbolic carvings. Outside, the towering walls glistened with a lustrous sheen produced by grinding crockery and old china, donated by the women, into the plaster. When it was finished, the words, "HOLINESS TO THE LORD" were printed on a plaque over the door. It was the most magnificent structure standing in that day, in the western part of the United States.

Today's visitors, accustomed to the white painted building, would take a second look if they were to see it in its original gunny-gray blue plaster, with a red roof and the doors painted apple green. The current caretaker of the building pondered aloud to the author that he wonders whether modern Saints would accept an authentic restoration. The miracle of it still standing more than a century and a half after it was built attests to its having been blessed of God, as surely it was.

Emma's Hymn Book

Emma must have experienced a personal sense of success at this time. Six years after she was directed by the Lord to make a collection of hymns for the Church, she held the finished volume in her hands. Final preparation of her collection had been done by William W. Phelps, who had been assigned to prepare it for printing. Notwithstanding the 1835 dating, it came off the press sometime in February 1836.[15]

How fervently Emma must have believed in the words of the hymn she had chosen for the beginning: "Know this, that every man is free, To choose his life and what he'll be."[16]

The right of agency—the freedom to choose one's own way—is a God-given privilege guaranteed to all citizens under the Constitution of the land. However, Emma was learning that it was a privilege with a responsibility and a price.

The Temple Dedication

The dedication of the temple took place on Sunday, 27 March 1836. Seating capacity for the building has been estimated to be between nine hundred and a thousand. According to reports of those who were present there were "between nine and ten hundred" in the room.[17] Apparently the Prophet had said that if children would be orderly and were willing to sit on their parents' laps, they could attend. When the room was as full as it could be, the doors were closed. The overflow went to the school house, and even that was not large enough. Some people had to remain out of doors.

The lengthy service included scripture reading from the Bible, singing of hymns, and discourses by Sidney Rigdon and others. Voting and sustaining of the Church leadership in their various offices was unanimous. After a short intermission, Joseph gave a brief address. He presented each of the various quorums, calling for the people to acknowledge the elders in their positions of leadership, and covenant to uphold them by their prayers of faith. When the Saints rose to their feet to show their acceptance of their leaders, again the voting was unanimous.[18]

The dedicatory prayer, given to Joseph by revelation, and presented by him, included a personal reference to Emma and his family:

> O Lord, remember thy servant, Joseph Smith, Jun., and all his afflictions and persecutions—how he has covenanted with Jehovah, and vowed to thee, O Mighty God of Jacob—and the commandments which thou has given unto him, and that he hath sincerely striven to do thy will.
>
> Have mercy, O Lord, upon his wife and children, that they may be exalted in thy presence, and preserved by thy fostering hand.[19]

Concluding his prayer, the Prophet asked the Lord to hear their petitions, "and accept the dedication of this house, . . . the work of our hands, which we have built unto thy name."[20]

What a thrill it must have been for Emma to stand, hymnal in hand, while the brass band and harp played, with the choir and that vast congregation singing, "The Spirit of God like a fire is burning; the latter-day glory begins to come forth!"[21]

At the end of the service, the proceedings were sealed by the congregation "shouting hosanna, hosanna, hosanna to God and the Lamb, three times, sealing it each time with amen, amen, and amen."[22]

This was a triumphant time for the Saints in Kirtland, and promised that great blessings were in store for the entire Church membership of 13,293.[23]

Sacred Experiences in the Temple

In the evening, after the dedication ceremonies, the priesthood quorums gathered to receive instructions concerning ordinances to be received the coming week. The meeting was opened to the congregation, and the Prophet told the Saints not to be afraid to prophesy, which many did. The meeting, which lasted until eleven that night, was a time like Pentecost in the New Testament. "A noise was heard like the sound of a rushing mighty wind, which filled the Temple, and all the congregation simultaneously arose, being moved upon by an invisible power; many began to speak in tongues and prophesy; others saw glorious visions; and I [Joseph] beheld the Temple was filled with angels, which fact I declared to the congregation. The people of the neighborhood came running together (hearing an unusual sound within, and seeing a bright light like a pillar of fire resting upon the Temple), and were astonished at what was taking place."[24]

Many who were present described seeing heavenly personages in the room. President Frederick G. Williams, "bore testimony that the Savior, dressed in his vesture without seam, came into the stand and accepted the dedication of the house; that he saw Him and he gave a description of his clothing, and all things pertaining to it."[25]

A few days later, the dedication program was repeated for those who had been unable to get into the building the first time.

The following Sunday, after the sacrament meeting was finished, Joseph and Oliver went together into the private place near the pulpit, and the curtains were dropped. While they were praying and meditating, suddenly the room was filled with light. These two men, who had received the priesthood under the hands of John the Baptist and Peter, James and John, now saw a glorious personage. Their testimony, written some time afterward, is quoted in part: "The veil was taken from our minds, and the eyes of our understanding were opened. We saw the Lord standing upon the breastwork of the pulpit, before us . . ."[26] The Lord spoke to them, saying:

Let the hearts of your brethren rejoice, and let the hearts of
all my people rejoice, who have, with their might, built this
house to my name.

For behold, I have accepted this house . . . yea, I will appear
unto my servants, and speak unto them with mine own voice, if
my people will keep my commandments, and do not pollute this
holy house.

Yea the hearts of thousands and tens of thousands shall
greatly rejoice in the consequence of the blessings which shall be
poured out, and the endowment with which my servants have
been endowed in this house.

And the fame of this house shall spread to foreign lands; and
this is the beginning of the blessing which shall be poured out
upon the heads of my people.[27]

This is but a small part of the revelation given to these men
during this sacred acceptance by the Lord.

Keys of Authority Restored

After this manifestation, the two men received a vision in which
some of the ancient prophets appeared to them. First was Moses, who
committed the keys of the gathering of Israel. Then Elias appeared,
committing the dispensation of the gospel of Abraham through
which all generations are to be blessed. Finally, the Prophet Elijah,
who was taken to heaven without tasting death, stood before them
and testified that he, as the Prophet Malachi had foretold, had come
"to turn the hearts of the fathers to the children, and the hearts of the
children to the fathers."[28]

Thus, on 3 April 1836, in the temple at Kirtland, Ohio, the keys
of this dispensation were committed into the hands of the Prophet
Joseph Smith and Oliver Cowdery.

Worship in the Temple

After the dedication, the Saints frequently met in the temple.
Occasionally, the Prophet would ask them to come late in the day,
after fasting. When they arrived, he would offer a prayer and then say,

"Now, as any of you are impressed by the Spirit, do what you are impressed to do."

At one such meeting, a "mother and a father" (perhaps implying there were whole families, including children present) not related to each other, and never having sung together previously, rose simultaneously and sang a duet in tongues.[29] Some journals contain entries which tell of people remaining through the night, with no one tiring and no one falling asleep, "feasting on what the Prophet called the fat things of the spirit."[30] In later years, Emma's grandchildren would recall that they often heard her singing hymns as she worked in her house and garden. One of the songs she sang was about the "feast of fat things."[31]

Joseph's Grandmother Arrives in Kirtland

In May, following the temple dedication, word came that Joseph's grandmother, Mary Duty Smith, was on her way to Kirtland in company of her sons John and Silas, and their families. Joseph and Hyrum left immediately to meet her.

Emma's baby was due very soon, so she waited at home for them. She must have had two excited youngsters on her hands, as young Joseph and Julia looked forward to the arrival of a grandmother whom they had never seen.

Grandfather Asahel Smith had died, and now Grandmother Smith arrived in Kirtland on 17 May 1836; her son Silas arrived the following day. Her coming was a cause for celebration. According to Joseph, as recorded in the *History of the Church*, "It was a happy day."[32] A family reunion was held, with Uncles John, Asahel, and Silas, and their families, Joseph, Sr., and Lucy, and all of their family. The Prophet's brother William had married Caroline Grant, 14 February 1833; Samuel married Mary Bailey, 13 August 1834; and Don Carlos married Agnes Coolbrith, 30 July 1835. With his sisters, Katharine, and Sophronia, and their husbands and children, there was a large crowd.[33]

Great-grandmother Smith expressed her joy at seeing all of her descendants. She was very aged and weak. A few days later, on 27 May, she retired to the bedroom to rest and quietly closed her eyes in death. They buried her in the graveyard beside the temple.[34]

Another Son

Not quite a month after Mary Duty Smith was laid to rest, Emma gave birth to a son. This baby was named Frederick Granger Williams Smith, after their close friend, Joseph's counselor in the First Presidency. Little Freddie, as the family called him, was welcomed into the family, 20 June 1836; his birth was an answer to prayers, but it was sandwiched between other momentous events and is barely recognized in the *History of the Church.*

Emma's devotion to the cause of Zion was not shallow, but her focus and her duty were clearly centered upon her husband, her children, and the security of their home. While she cradled her new baby in her arms, she was aware of the bittersweet taste of success. During these years in Kirtland, six children were added to her, four by birth and two by adoption, but only three survived. She surely rejoiced in the completion of her hymnal and the knowledge that Joseph had triumphed over tremendous obstacles and had received a glorious vision of the Savior's acceptance. Emma's faith did not aspire to grand visions; she asked only to be able to live peacefully and have the means of taking care of her children.

With the completion of the temple a torch had been lit—and in that torch burned the everlasting flame of truth, which beckoned the Saints to gather to Zion. The dedication of the temple was a milestone for the Church; however, Joseph's victory seemed all but swallowed up in the burden of debt he had taken upon himself and the Church in order to accomplish so much. In the coming turmoil, it would have required more than simple faith to withstand the persecution poured out upon the Saints. Certainly the flood of persecution could no more extinguish the flame embodied in the phrase "Holiness To The Lord" than could Elijah's righteous power be stayed—but like the priests of Baal, modern evil must have its day— and the Saints must be tried and purified through tribulation.

Notes

1. *HC,* 2:320; see also William Hartley, *They Are My Friends* (Provo, Utah: Grandin Book, 1986), p. 112.

2. *HC,* 2:396.

3. Andrew Ehat and Lyndon Cook, *The Words of Joseph Smith* (Provo, Utah: Religious Studies Center, Brigham Young University, 1980), pp. 347, 351.

4. *HC,* 2:323-44.

5. *HC,* 2:352.

6. *HC,* 2:352-54; see also Dean C. Jessee, *Personal Writings of Joseph Smith* (Salt Lake City: Deseret Book, 1984), p.121.

7. *HC,* 2:352-54. See also Jessee, *Personal Writings of Joseph Smith,* 1:121-22.

8. Ibid.

9. Ibid.

10. *HC,* 2:362

11. Kenneth W. Godfrey, Audrey M. Godfrey, and Jill Mulvay Derr, *Women's Voices: An Untold History of the Latter-day Saints 1830-1900* (Salt Lake City: Deseret Book, 1982), p. 51.

12. Ibid.

13. Heber C. Kimball papers, LDS Archives.

14. Truman Madsen, Education Week lecture, Brigham Young University, Provo, Utah, 1977. Author's personal notes.

15. Emma Smith, compiler, *A Collection of Sacred Hymns for the Church of Jesus Christ of Latter Day Saints* (Kirtland, Ohio: F. G. Williams & Co., 1835); copy of original in possession of Ruth Dirk, Eagle Rock, California; facsimile copies available from Herald Publishing Company, Independence, Missouri; hereafter cited as Emma Smith, *Hymns.*

16. Emma Smith, *Hymns,* no. 1; see also *Hymns of the Church of Jesus Christ of Latter-day Saints* (Salt Lake City: The Church of Jesus Christ of Latter-day Saints), no. 240.

17. *HC,* 2:410.

18. See Karl Ricks Anderson, *Joseph Smith's Kirtland Eyewitness Accounts* (Salt Lake City: Deseret Book, 1989), pp. 179-91, for an excellent chapter on the Kirtland Temple Dedication and events pertaining thereto.

19. Doctrine & Covenants 109:68-69.

20. Doctrine & Covenants 109:78.

21. Emma Smith, *Hymns,* no. 90; see also *Hymns of the Church of Jesus Christ of Latter-day Saints* (Salt Lake City: The Church of Jesus Christ of Latter-day Saints), no. 2.

22. *HC,* 2:427-28.

23. *Deseret News Church Almanac 1991-1992* (Salt Lake City: Deseret News, 1992), p. 333. See also HC, 2:28.

24. *HC,* 2:428.

25. *Journal of Discourses,* 26 vols. (Liverpool, 1854-1886), 11:10.

26. Doctrine & Covenants 110:1-2.

27. Ibid., 110:6-10.

28. Doctrine & Covenants 110:15; See also Malachi 4:6.

29. Truman G. Madsen, "The Kirtland Temple and Temple Worship," an oral presentation given at the Joseph Smith, Sr., Family Reunion, August 1977. Copy in Author's possession.

30. Ibid.

31. Buddy Youngreen, *Reflections of Emma, Joseph Smith's Wife* (Orem, Utah: Grandin Book, 1982). Part II, "The Notebook of Interviews" (pp. 53-133) is a collection of reminiscences by Emma's grandchildren. This is a wonderful collection of fragmented but interesting facts that the family recalled about Emma. See also Emma Smith, compiler, *A Collection of Sacred Hymns for the Church of Jesus Christ of Latter Day Saints* (Kirtland, Ohio: F. G. Williams & Co., 1835); copy of original in possession of Ruth Dirk, Eagle Rock, California; facsimile copies available from Herald Publishing Company, Independence, Missouri;

32. *HC,* 2:443.

33. Marriages of Joseph's brothers and sisters:

Sophronia to Calvin Stoddard, 2 December 1827. He died 19 November 1836, she married William McCleary, 11 February 1838, as her second husband.

Katharine to Wilkins Jenkins Salisbury, 8 January 1831

William to Caroline Grant, 14 February 1833

Samuel to Mary Bailey, 13 August 1834. She died 25 January 1841, and he married Levira Clark in Nauvoo, 29 April 1841.

Don Carlos to Agnes Moulton Coolbrith, 30 July 1835

Hyrum to Jerusha Barden, 2 November 1826. She died in 1837, and he married Mary Fielding, 24 December 1837.

Lucy to Arthur Millikin, 4 June 1840

Source for these dates is from copious family research/genealogical records in possession of the author.

34. *HC,* 2:443.

CHAPTER 7

Crisis

"If persecution would cease, [we] could live as well as any other family in the land . . . ." (Emma Smith)

Three years of unprecedented building in Kirtland had changed the face of the town. Membership in the Church had grown from 680 at the end of 1830, to over 13,000 by the end of 1836. There were two stakes, one in Kirtland and one in Missouri. Twenty-five wards and branches were organized in these two stakes, and twenty-nine mission branches were located outside of the stakes.[1] Many of these people were either in the process of moving to Kirtland or Missouri, or were making plans to do so. The temple, printing office, and many homes and businesses were built to accommodate the influx of converts to the Church from all parts of the country.

Much of the temple had been financed through loans obtained from individuals or banks. As Trustee for the Church, Joseph was personally liable for many of the notes which were coming due early in 1837. Sidney Rigdon and Newel Whitney had also borrowed heavily to finance Church projects.

Goods and merchandise bought on credit for the Whitney Store should have provided funds to defray some of the expenses; however, many of the store goods had gone out on credit to men who worked on the buildings. Thus, the leaders of the Church, and Joseph, especially, faced a serious financial crisis. Emma and Joseph must have worried a great deal about how they were going to pay the notes.

The Salem Incident

Presuming that the Lord would surely bless his Prophet with the means to pay his debts, Joseph expected to find a solution. A man named Burgess showed up with a story that there was a treasure, supposedly hidden many years ago, in a house in Salem, Massachusetts. It was hoped that the Lord would bless Joseph to find this treasure, perhaps like the apostles of old found a coin in the mouth of a fish, in order for the Lord to "render unto Caesar that which is Caesar's." On Monday afternoon, 25 July 1836, Joseph, Hyrum, Oliver, Sidney, and Sidney's son-in-law, George Robinson (who was serving as Joseph's scribe at the time), left by carriage for Salem, in hopes of finding the house, and the treasure, in order to provide badly needed funds to make the building of the Lord's kingdom possible. On 19 August, Joseph wrote to Emma that they had arrived.[2] While Joseph was away, Emma would have had to deal with many inquiries about where he had gone; those who knew what he was doing must have pressed her for news of his success or failure in this venture.

In Salem, the group was disappointed at every turn. After a time it became obvious that they were not going to find any treasure. Much disturbed and concerned, Joseph went to the Lord to inquire why. The answer came in the form of a revelation that informed Joseph the Lord was "not displeased" with them, notwithstanding their foolish attempt to find a treasure to finance the work.[3] He was informed that in spite of his folly, the Lord would bless them. They were instructed to preach the gospel in and around Salem, and to look into the records of the past, as the records of their ancestors were to be found in that city—a treasure of a different kind, to be sure.

The Lord told Joseph not to concern himself about the debts, assuring him that the means of paying them would be provided, not through finding treasure, but by an increase of members who would give abundantly to the cause. Clearly, the Lord let Joseph come to the understanding that He (the Lord) would build His kingdom through sacrifice and service, not through miracles.

By the time they arrived home in the middle of September, a new plan had been devised, which they felt could alleviate the financial crisis.

Since the Church had a great deal of land, it was hoped they could convert these solid assets into cash by opening a banking establishment in Kirtland. In November, papers were drawn up creating the Kirtland Safety Society. Orson Hyde went to Columbus to make application for Articles of Incorporation and to request a charter from the Ohio State Legislature. So sure were they of this plan, that Oliver was dispatched to Philadelphia to obtain plates to print notes for the Society.

The Kirtland Safety Society Bank

In January, the Prophet published an invitation to the public to "buy stock in our Safety Society."[4] Joseph, Oliver, and Sidney were to be the chief officers in the bank. Warren Parrish was to serve as manager and Frederick G. Williams as assistant clerk.

People bought shares, and the Kirtland Safety Society bank notes began to circulate. Emma was among the stockholders. According to the records of the bank, she bought $315 worth of stock. Others of Joseph's family also invested, along with nearly all the members of the Church.

Unfortunately, the legislature denied the banking charter. The entire country was in a financial crisis so no new charters were being issued. Failure to obtain a charter brought financial disaster to Kirtland, and consequently, to Joseph and Emma, as well as many others.

Marvin Hill, a prominent researcher, has noted:

> Joseph had large debts as a result of his business transactions, but he also had large assets with which he could have paid his debts, had the economy not collapsed. Joseph started his bank to transfer landed wealth into ready capital and, had he been able to secure a charter from the State Legislature, he could have established a modest but successful bank. But in 1836-37, for political and economic reasons, the State Legislature granted no new charters for banks, and Joseph had to improvise. He set up an anti-banking society that was in fact a simple corporation with note-issuing powers. He may have acted on bad legal advice here, but similar banks were being established elsewhere in the state at this time. . . .[5]

As these events were unfolding, there would surely have been a great deal of lively conversation around Emma and Joseph's dinner table, as well as much private conversation between the two, as they realized the ramifications of what was happening.

Church membership was increasing so rapidly, it was no longer possible to know each individual personally. Tensions were growing between the longtime members and the new ones. As eager new converts grasped the new ideas Joseph initiated, others murmured and dragged their feet, resentful that they had not been consulted. Old-timers in the area who were not members of the Church felt threatened by the overwhelming numbers of Church members coming into Kirtland, and they feared the influence Joseph had with them.

The influx of new people needing land and homes generated so much activity it gave the impression that business was doing fine. If the apparent economic prosperity had been real, and all individuals involved had been honest, the bank might have survived the financial crisis.

What pressures must have been put upon Emma, as she cared for her growing family and graciously welcomed everyone Joseph brought home to dinner. Records indicate that people often came to their house for a meal and stayed a week, or a month; in the case of both Oliver and Don Carlos, it was on and off for years. Frequently, Joseph's parents moved in and out again as their changing circumstances required. Always, Emma was on call to entertain and help nurse the sick or to give comfort, yet she seems to have kept her perspective centered upon her main concern—to give support and comfort to her husband.

Financial Disaster Foreseen, Conflict with Oliver

In February 1837, "by mutual consent," Oliver's printing office in Kirtland was dissolved. The entire establishment was transferred to Joseph and Sidney. Joseph signed a note to Oliver for the amount owed. Warren Parrish became the editor of the *Messenger and Advocate,* and William Marks took over the bindery.

Joseph intended to publish another edition of the Book of Mormon and print more hymnals. There was also a need for more copies of the Doctrine and Covenants, as well as the monthly newspaper, *Messenger and Advocate.* He also intended to publish another newspaper entitled *The Elder's Journal.*

These ambitious projects, along with a spacious new house Joseph and Emma needed in order to take care of their growing family and numerous guests, were exciting prospects on the horizon. Although he was optimistic, even jubilant, over the progress that had been made up to that time, Joseph tried to warn the people to be careful, honest, and wise. He urged them to avoid get-rich-quick schemes.

The spiritual development of the Prophet was increasing, and sometimes it was hard for members of the Church to separate the spiritual and temporal responsibilities of Joseph and the other leaders. Frederick Granger Williams, who was Joseph's counselor in the First Presidency, ran for the office of justice of the peace and was elected by a good margin of votes.

As business began to boom, a spirit of speculation seemed to take over.[6] The financial panic in the country triggered the failure of several banks. Suddenly, those banks still functioning refused to honor the Safety Society notes. Some note holders became angry with Joseph and threatened to sue him personally. Some members became embittered, left the Church, and began to actively and publicly spread their negative feelings toward him and the Church. This dissension aroused people in the neighboring communities against the Church. In the face of such troubles, Joseph found that many who had been his friends had suddenly turned against him.[7]

At the Church conference in April, he proceeded as if nothing was wrong. The Lord had directed him to open a mission in the British Isles. In June 1837, Orson Hyde, Heber C. Kimball, and Joseph Fielding were called and set apart for that great responsibility.[8]

Further organizational changes were made in the priesthood quorums, and there was much debate among the brethren as to exactly what duties belonged to what office. Sidney Rigdon and Frederick G. Williams were still Joseph's counselors in the First Presidency. Edward Partridge was Presiding Bishop, but he was in Missouri. There were others who were called as bishops, including Newel Whitney and Vinson Knight. Oliver Cowdery and David Whitmer still held presidential title in the Church leadership, but their status was vague and they were not entirely agreeable with all the changes Joseph was making in the quorums.[9]

A division began to develop in the Church community, and power struggles developed among the brethren. As the financial pressures increased, a mob spirit swept through the countryside. Emma must have had a constant feeling of dread, wondering where they would turn to obtain funds to meet their debts, certainly aware of the changing demands of Joseph's calling.

Personal Anguish

Not long after conference, the Prophet met young Wilford Woodruff. After looking keenly into his face, discerning the young man's good feelings toward him, Joseph exclaimed, "Brother Wilford, I am glad to see you. I hardly know when I meet those who have been my brethren in the Lord, who of them are my friends. They have become so scarce."[10]

When Wilford said he was soon to marry Phoebe Whitmore Carter and asked if the Prophet would marry them, Joseph invited them to have the wedding at his house. It was typical of Joseph to make this gesture; he simply knew Emma would welcome the couple and make a nice party for their wedding. The wedding day was set for 13 April 1837.

The day before the wedding, while Joseph was away from the house, he was warned of a plot to take his life. This necessitated him leaving town without even going home. Emma hosted the wedding alone, and Frederick G. Williams performed the ceremony.[11]

Emma later received a letter from Joseph telling her what had happened. Her reply, written on 25 April, says:

> Your letter was welcomed by friends and foes, we were glad enough to hear that you was well, and our enemies think they have almost found you by seeing where the letters were mailed. . . . Brother [Vinson] Knight will tell you better about the business than I can write, as there is but a moment for me to improve. I cannot tell you my feelings when I found I could not see you before you left, yet I expect you can realize them, the children feel very anxious about you because they don't know where you have gone. . . .[12]

Imagine Emma's feelings as she tried to explain to the children why their father had left without saying good-bye to them. Yet her words to Joseph gave him encouragement and reveal her confidence in him and her continued commitment to their divine mission. She wrote:

> I verily feel that if I had no more confidence in God than some I could name, I should be in a bad case indeed but I still believe that if we humble ourselves, and are as faithful as we can be, we shall be delivered from every snare that may be laid for our feet, and our lives and property will be saved and we redeemed from all unreasonable encumbrances. . . .[13]

When the danger was past, Joseph was able to return home, but they were not permitted to live in peace. Heber C. Kimball described the situation in Kirtland:

> Our enemies were raging and threatening destruction upon us. We had to guard night after night, and for weeks were not permitted to take off our clothes, and were obliged to lie with our firelocks in our arms, to preserve Brother Joseph's life and our own.
>
> Joseph was sued before a magistrate's court in Painsville, on a vexatious suit. I carried him from Kirtland to Painsville with four or five others, in my wagon, every morning for five days, and brought them back in the evening. We were often waylaid, but managed to elude our enemies by rapid driving and taking different roads. Esquire Bissel defended the prophet and he came off victorious.[14]

This kind of suit was not unfrequent. Those who filed the charges knew they were false, but engaged in the actions to incite public sentiment against the Mormons, which they succeeded in doing.

A Spirit of Speculation

Eliza R. Snow kept a precise record of events during this time. She wrote:

A spirit of speculation had crept into the hearts of some of the Twelve, and nearly, if not every quorum was more or less infected. Most of the Saints were poor, and now prosperity was dawning upon them—the Temple was completed, and in it they had been recipients of marvelous blessings, and many who had been humble and faithful to performance of every duty—ready to go and come at every call of the Priesthood, were getting haughty in their spirits, and lifted up in the pride of their hearts.[15]

Joseph tried in vain to get the people to be careful. He became suspicious that someone was embezzling funds from the bank and asked Justice of the Peace Frederick G. Williams for a warrant to search Warren Parrish's trunk. Frederick, also an officer in the bank (and counselor to Joseph in the presidency of the Church), undoubtedly resented the implication of wrongdoing in the bank. Deeply offended on behalf of his colleague, he refused to give the warrant. Joseph was extremely upset and told Williams that he would have the warrant or else he would be forced to "break him of his office."[16]

Frederick responded heatedly, "Break it is then!" and the two men shook hands on it.[17]

Although Joseph had no power to affect the office of justice of the peace, he could and did reject Williams as his counselor, and ceased to associate with him in any official capacity. This left Williams disgruntled and vulnerable to the persuasions of dissenters. In due time, Parrish, with some other apostates, became actively engaged in forming a "new" church.

The constant stress brought Joseph to a point of complete physical collapse. He was so ill for a time, it was feared he would not recover. He was forced to remain at home, in bed, for several weeks and required round-the-clock nursing. Emma was assisted by many friends during his illness.[18]

The Missionaries Leave for England

Notwithstanding the economic and social crisis, Heber C. Kimball, Orson Hyde, Willard Richards, and Joseph Fielding made ready to leave for their mission to England. Heber gave each of his children a blessing before he left them. He said they were crying so loud they could hardly hear what he said. Heber's wife, Vilate, like Emma, saw much less of her husband after he was called to the apostleship. The two women seem to have become friends, and one could wish Vilate had written about those early days.

On the morning of 13 June 1837, the four missionaries stopped at the Prophet's home to receive his blessing and say good-bye. Since he was too ill to lift his head from the pillow, Emma led the men into his bedroom. The parting was tender. They were leaving both their families and their Prophet sick. They had very little money or provisions for their journey. Nevertheless, they had faith. They had courage. They were missionaries. Three were Apostles of the Lord Jesus Christ, and they were going to take His restored gospel across the ocean.

Joseph Recovers But the Safety Society Is Doomed

Gradually, Joseph began to improve. Mary Fielding wrote to her sister Mercy Thompson, telling her of going to the Prophet's home for dinner. Joseph's condition had been "very serious," she said, and she wrote sympathetically of the terrible burden he and Hyrum carried, how she felt for their dear mother, and that his enemies were saying his illness was caused from his wickedness and was a judgment from God.[19]

It is interesting that nobody expresses sympathy for Emma. From reading through hundreds of bits and pieces collected from this period of their lives, it would seem that Emma was not a person who asked for or invited sympathy. She exhibited great personal strength, and she took care of her own business, and Joseph's, too, when he was forced to be absent.

Mary wrote that much to the disappointment of his enemies and the joy of his friends, Joseph recovered from his illness. She also said that she "took dinner with Joseph."[20] Presumably Emma prepared the meal on the day of Mary's visit; no doubt she and the children ate with Joseph and his guests. Mary reported that Joseph said during his illness he had been so low at times that the only comfort he received was when his wife or someone else prayed for him.[21] There is no information as to whether Joseph's estranged friend, Dr. Frederick Granger Williams came to his aid during his illness.

As Joseph began to feel better, another crisis flared. Most of the men who had been working on Joseph's and Emma's new house went out into the countryside to find work. One man, Jonathan Crosby, remained to work on the house and accepted payment in Kirtland Bank notes, which Joseph hoped would be honored at the local stores. When Jonathan went to buy food, he found no merchants who would accept the notes. He returned home empty-handed; that night he and his wife went to bed hungry. In their history they recorded that they had the comforting thought of "going to see the Prophet's wife in the morning."22 Such was the attitude of people toward Emma. If anything went wrong, they would go see Emma!

The next morning on their way to see her, the Crosbys met Joseph on the street and explained the problem to him. Caroline Crosby states that "Joseph arranged for him [Jonathan] to have some flour."23 It was Emma, however, who delivered the provisions. She came later that day to where Jonathan was working alone on the house. She thanked him for continuing his labors when the others had quit, and gave him a ham and some flour. As she walked around the spacious foundation and looked upon the unfinished building, perhaps she even wondered if it would ever be her home.

Johnathan's account of this incident states that "through no real fault of their own," Joseph and Emma had been reduced to poverty once again.24 He added that Joseph was also burdened with the responsibility of knowing that the financial ruin brought greater stress on relationships already stretched beyond the breaking point.25

According to Marvin Hill, "When Joseph learned that the notes would not circulate at face value, he withdrew his support from the bank."26

The following announcement by Joseph appeared in the *Messenger and Advocate:*

> I resigned my office in the Kirtland Safety Society, disposed of my interest therein, and withdrew from the institution; be fully aware, after so long an experiment, no institution of the kind established upon just and righteous principles for a blessing not only to the Church but the whole world would be suffered to continue its operations in such an age of darkness, speculation and wickedness. Almost all banks throughout the country, one after another have

suspended specie payment, and gold and silver have risen in value in direct ratio with the depreciation of paper currency.[27]

It would be early September before the issue of the bank's failure came up in a meeting of the general Church conference, and Church members were called upon to vote to sustain the twelve apostles. Three of the Twelve—Lyman E. Johnson, Luke S. Johnson, and John F. Boynton—were "rejected and disfellowshipped" for "leaving their calling to attend to other occupations."[28] Boynton, the only one of the three who was present, "attributed his difficulties to the failure of the bank, stating that he understood the bank was instituted by the will of God, and he had been told that it should never fail, let men do what they would." [29]

Joseph responded to this by informing them all that "if this had been declared no one had authority from him for so doing, for he had always said that unless the institution was conducted on righteous principles it would not stand."[30] Boynton was rejected by the vote of those attending the conference, but on 10 September, he, Luke S. Johnson, and Lyman E. Johnson, "made their confessions and were received into fellowship . . . also to retain their apostleship."[31]

But before any of these problems were resolved, the months of July and August held momentous events that must have affected Emma in a far more personal way than anyone can realize. She not only had to nurse Joseph through his illness, she had the care of her children, Julia, Joseph, and Little Freddie, who was about one year old.

Persecution Intensifies

Joseph "started from Kirtland in company with elders Rigdon and Marsh for the purpose of visiting the Saints in Canada," on 27 July.[32] Joseph was still far from well. It must have been hard for Emma to see him go, and it must have been an even greater surprise when he returned that same night, having gone no farther than Painsville.

Joseph would not have had to explain to Emma that Painsville was a center of anti-Mormon activity. She knew that Dr. Philastus Hurlbut often lectured there and he had a large following who took great pains to watch the roads and take any opportunity to harass Joseph. At Painsville, Joseph had been detained by a constable who served a warrant against him. The Justice of the Peace was found, and a hearing was arranged. The judge ruled that there were no grounds for the suit and dismissed the case. They had no sooner gone out the door than another warrant was served. This was followed by a third. Each suit was found to be without substance and was dismissed, but the enemies would not give up. Finally, late in the day, Joseph climbed wearily into the carriage to leave, but before he could take the reins into his hands, a fourth warrant was served. This time, there was some substance to the suit. It involved the traveling salesman who had insisted upon placing a stove in Emma's kitchen, hoping it would be good advertising. Since Joseph had not asked to have the stove installed and had not expected to buy it, when it was made a reason to harass him, he was exasperated and totally worn out. He left his watch for collateral, and he and Sidney returned to Kirtland.[33]

The next day, 28 July, they waited until evening, then, in S. B. Stoddard's wagon, they set out again, this time taking a lengthy and round-about route to Ashtabula, Ohio, a distance of thirty miles. It was not a small company who made this trip. Joseph, Sidney, Thomas B. Marsh, Albert Rockwood, and Brigham Young traveled through the night, arriving shortly after daybreak. They stayed at Ashtabula until afternoon, walking on the shore, bathing in the clear water of Lake Erie, enjoying a chance for some rare recreation and relaxation.[34] They boarded a steamer about four that afternoon and enjoyed a pleasant trip on deck passage, on Lake Erie to Buffalo. At Buffalo they parted; Brigham and Albert went to the Eastern States.[35] Joseph and the others went on the steamer, across Lake Ontario, to Toronto.

While they were in Canada, they met many Saints and preached many sermons. They baptized new members, blessed the Saints, and strengthened the branches. While they were gone, the missionaries in England were contending with the devil, but shortly they made some remarkable progress, opening the way for the conversion of many people. At this same time, the authorities of the Church in Missouri assembled in council at Far West, where they discussed the expectation of building a House of the Lord there.[36] In Kirtland, Emma held the creditors at bay, tended the children, and entertained visitors. In

Joseph's absence, Emma made visitors welcome. Her explaination of the records of Abraham apparently satisfied a Crosby relative, as Caroline notes, "He never seemed disposed to contend against it."[37]

Joseph Returns from Canada

Joseph's homecoming is described in a letter, dated 8 September 1837, written by Mary Fielding, who gives several interesting details of his experiences, which are left out of the official history.[38]

Some travelers, "Sisters Walton and Snider," arriving in Kirtland on Saturday around noon, had left Joseph and Sidney about 20 miles from Fairport, Ohio, and brought the news that Joseph should be arriving about ten o'clock that night.

We can be sure that Emma made great preparations for his arrival, but he did not come at the appointed time. Nor did he come at midnight. It was three in the morning before he got home. When he and Sidney came in, they were covered with mud, their clothes were torn, and they had a hair-raising story to tell.

About four miles from home, their carriage had been surrounded by a mob determined to take them back to Painsville. They were secured in a tavern, where a mock trial was planned. Fortunately, the housekeeper was a member of the Church and helped them make their escape, as Joseph said, "not by a Basket let down through a Window, but by the Kitchin Door."[39]

The night was pitch dark. They could hardly tell which way to go, but decided to hide in the woods. They ran as fast as they could and lay down in a swamp. The mob pursued them so closely that Joseph admonished Sidney not to breathe so loud. Then they ran on and on, being able to see where to go only because the mob carried lighted torches.

Climbing over fences, going through brush and corn fields, they finally found the road toward Kirtland. They estimated that by the time they reached home they had gone more than six miles on foot. Mary describes every detail as she must have heard it from the Prophet himself.

Sidney was too weak to get to meetings on the Sabbath, but Joseph came and went during several meetings that day.[40]

Extending the Stakes of Zion

One can scarcely comprehend the indomitable spirit of the Prophet Joseph. As his wife, Emma would have been the victim of circumstances when things went wrong, but she was also a firsthand witness to the incredible outpouring of inspiration that the Lord opened to him, from time to time. In the wake of the Safety Society's failure and facing financial ruin, apostasy among his closest associates, and physical abuse—including threats against his life—the Prophet Joseph, instead of turning inward with depression or recanting any of his professed beliefs, took bold steps to expand the foundation and enlarge the borders of the kingdom.

Writing on 7 October 1837, Mary Fielding recalls:

> Brother Joseph came to see us a few days since for the last time previous to his going on a journey to Missouri. . . . He, Brother Rigdon, Bro. Hyrum, William and others are all gone on a very important business and not expected back for some months. . . . Some important things were shown to Bro. Joseph in vision previous to his going off relative to the enlargement of our Borders which has indeed become indespensabley necessary, for the Inhabitants of Zion both here and in the West are crying [that] the Citys are too strait for us give place that we may dwell. The people are crowding in from all parts and as President Rigdon said in his last discourse, *"Here* they will gather and Earth and hell combined cannot hinder them, for *gather they will."* Hence the necessaty of planting new stakes which they received a command to do before they left and it is expected that after they have set in order the Church in the West they will fix upon 11 new Stakes before they return but this is not spoken of in public for reasons you will be aware of. If this were generally known it would probably make their way much more difficult.[41]

On Sunday, before leaving for the West, the Prophet addressed a large crowd in the temple. According to Mary Fielding, "not much less than 1500" faithful members were there to hear. She said that Joseph "looked over [the] congregation and considered what had been done and then what was still to be done . . . pouring his blessings upon all the sincere and faithful saints." To Mary, the events were "glorious," beyond her power to describe, for Joseph had testified in a powerful manner and, when he finished, the congregation said, "Amen!"[42]

That same day, Sidney gave a sermon in which he spoke about the future glory and purity of Zion. He said Zion would gather, "and earth and hell combined cannot hinder them for *gather they will* . . . ."[43]

Wilford Woodruff was also there and heard Joseph's testimony. He said, "[Joseph] seemed a fountain of knowledge from whose mouth streams of eternal wisdom flowed. As he stood before the people he showed clearly that the authority of God was upon him. . . . There is not so great a man as Joseph standing in this generation . . . [His enemies] look upon him, and he is like a bed of gold, concealed from human view. They know not his principle, his spirit, his wisdom, his virtue, his philanthropy, his calling. . . ."[44]

Emma, however, knew her husband's calling augured much for him and for the cause of the Church, and if she doubted his wisdom at this time, she is not quoted.

Joseph Goes to Missouri

It could not have come as a surprise to Emma that Joseph would have to leave again. His presence was needed in Missouri.

There, the Saints had been driven entirely out of Jackson County. For a time they had been allowed to live in Clay County, while making efforts to legally reclaim their land in Jackson County. But their attempts proved futile. In fact, the Jackson County people agitated the situation, insisting there was no room in any organized county in Missouri for the ever-increasing number of Latter-day Saints. There was a vast amount of empty land north, in Ray County. Alexander Doniphan, a lawyer, who had helped the Saints during their earlier troubles, and was now a representative in the legislature, led out in recommending that two new counties, Daviess and Caldwell, be formed from Ray County. Caldwell County was offered to the Mormons, and the Saints built the town of Far West; Independence, however, was still considered to be the "Center Place," or "Zion."

Joseph, Sidney, William Smith, and Vinson Knight, left on 27 September, for Missouri. Hyrum had gone there previously, leaving his family of four small children and his wife, Jerusha, about to give birth again.

When Joseph and the others arrived in Far West, about the first of November,[45] the apostles who were not traveling and the high council held a meeting. It was decided that there was sufficient room for the Church to continue to gather there and it was also decided that they would postpone efforts to build a temple there, for the time being.

Hyrum was sustained as a counselor to Joseph. Frederick G. Williams was dropped from the First Presidency.[46] For the moment, it seemed, the difficulties among the brethren were settled, and order was restored to the Church. Undoubtedly, Joseph hoped he and Oliver could resolve the problems that had developed between them.

Meanwhile, Emma was in Kirtland to help nurse Jerusha, who was extremely ill with pneumonia, following the birth of a baby. Lucy described what took place:

> . . . a calamity happened to our family that wrung our hearts with more than common grief. Jerusha, Hyrum's wife, was taken sick, and after an illness of perhaps two weeks, died, while her husband was absent on a mission to Missouri. She was a woman whom everybody loved that was acquainted with her. . . . The family were so warmly attached to her, that had she been our own sister, they could not have been more afflicted by her death.[47]

Jerusha died on 13 October 1837, just eleven days after she gave birth to her baby daughter. She left five small children. On her death bed, Jerusha said to one of her children, "Tell your father when he comes that the Lord has taken your mother and left you for him to take care of."[48]

Hyrum was still in Missouri, and Joseph was at Terre Haute, Indiana, on his way to Far West. It would be weeks before Hyrum could be told of the tragedy, and mid-December before he could return to Kirtland to attend to his little children. Mary Fielding, a friend of the family who had helped nurse Jerusha in her sickness, took care of the baby, and did the best she could for the others.

Apostasy in Kirtland

Emma had not only suffered the loss of a dear sister-in-law, but she and Joseph were also facing the worst financial crisis of their lives. Creditors continually confronted her, demanding that she pay Joseph's debts or give them his property in exchange. The Prophet had been away from home for some time when Jesse Crosby went to visit Emma to see if he might render some assistance. When he stated his purpose, "The Prophet's wife burst into tears and said that if persecution would cease, they could live as well as any other family in the land. . . ."[49]

Emma would have also known of the conspiracy going on to overthrow the Church and start a new church. Caroline Crosby remembers: "Warren Parrish was a sort of leader of a party of some 30 or 40 persons, among them was John Boynton and wife, Luke and Lyman Johnson, Harper Riggs, and others whose names I do not recollect. These were some of our nicest neighbors and friends. We had taken sweet counsel together and walked to the House of God as friends."[50]

In *The History of the Church* Joseph states: "Soon after my return this dissenting band openly and publicly renounced the Church of Christ of Latter-day Saints and claimed themselves to be the old standard, calling themselves the Church of Christ, excluding the word 'Saints,' and set me at naught, and the whole Church, denouncing us as heretics, not considering that the Saints shall possess the kingdom according to the Prophet Daniel."[51]

Realizing that the wives of these men who left the Church were Emma's friends and associates, we can better understand that this apostasy must have seemed a greater personal loss to Joseph and Emma than their financial losses, which were great. One woman, the wife of an apostate, when asked if it were true that she had apostatized, answered that she "was dissatisfied with some things in the Church, but . . . she still believed the Book of Mormon and thought she always should."[52]

Emma and Joseph's reunion on 10 December 1837 was almost certainly shrouded in deep sorrow and anxiety.

A New Sister-in-law

When Hyrum heard of Jerusha's death, he was devastated. His children needed him, and his calling as counselor in the First Presidency of the Church demanded his traveling extensively. He discussed his problem with Joseph. Joseph recommended Hyrum marry immediately, to give his children a mother and free him to continue his Church duties. Taking Joseph's counsel, he married Mary Fielding, who had been a close personal friend of the family for a long time.

They were married 24 December 1837. Thus Mary became a stepmother, something she had once told her sister she hoped to never be.[53] Her ready-made family consisted of five youngsters: Lovina, ten; John, four; Hyrum, Jr., three; Jerusha, twenty months; and Sarah, three months. In respect to his sudden marriage, Hyrum said, "It is not because I had less love or regard for Jerusha that I married so soon, but it was for the sake of my children."[54]

Mary and Hyrum developed a strong bond of love. She was devoted to him. Her strength of character and her faith in the divine mission in which they were engaged proved invaluable to Hyrum's ability to perform his ministerial duties.

Church Membership Increases—Kirtland Scene of Mob Threats

Even as these events unfolded in Kirtland, the first public conference in England was held on 25 December, with 300 Saints in attendance.

In the closing weeks of 1837, "apostasy, persecution, confusion and mobocracy strove hard to bear rule in Kirtland."[55] On the morning of 22 December, Brigham Young left Kirtland because his life was in danger. He said there were those who would take his life because "he would proclaim publicly and privately that he knew by the power of the Holy Ghost that [Joseph] was a Prophet of the Most High God, and that [he] had not transgressed and fallen as the apostates declared."[56]

In a letter to her sister, Hyrum's new wife, Mary, compares the apostasy in Kirtland to the Biblical account in the Numbers chapter

16: "I often have of late been led to look back on the circumstances of Korah and his company when they rose up against Moses and Aaron. . . . The feelings and conduct of many of the people and even the elders of Israel in these days [is] exactly described . . . ." Mary wondered if the Lord would deal with the Saints in Kirtland in the same manner, and prayed that he would have mercy. "I feel more and more convinced that it is through suffering we are to be made perfect and I have already found it to have the effect of driving me nearer to the Lord . . . ."[57]

Before the crisis was over, half of the twelve apostles, one of Joseph's counselors, and many of their oldest and dearest friends would become estranged from the Church. Sadly, this would include Oliver Cowdery and David Whitmer, with whom Joseph had been unable to reconcile. Joseph had warned Bishop Partridge, "Thus saith the Lord, let my people be aware of dissensions among them, lest the enemy have power over them."[58] When the people yielded to disunity and backbiting, the enemy had the power to overcome them.

On 12 January 1838, at his parents' home in Kirtland, Joseph met with Sidney Rigdon, Vinson Knight, and G. W. Robinson to discuss the question of how to deal with Oliver and David. The answer was clearly outlined in the revelations: a president could be removed from his office by vote of the high council and the majority of the membership. Undoubtedly, this meeting was intended to hedge up the way of the apostates who were claiming that David Whitmer was their president, and that they constituted the Church authority.

Joseph inquired of the Lord what course he should follow. The answer he received was straightforward: "Your labors are finished in this place for a season." He was told that he and Sidney were to take their families and go to the west as soon as possible. Joseph was also told , "Let all your faithful friends arise with their families also . . . and gather yourselves unto Zion."[59]

Flight from Kirtland

Since mobs were roving the area, Joseph and Sidney had to leave promptly. As he was leaving, Joseph said to his mother, "I shall see you again, let what will happen, for I have a promise of life and they cannot kill me until that time is expired."[60]

They left town in a covered wagon. As soon as they were out of danger, they mounted horses and rode sixty miles to Norton, in Knox County, Ohio, where they stopped to wait for their families.

Emma was left to pack up their belongings and prepare her children to flee from their home. Whatever else Emma took with her in her hasty departure, the Prophet's papers and manuscripts would surely have been included.[61]

Thus, we may understand that the assault upon Emma's peace and security was relentless. As she left Kirtland, she began an almost 900-mile trek in the dead of winter. She planned to meet up with the Saints, who were temporarily gathering on the prairie at Far West, Missouri. Joseph's youngest brother, twenty-two-year-old Don Carlos, brought Emma and her three children—Julia, not quite seven, little Joseph, who was five, and Frederick, six months short of two years old—to Knox County, where Joseph and Sidney waited about thirty-six hours for their families to arrive. From there, the Smiths and Rigdons began the long journey to Missouri.[62]

The histories give few details about the flight of the Smith family from Kirtland. It is known that they headed south and west, traveling through Dayton, Ohio, to Dublin, Indiana. They traversed the width of Illinois, crossing the Mississippi River at Quincy, into Missouri, turning south, then heading west again.

In the history of Jesse Taylor Jackson, there is an account of "Joseph the Mormon prophet bringing his family through Knox County, [Ohio]" where the Jackson family had a farm. They said that Joseph requested permission to use one of their vacant farm houses, and permission was granted. "They stayed there four days and left the house spotlessly clean." Jesse Taylor Jackson and his brother, Robert, were impressed with the message of the gospel, which they heard from Joseph during this time, and later they went to Nauvoo, where they united with the Church.[63]

At Dublin, Indiana, the travelers met Brigham Young, who was also going west. From his journal we learn that Joseph confided to Brigham, "I am destitute of means to pursue my journey." He asked for advice from Brigham, who said, "If you will take my counsel, it will be that you rest yourself and be assured, Brother Joseph, you shall have plenty of money to pursue your journey . . . ."[64]

According to Young's history, a man named Tomlinson sold his property and gave the Prophet three hundred dollars, which enabled him and his family to proceed.

Many years later, Joseph III described his memories of this trip. He does not give the detail one would wish; rather, these are the hazy and fragmented memories of an old man of something that happened when he was but a little boy of five. He recalled:

> Across the center of the covered wagon in which we rode, there was a division made up by fastening up blankets. . . . Father and someone else occupied the back of the wagon by turns. I remember we reached a river, which I now suppose was the Wabash in Indiana, and that the roads running through the low lands were of a kind called corduroy [logs laid crossways]. Some who had been riding in the wagons walked over these roads, and I also did so for a ways, stepping over the ridge poles, holding onto the hand of my mother.[65]

Emma, who was pregnant, probably preferred walking to riding over that bumpy road.

They traveled slowly; Brigham and some of the other families overtook them at Jacksonville, Illinois. After stopping to rest for a few days with members of the Church who lived there, the refugees from Kirtland caravanned on to Quincy, where they found the Mississippi River frozen.

Crossing the Frozen Mississippi, February 1838

Anxious to get their families to Far West, Joseph and Brigham went to the river and examined the ice to see if they could cross. The ice was not solid at the river's edge, but they found that by going through a long flatboat, which lay with the end to the shore, they could get onto the solid ice of the river. Finding the ice sufficiently sturdy to bear up the teams, they hauled their wagons over the flatboat and onto the ice. Then they led their horses onto the ice, hitched them up to the wagons, and proceeded across, with the women and children walking across.

Of this crossing, Brigham said, "After leaving the boat we struck out in a long string, and passed over in safety." Joseph's favorite horse, Charlie led out and "broke the ice at every step for several rods."[66]

Once across the river, they continued their journey, camping in their wagons at night. It appears as if they turned south, and then west. It took them a week to make their way to the Salt River. They found that the ice had broken up there, also, and the ferry had sunk, so they could not cross the river itself. After a few days, Joseph suggested they examine a pond which, if it were frozen solid enough, they could cross. Here they found that the old ice had sunk below the water, at the edge of the pond, but was still firm. By plunging their teams and wagons through a distance of two or three feet, at the edge of the pond, they managed to get their wagons onto the old ice and cross. They had to get off the ice on the other side in the same manner. A canoe was placed from the shore to the ice, and the families walked through the canoe to the solid ice and crossed, then got off in the same manner on the other side.[67] What a cold, miserable task it must have been to get everyone across this icy barrier.

Emma, in the fourth month of her fifth pregnancy had three small children to keep fed, warm, and if possible, clean. That Emma went at all speaks of her loyalty to Joseph. That she was able to endure speaks of her strength. Never again will I think of Emma's journey from Kirtland to Far West as "just another trip." It took two grueling months for her to travel what today we can do in a couple of days by car, or just a couple of hours by plane.

Notes

1. *Deseret News Church Almanac, 1991-1992* (Salt Lake City: Deseret News, 1992), p. 333.

2. Dean C. Jessee, *Personal Writings of Joseph Smith* (Salt Lake City: Deseret Book, 1984), pp. 349-50.

3. See Doctrine & Covenants 111.

4. *Messenger and Advocate*, January 1837, as quoted in *HC,* 2:473.

5. Marvin Hill, "Joseph Smith the Man: Some Reflections on a Subject of Controversy," *BYU Studies* (Spring, 1981), p. 185.

6. Matthias F. Cowley, ed., *Wilford Woodruff, History of His Life and Labors* (Salt Lake City: Bookcraft, 1964), p. 68.

7. *HC*, 2:488 ftnt.; see also *The Autobiography of Parley P. Pratt* (Salt Lake City: Deseret Book, 1985), pp. 183-84.

8. *HC*, 2:490-92.

9. Ibid. David Whitmer was not in the First Presidency of the Church, but in Missouri he served in the capacity we would define today as an Area President. Memo from Richard Anderson to the author, dated 11 March 1995.

10. Cowley, *Wilford Woodruff,* p. 68.

11. Ibid.

12. Emma Smith, letter to Joseph, 25 April 1837. Located in RLDS Archives. Copy in author's possession.

13. Ibid.

14. Orson F. Whitney, *Life of Heber C. Kimball* (Salt Lake City: Bookcraft, 1945), p. 31

15. *HC*, 2:487-88 ftnt.

16. Frederick G. Williams, "Frederick G. Williams of the First Presidency of the Church," *BYU Studies* (Spring, 1972), p. 255

17. Ibid.

18. *HC*, 2:492.

19. Mary Fielding Smith, Letter in LDS Archives.

20. Ibid.

21. Ibid.

22. Caroline Crosby History, unpublished family record in LDS Archives.

23. Ibid.

24. Ibid.

25. Ibid.

26. Hill, "Joseph Smith the Man," *BYU Studies* (Spring, 1981), p. 185.

27. *HC*, 2:497.

28. *HC*, 2:509.

29. *HC*, 2:510.

30. Ibid.

31. *HC*, 2:512.

32. *HC*, 2:502 .

33. Ibid.

34. *HC*, 2:502-503.

35. *HC*, 2:503.

36. *HC*, 2:505.

37. Kenneth W. Godfrey, Audrey M. Godfrey, and Jill Mulvay Derr, *Women's Voices: An Untold History of the Latter-day Saints 1830-1900* (Salt Lake City: Deseret Book, 1982), p. 52. Hereafter referred to as *Women's Voices.*

38. Mary Fielding Smith, letter in LDS Archives.

39. Godfrey, Godfrey, and Deer, *Women's Voices*, pp. 64-65, original copy in LDS Archives.

40. Mary Fielding Smith, letter in LDS Archives.

41. Godfrey, Godfrey, and Derr, *Women's Voices,* p. 67-68.

42. Ibid., p. 68

43. Ibid.

44. Cowley, *Wilford Woodruff,* p. 68.

45. *HC,* 2:521.

46. *HC,* 2:523.

47. Lucy Smith, *Biographical Sketches of Joseph Smith the Prophet and His Progenitors for Many Generations* (Independence, Mo.: Herald Publishing House, 1969), p. 246.

48. *HC,* 2:519.

49. In Hyrum L. Andrus and Helen Mae Andrus, *They Knew the Prophet* (Salt Lake City: Bookcraft, 1974), p. 143.

50. Godfrey, Godfrey, and Derr, *Women's Voices,* p. 56.

51. *HC,* 2:528.

52. Godfrey, Godfrey, and Derr, *Women's Voices,* Caroline Crosby Letter, p. 56.

53. Mary Fielding Smith letter, LDS Archives. Copy in author's possession.

54. Pearson H. Corbett, *Hyrum Smith, Patriarch* (Salt Lake City: Deseret Book, 1963), p. 164. For a more complete version of Jerusha's death and Hyrum's remarriage, see pp. 161-64.

55. *HC,* 2:529.

56. Ibid.

57. Godfrey, Godfrey, and Derr, *Women's Voices,* p. 64.

58. Revelation to Joseph Smith, compiled by Fred C. Collier, *Unpublished Revelations of the Prophet and Presidents of the Church of Jesus Christ of Latter-Day Saints* (Salt Lake City: Collier's Publishing Co., 1979), 1:86.

59. Ibid., p. 88

60. Lucy Smith, *Biographical Sketches,* p. 248.

61. Ibid., pp. 247-48.

62. Ibid.

63. Gracia Jones and Janice F. DeMille, *History of Fredonia, Arizona 1885-1985* (Hurricane, Utah: Homestead Publishers and Distributors, 1986), pp. 49-51.

64. Eldon Jay Watson, ed. *Manuscript History of Brigham Young 1801-1844* (Salt Lake City: Smith Secretarial Services, 1968), p. 26.

65. Mary Audentia Smith Anderson, ed., *Joseph III and the Restoration* (Independence, Mo: Herald Publishing House, 1952), p. 12.

66. Watson, *Manuscript History of Brigham Young,* p. 26.

67. Ibid.

CHAPTER 8

Crisis After Crisis

"*I hope there is better days to come to us yet. . . .*" (Emma Smith)

Power Struggle Among the Church Leaders

The controversies over the Kirtland bank failure in 1837 spilled over into further conflict in the leadership of the Church. When Oliver Cowdery had left Kirtland, he and Joseph were not on the most cordial terms; likewise, David and John Whitmer and W. W. Phelps, who constituted the area presidency in Missouri, were all affected by a spirit of resentment. David and John Whitmer and W. W. Phelps had apparently sold some lots in Jackson County for personal gain, and, it appeared, to non-Mormons. What made their actions even more questionable was that these men had previously signed a lengthy document in 1834, later published in the *Evening and Morning Star* and edited by Oliver Cowdery, which stated, . . . [To] sell our land [in Jackson County] would amount to denial of our faith, as that land is the place where the Zion of God shall stand . . . ."[1] In addition to both of the Whitmers, Oliver, and Phelps, the document was also signed by Edward Partridge, John Corrill, Isaac Morley, Parley P. Pratt, Lyman Wight, Newel Knight, Thomas B. Marsh, Simeon Carter, and Calvin Beebe.

The high council felt the accused had broken faith with the Church by selling land. The accused felt that their callings made them immune from the judgments of the council. But there were other issues as well.

The high council, headed by Apostle Thomas Marsh, sent a committee to visit with W. W. Phelps and John and David Whitmer to inform them that the Church was dissatisfied with their conduct in selling several lots in Jackson County, not keeping the word of wisdom, and not keeping the law of consecration.[2]

The committee found all three men hostile to the request to come to the council and answer these charges. In a letter to his brother Warren, Oliver observed that the Whitmers and Phelps "wont go" to the hearing. He indicated they felt they did not have to "answer to a tribunal which is no tribunal. . . ."[3] The council concluded unanimously that they did not want to accept the leadership of John and David Whitmer or W. W. Phelps any longer. Some felt that they should wait until Joseph Smith, Jr., and Sidney Rigdon got there before taking official action against Oliver Cowdery and David Whitmer, and placing Thomas B. Marsh, and David W. Patten, as interim area presidents of the Church in Missouri. However, the council voted to cut off Oliver and David from membership in the Church, and William W. Phelps and John Whitmer were cut off as well.[4] Since John Whitmer was one of the keepers of the Prophet's history, this would cause ongoing problems for Joseph in regard to his history.

The minutes of the council indicate that a letter was read from Joseph, sent from New Portage, Ohio, asking the brethren to assist him and his family to get to Far West. (He was unaware of the squabbles.) The letter had been long delayed but they acted on it immediately by assigning Bishop Edward Partridge, G. W. Harris, and Isaac Morley to form a committee to get wagons and teams and money to go and meet Joseph and Sidney and help them get to Far West.[5]

Arrival at Far West, Missouri

In March 1838, the brethren went to meet Joseph and Sidney at Huntsville with teams and money to help their families complete the remaining 120 miles. Brigham Young, Daniel S. Miles, and Levi Richards and their families arrived at the same time. Joseph's brother Samuel arrived with his family a few days later. The Rigdons were delayed several weeks, due to illness, but finally arrived on 4 April.

John P. Barnard took his carriage out to bring Joseph and his family to Far West.[6] On 13 March, Joseph and his family stayed the night with the Barnards, several miles from Far West. The next day, as they were nearing Far West, a large crowd came out to meet them. George W. Harris and his wife, Lucinda, opened their home to them. Blankets and provisions were brought and they were given every comfort.[7]

Joseph's Work—Emma's Home

With Emma and the children temporarily settled, Joseph immediately immersed himself in meetings with the high council in Far West. During the rest of March and into April, he was preoccupied with the serious business of setting in order the various priesthood quorums. Inherent in this business was the task of ascertaining who was willing and worthy to carry on the work of building the kingdom of God.

The day after they arrived, Joseph heard the minutes read and approved their previous actions of dropping the area presidency and excommunicating W. W. Phelps and John Whitmer. Joseph spent the next weeks ironing out organizational problems and attempting to unite the brethren and restore order to the Church leadership in Missouri. He had little time to spend with his family, being burdened with these matters.[8]

Historical records reflect this preoccupation; one can search in vain to find out what was done to provide a house for Emma and the children, though it is obvious a house was provided. We do not know if Emma's home was a frame house or log. One woman, Sarah Rich, who moved there in the early days recalled, "Far West was a place everybody lived in log houses so my husband had built a nice little hewed log hous[e] . . . ."[9] but she also mentions riding some distance to attend meetings, so she apparently did not live in the middle of town as Emma did. In his memory of events in Far West, Emma's eldest son, Joseph III mentions a "house" and a "gate," but does not describe the building. From these fragmentary bits of evidence we may get a mental picture of their home, with a fenced yard, which she must have appreciated because of her children. There was no need for Joseph to use Emma's kitchen as an office; there were other buildings where the brethren held their meetings and classes.

Oliver Cowdery and David Whitmer Excommunicated

About a month later, a list of nine complaints against Oliver were handed to the council.[10] After deliberation and much testimony, it was decided that Oliver was "no longer a member of the Church of Jesus Christ of Latter-day Saints."[11] With this action, the First Elder, one of the witnesses and the man who had baptized both Joseph and Emma, was stripped of his sacred calling and cut off from the Church.

The council followed Oliver's excommunication with another. They heard the case of David Whitmer, who had written a letter to the council claiming they had acted unlawfully. They determined that David had offered "contempt to the council by writing the letter" and after a few warm remarks concerning David's current behavior, it was decided that he, too, would no longer be considered a member.[12]

Recital of these bare facts cannot adequately indicate the heartbreaking reality that these old friends had become estranged. For more than eight years, Oliver and David had been like brothers to Joseph and Emma. John Whitmer and W. W. Phelps had played an important role in helping to publish Emma's hymnal and the revelations. As Joseph related the news of these excommunications to her, Emma must have experienced a mixture of feelings. Having a thorough knowledge of the dissenters' plans to take over the temple in Kirtland, and their accusations that Joseph was a fallen prophet, she undoubtedly burned with indignation against these men. At the same time, there must have been a cloud of immense sadness in the Smith home when the day of reckoning came and these old friends did not humble themselves, as Joseph had hoped they would.

Proposal to Provide Temporal Support for the First Presidency

Joseph and Sidney both faced the critical problem of supporting their families while devoting their full-time labors to their administrative duties in the Church. Joseph and Emma had been forced to depend upon the charity of others for their necessities on the trip, and in their getting settled in Far West. Now, any attempt to establish a new home without a secure income simply continued that embarrassing situation.

It was May before the problem of the destitute circumstances of the Presidency was brought up in council meeting. After some discussion, they all agreed some kind of arrangement had to be found to assure that the First Presidency had sufficient means to live without being beggars. They wanted to avoid any appearance of priestcraft (being paid for preaching), but realized at the same time that since the Presidency gave all of their time to Church work, they could not engage in other money-making occupations. The council discussed the fact that they might be paid for the work they did in the printing office and in translating. They proposed giving Joseph and Sidney each eighty acres of land adjacent to the city and $1100 a year. However, this generous offer did not materialize. Sidney's son-in-law, George Robinson, who was Joseph's clerk, stated many years later, in 1889, that "such an uproar followed the decision to pay the First Presidency annual wages that the request was finally dropped."[13] The struggle for cash flow was an ongoing crisis for the Church and its leaders in Missouri as it had been in Kirtland; only the generosity of individuals provided the necessities they could not obtain for themselves.

Since Emma was noted for her gardening in later years, it is likely that she planted vegetable seeds as soon as she had a plot of ground to use. An entry in the Prophet's history for May 1838 mentions him plowing his garden. According to Levi Hancock, the Saints raised pumpkins, beans, and corn in abundance, and many wild berries grew in the countryside, which also abounded in wild venison and wild pig.[14] With no supermarkets, all of their foodstuffs had to be produced by the labor of their hands. Food grown had to be preserved for the winter, and game had to be hunted and prepared. Clothing, likewise, from underwear to shoes, was a precious commodity. Keeping up with the food and clothing needs of her growing children was undoubtedly Emma's primary occupation.

Gathering to the Stakes of Zion

The Prophet saw his duty as one of gathering people into a center place where they could obtain the fullness the Lord had promised and where they would be strong enough to defend themselves while they fulfilled the commandment to take the restored gospel to the entire world. Although they had to leave Kirtland, Joseph did not abandon hope of retaining a foothold there. He had left agents to take care of the Church property and settle his just debts. But now in Missouri, he was faced with the need to stake out more territory to prepare for the harvest of souls he knew was coming.

On 18 May 1838, Joseph traveled north with Sidney Rigdon, Thomas B. Marsh, David W. Patten, Bishop Edward Partridge, Elias Higbee, Simeon Carter, Alanson Ripley, and many others, to "lay off a stake of Zion: making locations [for towns], and laying claim to lands to facilitate the gathering of the Saints. . . ." They camped out that night in tents, at the mouth of Honey Creek, a tributary of Grand River.[15] The next morning they traveled upriver, through timber, for about eighteen miles, to Lyman Wight's home.

On the prominent spot, overlooking the Grand River, which Joseph named Tower Hill, he examined a stone structure which he identified as an old Nephite altar.[16] He called the place Adam- ondi-Ahman and said that this was the place where Adam called his family together to bless them before he died. Joseph indicated that this place had been of great significance in ancient times, and so it would be again.[17] In this beautiful, fertile valley and the vast land of rolling hills, mostly empty of inhabitants, Joseph saw a place where the Church members could gather. Delighted with their success, he returned to Far West on 1 June. The time was rapidly approaching for the birth of Emma's new baby.

Alexander Hale Smith

A fine, robust son was born 2 June 1838.[18] His parents and sister, Julia, and brothers, young Joseph and Frederick, greeted Alexander with delight. Emma later jokingly remarked, using a play on words, that at the time he was born there "was a real hail storm in process," so they gave him the middle name of "Hale." He was named after Joseph's lawyer friend, Alexander Doniphan, who had been instrumental in helping the Saints establish the new county of Caldwell, which was to be the designated "Mormon County" in Missouri.

As soon as Joseph was sure all was well with his wife and new baby, he left again, this time with Hyrum and Sidney, to survey the area for the new town of Adam-ondi-Ahman, in Daviess County. They worked in a driving rain and were grateful for shelter at the Wights' cabin. They were back home before 16 June, when Joseph's Uncle John Smith and family, with six other families, arrived in Far West. After a joyful reunion, he sent them to settle at Adam-ondi-Ahman.[19]

On 28 June 1838, the same day that Queen Victoria was crowned queen of England, a stake of Zion was organized at Adam-ondi-Ahman, in Daviess County, Missouri.[20]

The Saints who heard Joseph's teachings about the place contemplated the revelations that designated this as an ancient and sacred place.[21] But the Missourians took a dim view of the Mormons expanding their settlement beyond the boundaries of Caldwell County. Trouble was brewing, and there would be a serious crisis in the near future.

Missionary Work Continues—Apostates Mingle with Saints

Notwithstanding the fact that Emma and Joseph's new home was in a primitive prairie town, on the western frontier of the United States, and their circumstances strained by debt and lack of income, they were young, healthy, and united with a growing organization committed to seeing their missionary work continue. Many brethren moved their wives and children onto farms in Missouri, where they would be able to provide for their own wants and needs, or into Far West; then two by two, as revelation directed, they went on missions to preach the gospel in the north, east and south, as well as in Canada and England. This labor bore fruit and served to swell the numbers of Saints coming to Missouri.

How the Smiths must have rejoiced to set a table in their wilderness home and share a meal with new converts as well as with tried and true friends. Perhaps Emma recalled the dinner in Kirtland when she had expressed fervent hope for this opportunity. Now it was here, but she and Joseph could not have been oblivious to the absence at their table of some who were no longer cordial to them, who had also moved to Missouri.

Some of these former friends had gravitated west with the body of the Saints and settled in the neighborhood. Among them was Frederick Granger Williams, with whom Joseph had quarreled in Kirtland. Frederick had been removed from his position as counselor in the First Presidency (not at Joseph's request), and Hyrum put in his place. The Prophet's reconciliation with Frederick had been tentative.

In spit of the conflict, both Frederick and his wife, Rebecca, remained committed to their testimonies of the Restoration and the Book of Mormon. Rebecca's father, having heard that they were disenchanted with the Church leaders, wrote to invite her back home. She informed her family that notwithstanding their differences, they would remain faithful to the Church.[22] Frederick brought his family to Far West and built a cabin across the street from the Prophet.[23] He and Rebecca still wanted to be of service to the Prophet's family as he had done ever since he became a member.

In the wake of the financial panic in Kirtland and the persecution that ensued, half of the original Apostles, three of the witnesses, and dozens of men who had been in the leading councils, left the Church. Their excommunication severed their privileges as Church members, canceling their ministerial authority in the Church. The Cowderys, John and David Whitmer, W. W. Phelps, John F. Boynton, and others were excommunicated from the Church in 1838, for various manifestations of their refusal to comply with Church policies. These families continued to live among the Saints in Caldwell County, or in the vicinity, after their ejection from Church membership, the brethren having been stripped of their offices. Reluctant to relinquish their claim of authority, several claimed to be rightful leaders, calling Joseph a "fallen" prophet. Their apostasy did not stop the Church's progress, but it lent support to the claims made by enemies, giving credence to the accusations leveled against Joseph.

It may be worth noting here that in a church overseen by modern revelation, change is a constant event. This is a radical difference from the rigidity to tradition that governs most religious sects. In the LDS Church, policy changes are common. Considering that many of the early leaders had been previously involved in Protestant organizations, it is not too surprising that they would at times find it difficult to adjust to change. To this day, this problem continues to affect some members. When changes are made, they assume an attitude of judgment, insisting that previous policies should be maintained. Such resistence to accept new revelation and change is the same spirit that prevailed among those who crucified Jesus Christ. It is the fuel that feeds the fire of apostasy.

Significantly, most of the men who apostatized retained a testimony of the divine origin of the Book of Mormon, even as they ridiculed the man who translated it. William E. McLellin, who in May had been tried in Church court for "lustful desires and for lack of confidence in Church leaders,"[24] would testify many years later, "I have no faith in Mormonism as an ism, even from its start . . . but when a man goes at the Book of Mormon he touches the apple of my eye. He fights against truth—against purity—against light—against the purest, or one of the truest, purest books on earth."[25] Likewise, David Whitmer and Oliver Cowdery, estranged from the Church for many years, to their dying breath, remained steadfast to their testimony that they had seen the plates and were convinved of the divine origin of the Book of Mormon. Many years after Joseph was dead, Oliver returned to seek rebaptism. But, in 1838, the Whitmers and the Cowderys had hardened their hearts and displayed nothing but haughty indignation toward all that Joseph was doing.

Some members of the Church who took issue with those they considered to be apostates living among them, took it upon themselves to warn the Cowderys, Whitmers, Phelpses, and Luke E. Johnson to leave Missouri at once. Joseph did not participate in this offense, nor did he know about it until afterward. The Cowdery home was ransacked, and many of its contents were thrown into the street. The Cowderys moved for a time to Richmond, then later moved out of the state. Many years later, Oliver wrote in a letter regarding these events, "The circumstances under which I left Far West, in June 1838, and immediately following are . . . always painful to reflect on."[26] The Whitmers also moved to Richmond.

One of the main objections the apostates had was that Joseph used his position as president of the Church to exercise control over temporal matters such as property or wealth. In other words, they rejected the law of consecration.

Joseph's Family Arrives in Far West from Kirtland

After Joseph and Sidney left Kirtland the night of 12 January 1838, Joseph's parents went through a terrible ordeal. The following day, Luke Johnson, who was the constable, and an apostate from the Church, served a summons on Father Smith for performing a marriage. Ignoring Lucy's pleas, Luke bustled about preparing the papers and making a great thing of it. When an opportunity presented itself, however, Luke went to Hyrum and told him he would put Father Smith in a certain room, from which they could get him out. With the help of Hyrum and John Boynton, another apostate (who was nevertheless a friend to Father Smith), Joseph Sr. escaped. He went to the home of Oliver Snow, father of Eliza Snow, where he hid for some time.[27]

Lucy had no idea what had happened to her husband. When Johnson came later, as if he expected to find Father Smith returned home, she cried, "Luke, you have killed my husband." He denied having done that, but didn't explain.[28] Lucy described the ordeal so movingly that one is moved to anger at the incredible ferocity of the antagonists in Kirtland toward a gentle old man. They posted handbills in every public place, offering a reward for his return, as though he were a dangerous criminal instead of a gentle old man who had never done harm to anyone. His youngest son, Don Carlos, took him to New Portage, where he stayed with the Taylors; Joseph Sr. even went with Edwin Wooley to Rochester for a while. Hyrum was already there with his family, and eventually Lucy was able to get the rest of the family notified, and all began to prepare to make the journey to Missouri.[29]

After a considerable time, the entire family gathered at New Portage, Ohio, from whence they began their journey to Missouri. After crossing the Mississippi River, they found shelter from the rain in an abandoned hut, where Joseph's sister, Katharine Salisbury, gave birth to a baby boy.[30] Her husband, Wilkins, and Sophronia and William McCleary stayed behind to take care of her while the rest of the group hastened on to Huntsville, Missouri. They waited there for the Salisburys, who drove a day and a half to get there; Katharine was wet and cold, and suffered chills and fever for some time, but she and the baby survived.

Lucy's account of their trip provides a practical view of how they met the daily tasks in spite of sickness, bad weather, and difficult travel conditions. "I washed a quantity of clothes," Lucy said, "and then we proceeded on our journey, and with no further difficulty until we arrived at Far West."[31]

They stayed for a short time with Joseph and Emma; then, as soon as arrangements could be made, they took over running a two-story hotel. Samuel had moved to Missouri previously, and settled in a place called Marrowbone, in Daviess County.[32] Don Carlos settled his wife, Agnes, and their little girls on a farm farther north, not far from the Grand River. William and his wife, Caroline, moved thirty miles in another direction.

Emma must certainly have welcomed her mother-in-law and her sisters-in-law with open arms. Lucy makes reference in her history to Emma's kindness to her husband's family. It had to have been a joyful time for the entire family as the new mothers compared their babies in the company of grandmother Lucy once again. Arriving in the first week of July, they were there in time to share in the dedication of the temple grounds, which was to take place in conjunction with the celebration of Independence Day—July Fourth.

Fourth of July, 1838

The Saints, who were very patriotic, celebrated the sixty-second birthday of their country with great enthusiasm. Church members from throughout the state came to participate. Solomon Hancock had been asked by the Prophet to write a song for the program, which he did.

July Fourth was chosen as the day for dedicating the ground for the Far West Temple site. The ground had already been broken for the building; the excavation around the building site was five feet deep. The ceremonies started with a parade, lined up around the perimeter. The Presidency—Joseph, Sidney, and Hyrum—were in the lead, then came the patriarchs—Joseph Smith, Sr., Joseph Knight, Sr., and Isaac Morley. They were followed by the Twelve Apostles and the high council. Behind the brethren came "the Ladies" and children, and finally, the cavalry.[33]

At the time of these festivities, Emma's baby, Alexander, was just a month old. We have no idea what part Emma may have played in the day's events. If she felt up to it, she would probably have been among the "ladies" in the crowd, if not one of those in the parade. We may fantasize a moment, picturing the ladies in their long skirts, bonnets of various design, babes in arms or at the knee. July in Missouri tends to be hot and humid. We know from records of the event there were thunder showers in the vicinity; perhaps the blue of the sky was spotted with thunderheads.

After the parade had encircled the entire circumference of the excavation, the procession stopped, and with great ceremony the various quorums laid the cornerstones for the temple. The jubilant Saints cheered, while Missourians who had come out of curiosity looked on with varying degrees of interest and perhaps some apprehension. The Mormons were already spilling over beyond the borders of Caldwell County, which had been assigned to them.

About two weeks earlier, Sidney Rigdon had delivered a sermon in Far West, which he had based upon Matthew 5:13, and warned the apostates that they, like the salt, " have lost his savor . . . it is thenceforth good for nothing but to be cast out and to be trodden under foot of men." Sidney implied that the apostates would be literally trodden underfoot if they didn't move out at once.[34]

On the Fourth of July, he gave another rousing speech, declaring the Saints' independence, expanding somewhat upon the ideas he had addressed in the previous sermon. Most of the Saints were in solemn agreement with what he said. He said:

> We have not only when smitten on one cheek, turned the other, but we have done it, again and again, until we are weary of being smitten, and tired of being trampled upon. . . . We will never be the aggressors; we will infringe on the rights of no people; but shall stand for our own until death. . . . We this day then proclaim ourselves free, with a purpose and a determination, that never can be broken, No never! No Never!! NO NEVER!!![35]

Some passages in his talk threatened a war of extermination upon mobs should they again arise to plague the Saints. Rigdon's words have been severely criticized as ill-advised,[36] as undoubtedly they were; but it is small wonder that the old man should express himself in such indignant terms, considering all the Saints had suffered, having been denied the justice that should have been guaranteed them under the Constitution of the land. But it is also true that it would have been wiser to turn the other cheek, remembering that old proverb, "a soft word turneth away wrath." By claiming to be Latter-day Israel, perhaps the Mormons called to the Missourians' minds, the clearing out of those people who occupied the land of Jerusalem when Moses brought them out of Egypt. By a certain lack of humility and wearing a mantle of assurance that God was giving them the land, regardless of others' prior presence there, perhaps the Saints revisited the same attitudes which had brought ejection of the Church from Jackson County in 1833.

Children who were present at this great July 4th celebration recall an incident which indicates Joseph's recognition that the jubilant celebration was but an island of peace in a wide sea of tribulation. Mosiah Hancock, who was a youngster at the time, later recalled that lightning struck the Liberty Pole that day. Eight-year-old Oliver DeMille remembered that the pole was slivered to pieces; and in later life, he said, "I heard the prophet say, 'Just as that has been stricken down, our liberty shall be taken from us, every vestige.'"[37]

Law of Tithing Replaces Law of Consecration

Joseph had been commanded by revelation to establish a community where the people would live God's laws, a people who would come from all parts of the world. Obviously this would require funds. Joseph had learned through his experience in Salem, that the gathering would be by covenant and sacrifice, not by finding treasure—in other words, not by obtaining easy money. The law of consecration, initiated earlier in Kirtland, required more than an ordinary process of giving. It had been designed to combine and maximize the available wealth for the good of all, and to expiate selfishness from the Saints. Through the failure of some to deal honestly and unselfishly, it became apparent that the Saints could not, or would not, live the law of consecration. The Lord had revealed the principle of tithing earlier; but starting in July 1838, it became the means of providing for the financial needs of the Church.[38]

Mob Rule, Missionary Zeal

As many thousands of new converts were streaming into Missouri, signaling the success of missionary work abroad, their very numbers brought persecution upon them. Undoubtedly, their political clout was feared more than their religious ideology. Notwithstanding there were many good, law-abiding citizens in Missouri who had no grudge against the Mormons, certain ministers throughout the state feared losing members of their congregations to a religion they considered blasphemous. Some of these ministers became leaders and organizers of an element of Missouri society who became committed to an unholy pogrom designed to drive the Mormons entirely out of the state. These people traveled the state, hounding the Mormons, trying to provoke them to defend themselves, then accusing them of causing a fight; they even stopped the migrating trains and deflected some of them from arriving in Far West at all. In some cases, the civil authorities were committed to the cause of the mobs.

Given the state of confusion and distress all around them, it is easy to become engrossed in the political upheaval surrounding the Saints and forget that Joseph was never out of touch with his mission, that the task he was sent to perform was in God's hands, not man's.

On 8 July Joseph petitioned the Lord concerning several problems. Specifically, he addressed the question of how much the Lord required of his people. He also asked concerning how the Church was to pay its debts (in most cases, the debts and property were all in the names of the leaders) and what the Lord wanted done with the property in Kirtland. They were instructed to sell their property in Kirtland, but not the temple at that time. To the Saints in Kirtland, the command was to "remember the Lord their God, and mine house also, to keep and preserve it holy, and to overthrow the money-changers in mine own due time."[39]

The Lord directed that the vacancies left in the Council of the Twelve be filled. John Taylor, John E. Page, Wilford Woodruff, and Willard Richards were named to this calling. The Apostles were directed to leave in the coming spring, 26 April, from the Temple Site at Far West, to further the missionary work across the ocean.[40]

In another revelation the same day, in answer to the question of how much the Lord required of his people for a tithe, the answer was a short one which spelled out the simplicity of God's financial plan for his people. They were to give "all their surplus property" to the bishop, to be used "to lay the foundation of Zion" and provide for the payment of debts owed by the Presidency of the Church. (Purchase of all Church property was done by individuals; therefore, their debts were Church debts.) Beyond their surplus, the Saints were to give one-tenth "of all their interest annually," and this was to be a "standing law" forever.[41] This left to the individual the decision of what was his and what was the Lord's. It freed the bishop and the Church from the burden of holding deeds from every family, with the risk that if they reneged, they would come after the Church leaders with suits and warrants. It also placed the responsibility upon each individual to deal honestly with the Lord in giving his tenth. Although it was far less encompassing than the law of consecration, it still required faith and sacrifice on the part of the membership.

Another revelation, given the same day, was not published with the others, but was found many years later and included as a footnote in *The History of the Church*. It bears mention here because it makes known the duty of two men, Frederick Granger Williams, and W. W. Phelps, who had been extremely close friends to Joseph and Emma. Both had been excommunicated, and it seems both were struggling at this time. The revelation was as follows: "Verily, thus saith the Lord, in consequence of their transgressions their former standing has been taken away from them, and now, if they will be saved, let them be ordained as Elders in my Church to preach my gospel and travel abroad from land to land and from place to place, to gather mine elect unto me, saith the Lord, and let this be their labors from henceforth. Amen."[42]

On 5 August, Frederick Granger Williams was confirmed, having been previously re-baptized. There seems to be no record of Phelps being restored to the Church at this time, but the two men left their families in Far West, traveled to Burlington, Iowa, and undoubtedly preached along the way.

Some Thoughts on a Friendship That Was Tried by Fire

Frederick Williams continued to practice medicine and bought land at the Prophet's request. One biographer comments, "Since he was only a lay member of the Church at this time he did not think it necessary to consult the leaders as to where he was going."[43] His failure to let the brethren know his intentions probably laid him open to the suspicion which led, in March 1839, to his being excommunicated again. The calamities that continued to plague him seem not to have deflected him or his wife, Rebecca, and later their son, Ezra, from remaining loyal friends to Joseph and Emma. Rebecca would be Emma's neighbor in Far West, and later in Nauvoo, although eventually, after both were widowed, they would part, Rebecca going to the West, Emma staying in Nauvoo. But there is no whisper of dissension between these two women that I can find. We can only wish the intimate conversations they may have shared could have been preserved.

Each of these women had given up a great deal for her faith. Each had been estranged from her father for having believed in the Book of Mormon. Each had chosen the difficult path of sacrifice and service in God's kingdom, and each was undeviatingly loyal to the Prophet Joseph. Emma came from the pastoral green land of Pennsylvania. Rebecca came from the area near Niagara Falls, New York. As a teenager Rebecca had been driven from her home by the British when they captured that section of the country in the war of 1812. During the fall and winter of 1838, both would now endure the infamous persecution, and be driven from their homes by their own countrymen.

Undoubtedly, they each watched the dedication of the Far West Temple Site with hope for the future. Each must have hoped for complete healing of the rift that had occurred between their husbands. Each must have listened to Sidney Rigdon's passionate oration at the July 4th celebration, with grim concern for what the future might hold for them and their children.

Political Oppression

Just one month after the July 4th celebration, elections were held at Gallatin, in Daviess County, not far from Adam-ondi-Ahman. A number of the brethren went to cast their vote, even though they had been warned to stay away.[44]

As expected, a mob tried to stop them from voting, and a fight ensued. Exaggerated accounts of this fight reached Joseph the next day. He left for Gallatin with Sidney, Hyrum, and fifteen or twenty armed men, believing that several members of the Church had been killed. Arriving at Lyman Wight's cabin, they learned that the reports were false.

An equally false report was sworn before Judge Austin A. King against Joseph and Lyman Wight, stating that they had an army of five hundred armed men and had threatened the life of Justice Adam Black. Actually, Joseph had merely asked Adam Black for an affidavit stating that he (Joseph) had not been involved in the ruckus at Gallatin. Black later claimed he had been forced to sign the affidavit.[45]

On 13 August, a mob chased Joseph about twelve miles. Later he learned that Judge King had issued a warrant to arrest him and Lyman Wight. When the sheriff and Judge Morin came to arrest Joseph, he meekly submitted to them, saying that he "intended always to submit to the laws of [the] country." After some discussion, the sheriff decided not to serve the warrant on Joseph. However, when Lyman Wight attempted to defend the rights of Church members against the mob, it was publically assumed that he had defied the sheriff's authority. This set the stage for state officials to take immediate action against the Saints.[46]

An Ironic Circumstance

When Governor Lillburn Boggs heard of Wight's actions (which were interpreted as being in defiance of the law), it was just the excuse he needed to take military action against the Mormons. Governor Boggs had once befriended the Saints in Jackson County, but then turned against them for political expediency. Now he ordered General

Atchison to call out four hundred of the militia in preparation for a campaign against the Mormons, if it proved necessary. The Mormons, believing themselves legally justified in defending themselves if attacked by mobs—having been so advised by Alexander Doniphan—formed two armed units. The unit in Caldwell County was a unit of the state militia; the one in Daviess County had no official status, but was for the purpose of self-preservation. General Doniphan, in Caldwell County, and General Parks, in Daviess County, both officers in the state militia, were struggling to keep the peace in their respective counties.

The Prophet noted that in spite of the rising storm around them, the Saints had been very peaceable. He was often at home working on his history, and he had a new scribe, James Mulholland, who became his and Emma's trusted friend.[47]

The Press Debates "Mormon Question"—Rumors Lead to Political and Military Action

Rumors about the Mormons traveled at a much greater rate of speed than truth, and the newspapers in Missouri took up the issue with alacrity. Some accounts accused the Mormons of violating their promise to stay within Caldwell County by spreading to other counties. Others defended them, saying that a law requiring that members of any religion stay within a certain county was unconstitutional. The unlawful attempt to prevent them from voting in Daviess County was lost in the muddle of conflicts, real and imagined.

Some of the men in the units that Generals Atchison, Doniphan, and Parks headed were bent on driving the Mormons out of the area. When the leaders found that they were unable to control these hostile men, they disbanded some of the units. Many of the men traveled fifty miles south to join a band led by a Dr. Austin, in Carroll County. No area was exempt from the activities of these mobocrats, including the counties of Ray, Clay, and others. The Saints called these militia men "mobocrats," because they used their position in the state militia to cause as much injury as possible to the Mormons, hoping to obtain the improved land, houses, and belongings the Saints had accumulated.

Several of the generals in command of state troops found the Mormons peaceable and law abiding, not at all as they had been expecting when they were assigned the duty of quieting the disturbance reportedly caused by them. During September, an effort was made to quiet the hostilities. General Parks, in charge of the Daviess County Militia, wrote to Governor Boggs, on 25 September:

> Whatever may have been the disposition of the people called Mormons, before our arrival here, since we have made our appearance they have shown no disposition to resist the laws, or of hostile intentions. There has been so much prejudice and exaggeration concerned in this matter, that I found things entirely different from what I was prepared to expect. . . .[48]

A day later he wrote again, this time to General Atchison, reporting that there was to be a meeting between "a committee from Daviess County and a committee of the Mormons at Adam-ondi-Ahman, to propose to them to buy or sell. . . ."[49] It appeared as if the Mormons were going to be able to buy out the discontented Missourians.

On 26 September, the meeting took place. An agreement was reached for the brethren to purchase all the lands and possessions of those who desired to sell and leave Daviess County.

It was late in the evening when this was reported to Joseph. With the hope of reaching a peaceful agreement, Joseph and Emma must have felt some relief. Joseph needed men he could trust to make a quick and, hopefully, successful trip, to accomplish an important mission. He called Don Carlos Smith, George A. Smith, Lorenzo D. Barnes, and Harrison Sagers, to leave at once to go to the "south and east and raise men and means to fulfill the contract."[50]

We have a great advantage, researching these events more than 100 years after the fact. We can refer to published copies of letters written by those who were on the scene, on both sides of the issue, but could not have had full communication with one another at the time. In a letter from Liberty, Missouri, written 27 September, General Atchison wrote to Governor Boggs: "Things are not so bad in the county as represented by rumor, and, in fact, from affidavits I have no doubt your Excellency has been deceived by the exaggerated state of alarm on account of the Mormons; they are not to be feared; they are very much alarmed."[51]

On 1 October, Atchison, Doniphan, and Parks disbanded most of the militia, keeping only enough men to secure peace in the area. Apparently many of these men headed southeast to Carroll County, where they also joined the band led by Dr. Austin.

The next day, a large company, known as the Kirtland Camp, obedient to the revelation directing the Saints to move west, arrived at Far West.

Kirtland Camp Arrives in Far West

The group called "Kirtland Camp" consisted of 105 families from Kirtland, comprising more than 500 souls, who had come to Far West in obedience to the inspired instructions and organization of Hyrum Smith, when he had addressed a full house at the temple in Kirtland. They had been brought through, after untold hardship. Now they camped on the public square in Far West, Missouri, "round the foundation of the Temple," after having traveled eight hundred and seventy miles since leaving Kirtland.[52] Food was prepared for them, which the travelers welcomed as they had had little to eat for several days. The sick were provided with a supper by Sidney Rigdon.

With the expectation that peace had been assured by the brethren having agreed to buy out the Missourians in Daviess County, this company of Saints was sent to Adam-ondi-Ahman. They left 3 October, arriving that evening at Ambrosia Creek, and the day following arrived at their destination about sunset. They pitched their tents, and one of the brethren in that place proclaimed, "Brethren, your long and tedious journey is now ended; you are now on the public square of Adam-ondi-Ahman. This is the place where Adam blessed his posterity, when they rose up and called him Michael, the Prince, the Archangel, and he being full of the Holy Ghost predicted what should befall his posterity to the latest generation."[53]

The public square of Adam-ondi-Ahman was nothing but a wide meadow atop a large hill in a vast wilderness above the Grand River. Situated beneath that hill, Lyman Wight's house, near the ferry across the Grand River, would have been a busy place, as the group moved to the new town. Soon the brickyard would have to step up its pace to make enough bricks for all the chimneys needed for the new homes that would be built.

Even as the men, women, and children lighted from their wagons, hopeful of standing on ground that would become their home in Zion, terrible things were happening to some Saints who had, not long before, settled in De Witt, Carroll County, about fifty miles to the southeast of Far West.

Devilish Actions by Mobs

On 2 October 1838, Dr. Austin, perhaps fired by having noted the passing of Kirtland Camp through Carroll County several days before, led a mob in an attack on the Saints in the town of De Witt, in Carroll County. His band had swelled, due to the disbanded militia from Clay, Daviess, and Caldwell Counties. Austin surrounded the town, then provoked a fight, and eventually fired on them. The Saints returned the fire in self-defense. Rumors of this situation reached General S. D. Lucas, an old enemy of the Saints since the Jackson County expulsion of 1833. Lucas wrote to Governor Boggs on 4 October, claiming that he had seen a large force of Mormons at De Witt, under arms. He claimed their commander, Colonel Hinkle, formerly of Caldwell County, "informed me that there were two hundred, and that they were . . . determined to fight." Colonel Hinckle, in turn, said he got his information from a "gentleman of respectability." Lucas claimed that "there had been a fight the day before, and that several persons were killed." Then he warned, "If a fight has actually taken place, of which I have no doubt, it will create excitement in the whole of upper Missouri, and those base and degraded beings [referring to the Mormons] will be exterminated from the face of the earth. If one of the citizens of Carroll should be killed, before five days I believe there will be from four to five thousand volunteers in the field against the Mormons, and nothing but their blood will satisfy them."[54]

In this epistle, Lucas was subtly reminding Boggs (in an election year) that four or five thousand Missourians would not be pleased if the governor should give any support to the Mormons, whom he dismissed as "base and degraded." Understandably the Mormons felt this was a rather biased description for a community of people who were notably neat, clean, and who actually had erected and staffed the first schoolhouse in Jackson County. Lucas knew very well the mob had fired on the Saints, and he knew the Saints would only fight in self-defense; but he wrote this letter to influence the governor's mind, which it did, for it gave the governor an excuse to assume a hard attitude toward the Mormons, whom he wanted removed from his state.

> An affidavit, prepared by John W. Price and William H. Logan, was sent by the citizens of Chariton County, to find out the nature of the difficulties between the citizens of Carroll and the Mormons. The affidavit was sworn before Justice of the Peace John Morse, on 5 October 1838; conditions in De Witt were described and a conversation with one of the mobbers related:
> We arrived at the place . . . and found a large portion of citizens of Carroll and the adjoining counties assembled . . . well armed. We inquired into the nature of the difficulties. They said that there was a large portion of the people called Mormons embodied in De Witt, from different parts of the world. They were unwilling for them to remain there, which is the cause of their waging war against them. To use the gentleman's language, "they were waging a war of extermination, or to remove them from the said county."[55]

Price and Logan went into De Witt "to see the situation of the mormons." They "found them in the act of defense, begging for peace, and wishing for the civil authorities to repair there as early as possible, to settle the difficulties between the parties." It was the opinion of these men that the hostilities would continue until stopped by the civil authorities.[56]

This viewpoint was confirmed the same day. From Carroll County, General Atchison wrote the governor that the "citizens were in arms for the purpose of driving the 'Mormons' from the county."[57]

At this time the third quarterly conference of the Church in Caldwell County was being held at Far West. Brigham Young presided. Since there were not enough people present to accomplish much business, they adjourned till the next day. Joseph and some others took time out to look for a place to locate a new town in the southern part of Caldwell County. While they were away on this errand, one of the brethren from De Witt found him and informed him that the Saints in De Witt were "surrounded by a mob who . . . threatened their lives, and had shot at them several times."[58]

Joseph stated, "I was surprised on receiving this intelligence, although there had, previous to this time, been some manifestations of mobs, but I had hoped that the good sense of the majority of the people, and their respect for the Constitution, would have put down any spirit of persecution which might have been manifested in that neighborhood."[59]

Joseph—A Man of Peace But Facing War

Because the mobs were guarding the main roads, Joseph took the back roads to De Witt, where he found the Saints in desperate circumstances. He immediately sent an urgent plea to Governor Boggs, requesting protection from the mobs who were, in some cases, members of the state militia. He noted that "several gentlemen of standing and respectability, . . . not in any way connected with the Church of Later-day Saints, who had witnessed the proceedings . . . came forward and made affidavits . . . and offered their services to go and present the case to the governor . . . ."[60]

Arriving outside of De Witt, General Parks observed, "I found a body of armed men under the command of Dr. Austin, encamped near De Witt, besieging that place . . . with a piece of artillery ready to attack the town of De Witt." He observed that Austin had two or three hundred men. The Mormons, on the other side, had three or four hundred men. "The Mormons say they will die before they will be driven out, etc.," he continued. "As yet they have acted on the defensive, as far as I can learn. It is my settled opinion, the Mormons will have no rest until they leave; whether they will or not, time only can tell."[61] This was his report to the governor.

The mobbers sent an appeal to Howard County, asking for help to "rescue the citizens of Carroll County, as the 'Mormons' were firing upon them." Without checking to see if this was true, the representative from Howard County made a certificate attesting to these lies. General Clark wrote to the governor swearing that these mobbers were "worthy, prudent and patriotic citizens."

A Mr. Caldwell, who was sent to ask the governor for assistance on behalf of the Saints, came back with unpleasant news. Governor Boggs' response to the information that the mobs were the aggressors, and the Saints needed help from the civil authorities, was simply that "the quarrel was between the Mormons and the mob," and they "might fight it out" on their own.[62]

The De Witt Saints were running out of food and were refused protection by the authority of the state. The general in charge of the militia in the area could not even control the units, which were led by mobocrats. Each hour the number of mobbers was growing, and Parks informed the Church leaders that the "greater part of his men under Captain Bogart had mutinied," so he was afraid they would join the mob rather than help keep the peace.

Joseph said, "I was there. . . . [Our enemies] fired at us a great many times. Some of the brethren perished from starvation; for once in my life, I had the pain of beholding some of my fellow creatures fall victims to the spirit of persecution."[63]

In time, word was brought, that if the Saints would leave the place, they would not be hurt, and a pledge was made that they would be compensated for any losses they incurred.

Outgunned by a mob led by militia, with cannon, the Saints realized it would mean certain extinction if they tried to stand and fight for their rights. Furthermore, in the face of the governor's refusal to defend their rights, the Saints decided to leave Carroll County.

Destitute Saints from De Witt Arrive in Far West

What might Emma have thought as she saw seventy wagons, loaded with the destitute Saints from De Witt, roll into Far West that autumn day in October 1838? In spite of all the advice given them by Alexander Doniphan, in spite of their great care to keep their activities in strict accord with state laws, the Saints had been shot at, mobbed, and driven away. Where would it end? Perhaps she took comfort in knowing there was a strong Mormon unit of the state militia in Caldwell County, led by Colonel George M. Hinkle.[64]

Was Emma's dooryard and her house filled with homeless, hungry, frightened Saints? In the past, she had comforted many who were homeless and fleeing persecution since joining the Church. The Saints who had been driven out of De Witt arrived in Far West on 12 October. Having similarly been driven from her home, Emma would know how to comfort the De Witt Saints. Familiar with mobs, were Emma's little children frightened? Did Rebecca Williams, Phebe Woodruff, Mary Ann Young, and the other women in Far West rush forward to comfort and help the sick, the weary, and the injured? Such compassionate service rarely makes the pages of history, but we can imagine it was rendered in abundance in this instance.

Emma surely must have listened to Joseph relating the terrible things he had seen at De Witt. This may well have been one of those times when she was called upon to comfort her husband in his time of great affliction. Was Emma's compassionate heart wrenched by the sorrow her husband, the Prophet, was feeling? How he must have suffered to see these new converts to the Church, who had come to Zion with hope, some of them from across the ocean, being robbed of the rights and freedoms supposedly guaranteed in America. Many barely understood English and could not comprehend this devastating strike against them in their new home.

With nearly 15,000 people to shepherd safely through this strange impasse with mobs and self-serving politicians, Joseph knew he had made every effort he could to obtain justice through proper channels. He knew he had enough men to stand and defend Far West, yet he still hoped it would not come to such a state.

Almost immediately after returning from De Witt, Joseph was warned by General Doniphan of Clay County that "a company of mobbers, eight hundred strong, were marching toward a settlement of our people in Daviess county." Mobs were also rising in Platte and Clinton Counties, under a man named Sashiel Woods, who suggested that they could "get the Mormons driven out . . . [and] get all the lands entitled to pre-emptions."[65]

Joseph had sent word to the outlying Mormon communities to consider coming to Far West; some who had ignored the warning came now with reports of burned houses, brutal abuse, and threats if they didn't leave the state.

Emma and the other women in Far West would have again provided comfort and food for these Latter-day Saints, who, like the early Christians, were being driven and persecuted.

Doniphan ordered a company from Far West to go to Adam-ondi-Ahman to protect the Saints there. He advised them to "defend our people from the attacks of the mob, until he should raise the militia in his [own] and adjoining counties to put them down."[66]

On 14 October, a Sunday, Joseph preached from the words of the Savior, "Greater love hath no man than this, that he lay down his life for his brethren." When he closed his sermon, he called upon all who would, to meet him in "the public square the next day."[67]

Perhaps Emma was there to hear him when, on Monday, 15 October, in terrible anger, Joseph spoke to the men who had gathered, all prepared to go to the aid of their fellow Saints in Daviess County. He is quoted as saying: "All are mobs; the governor is mob, the militia is mob, and the whole state is mob. . . . I am determined that we will not give another foot and I care not how many come against us."[68]

Settling Accounts

In the midst of a heavy snowstorm, the brethren marched their defense unit north. They felt completely justified in defending themselves and their towns. About one hundred men, under Colonel George M. Hinkle, took part. Joseph went with them because he had property there in Daviess County, and a house in the process of being built.[69]

Up until now, Joseph seems to have believed the law would eventually bring justice to bear and they would be able to return to their property in Jackson County, as well as live in peace in the other towns they had established in the state of Missouri. As he rode north with the militia, he must have contemplated the fact that blood had been shed already; and with mobs continuing to raid, there would be more and more. His hope now rested in the brave men with whom he rode and in his faith in God's promise that He would redeem Zion, in His own way and in His own time.

Meanwhile, undisciplined mobs, unfettered by any worry of legal action against them, attacked wherever they pleased, picking on isolated homes in particular. Agnes Smith was alone with her little children after her husband, Don Carlos, left on his mission to Tennessee. She and the children were driven outside, and their house was burned. There was snow on the ground and the weather was extremely cold. Agnes made her way on foot, about three miles, to the Grand River. Since the ferry wasn't running, she waded the river with her two little girls in her arms. When she arrived at Lyman Wight's cabin, she was in a pitiable condition. The Wights took care of her and the children and they all survived. Samuel Smith's wife, Mary, suffered the same treatment, being driven from her cabin in a driving rain when her baby was only three days old. She went to Far West and was cared for by her mother-in-law, with Emma's help. Understandably, this inhumane treatment of women and children riled the emotions of the brethren.[70]

It was into this dangerous setting that young Benjamin F. Johnson, age nineteen, came with his sisters and their husbands. They took up residence at Adam-ondi-Ahman, now called Diahman. Because he was young and unmarried, he was one of the last men to be assigned a lot. He recalls, "When it was my choice I found I must take the top lot on the promontory overlooking the Grand River valley, or go farther away and lower down than I wished to. So I chose the upper, which at first appeared rocky, which made the other lots almost enviable." A few days later Joseph accompanied him to the spot and told Benjamin this was the spot where Adam "built an altar and offered sacrifice . . . where he stood and blessed the multitude of his children, when they called him Michael, and where he will again sit as the Ancient of Days, then I was not envious of anyone's choice for a city lot in Adam-ondi-Ahman."[71]

Benjamin tells of the hardships they encountered in November, when winter set in, and there was no food available. He said they had to forage the best they could. He was also one of those who joined in the defending parties, whose efforts so enraged the Missourians.

Emma was so surrounded with danger now in Missouri, it may have been small comfort to her when word came from Oliver Granger that he had done his best to settle and clear Joseph's old debts in Kirtland. The news cheered the Prophet, as he had smarted under accusations that he had run out on his debts there. When he returned to Far West on 22 November, he could report to Emma that he felt the brethren from Diahman, and the Far West Unit were sufficiently formidable to scare the mob out of Daviess County without a fight. It was evening when he got home and he was probably hoping to enjoy some peace at least for a time, but the minute he arrived he was informed of trouble on the border of Caldwell County. Several brethren had been taken prisoner and some houses were burned. It was reported that the prisoners were to be killed that night.[72]

Judge Elias Higbee responded to this by ordering Colonel Hinkle to "send out a company to disperse the mob."[73] Because it was rumored they would be killed, emotions ran high. Elias Higbee hoped to rescue the prisoners.

Emma and Joseph must have been reeling with the onslaught of bad news.

Thomas B. Marsh, formerly president of the Twelve who had apostatized, had moved to Richmond. Another apostle, Orson Hyde, also at Richmond, attested to most of the statements made in an affidavit Marsh had signed, accusing Joseph of secretly backing a group called the Danites. The affidavit, signed by Marsh on 24 October, gave the Missourians the justification they needed to strike down the Mormons without mercy.[74] Both of these men lost their membership and their apostleship over this incident. Both repented and years later returned to the Church and were forgiven; but their signatures at that time paved the way for Joseph to be arrested and imprisoned for many months, and jeopardized the security of all members of the Church in Missouri.

This affidavit supplied all the "proof" needed to build a case against Joseph Smith and the other Church leaders, when coupled with the claims of the mob who had been scared out of Daviess County by the brethren from Adam-ondi-Ahman. Before the perpetrators had fled Daviess County, they burned their own cabins, then raced to tell the governor the Mormons had done it. The mobbers also claimed that the Mormons had a large army and were going to march on Richmond. This was a lie, but it served to rile up the civil authorities and, once again, militia were ordered for the purpose of putting down the perceived Mormon threat.[75]

If this had not been enough, the company—sent out from Far West by Judge Higbee, and led by Captain David Patten—found Bogart's force of Missourians where they had camped on Crooked River. As the company drew near the camp, they split up. At dawn on 25 October, some of the Mormons were leading their horses near the ford of Crooked River. Suddenly a shot rang out, and one young Latter-day Saint, Patrick O'Banion, fell to the ground. Patten ordered the men to charge, and very soon were within fifty yards of the camp. Suddenly they were fired on again, and four men fell. Gideon Carter was killed; the others were wounded severely. The survivors fired back. After a couple of exchanges of fire, Patten cried, "God and Liberty," which was the watchword, and the company charged the camp. In hand-to-hand combat, they routed the mob, but one man fired a shot as he fled, hitting David Patten and mortally wounding him.[76]

Patten was taken to the Winchester home, about three miles from Far West. Joseph and Hyrum, along with Lyman Wight, went to meet the brethren who had been involved in the battle at Crooked River. Joseph found David Patten in a bad way. His wife was brought to him, and before he died, David said to her, "Whatever you do else, O! do not deny the faith."[77]

A poignant memory recorded by Joseph III in his *Memoirs* shows how unshielded the children were from the carnage. "There is a faint memory . . . of hearing about the wounding of David Patten. I remember going with someone to the house where he lay. While not permitted to enter the house, I looked in at the door and saw him lying on his bed, and heard some talk about his wound, as if it were in the body, and of its being cleansed with a silk handkerchief."[78]

Given the hostility and unreasoning fear on all sides, there was no way to end the conflict peaceably; the Mormons believed they were a legal unit of the state militia, and the mob likewise claimed militia status. In the battle at Crooked River, Bogart's force lost one man; seven Saints were wounded and three died.[79] Among the community of the Saints, these men were mourned by their friends and families.

It is a strange fact of written history, that although David Patten's wife must have been a close friend to Emma, as David was to Joseph, we are not even told her name. When Joseph went to the Patten home to pay his respects, did he take Emma with him? Was she there to hear him when he pointed "to [Patten's] lifeless body," and testified, "There lies a man that has done just as he said he would—he has laid down his life for his friends."[80]

Blood had been shed. The price of the land of Missouri had been established. The warning given by the Prophet years before was being realized—that if blood was shed, the Saints would be scourged from city to city. Nor was the end in sight. It was becoming evident that Zion would not be redeemed in the foreseeable future. Even as David Patten was being buried, an order was being prepared, directing that the Mormons be "treated as enemies and . . . exterminated or driven from the state."[81]

Notes

1. *HC,* 2:127.

2. *Far West Record: Minutes of The Church of Jesus Christ of Latter-Day Saints, 1830-1844.* Edited by Donald Q. Cannon and Lyndon W. Cook. (Salt Lake City: Deseret Book, 1983), p. 140 ftnt. 5.

3. Ibid, pp. 164-66 letter from Oliver Cowdery; also Oliver Cowdery's letter quoted in *Far West Record,* p. 140 ftnt. 5.

4. *Far West Record,* p. 149.

5. Ibid.

6. Elden J. Watson, *Manuscript History of Brigham Young* (Salt Lake City: Smith Secretarial Services, 1968), p. 27, as quoted in the *Far West Record,* p. 144.

7. *HC,* 3:9.

8. *Far West Record,* p. 149 and thereafter.

9. Kenneth W. Godfrey, Audrey M. Godfrey, and Jill Mulvay Derr, *Women's Voices: An Untold History of the Latter-day Saints 1830-1900* (Salt Lake City: Deseret Book, 1982), p. 98. Hereafter referred to as *Women's Voices.*.

10. See *Far West Record,* p. 163, for a list of charges.

11. Ibid., p. 178.

12. Ibid., pp.176-77. Joseph is quoted in the minutes of the meeting that followed Oliver's trial; the council heard the case of David Whitmer. David seems to have assumed that his previous assignment to serve in the Presidency of the Church could not be rescinded, no matter what his attitude might be. David had written a letter to the council claiming they had acted unlawfully, saying, "I have been deprived of my office as one of the Presidents of this Church." He felt their actions "were not agreeable to the revelations of God." Therefore, "to spare you any further trouble I hereby withdraw from your fellowship and communion— choosing to seek a place among the meek and humble, where the revelations of Heaven will be observed and the rights of men regarded."

13. *Far West Record,* p. 187-88.

14. Levi Hancock Journal, copy in possession of author.

15. *HC,* 3:34.

16. *HC,* 3:35; see also *HC,* 3:38-9 and ftnts. 39-40. For a discussion of this area in Missouri, see Leland H. Gentry, "Adam-ondi-Ahman, A Brief History Survey," *BYU Studies* (Summer 1973), pp. 553-76.

17. *HC,* 3:40

18. Joseph and Emma Smith Family Records. In author's possession.

19. *HC,* 3:38

20. *HC,* 3:39-40 ftnt.

21. *HC,* 3:40 ftnt. It is recorded here, "Three years previous to the death of Adam, the Patriarchs Seth, Enos, Cainan, Mahalaleel, Jared, Enoch, and Methuselah, together with all their righteous posterity, were assembled in this valley . . . and their common father, Adam, gave them his last blessing."

22. Frederick G. Williams, "Frederick Granger Williams of the First Presidency of the Church," *BYU Studies* (Spring, 1972), pp. 243-61.

23. Nancy Clement Williams, *After 100 Years* (Independence, Mo.: Zion's Printing & Publishing Co., 1951), p. 118

24. *HC,* 3:31-32.

25. "Letter of W. E. McLelland, M.D., to Mr. J. T. Cobb, Independence, Mo., August 14, 1880," *BYU Studies* (Summer 1970), p. 486. This letter reveals a great deal about this contradictory man.

26. Oliver Cowdery, Letter to Brigham Young, 25 December 1843; Huntington Library; microfilm copy in LDS Church Archives.

27. Lucy Smith, *History of the Prophet Joseph Smith by His Mother,* ed. Preston Nibley (Salt Lake City: Bookcraft, 1958), p. 248.

28. Ibid., p. 249.

29. Ibid., p. 149.

30. Ibid., p. 252.

31. Ibid., p. 253.

32. Ibid.

33. *HC,* 3:41.

34. J. Christopher Conkling, *A Joseph Smith Chronology* (Salt Lake City: Deseret Book, 1979), p. 112.

35. *HC,* 3:42 ftnt. This oration is published in a pamphlet; see "Sidney Rigdon, Oration," *BYU Studies* (Summer 1974), pp. 517-27.

36. *HC,* 3:42 ftnt.

37. Isaac M. R. Teeples Stapley, *DeMille Family History and Genealogy* (Private Printing, 1953), p. 131.

38. Law of tithing, Doctrine & Covenants 119; see also 119:4; 120; 64:23; 85:3; 97:11-12.

39. Doctrine & Covenants 117:16.

40. Doctrine & Covenants 118.

41. Doctrine & Covenants 119.

42. *HC,* 3:46.

43. Nancy Williams, *After 100 Years,* p. 120.

44. *HC,* 3:56.

45. *HC,* 3:60-61

46. *HC,* 3:63; see also Conkling, *Joseph Smith Chronology,* pp. 116-17.

47. Ibid. For details about Joseph's scribes and other information about Joseph Smith's history-keeping efforts, see Howard S. Searle, "Authorship of the History of Joseph Smith: A Review Essay," *BYU Studies* (Winter 1981), pp. 101-122.

48. *HC,* 3:84.

49. Ibid.

50. Ibid.

51. Ibid.

52. *HC,* 3:85

53. *HC,* 3:147.

54. *HC,* 3:148.

55. *HC,* 3:150.

56. *HC,* 3:151.

57. Ibid.

58. *HC,* 3:152.

59. Ibid.

60. *HC,* 3:153.

61. *HC,* 3:156.

62. *HC,* 3:157.

63. *HC,* 3:158.

64. Conkling, *Joseph Smith Chronology,* pp. 119-20; see also *HC,* 3:149-50.

65. *HC,* 3:161.

66. Ibid., 3:161-62.

67. Ibid, 3:162.

68. Conkling, *Joseph Smith Chronology,* p. 120, quoting *HC,* 2: 231-32.

69. *HC,* 3:162.

70. Lucy Smith, *Biographical Sketches of Joseph Smith the Prophet and His Progenitors for Many Generations* (Independence, Mo.: Herald Publishing House, 1969), p. 265.

71. Benjamin F. Johnson, *My Life's Review* (Zion's Printing and Publishing Company, Independence, Mo., copyright by Wilbern Johnson in 1947), pp. 34-37, discusses this spot, which he received as his lot, at Diahman. He arrived there with his sisters and husbands, Delcena and L. R. Sherman, and Julia and A. W. Babbitt, in October, shortly after the massacre which took place at Haun's Mill in October 1838. Patsy Lamb, a descendant of Benjamin, provided details on his family.

72. *HC,* 3:169-70.

73. Ibid.

74. Conkling, *Joseph Smith Chronology,* p. 121.

75. *HC,* 3:165-68. There were numerous reports including those made by Woods and Dickson to Governor Boggs on 24 October 1838.

76. *HC,* 3:170-71.

77. Ibid.

78. Mary Audentia Smith Anderson, ed., *Memoirs of President Joseph Smith III—1832-1914,* (Independence, Mo.: Herald Publishing House, 1979), p. 3b.

79. Ibid., pp. 170-71.
80. *HC,* 3:175.
81. Ibid.

The Extermination of the Latter Day Saints from the State of Missouri in the Fall of 1838
by the Cruel Orders of Governor L.W. Boggs

Lith of H.R. Robinson 143 Warsaw St. N.Y.   Published by S. Brennan Prophet Office New York.

Entered according to Act of Congress in the year 1886, by Chas. W. Carter,
in the Office of the Librarian of Congress at Washington.

(No. 1) Genl Clarke, Gentlemen you shall have the honor of shooting the Mormon leaders on Monday morning at 8'oClock!

(2) McCary. Had his brains knocked out by the butt end of a musket in a general massacre!

(3) Rev. S. Bogard. It is my opinion they should all be shot!

(4) Genl Lucas. Your verdict gentlemen is that the mormons shall be shot tomorrow morning I fully concur with you in your sentense!

(5) Rev. I. McCoy. It is my opinion also that they should be shot or otherwise disposed of! (6) Genl Atcheson. I am against shooting men that have committed no crime!

(7) Genl Graham I am decidedly opposed to the determination of the court Martial

(8) Genl Doniphan By God you have been sentenced to be shot by the Court Martial this morning but Ill be damd if Ill have any of the honor of it. I consider it to be cold blooded murder and I bid you farewell!

(9) Genl Wilson Your die is cast. Your doom is fixed. You are sentenced to be shot tomorrow morning on the public square in Far West at 8 oClock!

(10) Lyman Wight, Shoot and be damd

(11) Wm B. McClellen I think Col we ought not to have left the Mormons. I am sorry for it I hate to be called a Traitor!

(12) Col Geo Hinckle I would rather be called a Mormon traitor than to be shot like a squirrel!

(13) Brest Work!

(14) City of Far West

Original in both LDS Archives and RLDS Archives.

CHAPTER 9

Mobbing, Extermination, and
Expulsion from Missouri

"The Mormons must be treated as enemies and must be exterminated or driven from the state. . . . " (Governor Lilburn W. Boggs)

From the beginning of the Mormon troubles in Missouri, Joseph had urged the Saints never to fight unless it was in self-defense. Knowing this, they tried to be peaceable, although they were frequently harassed and bedeviled. When, at last, one of them would retaliate in some manner, it would be reported as aggression on their part and consequences followed. But in the closing days of their trials in Missouri, Joseph would learn of an even more sinister situation which would sicken his soul.

Some members of the Church had secretly taken it upon themselves to organize a vigilante party. They called themselves Danites.[1] Unknown to Joseph (at the time), they operated using secret oaths, maintaining complete loyalty among themselves. These misguided individuals, many of them believing they were obeying directions given by Joseph, through their leader, Dr. Samson Avard, had been taking revenge, burning houses, and terrifying Missourians.

This group, it is said, were the ones who instigated frightening the Whitmers, Phelps, and Cowderys out of Far West, in June. Although Joseph had never sanctioned such a group, Avard, claimed to have authority from Joseph. By subtle and clever insinuation, he managed to convince those who signed on with him that he acted with Joseph's knowledge and approval. These men ought to have known better, for everyone, including the Missourians, knew Joseph had always urged the Saints to be peaceful. However, by perpetrating this fraud, Avard and his cohorts placed the Prophet in an indefensible position; in some ways, it would seem to lay the burden of responsibility for the death and destruction of many souls directly upon Joseph's shoulders.

What does a Prophet do when he finds that the people he has labored for and with, for more than eight years, reject his counsel and his warnings, and become vengeful, vile, and false swearers? And what does a governor do, when his state is being ravaged by war and he faces almost certain political destruction should he side with the Mormons?

Extermination Order

Like rulers of ancient times, confronted by prophets who attempted to overthrow evil by reintroducing God's laws, Governor Boggs chose not to listen. Bombarded with claims against the Mormons by his military leaders and associates, he made a decision of political expediency: to force the Mormons to leave the state under threat of extermination. Using his authority as governor of the state, he set that awful process in motion.

Although Governor Boggs understood the actual and real purpose behind the mobbings, he accepted the incidents reported to him without investigating the possibility of bias, exaggeration, and even falsehood: the report by Bogart stated that ten of his company were killed by the Mormons. In a grossly exaggerated fashion, the report told of women and children fleeing out of Richmond, fearful of the attack by the Mormons that was expected within hours. Every detail of Bogart's report was contradicted by information the governor had received from generals in the field, and contrary to the spirit of pleading in the Prophet's earlier requests for protection for his people in their homes and communities.

Governor Boggs' act of committing himself against truth and against law and order was cloaked in a short letter to General Clark, written on 27 October. The letter was the ultimate in false witness, written by a man who knew better, providing legal sanction for one of the most diabolical acts of civil injustice to ever take place upon American soil.

Because of the impact this order had upon Emma and Joseph, the Church, and the future of Missouri in the eyes of the Saints, the text of the letter containing the order to exterminate or drive the Mormons from the state of Missouri is given here in its complete form (as reported in *The History of the Church*).

Headquarters Militia, City of Jefferson

October 27, 1838

> SIR:—Since the order of the morning to you, directed you to cause four hundred mounted men to be raised within your division, I have received by Amos Rees, Esq., and Wiley C. Williams, Esq., one of my aids, information of the most appalling character, which changes the whole face of things, and places the Mormons in the attitude of open and avowed defiance of the laws, and of having made open war upon the people of this state. Your orders are, therefore, to hasten your operations and endeavor to reach Richmond, in Ray County, with all possible speed. The Mormons must be treated as enemies and must be exterminated or driven from the state, if necessary for the public good. Their outrages are beyond all description. If you can increase your force, you are authorized to do so, to any extent you may think necessary. I have just issued orders to Major-General Wallock, of Marion County, to raise five hundred men, and to march them to the northern part of Daviess and there to unite with General Doniphan, of Clay, who has been ordered with five hundred men to proceed to the same point for the purpose of intercepting the retreat of the Mormons to the north. They have been directed to communicate with you by express; and you can also communicate with them if you find it necessary. Instead, therefore, of proceeding as at first directed, to reinstate the citizens of Daviess in their homes, you will proceed immediately to Richmond, and there operate against the Mormons. Brigadier-General Parks, of Ray, has been ordered to have four hundred men of his brigade in readiness to join you at Richmond. The whole force will be placed under your command.
>
> *L. W. Boggs,*
> *Governor and Commander-in Chief.*
> *To General Clark*[2]

When the Extermination Order was made public, former Mormon-hating Missourians volunteered almost immediately and gathered at Richmond from all parts of Missouri, prepared to go against the Mormons. Certainly other Missourians were disgusted, knowing it was all a creation for political manipulation to pander to a certain element of the state.

Although the state militia had been earlier ordered to keep the peace, those who were bent on driving the Mormons out of Missouri now had "official" orders. They began this action on 30 October, with an attack on the Mormon community of Haun's Mill. This small, unimportant community, a few miles east of Far West, was enjoying a quiet October day. When the militia rode in, alarm spread. An old man approached with a white flag, ready to talk things over. He was answered by a deadly barrage of rifle fire, killing him where he stood. Men, women, and children fled across the stream and hid in the hills. One woman reported bullets raining around her as she fled. Another woman was wounded. Many men and boys barricaded themselves in the blacksmith's shop. The mob stuck their gun barrels through cracks between the logs and fired point blank until most of the people in the building were dead. Among those killed were boys under ten and men over seventy-five. One young boy, crying for help, was shot point blank. The man who did it said, "Nits make lice, he would just grow up to become a Mormon."[3]

When the Missourians had killed all the men and boys they could find, they left as quickly as they had come. In great fear that the militia would return, the survivors did not take time to bury their dead, but they tossed the bodies into a hole being dug for a well. The militia had accomplished a full scale massacre with 1600 rounds of ammunition fired at forty people. Eighteen or nineteen people were killed and fourteen wounded, including one woman.[4]

There is no information about Emma's reaction to the terrible news of the massacre at Haun's Mill. Most of the people at Haun's Mill were fairly recent arrivals in Missouri. Joseph had warned them to leave that place, saying they were not safe there and to come to Far West. However, they had refused, apparently assuming that since they were not directly involved in the troubles going on, they would be left alone if they minded their own business. Now, these innocent people were dead, not for any act of offense on their part, but for simply being Mormons who had moved to Missouri. Emma and Joseph must have felt an awful responsibility, although at the same time they must have expected that Far West would surely be the scene of a showdown with the officials of the state.

Within a few days after the order was made public, Generals Atchison and Lucas wrote to Boggs, asking for his presence at the seat of war—Far West, Caldwell County.

HEADQUARTERS OF THE 3RD AND 4TH DIVISION, MISSOURI[5]

MILITIA, RICHMOND, October 28, 1838.

To the Commander-in-chief, Missouri Militia:
SIR:—From late outrages committed by the Mormons, civil war is inevitable. They have set the laws of the county at defiance, and are in open rebellion. We have about two thousand men under arms to keep them in check. The presence of the commander-in-chief is deemed absolutely necessary, and we most respectfully urge that your excellency be at the seat of war as soon as possible.
Your most obedient servants,
David R. Atchison, M. G. 3rd Div.
Samuel D. Lucas, M. G. 4th Div.

According to General Doniphan, the governor sent General Atchison back to the town of Liberty before the actual assembly at Far West, because "[Atchison] was inclined to be too merciful to the 'Mormons' so that he was not active in the operations about Far West."[6] Generals Clark and Doniphan would both be there when General Lucas took over command and led 2,000 volunteers to surround Far West.[7]

Far West under Siege

Church history documents Joseph's fortification of Far West. After the tragedy at Crooked River and the massacre at Haun's Mill, Far

West prepared earnestly for an attack. Under Colonel Hinckle, the militia unit he commanded was armed and committed to making a stand to defend their homes and the lives of their families and friends. The majority of the Saints were united in loyalty to their Prophet.

When the militia surrounded Far West, Colonel George M. Hinkle went out to talk with Generals Lucas and Clark. Colonel Hinckle was in a position nobody could envy. He commanded a bona fide unit of the Missouri state militia, yet he, and his militia unit, stood to be charged with treason if they defended the city against the army sent by Governor Boggs, which was now amassed just outside the pitifully fragile barriers the Mormons had attempted to erect to fortify their city. Clearly, the Missouri officials wanted Joseph first, and they must have put it to Hinkle very bluntly. When Hinkle returned from talking to the generals, he requested that Joseph come out and talk with the generals. Believing that if he could talk with the officers in charge, he could make them understand the peaceable intent of the Mormon people, Joseph agreed to the meeting.

Joseph, Sidney, and several other men accompanied Hinkle. As soon as they were a short distance outside the line of defense, a company of soldiers surrounded them. Suddenly, without a word of explanation, the Church leaders were taken by armed guard, bound and left lying on the ground, where they suffered exposure to the driving rainstorm with no protection from the elements.

After they were taken, people in Far West could hear guns discharged; they also heard yells and whoops made by some members of the mob who were watching and celebrating the capture of Joseph Smith. While the militia guarded the prisoners, the generals conferred. They were committed to hunting down all Mormons who had been at the battle of Crooked River, or anyone who could be tied to any of the conflicts that were purported to have occurred. Those brethren who could, hastily made their escape. Unfortunately, Amasa Lyman and Hyrum Smith were not able to get away. They were also arrested and joined the others on the ground. When Joseph protested the harsh treatment, saying he had "always been a supporter of the Constitution and of democracy," General Wilson, who was guarding them, answered, "I know it, and that is the reason why I want to kill you, or have you killed." [8]

Later that night, under cover of darkness and in secret, a "court-martial" was held. Out of this peculiar trial, wherein the defense had no hearing, General Lucas gave his verdict: He commanded General Alexander Doniphan to ". . . *take Joseph Smith and the other prisoners into the public square in Far West, and shoot them at 9 o'clock tomorrow morning.*"9

To this, Doniphan replied, "It is cold-blooded murder. I will not obey your order. . . . If you execute these men, I will hold you responsible before an earthly tribunal, so help me God."

This brave man also informed Lucas that he would march his men at eight o'clock10 the next morning to Richmond and make public the illegal proceedings over which Lucas presided. Because of his belief that Doniphan would fulfil his threat, Lucas was forced to spare the lives of Joseph and the brethren. It was decided then to take the prisoners to Independence.

During the long hours since they had been taken, and through the night, after hearing the boisterous revelry and shooting, Joseph's family and all the Saints believed that he and the others had certainly been killed.11 In the morning, the prisoners, believing they would, in fact, be going to their death, asked to be allowed to say good-bye to their families.

At his house, Joseph found Emma and his children in anguish, weeping, because they thought he was dead. But there was no chance for them to rejoice that he was alive, nor to exchange tender words. As a seven-year-old, Joseph III recalled that he was prevented from embracing his father's knees. He wrote,

> I vividly remember the morning my father came to visit his family after the arrest. . . . When he was brought to the house by an armed guard I ran out of the gate to greet him, but was roughly pushed away from his side by a sword in the hand of the guard and not allowed to go near him. . . . My mother also was not permitted to approach him and had to receive his farewell by word of lip only. The guard did not permit him to pass into the house nor her to pass out, either because he heard an attempt would be made to rescue his prisoner or because of some brutal instinct in his own breast.12

Denied so much as a final touch of his hands, Emma was weeping, and as the Prophet was taken away, he heard his son calling, "Father! Father! Why are they taking you?"[13]

The prisoners were put into a wagon, which was closed tightly. When Joseph's parents heard what had happened to their sons, Joseph Sr. collapsed from the shock of emotions overcoming him, his body drained of all strength. "Oh, my God! my God!" he cried. "They have killed my son! They have murdered him! and I must die, for I cannot live without him!" He fell upon his bed in a terrible state. Lucy said of this experience, "I had no word of consolation to give him, for my heart was broken within me—my agony was unutterable."[14] Although Lucy was horrified, the shock put her into action rather than laying her low. She and her daughter, Lucy, ran to try to see them before they were taken away. In the crush of soldiers and other people, they could hardly get near the wagon. When they did, they managed a brief handclasp under the edge of the canvas before the wagon was gone.

The wagon proceeded toward Independence. As they crossed into Jackson County, a crowd gathered. One woman asked the guard, "Which of the prisoners was the Lord whom the 'Mormons' worshiped?" When Joseph was pointed out to her, she asked him whether he professed to be the Lord and Savior. Joseph answered that he "professed to be nothing but a man, and a minister of salvation, sent by Jesus Christ to preach the Gospel."[15] While still in bonds, he preached a sermon, thus fulfilling a prophecy he had made earlier that he would yet preach a sermon in Jackson County.

In due time they were taken to Richmond and arraigned on charges of treason. By order of the governor, many Mormons were arrested in Daviess and Ray Counties, but were later cleared of wrongdoing.[16]

Far West under Militia Occupation

With Joseph's arrest, Emma was left to face the loneliness and the hazards of the coming winter, in occupied Far West, without her husband. She was not alone in that condition, however. Dozens of men had been forced to leave their families there and flee beyond the reach of the warrants for their arrest for their efforts to defend their communities from being plundered and burned.

The Saints who remained in Far West were required to turn in all firearms. The men who occupied the town, although under militia command, were not trustworthy; some were mobocrats, who were responsible for the persecution of the Saints and Joseph's arrest. While these men proceeded to search for arms and for the men who had escaped, they harassed the women and helped themselves to whatever they wished from the homes of the frightened citizens. Some of the women were raped.

General Clark, Governor Boggs' appointed commander of the entire Mormon War, came to Far West, breathing a spirit of haughty superiority and ordering the people to stay in the city. When he addressed them on 6 November, he indicated that they would not be forced to leave the state in the depths of winter. He said: "For this lenity you are indebted to *my* clemency. I do not say that you shall go now, but you must not think of staying here another season, or of putting in crops. . . . As for your leaders, do not once think—do not imagine for a moment—do not let it enter your mind that they will be delivered, or that you will see their faces again, *for their fate is fixed—their die is cast—their doom is sealed.*"[17]

Emma must have heard this reported, if she did not hear it firsthand. Notwithstanding her grief and fear, this thirty-four-year-old mother was forced to look to the immediate concern of daily bread. Food was scarce in the city. Although game may have been plentiful, they had no firearms to obtain meat. Albert P. Rockwood said most crops around Far West were unharvested because men had been too busy for eight weeks doing military duty to work the farms. Potatoes still in the ground were "froze solid." Rockwood further stated, "Our houses are rifled and our sheep and hogs, and horses [are] drove off before our eyes by the Missourians who come in small companies well armed. Here [there] is no law for poor Mormons."[18]

In his *Memoirs*, Joseph III remembered one humorous incident from this time. He said one of the brethren came to their house and Emma served what they had—corn bread and sorghum molasses. The boy couldn't recall who it was, but remembered the man complimented Emma's cooking by saying a person could take a piece of her cornbread out to the "northwest corner in a stiff breeze and chew up a sweat."[19]

Apostates Return and Boldly Assert Dominion

Not only the militia, but former members of the Church, now having turned bitter and vicious in their apostasy, plagued the people in Far West. They enjoyed immunity from any possible retribution, legal or otherwise. Caroline Butler, one of the women whose husbands had to escape, remained in Far West. She relates several experiences connected with Joseph's family. Her husband, John, later said Caroline told him that in December, Joseph Smith, Sr., had announced a prayer and fast meeting, to be held for the purpose of petitioning God in Joseph and Hyrum's behalf, that they would be able "to bear the cruelties that they had to suffer."

The meeting was to take place about sunrise. But when the people arrived at the building they found the door locked and people inside who refused to open the door or acknowledge their presence. John Butler said that Joseph Sr. "called to them to open the door, but no one answered or took any notice whatever." By this time several had gathered together and some of them wanted to take an ax and cut the door down, so that they could get [in]. But Father Smith said, "No, we must not do that."

John Taylor was there and suggested although they might be deprived of the house to meet in, they could not be deprived of "praying to God our Heavenly Father to look down in tender mercy upon His servants and enable them to bare their afflictions and the wrongs that they had to pass through."

A smaller building was found; Father Smith told the crowd that those who were unable to get inside could stand outside and listen. The meeting was described as being exceptional. "The Lord was with them to bless and answer their prayers."

Those who had occupied the other building were the Whitmers, Thomas B. Marsh, and "a great many more." John Butler "presumed it was some plan to help . . . destroy Mormonism."[20]

Prisoners for Christ's Sake

Emma received a letter from Joseph written on 4 November. How she must have rejoiced as she recognized the familiar scrawl—

evidence that her husband was alive. He wrote that they had arrived in Jackson County and were at Independence. They were all alive and were being treated well. He said, "I have great anxiety about you, and my lovely children, my heart mourns and bleeds for the brethren, and sisters, and for the slain of the people of God . . . ."[21]

He informed Emma of the treachery of Colonel Hinkle and John Corrill, who he said had tricked him. He warned, "I mention this to have you careful not to trust them. . . ."[22]

As Joseph wrote, he tried to be hopeful for a peaceful resolution of all the difficulties, but he had to recognize the extreme danger: "It is said by some that General Clark is determined to exterminate. . . . God has spared some of us thus far perhaps he will extend mercy in some degree towards us [yet] some of the people of this place [Independence] have told me that some of the mormans may settle in the county as others do I have some hopes that some thing may turn out for good to the afflicted Saints."[23]

He hoped to be able to send for his family and have them brought to him, but for the moment, he wrote, "I want you to stay where you are until you hear from me again. . . . I hope you will be faithful and true to every trust. . . . Conduct all matters as circumstances and necessities require, may God give you wisdom and prudence and sobriety which I have every reason to believe you will. . . ."[24]

No doubt Joseph was nearly overcome with emotion as he finished with a pathetic plea: "O Emma for God sake do not forsake me nor the truth but remember me, if I do not meet you again in this life may God grant that we may meet in heaven, I cannot express my feelings, my heart is full, Farewell oh my kind and Affectionate Emma I am yours forever. Your husband and true friend."[25]

As Emma read this letter, what must her feelings have been? She received another letter on 12 November. This letter provides us with one of the most personal insights into the character and feelings of Joseph Smith.

> Dear Emma . . . We are prisoners in chains for Christ's sake and for no other causes. . . . Oh god grant that I may have the privilege of seeing once more my lovely family, in the enjoyment of the sweets of liberty and solace of life; to press them to my

bosom and kiss their lovely cheeks would fill my heart with unspeakable gratitude. Tell the children that I am alive and trust I shall come and see them before long. Comfort their hearts all you can, and try to be comforted yourself, all you can. . . . We are in good spirits and rejoice that we are counted worthy to be persecuted for Christ's sake. Tell little Joseph he must be a good boy; Father loves him with a perfect love; he [who] is the Eldest must not hurt those that are smaller than him but comfort them. Tell little Frederick, father loves him with all his heart; he is a lovely boy. Julia is a lovely little girl; I love her also, she is a promising child; tell her, Father wants her to remember him and be a good girl, tell all the rest that I think of them all. . . . Alexander is on my mind continually. Oh, my Affectionate Emma, I want you to remember that I am a true and faithful friend to you, and the children forever. My heart is entwined around yours forever and ever; oh, may God bless you all. Amen. I am your husband, and am in bonds and tribulation etc. . . . Joseph, Jun. [26]

Though he was "the Prophet," in this instance he was communicating as any desperately homesick father and husband would, trying to give his family and himself courage, through his uninhibited outpouring of love.

While the Prophet and his fellow prisoners were confined in Richmond, they were chained together, subjected to inhuman treatment by the guards who swore and bragged about the things they had done to the Mormon women. Their language was so rude and blasphemous Joseph could stand it no longer. His rebuke, which silenced these men, is described by Parley P. Pratt:

In one of these tedious nights we had lain as if in sleep till the hour of midnight had passed, and our ears and hearts had been pained, while we had listened for hours to the obscene jest, the horrid oaths, and dreadful blasphemies and filthy language of our guards, Colonel Price at their head, as they recounted to each other their deeds of rapine, murder, robbery, etc., which they had committed among the Mormons while at Far West and vicinity. They even boasted of defiling by force, wives, daughters and virgins, and of shooting or dashing out the brains of men, women and children. I had listened till I became so disgusted, shocked, horrified, and so filled with the spirit of indignant justice that I could scarcely refrain from raising upon my feet and rebuking the guards; but had said nothing to Joseph, or anyone else, although I lay next to him and knew he was awake. On a sudden he arose to his feet, and spoke in a voice of thunder, or as the roaring lion, uttering, as nearly as I can recollect, the following words: "Silence, ye fiends of the infernal pit! I will not live another minute and hear such language. Cease such talk, or you or I die this instant!"

He ceased to speak. He stood erect in terrible majesty. Chained, and without a weapon; calm, unruffled and dignified as an angel, he looked upon the quailing guards, whose weapons were lowered or dropped to the ground; whose knees smote together, and who, shrinking into a corner, or crouching at his feet, begged his pardon, and remained quiet till a change of guards.[27]

The prisoners were invited to give names of witnesses who might testify in their behalf, but anyone they named was promptly arrested. In due time, Joseph and five others were taken to Liberty, Clay County, to await trial for treason and murder.

Of this charge, Joseph said, "Our treason consisted of having whipped the mob out of Daviess County, and taking their cannon from them; the murder, of killing the man in the Bogart battle; also Parley P. Pratt, Morris Phelps, Lyman Gibbs, Darwin Chase, and Norman Shearer, who were put into Richmond Jail to stand . . . trial for the same crimes."[28] Others, besides Joseph, were Lyman Wight, Caleb Baldwin, Hyrum Smith, Alexander McRae, Sidney Rigdon.

General Doniphan and Amos Rees warned Joseph not to bring witnesses in, since there wouldn't be any left for the final trial, "for no sooner would Bogart and his men know who they were than they would put them out of the country."[29] Doniphan made a comment to Joseph about Judge King, to the effect that if a cohort of angels were to come down and declare them innocent, it would be all the same, for he (King) had determined from the beginning to cast them into prison.[30]

Emma Visits Joseph in Prison

On 1 December 1838, Joseph wrote to Emma: "My Dear companion I take this opportunity to inform you that we arrived in Liberty and committed to gaol this evening but we are all in good spirits Captain Bogart will hand you this in my respects to all remain where you are at present yours & c. . . . . Joseph Smith.[31]

One can scarcely imagine what Emma thought when she opened her door to the mob leader himself, now militia captain Bogart. A week later, on 8 December, Emma went to visit Joseph in prison.[32]

Little is known about Emma's visits to Liberty. Many years later, Sidney Rigdon's son, John, who was about eleven at the time of the raid on Far West, related:

> When they went away we supposed it was the last time we would ever see them. . . . A Dr. Madish of Terra Haute, Indiana came to Far West . . . in a two- seated carriage, drawn by a beautiful span of cream horses and he tendered his carriage to My Mother & Joseph Smith's wife for the purpose of going to jail if they could get someone who would drive the horses. Joseph Smith's wife took her oldest son along & My Mother took me. We started rather late in the morn & did not get to the jail til after dark & they would not let [us] go in till the next morn. After taking breakfast at the hotel we were taken to the jail & there remained for three days. When the jailer let me go out to go round the town young Joseph Smith went with me & when I went back he always went with me as he was a little afraid to stay out alone thinking there might be danger. My father Sidney Rigdon was taken out of the Liberty Jail to be tried. Burr Riggs [son-in-law of Rebecca and Frederick Granger Williams] stated he told him that Rigdon had killed a man & hid his body in the bushes. Riggs could produce no body so the judge discharged My Father.
>
> The Missourians said he [Sidney] would not go free and they were going to kill him, he was taken back to jail. He remained there a few days, one night a friend of Fathers came riding to the back door of the jail with a horse all saddled. The man in charge of the jail was friendly and helped him away. He bid his fellow prisoners goodbye got on the horse & with his guide got safely to Quincy Ill. We knowing he had left the jail went to Quincy and joined him.[33]

Emma returned to the jail at Liberty on at least two other occasions: 20 December 1838, and again on 21 January 1839.[34]

On one of the visits, Emma went with the wives of Caleb Baldwin and Alexander McCrae. At least once she went with Hyrum's wife, Mary Fielding Smith, and Mary's sister, Mercy Thompson. Don Carlos drove the wagon and took Mary and her new baby, Joseph F. Smith. Mary was too ill to get out of bed so they put her bed into the wagon. The weather was cold and rainy. They suffered terribly as they made the trip of more than thirty miles. According to Joseph III:

> I remember that . . . I visited the jail at Liberty. . . . There were present in that prison several men, among them Uncle Hyrum Smith, Caleb Baldwin, Lyman Wight, Alexander MacRae, Sidney Rigdon and a singer . . . He sang two ditties or ballads characteristic of the times, which made an impression upon me. One was called "The Massacre at the River Raisin," and the other was a parody called "Mobbers of Missouri," sung to the tune of "Hunters of Kentucky'. . . . I, being very fond of music, well remember this circumstance of his singing to entertain those in the jail the time I was left by my mother to spend the night there with my father.[35]

He also recalled that his mother carried a permit to visit her husband in the jail, and that Emma herself stayed overnight in the jail more than once.[36] However, Joseph III, being so young at the time, recalled few specific details. He did remember being blessed by his father in Liberty Jail; he did not claim this to be an ordination, but rather a father's blessing.[37]

Young Joseph did not recall who took them to Liberty. It is possible that James Mulholland drove them on at least one occasion, since both his and Emma's signatures appear on the statements regarding the ransacking of Emma's house.[38] These affidavits were written during one of her visits:

> William E. McLellin is guilty of entering the house of Joseph Smith Jun., in the city of Far West, and plundering it. . . . Said McLellin was aided and assisted in the above transactions by Harvey Green, Burr Riggs and Harlow Redfield.[39]
>
> The above mentioned William E. McLellin also came to and took away from the stable of the said above mentioned Joseph Smith, Jun., one gig and harness, aided and assisted by Burr Riggs— which can be proven by the following witnesses. (Signed Caroline Clark, James Mulholland, Mrs. Sally Hinkle, Joanna Carter.)

> J. Stollings is guilty of entering the house of Joseph Smith, Jun., in the city of Far West, in company with Sashiel Woods and another man not known, and taking from a trunk, the property of James Mulholland, an inmate of said house . . . . besides tossing and abusing the rest of the contents of said trunk; which can be proven by the following persons (Signed Mrs. Emma Smith, Mrs. Sally Hinkle, Caroline Clark, James Mulholland.[40]

These affidavits shed light on some of the comments made by John Rigdon. It appears that Emma's house was entered more than one time. There is an oblique comment in Frederick Granger Williams' story, as told by Nancy Williams, to the effect that some of Dr. William's belongings were stored in the Smiths' stable, in Far West. The affidavit naming Burr Riggs as one who obtained goods from the stable may be explainable with further research. The bald facts stated in the affidavits reflect that things were taken from Joseph's house and stable without proper permission. Obviously there was sometimes a confused and often distorted view of every event by those who were involved. The main interest here is to show that Mulholland undoubtedly went with Emma to make these affidavits.

None of the accounts of Emma's visits to the jail mention what she did with her other children while she was on the trip. Her seven-month-old baby, Alexander, would still be nursing. If she did not take him along, both she and the baby must have suffered during these trips. A nursing mother cannot simply suspend her milk supply for a week and then resume nursing as though nothing had happened. Julia and little Freddie are likewise unaccounted for. How did Emma manage these difficult circumstances and still take care of her little ones? Who cared for her little ones?

When Emma was not traveling to see her husband, she was caring for her four children in a city that was ill prepared for winter. When Joseph sent asking Emma to send him some blankets, she wept because most of her bedding had been taken. John Butler records this incident, showing how compassionate the Saints were to Emma:

> My wife [Caroline Butler] was up there when the word came, and she said that Sister Emma cried and said that they had taken

all of her bed clothes, except one quilt and blanket, and what could she do? So my wife, with some other sisters said, "Send him them and we will see that you shall have something to cover you and your children." My wife then went home and got some bed clothes and took them over to her.[41]

Under General Clark's "lenity," people were permitted to return to various towns, with explicit instructions that they were forbidden to plan to plant another season in Missouri. His November discourse had revealed his ignorance concerning their faith, and the blind prejudice he held toward them for their religion. He had said:

> I am sorry, gentlemen, to see so great a number of apparently intelligent men found in the situation that you are; and oh! that I could invoke that Great Spirit, the unknown God, to rest upon you, and make you sufficiently intelligent to break that chain of superstition, and liberate you from those fetters of fanaticism with which you are bound—that you no longer worship a man. . . . I would advise you to scatter abroad, and never again organize yourselves with Bishops, Presidents, etc., lest you excite the jealousies of the people, and subject yourselves to the same calamities that have now come upon you . . . .[42]

It was obvious from Clark's words, spoken as the general in charge of the entire campaign, the only thing they could do was comply as quickly as possible with the order to leave the State.

Preparations to Leave Missouri

People in Illinois had heard and were shocked by the plight of the Latter-day Saints, now almost universally known to outsiders by the name "Mormons." Citizens and the press in Illinois indignantly denounced the injustice being done by the Missourians. Their invitation to the Mormons to move into Illinois held political overtones, as Illinois was a free state. In contrast, Missouri was a slave state, and a national controversy on the subject of slavery had been rapidly developing. The Saints represented an impressive voting contingency, guaranteed to oppose slavery. Illinois wanted them—Missouri did not.

The desperate members of the Church immediately began their exodus from Missouri; those who had means were able to leave without hindrance. Many were so poor they could not go. Brigham Young, president of the Twelve Apostles, organized a committee for the removal of those too poor to help themselves. Joseph's uncle John Smith was chosen as chairman and Elias Smith as secretary of this committee. On Tuesday, 29 January 1839, they wrote: "On motion of President Young, it was resolved that we this day enter into a covenant to stand by and assist each other to the utmost of our abilities in removing from this state, and that we will never desert the poor who are worthy, till they shall be out of the reach of the extermination order. . . ."[43]

A committee of seven men was appointed to supervise the removal: William Huntington, Charles Bird, Alanson Ripley, Theodore Turley, Daniel Shearer, Shadrach Roundy, and Jonathan H. Hale.

Eighty men subscribed to this covenant the first day, and three hundred the second day.[44] A bill was passed in the Missouri legislature ordering an investigation into the situation. This coincided with the decision by the committee for removal, that the first families to be moved would be those of the Presidency and the other prisoners.[45] From 1 February on, every effort was made to get every man, woman, and child who wanted to leave Missouri, out of the state.

When there was a wagon ready for Emma, she put what possessions she could into it. James Mulholland had taken Joseph's papers, including the manuscript of the inspired translation of the Bible, to his sister, who made a muslin pocket apron and sewed them into it. Just before Emma was ready to leave, the bundle was brought to her so she could take it out of the state. A popular story has her carrying Joseph's papers and the manuscript copy of the inspired translation of the Bible under her dress. Perhaps she did carry some of his valuable papers there, but the large Bible and manuscript that constitutes the Joseph Smith's translation of the Bible would have been large enough in bulk and weight to suggest that it is improbable she could have had them all on her person—but certainly she had them in her care and considered herself a guardian of them.

Emma's Second Crossing of the Mississippi, February 1839

Emma left Far West on 7 February 1839. Stephen Markham drove the team and wagon which carried Emma, the children, and the Jonathan Holmes family.[46] They arrived at the Mississippi, opposite Quincy, on 15 February. Almost one year after Emma had crossed the frozen Mississippi, going west, she now faced the return journey. Nine days of travel through bitter cold, rain, and sleet brought her face-to-face once again with the ice-choked Mississippi. Crossing the ice on foot, she carried eight-month-old Alexander; two-year-old Frederick clung to her neck, and little Joseph and Julia held onto her skirts. Others traveled with her, yet she must have felt very much alone.

After Markham delivered them safely to Quincy, he returned to Far West. The committee for removal of the Saints had ascertained that thirty-nine families were utterly destitute of teams or provisions for the trip. Most of the Saints were able to obtain their own conveyance, but had few provisions to take with them.

Every able-bodied man in the Church assisted in moving the besieged Saints from Missouri.[47] On 14 February, Don Carlos Smith is said to have petitioned the mob to take up a collection to assist Joseph Sr. and Lucy. Perhaps he was being sarcastic. There is no information as to whether any assistance was forthcoming. Joseph Sr. and Lucy departed that day with Don Carlos, and arrived at last in Quincy after a difficult journey.[48]

Exodus from Missouri

From the end of January through the rest of the winter and spring, wagons rolled across northern Missouri and southern Iowa, toward Illinois. Between twelve and fifteen thousand people were exiled from their homes through the extermination order. The legislature, which had been petitioned to protect the Mormons, refused to act.[49]

The suffering brought upon the exiles goes beyond all description. One youngster, Mosiah Hancock, whose family followed close on the heels of the first group, later recalled the hardships they endured and described seeing the break-up of the ice on the Mississippi.

> We gathered elmbark to eat with our corn. . . . Elmbark and
> buds helped us get along until we came to the Mississippi River.
> There we camped for the night because we didn't know how to
> cross the river. Oh! what a cold night that was! We found some
> herbs growing on strings which we discovered to be wild pota-
> toes—they were good roasted, but I was glad to eat what I could
> find raw. . . . The next morning the river was frozen over with
> ice—great blocks all over the river, and it was slick and clear.
> That morning we crossed over to Quincy, Illinois. I being bare-
> footed and the ice so rough, I staggered all over. We finally got
> across, and we were so glad, for before we reached the other side,
> the river had started to swell and break up. Father said, "Run
> Mosiah," and I did run! We all just made it on the opposite bank
> when the ice started to snap and pile up in great heaps, and the
> water broke thru![50]

Others describe making it across the ice flow in canoes, pushing the
blocks away with the oars, wending their way between the ice blocks, in
great peril all the way. Joseph's sisters walked in ankle-deep mud, slept
under a blanket of snow on the west bank of the Mississippi, and
crossed on the ferry. Exposure to the cold, snow, and rain, which was
more like sleet, took a terrible toll on everyone's health.

Not everyone went to Illinois right away. Emma's neighbor, Rebecca
Williams, had gone previously to Burlington, Iowa, and later Frederick
Granger Williams and his family purchased a place in Quincy.

Refuge in Quincy

Emma and the children found refuge in Quincy in the home of
Judge John Cleveland and his wife, Sarah. They had a farm about
three miles from town, where several other families were staying as
well. Whether they moved into existing buildings or threw up shacks
to shelter them is not clear. They crowded together and situated
themselves the best they could.

On 27 February, the Democratic Association of Quincy met to
discuss how they should receive the refugees from Missouri. They
resolved: "That the strangers recently arrived here from the state of
Missouri, known by the name of the 'Latter-day saints,' are entitled to

our sympathy and kindest regard, and that we recommend to the citizens of Quincy to extend all the kindness in their power to bestow on the persons who are in affliction."[51]

On 6 March 1839, Don Carlos Smith wrote to his brothers who were being held in Liberty Jail:

> Brothers Hyrum and Joseph . . . Father's family have all arrived in this state except you two; and could I but see your faces this side of the Mississippi, and know and realize that you had been delivered from your enemies, it would certainly light up a new gleam of hope in our bosoms; nothing could be more satisfactory, nothing could give us more joy.
>
> Emma and the children are well; they live three miles from here, and have a tolerable good place. Hyrum's children and mother Grinold are living at present with father; they are all well. Mary [wife of Hyrum Smith] has not got her health yet, but I think it increases slowly. . . . We are trying to get a house, and to get the family together; we shall do the best we can for them, and that which we consider to be most in accordance with Hyrum's feelings.
>
> Father and mother stood their journey remarkably well. They are in tolerable health. Samuel's wife has been sick ever since they arrived. William has removed forty miles from here, but is here now, and says he is anxious to have you liberated. . . . My family is well: my health has not been good for about two weeks; and for two or three days the toothache has been my tormenter. It all originated with a severe cold. . . . We just heard that the governor says that he is going to set you all at liberty; I hope it is true. . . . I close by leaving the blessings of God with you, and praying for your health, prosperity and restitution to liberty. . . . This from a true friend and brother, Don C. Smith.[52]

William also wrote saying he dared not go to visit Joseph at Liberty for fear of making things worse for them (and for himself as well, undoubtedly). His heartfelt hope was "that you will be permitted to come to your families before long. Do not worry about them, for they will be taken care of . . . ."[53]

Emma wrote to Joseph by the same mail:

> Dear Husband . . . I shall not attempt to write my feelings altogether, for the situation in which you are, the walls, bars and

bolts, rolling rivers, running streams, rising hills, sinking valleys
and spreading prairies that separate us, and the cruel injustice
that first cast you into prison and still holds you there, with
many considerations, places my feelings far beyond description.
Was it not for conscious innocence and the direct interposition
of divine mercy, I am very sure I never should have been able to
have endured the scenes of suffering that I have passed through
since what is called the Militia, came into Far West under the
ever remembered Governor's notable order; an order fraught with
as much wickedness as ignorance and as much ignorance as was
ever contained in an article of that length; but I still live and am
yet willing to suffer more if it is the will of kind heaven, that I
should for your sake. . . . No one but God knows the reflections
of my mind and the feelings of my heart when I left our house
and home and almost all of everything that we possessed except
our little children and took my journey out of the State of
Missouri, leaving you shut up in that lonesome prison. But the
reflection is more than human nature ought to bear . . . and if
God does not record our sufferings and avenge our wrongs on
them that are guilty, I shall be sadly mistaken. . . .

You may be astonished at my bad writing and incoherent
manner, but you will pardon all when you reflect how hard it
would be fore you to write when your hands were stiffened with
hard work and your heart convulsed with intense anxiety . . . but
I hope there is better days to come to us yet. . . . I am ever yours
affectionately. Emma Smith.[54]

Meanwhile, in Missouri, Apostles Heber C. Kimball and Alonson
Ripley, were "importuning at the feet of the judges." On a weekly
basis they met with Judge Hughes, who on one occasion, "starred
them full in the face and observed to one of his associates, 'By the
look of these men's eyes, they are whipped, but not conquered; and
let us beware how we treat these men; for their looks bespeak innocence.'" Judge Hughes entreated his associates to let the prisoners out
on bail, but " the hardness of their hearts would not admit to so char-
itable a deed." They were told that no ruling on the part of the
committee disputed the innocence of the prisoners, but "in consequence of the fury of the mob, that even-handed justice could not be
administered." In other words, they were afraid that if they let the
prisoners out of jail, the mob would turn upon them for doing it.[55]

Notes

1. *HC*, 3:179-82.

2. *HC*, 3:175.

3. Edward Tullidge, *Women of Mormondom* (New York: Tullidge & Crandall, 1877), p. 127.

4. J. Christopher Conkling, *A Joseph Smith Chronology* (Salt Lake City: Deseret Book, 1979), pp.122-23.

5. *HC*, 3:176.

6. *HC*, 3:176 ftnt.

7. Conkling, *Joseph Smith Chronology*, p.123.

8. *HC*, 3:191.

9. *HC*, 3:190-91, ftnt.; italics added. *The History of Caldwell County* says the following:

> Yielding to the pressure upon him, it is alleged that General Lucas, at about midnight, issued the following order to General Doniphan, in whose keeping the hostages were:

> Brigadier-General Doniphan:
> SIR:—You will take Joseph Smith and the other prisoners into the public square of Far West, and shoot them at 9 o'clock to-morrow morning.
> SAMUEL D. LUCAS,
> Major-General Commanding.

> The Caldwell County history continues:
> But General Doniphan, in great and righteous indignation, promptly returned the following reply to his superior:
> It is cold-blooded murder. I will not obey your order. My brigade shall march for Liberty tomorrow morning, at 8 o'clock; and if you execute these men, I will hold you responsible before an earthly tribunal, so help me God.
> A. W. DONIPHAN,
> Brigadier-General

10. *HC*, 3:190-91. For more information on Alexander Doniphan, see Gregory Maynard, "Alexander William Doniphan: Man of Justice," *BYU Studies* (Summer, 1973), pp. 462-72.

11. Hyrum Smith wrote, "The whoopings, howlings, yellings, and shoutings of the army, . . . were so horrid, that they frightened the inhabitants of the city [Far West]. It is impossible to describe the feeling of horror and distress of the people," in Scot and Maurine Proctor, *The Revised and Enhanced History of Joseph Smith by His Mother* (Salt Lake City: Bookcraft, 1996), p. 405.

12. Mary Audentia Smith Anderson, ed., *Joseph III and the Restoration* (Independence, Mo: Herald Publishing House, 1952), p. 2.

13. See Doctrine & Covenants 122:6.

14. *HC,* 3:193 ftnt. See also Proctor and Proctor, *The Revised and Enhanced History of Joseph Smith by His Mother,* pp. 382-83 and Lucy Mack Smith, *History of Joseph Smith by His Mother,* ed. Preston Nibley (Salt Lake City: Bookcraft, 1958), p. 289.

15. *HC,* 3:200-201.

16. *HC,* 3:204-211.

17. *HC,* 3:203; emphasis in original.

18. Quoted in William Hartley, *My Best for the Kingdom* (Salt Lake City: Aspen Books, 1993), p. 85, from Albert Perry Rockwood Journal, November 1838, pp. 28-29.

19. Anderson, *Memoirs of Joseph III,* p. 3.

20. Hartley, *My Best for the Kingdom,* p. 86.

21. Dean C. Jessee, *The Personal Writings of Joseph Smith* (Salt Lake City: Deseret Book, 1984), pp. 361-63; quoted from Joseph Smith's letter to Emma, 4 November 1838.

22. Ibid.

23. Ibid.

24. Ibid.

25. Ibid.

26. Jessee, *Personal Writings of Joseph Smith,* pp. 367-69.

27. *HC,* 3:204 ftnt.; quoted from *The Autobiography of Parley P. Pratt* (Salt Lake City: Deseret Book, 1938), p. 179.

28. *HC,* 3:210-213.

29. Ibid.

30. Ibid.

31. Joseph Smith, Letter to Emma; original is in LDS Church Archives; copy in LDS Archives.

32. Anderson, *Joseph III and the Restoration,* p. 14.

33. John Rigdon, *The Sesquecentennial Times* (25-31 July 1965), Friendship, New York.

34. Anderson, *Joseph III and the Restoration,* p. 14.

35. *Memoirs of Joseph III,* p. 2.

36. Ibid., pp. 2-3.

37. Ibid., p. 2.

38. *HC,* 3:288.

39. Redfield was later cleared. See *HC,* 3:287 ftnt.

40. *HC,* 3:286-88.

41. Hartley, *My Best for the Kingdom,* p. 86. See also *History and Biography of John Lowe Butler, a Mormon Frontiersman* (Salt Lake City: Aspen Books, 1993).

42. *HC,* 3:204. General Clark's speech is found in the *History of Caldwell and Livingston Counties, Missouri* (St. Louis National Historical Company, 1886), p. 140.

43. *HC,* 3:250.

44. *HC,* 3:251-34. This list of names is very impressive. Due to these men, many lives were saved.

45. *HC,* 3:255.

46. *HC,* 3:256.

47. *HC,* 3:250-51. This gives the minutes for the meeting of the committee for removal and the names of those who covenanted to help bring the Saints out of Missouri, as noted in Note 45 above.

48. *HC,* 3:261.

49. In Richard Anderson's memo to author.

50. Mosiah Hancock Journal; typescript copy in possession of author.

51. *HC,* 3:268.

52. *HC,* 3:273-74.

53. *HC,* 3:274.

54. Emma Smith, Letter to Joseph Smith, March 1838, RLDS Archives.

55. *HC,* 3:264-65.

Letter from Joseph to Emma, 1 December 1832.
Courtesy of LDS Archives.

CHAPTER 10

Liberty, Sweet Liberty

"Peace be unto thy soul; thine adversity and thine afflictions shall be but a small moment." (Doctrine & Covenants 121:7)

For a man of Joseph's nature, five months in a prison under guard by men who were vile in their language and almost sadistic in their delight in causing misery was a physical, mental, and spiritual ordeal. Rather than break his spirit, however, this ordeal seems to have served to refine his soul and magnify his spiritual powers. But it was a process over time, which held some of the darkest days of his life.

All the prisoners suffered greatly from living in the filthy, cramped circumstances afforded them in Liberty Jail. The damp cold and miserable dimness of the closed-up building was overwhelming to men who were used to being out of doors. They bore with their confinement through December and January, but finally, desperate for freedom, they made two separate unsuccessful attempts to escape, one on 9 February, and one on 4 March. After that, their confinement became even more difficult; they were more closely guarded than before, and at times their friends were prevented from visiting.

On 19 March 1839, Emma's letter arrived along with letters from Don Carlos and Bishop Edward Partridge. Joseph's response was a lengthy letter on 20 March. Fellow prisoner Alexander McCrae served as his scribe. Sections of this letter were later published in *Times and Seasons* and were incorporated in the Doctrine and Covenants as sections 121-123. The letter is too lengthy for full inclusion here, but some excerpts shed light on many aspects of the Prophet's nature.

> To the church of Latter-day saints at Quincy Illinois and scat-
> tered abroad, and to bishop Partridge in particular, your humble
> servant Joseph Smith, Jun., prisoner for the Lord Jesus Christ's
> sake and for the saints taken and held by the power of mobocracy
> under the extermination reign of his excellency the Governor
> Lilburn W. Boggs in company with his fellow prisoners and
> beloved Brethren, Caleb Baldwin, Lyman Wight, Hyrum Smith
> and Alexander McRae send unto you greeting. May the grace of
> God the father and of our Lord and savior Jesus Christ rest upon
> you all and abide with you for ever. May knowledge be multiplied
> unto you by the mercy of God. And may faith and virtue and
> knowledge and temperance and patience and Godliness and
> Brotherly kindness and charity be in you and abound that you
> may not be barren in anything nor unfruitful. . . .[1]

This letter took several days to compose. When it was finished
Joseph and all the prisoners signed it. In it we find lamentations,
prayers, and prophecies. It is a document of immeasurable worth to
the Church.

Joseph identifies the terrible persecution of the Latter-day Saints as
preliminary events to the tribulations prophesied to come in the last
days—"terrible storms that are now gathering in the heavens with darkness and gloominess and thick darkness as spoken of by the Prophets."[2]

He observes that God is not unaware of what is happening to his
people through the wrongful acts of the mobs and corrupt politicians. It
was Joseph's conviction that the spirits of the Saints who had been slain at
Haun's Mill and elsewhere were bearing testimony in heaven concerning
the events that had transpired. He noted, "There seems to be a whis-
pering that the angels [of heaven] who have been entrusted with the
council of these matters for the last days have taken counsel together."[3]

He revealed his conviction that a decision was being made in
heavenly councils; in due time that decision would be made known
and all things that offend would be taken into consideration—particularly evil behavior against the innocent.

Joseph lamented, "Oh! the unrelenting hand of the inhumanity
and murderous disposition of this people shocks all nature, it beggars
and defies all description. It is a [tale] of woe, a lamentable [tale], yea
a sorrowful [tale]. Too much to tell, too much for contemplation, too
much to think of for a moment, too much for human beings."[4]

He was indignant over the atrocities enacted upon his people, because of their religious beliefs; that no enforcement of law was attempted to prevent the violation of their constitutional rights. It is hard to determine whether he was most horrified at the acts of cruelty or at the failure of the duly constituted law enforcement officials to protect innocent people from such acts or to punish the offenders. From his pen flowed a veritable tirade of emotion.

> I think it cannot be found among the wild and ferocious beasts of the forest that a man should be mangled for sport, women be [robbed] of all that they have, their last morsel for subsistence, and then be violated to gratify the hellish desires of the mob, and finally left to perish with their helpless offspring clinging around their necks. But this is not all; after a man is dead he must be dug up from his grave and mangled to pieces for no other purpose than to gratify their spleen against the religion of God.
> They practice [these] things upon the saints who have done them no wrong, who are innocent and virtuous, who loved the Lord, their god, and were willing to forsake all things for [Christ's] sake. These things are awful to relate, but they are verily true—it must needs be that offenses come, but WOE! to them by whom they come.[5]

Is it any wonder Joseph's next words are as a cry of agony? Why he turned to prayer?

> O God where art thou and where is the pavilion that covereth thy hiding place how long shall thy hand be stayed and thine eye yea thy pure eye behold from the eternal heavens the wrongs of thy people and of thy servants and thine ear be penetrated with their cries, yea, O Lord, how long shall they suffer these wrongs and unlawful oppressions before thine heart shall be softened towards them and thy bowels be moved with compassion towards them . . . .[6]

Reading from the original text of the letter expands our understanding of the setting which gave rise to the profound verses we now have in the Doctrine and Covenants. Clearly, receiving his friends' letters inspired in the prophet an urgent spiritual reaching that yielded gratifying reassurance.

Within the text we find Joseph's expression of how he felt having "received some letters last evening, one from Emma, one from Don C. Smith, and one from Bishop Partridge, all breathing a kind and consoling spirit. We were much gratified with their contents. We had been a long time without information, and when we read those letters, they were to our souls as the gentle air is refreshing—but our joy was mingled with grief because of the suffering of the poor and much injured saints . . . the floodgates of our hearts were hoisted and our eyes were a fountain of tears . . ."[7] Joseph continued:

> Those who have not been inclosed in the walls of a prison without cause or provocation can have but a little idea how sweet the voice of a friend is; one token of friendship from any source whatever awakens and calls into action every sympathetic feeling. It brings up in an instant everything that is passed; it seizes the present with a vivacity of lightning; it grasps after the future with the fierceness of a tiger. It retrogrades from one thing to another until finally all enmity malice and hatred and past differences misunderstandings and mis-managements be slain victims at the feet of hope—and when the heart is sufficiently contrite [then] the voice of inspiration steals along and whispers *my son peace be unto thy soul thine adversity and thy afflictions shall be but a small moment and then if thou endure it well God shall exalt thee on high thou shalt triumph over all thy foes thy friends do stand by thee and they shall hail thee again with warm hearts and friendly hands, thou art not yet as Job . . . .*[8]

Emma's heart must have filled with emotion as she read what would become one of the most precious examples of prayer in latter-day scripture. The Prophet's prayer, uttered from a filthy dungeon in Liberty, Missouri, echoed the cry of early Christians; it forespoke the anguish of the Jews under Hitler's rampaging genocide; of Catholics and Protestants locked in conflict in Northern Ireland; of Arab and Jew in Israel and Palestine; of persecuted people in any land, in any era.

Was it written in candle light or the shadowy shaft of daylight that passed through the narrow, barred window high in the cell room wall?

Joseph added an admonition and a promise; they must all become meek, and God would give them knowledge, through the gift of the Holy Ghost. Then the time would come which, "our fathers have waited with anxious expectation to be revealed in the last times . . . the fullness . . . a time to come in the which nothing shall be with held. . . ."9 Here the Prophet was stating plainly that the dispensation of the fulness of times had come.

With joy, the Prophet declared that the Restoration had begun to do its work on the earth. He likened the situation to that of a torrential rain flooding down the mountains, washing debris and filth into the streams, leaving fallen trees along the hillsides. The flood will pass, and the flood of truth "as time rolls on may bring us to the fountain as clear as crystal and as pure as snow while all the filthiness . . . is left and purged out by the way. . . . How long can rolling waters remain impure? What power shall stay the heavens? Men might as well stretch out a puny arm to stop the Missouri River in its decreed course . . . as to hinder the Almighty from pouring down knowledge from [heaven] upon the heads of the Latter day saints. . . ."10

He said that Boggs and his murderous party would be caught in the flood and left behind, while the pure stream of the gospel would roll on and on. Joseph also declared that "God is the author of truth and 'mormonism' He is our shield it is by him we receive our birth, it is by his voice that we were called to a dispensation of his gospel in the beginning of the fullness of times, it was by him we received the Book of Mormon, and it was by him that we remain unto this day; and by him we shall remain, if it shall be for our glory and his almighty name, we are determined to endure tribulation as good soldiers. . . ."11

He gave the brethren instructions concerning the general conference of the Church, which would be held in April. He warned, "If there are any among you who aspire after their own aggrandizement and seek their own opulence while their brethren are groaning in poverty and are under sore trials and temptations they cannot be benefitted by the intercessions of the holy spirit which maketh intercession for us day and night. . . . We ought at all times to be very careful that such highmindedness never have place in our hearts . . . with all long suffering bare the infirmities of the weak."12

His words were of warning and admonition.

> "Behold there are many called but few are chosen. And why
> are they not chosen? Because their hearts are set so much upon
> the things of this world and aspire to the honors of men that
> they do not learn this one lesson. That the rights of priesthood
> are inseparably connected with the powers of heaven and that the
> powers of heaven cannot be controlled nor handled only upon
> the principles of righteousness that they may be conferred upon
> us it is true but when we undertake to cover our sins or to gratify
> our pride or vain ambition or to exercise control or dominion or
> unrighteousness behold the heavens with draw themselves the
> spirit of the lord is grieved and when it has withdrawn amen to
> the priesthood or the authority of that man. . . ."[13]

Joseph requested that they write to him a full report of all that
occurred at the conference. He also asked them to obtain testimony
of all who had suffered and apply to the United States government for
redress from the state of Missouri.

Reassurance that his family and the Church were faithful in spite
of all they had endured must have infused his soul with new hope,
new vigor, and a surge of longing to be free to go to them. This hope
was confirmed in revelation: "Thy friends do stand by thee, and they
shall hail thee again with warm hearts and friendly hands."[14]

Joseph's more personal letter to Emma was penned by his own
hand, dated 21 March 1839:

> Affectionate Wife I have sent an Epistle to the church
> directed to you because I wanted you to have the first reading of
> it, and then I want Father and Mother to have a copy of it. Keep
> the original yourself as I dictated the matter myself. . . . I want
> you [to] have the Epistle copied immediately and let it go to the
> Brethren firs[t] into the hands of Father for I want the produc-
> tion for my record. . . . I want to be with you very much but the
> powers of mobocra[c]y is too many for me at present. . . . My
> Dear Emma I very well know your toils and simpathise with you.
> If God will spare my life once more to have the privilege of
> taking care of you I will ease your care and indeavour to cumfort
> your heart. . . . I want you to try to gain time and write to me a
> long letter and tell me all you can and even if old major [the dog]

is alive yet and what those little pratlers say that cling around you[r] neck. Do you tell them I am in prison that their lives might be saved. I want all the church to make out a bill of damages and apply to the united states court as soon as possible. . . . You expressed my feelings concerning the order and I believe that there is a way to git redress for such things but god ruleth all things after the council of his own will my trust is in him the salvation of my soul is the most important to me for as much as I know for a certainty of Eternal things if the heavens linger it is nothing to me I must stear my bark safe which I intend to do I want you to do the same. Yours forever. Joseph Smith, Jun.[15]

On a second page he asked her, not in a plaintive way, but tenderly, "My Dear Emma, do you think that my being cast into prison by the mob renders me less worthy of your friendship no I do not think so but when I was in prison and ye visited me inasmuch as you have done it to the least of these you have done it to me. . . ."[16]

His letter to the Church reveals Joseph praying on and on—his spirit gradually moving from depression and misery to recognition that the time would indeed come when the Savior will return to earth, bringing His perfect order of justice. The Prophet solemnly reflected some well-honed wisdom when he warned them to beware of "a fanciful and flowery and heated imagination because the things of God are of deep import and time and experience and careful and ponderous and solemn though[t]s can only find them out. . . ."[17]

Each word, like manna to her soul, must have touched Emma deeply, infusing her with confidence that Joseph would be with her and the children again on this earth, after all.

An Apostate Testifies of the Book of Mormon

Early in April, pressure was mounting in Daviess County for the removal of every Mormon from the state. The Committee for Removal had been summarily directed to have all the Mormons out of Missouri by the next Friday.

Brother Turley reported an incident that occurred at this time. After he and Heber C. Kimball were back in Far West, eight men, including Captain Bogart (who was the county judge) and John Whitmer, entered the room where the Church Committee for

Removal had its office. The men "presented a paper containing Joseph's revelation of 8 July 1838, in which he directed the Twelve to take their leave of the Saints in Far West on the building site of the Lord's House on the 26th of April, to go to the isles of the sea."[18]

Turley acknowledged it, saying, "Gentlemen, I am well acquainted with it."[19]

They taunted Brother Turley, suggesting that if he were a rational man he would give up his faith in Joseph Smith's being a prophet and an inspired man. They declared, "He and the Twelve are now scattered all over creation; let them come here if they dare; if they do, they will be murdered. As that revelation cannot be fulfilled, you will now give up your faith."[20]

Turley jumped up and said, "In the name of God that revelation will be fulfilled."

Some of the men laughed scornfully, saying again, the Twelve dared not try to take leave from Far West, for if they came there they would all be killed. John Whitmer hung his head.

Turley then directed a question at Whitmer, asking him if he believed the Book of Mormon to be true. He challenged Whitmer about the fact that there was a double message coming from the dissenters. Pointing out that one of the dissenters, John Corrill, was about to publish a book against the Church, Turley said, "Gentlemen, I presume there are men here who have heard Corrill say, that 'Mormonism' was true, that Joseph Smith was a prophet, and inspired of God. I now call upon you, John Whitmer: you say Corrill is a moral and a good man; do you believe him when he says the Book of Mormon is true, or when he says it is not true?"[21] This inquiry hit home to the recalcitrant witness of the Book of Mormon.

"Do you hint at me?" Whitmer asked.[22]

Turley snapped, "If the cap fits you, wear it; all I know is that you published to the world that an angel did present those plates to Joseph Smith."

Whitmer replied: "I now say, I handled those plates; there were fine engravings on both sides. I handled them."[23] Despite ridicule, he stood firm that what he had seen was genuine and from a divine source. When he was pressed to explain why he now seemed to not believe in the translation of the Book of Mormon, Turley said John

Whitmer answered that he "could not read the original, so he did not know whether the translation was true."[24]

Had Joseph or Emma heard the details of this testimony, what would they have thought, considering their knowledge of his intimate association with the coming forth of the Book of Mormon?

Prisoners are Moved from Liberty Jail to Daviess County

On 4 April 1839, Judge King learned that Heber C. Kimball and Theodore Turley had met with the governor to demand justice for the prisoners. King was furious with them and told them that he himself would have released all but Joseph, if they had asked him. He said Joseph was not fit to live, and he refused to allow them to visit inside the jail. Through the grate of the window, Joseph reassured Kimball and Turley, saying, "We shall be delivered; but no arm but God's can deliver us now. Tell the brethren to be of good cheer and get the saints away as fast as possible."[25]

Judge King ordered a guard of about ten men, commanded by Samuel Tillery, deputy jailer of Clay County, to take the prisoners to Daviess County for trial. The prisoners later recalled they were very feeble and found the trip difficult.[26] Although they had been promised they would go through Far West on the way to Gallatin, the guards took them miles around Far West, keeping them away from any contact with their friends.

According to Church history, the atmosphere of hostility in Daviess County increased as the day for the trial drew near. Brothers Turley and Kimball reported observing that about fifty men in Daviess County had sworn they would never eat or drink until they had seen "Joe Smith" dead. Their captain, William Bowman, stated it even more bluntly; as soon as he saw Smith, he said he intended to kill him.[27]

On 8 April, the prisoners arrived in Daviess County. Within a mile of Gallatin, the Clay County Guard left them in the hands of Sheriff Morgan, with guards John Brassfield and John Pogue, and the prisoners' avowed enemy, William Bowman.

The Prisoners Are Freed

The trial at Gallatin convened on 9 April, with none other than Judge Austin A. King, presiding. The jury was drunk—so was the judge. Stephen Markham had been sent by the brethren at Far West, bringing money and a copy of a statute that had passed the Missouri legislature, granting the prisoners permission to obtain a change of venue.[28] Another welcome visitor was Judge Morin, from Mill Port, who was favorable to their obtaining such a change.

That night, the prophet was warned by the Spirit of danger to Stephen Markham. He woke Stephen up and told him he should leave in the morning before dawn; if he did not, he would surely be shot. Stephen took the warning and though he was pursued, he got away safely. Words cannot describe the bravery of men such as Stephen Markham, Heber C. Kimball, Theodore Turley, and many others who put their lives on the line for the sake of the Lord's prophet during the proceedings.

The trial continued until 14 April. The outright abuse of defense witnesses by the mob, of which the jury seemed to approve, rendered the entire proceedings a farce; there was no justice to be had for the prisoners, now indicted for "murder, treason, burglary, arson, larceny, theft, and stealing."[29] The charges were, of course, false. None of these men had performed any such acts. Nevertheless, it was the stated intent of this court to condemn the prisoners to death.

During this time the Committee for Removal worked feverishly to remove all the Latter-day Saints remaining in the area. The brethren also worked feverishly to obtain a change of venue for the prisoners. But it took time to obtain the necessary documents, and time was running out.

In the midst of these trials, Joseph and Hyrum were greatly comforted by a letter from Agnes Smith, wife of Don Carlos.

> Beloved Brothers, Hyrum and Joseph . . . My prayer is to my Heavenly Father for your deliverance. It seems as though the Lord is slow to hear the prayers of the Saints. But the Lord's ways are not like our ways; therefore He can do better than we ourselves. You must be comforted . . . and look forward for

better days. Your little ones are as playful as little lambs; be comforted concerning them, for they are not cast down and sorrowful as we are. . . .[30]

This letter speaks volumes concerning Emma's and Mary's care of the children through all they had suffered.

Elias Higbee wrote on 16 April that he had "seen Sister Emma yesterday." She was living with the Cleveland family, at Quincy.[31] Higbee's letter would not reach Joseph at Gallatin. On 15 April, the plan of the mobbers to "legally" condemn the prisoners to death was blocked by the arrival of a change of venue to Boone County, Missouri.[32] On 16 April, the prisoners started for Boone County, a considerable distance east of Daviess County. During the move, the prisoners made their escape.

Emma and the Children in Quincy

Joseph III, in his *Memoirs,* gives some interesting glimpses of the Smiths' stay at the Cleveland farm. He described George Cleveland as a "middle-sized man, with a kind face and soft, even voice. I do not remember him speaking harshly or exhibit[ing] any temper or impatience. His wife was a fine-looking woman, approaching middle age. . . ."[33]

Two incidents are recorded by Joseph III, which give us a vivid view of Emma and her dealings with her children. It also sheds light on their living situation. Although he did not remember if Sidney and his sons, John and Sidney Jr., were there, he is certain Mrs. Rigdon and her young daughter, Lucy, lived there with them.

> The Cleveland farm was located about three or four miles out from Quincy. Emma and the children, and some, or all of the Rigdon family, made up a part of the household. . . .
> One day Julia came in and began teasing for something which Mother did not think proper to grant just then; I think it was for something to eat. Mother told her to wait; but the child, too impatient to do so, threw herself down upon her back on the floor and with a very good imitation of weeping began pounding her heels and bumping her head on the floor, accompanying the tattoo with a series of screams.

Mother stepped quickly to her, caught the young miss by the
shoulder[s] and straightened her to her feet with the sharp
command, "Stop that! If you want anything, ask for it, but don't
try any of that nonsense if you can't have it right away. You just
can't come Lucy Rigdon on me!"[34]

Joseph III, then explains, "The childish tactics my sister
attempted at that time were indeed almost a daily occurrence with
Mrs. Rigdon's Lucy, who ruled her mother through inspiring a fear
that she would injure herself by bumping her head on the floor in
that fashion. Mother's Julia, however, never tried the experiment on
Mother again; it did not work."[35]

The next story broadens our understanding of Emma's fears and
sense of responsibility; we also can appreciate her method of disci-
plining her son, who was obviously a very strong-willed child.

Dimick Huntington and his wife and children had moved into a
home not far from the Clevelands. They had several children, the
eldest being Allen. Allen was several years older than Joseph III, and
was permitted to take his father's rifle out to hunt rabbits in the fields.
The Clevelands also had a boy about the same age as Joseph III, and
all the children liked to go with Allen to look for rabbits. Joseph III
recalls, "We used to form quite a little band of players, ranging the
farm at will."[36]

Emma didn't object to Joseph III and Freddie playing with the
Huntington children until she discovered Allen was taking his father's
rifle out with him when they were there. Fearful of an accident, she
told her boys to stay away from the Huntingtons' place.

But young Joseph was hooked. The next day, despite his mother's
direct order, he wandered over to the Huntingtons and spent a
delightful day following Allen around, hunting rabbits. It was quite
late in the day when he returned. When questioned by his mother, he
admitted he had been out hunting rabbits. Allen, he said, "had
carried the rifle. Thereupon, with the aid of a ready hazel switch,
[Emma] promptly administered punishment."

But that was not the end of it. Next morning, when Joseph and
Freddie were heading outside to play, she said, "Joseph, I will not say
you must not go to Mrs. Huntington's today, but I will say that if you

do go I shall punish you when you return." She again explained as she had previously, "It is a dangerous thing to play with Allen when he carries the rifle, and I am not going to be responsible for any harm that may come. So just remember what I tell you." Joseph III continues:

> Again, either forgetful or neglectful of the mandate, I ventured into the forbiden region and spent a portion of the day with the Huntington boys in the hazel brush after rabbits, staying late enough in the afternoon to see the little animals at play on the hillside and to hear the crack of the rifle.
>
> When I returned home Mother had company at supper and nothing was said to me about my visit to the Huntingtons; hence I went to bed thinking it had escaped my mother's notice and that I was safe from punishment. However, after the guests departed, I discovered my error, for Mother found me and I received the punishment she had promised, applied vigorously enough to make me feel sorry I had undressed as I went to bed!
>
> When morning came Mother repeated her charge, saying, "I will not say you shall not go to play with the Huntingon boys while their mother allows Allen to take his father's gun with him to play, but if you do go, I will punish you; and I shall punish you harder and harder until you stop."
>
> Once more the allure of the pastime seemed stronger than my mother's counsel and her efforts to deter me, and again I went to the Huntingtons and spent the day with the boys and their rifle. When I returned my mother punished me with such decidedly increased severity that I—well, comment is needless! I did not go again, for I found that my mother was indeed a woman of her word.[37]

And so, as Joseph III remarked, "the winter passed away" and Emma heard from Joseph "at intervals more or less extended," until the wonderful day he returned to them.

Together Again

A ragged, dirty, emaciated Joseph approached the gate of the Cleveland house, on 22 April 1839. A witness to his homecoming, Dimick Huntington saw Emma look out the door and rush into Joseph's arms before he could get halfway up the path to the house.[38]

Joseph's record tells us, ". . . after suffering much fatigue and hunger, I arrived in Quincy, Illinois, amidst the congratulations of my friends, and the embraces of my family, whom I found as well as could be expected, considering what they had been called to endure."[39]

The Prophet must have given his family an expansive description of the escape. To the family and the church it seemed like nothing short of a miracle.

Joseph explained that some of the officers in Daviess County, realizing there was no hope for a fair trial for these men, had connived to set the prisoners free. Judge Birch made out a *mittimus*, or warrant, without a name, date, or place, and sent the five prisoners in a two-horse wagon, with four guards in addition to the sheriff. They started from Gallatin, early in the morning. After an all-day trip they arrived at Judge Morin's, where they rested until morning. At some point, William Bowman left to return to Daviess County, leaving Morgan and the others to carry on.

In an affidavit prepared by Hyrum Smith, the "escape" is fully described.[40] Hyrum says that next day they traveled twenty miles and having stopped and bought a jug of whiskey, they "treated their guards." The sheriff showed them the unsigned warrant and told them that Judge Birch had said not to take them to Boone County. Sheriff Morgan said, "I shall take a good drink of grog, and go to bed, and you may do as you have a mind to." All the guards drank whiskey and fell asleep. The prisoners did what they "had a mind to" and departed post haste. Two horses had been left saddled and bridled. The Smiths rode fast for the Illinois border. The prisoners split up, each making his own way to Quincy.

It was later learned that Sheriff William Morgan, and also, ex-sheriff William Bowman, received harsh treatment at the hands of the citizens of Gallatin when it was learned that the prisoners had escaped. "They [the Daviess County mob] rode the sheriff on a rail, and Bowman was dragged over the square by the hair of the head."[41] Such treatment of William Bowman, who had been as determined to see Joseph dead as any of them, shows the irrational mentality of the mob. They were so incensed that Joseph had escaped, they assumed Bowman must have let them go in exchange for money, which he had not done. Not surprisingly, none of the mob was ever punished for their treatment of Bowman and Morgan.

Happily, the Prophet, now free to be with his family, must have marveled at the growth five months could bring to his children. Little Alexander, just a tiny infant when Joseph had been put in jail, was now a big, husky fellow, walking around chairs. Young Joseph was a solemn child who took his mother's word as "law." Julia had grown tall. Little Freddie, never very strong physically, was a two-year-old with a new command of the language. The Prophet's delight with his children has been attested to by many journal entries. We can sympathize with them all when we realize that the pressures of business, Church, and well-wishing Saints drew him away almost immediately. But Emma could rest, knowing he was safe, at least for the present.

A Prophecy Fulfilled

There was a great determination by the mob to prevent the Twelve from returning to Far West for the meeting Joseph had said they should have at the Far West Temple Site on 26 April. The brethren were equally determined that they would fulfill every statement made by Joseph. Elders Clark and Turley joined Alpheus Cutler, Brigham Young, Orson Pratt, George A. Smith, John Taylor, Wilford Woodruff, John E. Page, and Daniel Shearer as they made their way to Far West. Stephen Markham also returned to Far West. Minutes of the meeting indicate that those gathered at the Far West Temple Site were "the Twelve, High Priests, Elders, and priests, on the 26 day of April, 1839."[42] This was a representation from every priesthood quorum.

Like the apostles of old, these modern day apostles stood in great danger, yet they did not hesitate to proceed with the business before them. They sang a hymn, "Adam-ondi-Ahman," and offered prayer. They ordained two new apostles, Wilford Woodruff and George A. Smith, who had previously been issued the call by the First Presidency; they also ordained several men to the office of Seventy. Their next important act was to finish laying the fourth cornerstone; Brigham Young, Heber C. Kimball, Orson Pratt, John E. Page, and John Taylor, placed the stone in its position, after which the conference adjourned, and they all dispersed to safer ground.

Before leaving the state, Elders Turley, Page, and Woodruff could not resist stopping by an old friend's house to say good-bye. Perhaps they hoped word would get around that the Twelve had fulfilled the prophecy that they would dedicate the site and take leave of their friends on the foundation of the Lord's House, as they set out for the islands of the sea.

Within a few months, several of the brethren would embark upon their missions, but the first order of business for the Saints was to find another place to gather.

Commerce

A land speculator by the name of Galland offered the Mormons a parcel of land about fifty miles north of Quincy, at a place called Commerce—an all but abandoned town set in a swamp, on the Illinois side of the Mississippi. According to Cecil McGavin, "a tract of farm land comprising one hundred and thirty-five acres was purchased from Hugh White for the [sum] of $5000. Dr. Isaac Galland sold his adjoining farm for $9,000. . . . the exiles poured into this new settlement, additional land titles were secured, until a vast belt of virgin soil extending far from the bogs of Commerce, was forced to yield its treasures of grain and hay to the breakers of the wilderness."[43]

This land was purchased on credit, as attested to in a letter written by Galland to a friend on 22 July 1839, describing the deal as well as predicting the eventual expulsion of the Mormons from Illinois. He wrote:

> I disposed of my halfbreed lands (so called because it was gotten originally from the Indians), for about 50 thousand dollars, that is to say $2500 annually for 20 years, and above sales were made to the people called Mormons who were last winter expelled from the state of Missouri by a proclamation from Gov. Boggs of that state, of which brutality and villainy you have probably heard. These people (the Mormons) have also bought out Hugh White and some others, and will probably continue to buy out the settlers in that neighborhood, until they again acquire a sufficient quantity of "honey comb" to induce the

surrounding thieves to rob them again; at which time they will no doubt have to renounce their religion, or submit to a repetition of similar acts of violence, and outrage, as have already been inflicted on them. . . .[44]

Galland was baptized by the Prophet and ordained an elder by him.

The townsite of Commerce was in the middle of a swamp. Young Mosiah Hancock recalled, "The water stank in Commerce because of the many sloughs."[45]

Because of the swampy nature of the place, other people had shunned living there. Joseph recognized the possibilities of the location, although it was not noted for being a healthful area to live. Perhaps the most attractive feature was that nobody else wanted it. Over time, Church members purchased many other tracts of land in the area.

Recalling the move to Commerce, Joseph III said, "We stopped on the way at what I now believe was the Morley settlement near Lima. The record shows that Father and his family left Quincy May 9, arrived at Commerce the following day."[46]

The Prophet and his family moved into a block house on the White farm. Built in 1823 by Captain White, the house had been constructed to serve as the post for the first Indian agency established in Illinois. The hewn-log structure consisted of one room below and one above. There was a summer kitchen at the back of the house which had an oven and fireplace for cooking.

Of his new home, Joseph III wrote, "The Hugh White farm was a veritable plantation. . . . We were comfortably located in our log house. . . . There was a spring near by from which we obtained our drinking water. It issued out from under the hillside on the bank of the river, not far from the large oak tree." Not long after they settled into the log house near the river, Joseph III continued, "Grandfather Joseph Smith and Grandmother Lucy Smith reached the place and were for a time located nearby."[47]

Joseph eventually added a large room to the west and one to the rear of the log structure. This would be their home until 1843. The family always have referred to it as the "Old Homestead."

In Liberty, Joseph had matured in his understanding of temporal and spiritual matters. His escape had been facilitated partly by the growing public sentiment in his favor, as the behavior of Judge King and the antagonists became public. Many people were opposed to the mob rule that drove the Mormons out of Missouri. Although no action was taken to punish the mob or make reparation for the damage done to the Saints, there was no general approval of the actions of the mob.

One of the things Joseph took from Liberty was a vast practical experience which showed him and the Church how committed he and his family were to his sacred mission. The revelation he had received in the jail was to find fulfillment in every aspect.

> The ends of the earth shall inquire after thy name, and fools shall have thee in derision, and hell shall rage against thee, while the pure in heart, and the wise, and the noble, and the virtuous, shall seek counsel, and authority and blessings constantly from under thy hand, and thy people shall never be turned against thee by the testimony of traitors; and although their influence shall cast thee into trouble, and into bars and walls, thou shalt be had in honor, and but for a small moment and thy voice shall be more terrible in the midst of thine enemies, than the fierce lion, because of thy righteousness; and thy God shall stand by thee forever and ever.[48]

Notes

1. The full text of this letter is published in Dean C. Jessee, *The Personal Writings of Joseph Smith* (Salt Lake City: Deseret Book, 1984), pp. 388-413; see also *HC*, 3:289-305. Spelling and punctuation corrected for clarity. The benefit of Dean Jessee's book is that the text is in bold when anything was in Joseph Smith's own handwriting. Because of this advantage, I have cited Jessee rather than *HC* in many instances. The original letter was handwritten, with almost no punctuation, and spelling was phonetic, according to the pronunciation of the person speaking.

2. Jessee, *Personal Writings of Joseph Smith*, p. 400.

3. Ibid.

4. Ibid., p. 391.

5. Ibid. Spelling and punctuation corrected.

6. Ibid. From this we see the context of the Prophet's prayer, now found in Doctrine & Covenants 121.

7. Ibid., p. 393.

8. Ibid., p. 394; italics added.
9. Ibid., p. 397.
10. Ibid., p. 398.
11. Ibid., p. 399.
12. Ibid., p. 401.
13. Ibid., p. 394.
14. Ibid.
15. Letter, Joseph Smith, Jr., to Emma, 21 March 1838.
16. Dean C. Jessee, *Personal Writings of Joseph Smith*, p. 409.
17. Ibid., p. 396.
18. *HC,* 3:307.
19. Ibid.
20. Ibid.
21. Ibid.
22. Ibid.
23. Ibid.
24. *HC,* 3:308.
25. *HC,* 3:306.
26. *HC,* 3:309.
27. *HC,* 3:306.
28. *HC,* 3:314.
29. *HC,* 3:315.
30. *HC,* 3:314.
31. *HC,* 3:319.
32. Ibid.
33. Mary Audentia Smith Anderson, ed., *Memoirs of President Joseph Smith III—1832-1914* (Independence, Mo.: Herald Publishing House, 1979), pp. 4-5.
34. Ibid.
35. Ibid.
36. Ibid.
37. Ibid.
38. Dimick B. Huntington statement, LDS Archives, as quoted in David E. Miller and Della S. Miller, *Nauvoo: The City of Joseph,* p. 26.
39. *HC,* 3:327.
40. *HC,* 3:321 ftnt.
41. Ibid.
42. *HC,* 3:336.
43. E. Cecil McGavin, *Nauvoo the Beautiful* (Salt Lake City: Bookcraft 1972), p. 5.
44. Ibid.
45. Mosiah Hancock Journal, p. 14; typescript copy in possession of author.
46. Joseph Smith III, *Memoirs,* p. 5.
47. Ibid.
48. *HC,* 3:301; see also Doctrine & Covenants 122:1-4.

Joseph Smith, Jr., in his Nauvoo Legion uniform.
Watercolor by Sutcliffe Maudsley. Courtesy of Buddy Youngreen.

CHAPTER 11

Beautiful Resting Place

"It will be a long, lonesome time during my absence from you and nothing but a sense of humanity could have urged me on so great a sacrifice. . . ." (Joseph Smith to Emma)

Emma and Joseph welcomed the Saints who began gathering at Commerce from Quincy and the outlying communities as soon as they learned Joseph was there and proposed to continue the work of building up The Church of Jesus Christ of Latter-day Saints. By the following year the town would be renamed, "Nauvoo," meaning "beautiful resting place," and it would become a fast-growing city, boasting attractive homes, gardens, and businesses.

But during the spring and summer of 1839, many families camped near the Homestead, where they had ready access to the spring, which had good water. Among those who gathered to camp in Joseph and Emma's yard were tried and true friends, including the Whitneys, who had lost everything for the sake of following their faith, and the Knights, who had given Joseph so much support in the early days and had endured the Missouri persecutions. The Partridges, the Woodruffs, the Youngs, the Rigdons, and hundreds of other families whose names deserve mention and acknowledgment also came to settle in various locations along the "halfbreed" tract, which included land in Illinois and across the Mississippi River in Iowa territory as well. One of the first orders of business was to lay out lots in the township, to give every family a spot to call their own.

The new settlers experienced widespread sickness. The boggy terrain bred mosquitos, and many people contracted malaria. The humid climate, with its intense heat in summer and cold in winter, magnified any incidence of lung or bronchial problems. Many who had endured deprivation of proper food, clothing, and bedding also suffered emotional and spiritual stress and succumbed to serious illness. Joseph and Emma moved out of the Homestead into a tent, to make room for the sick who overflowed the house and lay on pallets in the yard. This condition lasted for weeks.

Emma's compassion, manifest in her constant and gentle nursing of the sick, stands out as perhaps the most notable memory her contemporaries had of her. Her older children, Joseph and Julia, also assisted in the care of the sick. The Prophet Joseph, having exhausted himself in helping to care for the sick, fell sick as well, and had to remain in bed for several days. While confined to bed, he meditated upon his situation; then he arose from his bed and began to lay his hands on the sick to bless them in the name of the Lord. Wilford Woodruff records Joseph's going among the sick lying on the bank of the river to the stone house where Sidney Rigdon lived. All along his way, he saw the sick along the bank of the river. He healed all that lay in his path, commanding them "'in the name of the Lord Jesus Christ to arise and be made whole'; and the sick were healed upon every side of him."[1]

He called upon Heber C. Kimball and others to accompany him across the river to Montrose, Iowa Territory. There he found the same conditions. Among the sick he found several of the Twelve Apostles, including President Brigham Young. Healing Brigham, "in the name of the Lord," the two went along and found John Taylor, Wilford Woodruff, and Orson Pratt, who were also living in Montrose. Joseph directed the apostles to come with him, and they witnessed the healing of Elijah Fordham. Brother Fordham was so far gone,

> [He] was unable to speak, his eyes were set in his head like glass, and he seemed to be entirely unconscious of all around him. Joseph held his hand and looked into his eyes in silence for a length of time. A change in the countenance of Brother Fordham was soon perceptible to all present. His sight returned, and upon Joseph asking him if he knew him, he, in a low whisper, answered "Yes." Joseph asked him if he had faith to be healed. He answered, "I fear it is too late; if you had come sooner

I think I would have been healed." The Prophet said, "Do you believe in Jesus Christ?" He answered in a feeble voice, "I do." Joseph then stood erect, still holding his hand in silence several moments. Then he spoke in a very loud voice, saying, "Brother Fordham, I command you, in the name of Jesus Christ, to arise from this bed and be made whole."2

To those present, it seemed that the house shook, and to the astonishment of all, Brother Fordham was immediately made whole. He kicked off the poultices which had been bound upon his feet, and sat up and ate a bowl of bread and milk. After this he followed Joseph to another house, where more healing took place. Believers and nonbelievers observed these events.

As Joseph and the Apostles were waiting for a boat to cross the river, a man who had seen the sick and dying healed told Joseph that he had two children who were very ill, and he asked the Prophet to go with him to heal them. Joseph said he could not go himself, but he would send someone to heal the children. He then asked Wilford Woodruff to go with the man and heal them. He gave Wilford a silk bandanna handkerchief, telling him to use it to wipe the children's faces. Wilford did as he was told, and the children were healed.

There were more sick people than Joseph could visit so he sent the Twelve to visit them and administer to them. Many were healed. The next day, Joseph sent his cousin George A. Smith and his brother Don Carlos up the river to administer to the sick. Obedient to their duty, they went as far as Ebenezer Robinson's house, perhaps a mile or so, blessing the sick along the way by the power of the priesthood. Again, the sick were healed.

By this experience, the power of the priesthood began to take shape in their understanding. Men, women, and children recognized this manifestation of God's power as miraculous.

A Temporary Resting Place

The Latter-day Saints, having been driven out of the land designated by the Lord as the center Stake of Zion, and temporarily forced to abandon the project of building the Lord's House in Jackson

County, Missouri, were disappointed, but cheerful, as they waited for direction from the Lord through the Prophet Joseph. The vision of Zion still hovered, undimmed, in their dreams and hopes. They looked upon Nauvoo as only a temporary resting place for the Saints until they could return to Missouri in peace.

Joseph's house must have been a beehive of activity. There were meetings for establishing the town, meetings with the Twelve concerning Church organization and missionary work (they were still planning to leave for England), meetings for dividing land so every family would have space for a house and garden. There were also letters to write regarding the legal situation Joseph and the other former prisoners faced because of their "escape" in Missouri.[3]

Church history indicates that Joseph was often away from home. Even when he was home, the place was filled with people who had a quest to see the Prophet. His attention was constantly pulled beyond his personal life by the demands of his calling.

What did Emma do with the children to keep them out from underfoot? How did she manage to accomplish her household tasks of laundry, baking, candle making, spinning, weaving, and sewing, with her small house constantly full of people? Although we don't know when, we do know that eventually an addition was added to both front and back, which more than doubled the living space of the Old Homestead. Once again, Emma had a real home of her own. It is doubtful she minded that Joseph's church business was conducted, for the most part, in her kitchen.

One of the letters Joseph dictated on 22 May 1839, with the services of a scribe, was to William W. Phelps, who had been among those who testified against the Prophet and his fellow prisoners before Judge Austin King at Richmond. For some reason, Phelps had begun to show interest in the business affairs of the Saints regarding the property in Missouri. Joseph's response was very curt:

> We would be glad if you can make a living by minding your own affairs; and we desire (so far as you are concerned) to be left to manage ours as well as we can. We would much rather lose our properties than to be molested by such interference; and, as we consider that we have already experienced much over-

officiousness at your hands, concerning men and things pertaining to our concerns, we now request, once [and] for all, that you will avoid all interference in our business or affairs from this time henceforth and forever. Amen. Signed by Joseph Smith, Jun.[4]

Undoubtedly, Emma was aware of his testy feelings toward Phelps and probably agreed with him.

Emma and the children went with Joseph on 15 June to visit Don Carlos and Agnes, who had settled in McDonough County, near the village of Macomb, a considerable distance east of Commerce. On the way, about four miles from Carthage, they met Joseph's brother William and stopped at his house in Plymouth. They went on to Don Carlos' home the next day. While they were there, Samuel arrived with his wife and children. This was the first time these families had been able to indulge in a social visit together since Joseph's release. More than likely Joseph discussed the idea of Don Carlos coming to Commerce to help establish a Church newspaper. The children surely raced about, playing happily, as children will do, while their mothers caught up on all the latest news each had to share.

Joseph Goes to Washington, D.C.

Emma said good-bye to her husband again on 27 October 1839. A group of the brethren were leaving at the same time, some to go on missions, but Joseph, Sidney Rigdon, and Elias Higbee were going to Washington, D.C., to ask the United States government to intervene, hopefully, and make it possible for the Saints to obtain redress from the state of Missouri for the lost property and damage done to the Church members there. Perhaps they hoped they might even be restored to their property in Jackson County.

Emma had spent the winter of 1838-39 in Missouri and Illinois without Joseph. It was a great sacrifice for them both for him to leave again. She received a letter from him, written en route, 9 November, from Springfield, Illinois. Joseph told her:

I shall be filled with constant anxiety about you and the children until I hear from you and in a particular manner little

> Frederick it was so painful to leave him sick. I hope you will
> watch over those tender offsprings in a manner that [is] be-
> coming a mother and [a] saint and try to cultivate their minds
> and learn to read and be sober do not let [them] be exposed to
> the whether to take cold and try to get all the rest you can it will
> be a long and lonesome time during my absence from you and
> nothing but a sense of humanity could have urged me on so
> great a sacrifice. . . . [5]

There is no indication that she ever allowed herself to behave in a way that would have given the children the impression she was dissatisfied with their father and his ministry. Joseph's travels were something they had all come to accept. Young Joseph seems to recall that winter as a fairly comfortable and pleasant time. On one occasion, the brethren drove a herd of wild pigs into town and slaughtered them, giving each family a supply of meat.[6]

Meanwhile, Joseph had an interesting adventure on his way to Washington. Sidney Rigdon started out on the trip, but fell ill and was unable to travel. Joseph and Elias Higbee continued their journey by stage, as they had appointments to keep.

One day, the driver left the stage to go into a tavern. For some reason the horses ran away, with the passengers still inside the coach. Joseph climbed out of the driverless coach and up to the front. He got hold of the reins and stopped the horses, thus preventing a serious accident. His courageous actions brought sincere appreciation from his fellow passengers. There happened to be some members of Congress in the stage at the time, and some of them thought the heroic deed should be mentioned in their congressional meeting. However, according to Joseph, "on inquiring my name, to mention as the author of their safety, and finding it to be Joseph Smith the 'Mormon Prophet,' as they called me, I heard no more of their praise, gratitude, or reward."[7]

The Prophet Meets the President of the United States

On 29 November, Joseph and Elias met with President Van Buren. After they related the purpose of their visit, he said, "What can I do? I can do nothing for you! If I do anything, I shall come in contact with the whole state of Missouri."[8] He certainly had no intention of damaging his re-election chances by siding with an unpopular religious group, so, in effect, he simply washed his hands of them.

The Prophet Visits Congress

Failing to obtain any support from President Van Buren, they prepared to go before Congress on 7 December 1839. They wrote to Hyrum reporting on the congressional meetings. Emma undoubtedly read this letter, which reveals Joseph's sarcastic disgust, cloaked in humor: "There is a great deal of wind blown off on the occasion on each day. . . . There is such an itching disposition to display their oratory on the most trivial occasion—and so much etiquette, bowing and scraping, twisting and turning, to make a display of their witticisms."[9]

Joseph felt he had made a respectable presentation of the facts, setting before Congress the injuries they had sustained and the fact that they had been refused proper judiciary protection by the governor of Missouri. Most of the congressmen listened with interest and some sympathy. They requested affidavits be sent regarding Joseph and others being refused the privilege of habeas corpus by the authorities in Missouri. Joseph asked in his letter to Hyrum that all who had endured persecution in Missouri should make affidavits and send them to Washington as quickly as possible.[10]

He also asked Hyrum if they could raise some money to help him remain in Washington until he and Higbee could accomplish what they had gone there to do. Hyrum issued a call for financial help, but nobody had any money. He was at last able to obtain assistance from Church members at Quincy. Among those who pledged financial assistance was William Law, who had arrived the previous fall with a large number of converts from Canada.

On 6 December, Emma wrote to inform Joseph of various situations. She told of people coming and going at their house. She was forthright in explaining about sicknesses the children and others had overcome. She must have dreaded telling Joseph of the death of their good friend, and Joseph's clerk, James Mulholland. She reported that Hyrum had put Robert B. Thompson in his place as clerk, but didn't see him getting much done. She relayed a request from Don Carlos asking Joseph where he could find a letter with names and addresses of subscribers for the newspaper, *Times and Seasons*. She told him his parents were doing fairly well and related news of goings-on in Missouri.

Emma concludes, "There is great anxiety manifest in this place for your prosperity; and the time lingers long that is set for your return. The day is wandering, and night is approaching so fast, that I must reserve my better feelings until I have a better chance to express them. Yours affectionately, Emma."[11] She must have hastened to close her letter as candles were scarce. Everything was scarce. She does not mention in her letter that she is expecting a baby; we have no idea whether Joseph knew.

A month later, Hyrum wrote to Joseph on 3 January 1840: "The Mississippi is frozen up. The weather is very cold, and a great quantity of snow is on the ground, and has been for some time. Your family is in tolerable good health, excepting one or two having the chills occasionally."[12]

The Prophet Preaches in Philadelphia

Having nothing to do but wait until he had the necessary affidavits to submit to Congress, Joseph went to Philadelphia, where he visited many members of the Church and preached to large congregations. A man who attended one of the Prophet's sermons reported in a letter to his wife:

> I went last evening to hear "Joe Smith," the celebrated Mormon, expound his doctrine. . . . He is not an educated man; but he is a plain, sensible, strong minded man. Everything he says, is said in a manner to leave an impression that he is sincere. There is no levity, no fanaticism, no want of dignity in his deportment. He is apparently from forty to forty-five years of age, rather above the middle stature, and what you ladies would call a very good looking man. In his garb there are no peculiarities; his dress being that of a plain, unpretending citizen. He is by profession a farmer, but is evidently well read.[13]

On 20 January, Joseph wrote to Emma, saying, "I am making all hast[e] to arrange my business to start home I feel very anxious to see you all once more in this world, the time seems long that I am deprived of your society. . . . I pray God to spare you until I get home my dear Emma my heart is entwined around you and those little ones. . . ."[14]

Missionary Work Goes On

While Joseph was in Washington, the work of the Church was going forward under the direction of Hyrum, who was co-president, having taken the place of Oliver Cowdery.

The first issue of the *Times and Seasons* was printed in November 1839. The Twelve were on missions in England, and many others were preaching the gospel throughout the United States and Canada. Not only did the men consent to being called on missions, they performed them well, and the women consented to their husbands leaving. Many times the women provided their own support and even tried to send their husbands a few dollars to help them on their missions. In spite of the privations, persecution, and difficulties they had endured, the Saints took the command to take the message of the restored gospel to all people more seriously than they took their own livelihood.

Bad News from Washington

On 26 February 1840, Elias Higbee wrote from Washington that the decision of Congress was against them; they would not act on the petitions until the Missouri legislature had acted upon them—and the Missouri legislature refused to act on any petitions for redress for the Mormons. It was a standoff, with both Missouri and the U.S. Congress. Having done all he could, Higbee wrote: "I feel a conscience void of offense towards God and man in this matter. . . . I have discharged my duties here. . . . I feel now that we have made our last appeal to all earthly tribunals; that we should now put our whole trust in the God of Abraham, Isaac, and Jacob. We have a right now which we could not heretofore so fully claim—that is, of asking God for redress and redemption, as they have been refused us by man. Elias Higbee"[15]

When Joseph returned on 4 March 1840, he had little time for a peaceful reunion with Emma and the children. There were many challenges for him to meet—the chief one being that he needed a faithful scribe and clerk. The entry recorded in *The History of the Church* on the day of Joseph's return makes no mention of his wife or children:

> I arrived safely at Nauvoo, after a wearisome journey, through alternate snow and mud, having witnessed many vexatious movements in government officers, whose sole object should be the peace and prosperity and happiness of the whole people; but instead of this, I discovered that popular clamor and personal aggrandizement were the ruling principles of those in authority; and my heart faints within me when I see, by the visions of the Almighty, the end of this nation, if she continues to disregard the cries and petitions of her virtuous citizens, as she has done, and is now doing.[16]

Joseph was heartsick at the evidence he had seen in Washington, of the same spirit of what he called "popular clamor and personal aggrandizement," which seemed to rule there as it had in Missouri. In this, he foresaw danger to this nation. As for President Martin Van Buren, Joseph felt obligated to influence anyone he could, against supporting him in future elections.

Nauvoo City Charter

Notwithstanding this gloomy prediction, the next few months proved to be good ones for the family and the Church. No effort was spared in building a secure place for the Saints. For Joseph, this meant a broad city charter. This charter was drafted with the help of a new convert, John C. Bennett, who boasted considerable knowledge and skill in city and state government. At the end of 1840, Bennett carried the petition for a city charter to the legislature in Springfield, where it passed without opposition.

Times and Seasons announced the incorporation of the City of Nauvoo on 16 December 1840. This incorporation allowed them to have a militia, which was called the Nauvoo Legion, and to establish the University of the City of Nauvoo.

Joseph took full responsibility for the contents of the Charter, saying, "The city Charter of Nauvoo is of my own plan and device. I concocted it for the salvation of the Church, and on principles so broad, that every honest man might dwell secure under its protective influence without distinction of sect or party."[17]

Joseph's new scribe, Howard Coray, who was hired in April 1840, was there when the charter was being prepared and attested to the inspired nature of the charter: "I was seated . . . six or eight feet on Joseph's left side, so I could look almost squarely into the side of his eye. The Spirit of God descended upon him, and a measure of it upon me, insomuch that I could fully realize that God, or the Holy Ghost, was talking through him. I never, neither before or since, have felt as I did on that occasion. . . . Joseph dictated much of the charter. I could overhear the instruction he gave Bennett and I know it was gotten up mainly as Joseph required."[18]

For Emma, his hiring Howard Coray would add to her household. One day while he and Joseph were joking together, Joseph had pretended to trip the young man and when Coray fell, he broke his leg. Joseph took Coray into his own house and nursed him until the leg was healed. Despite his injury, he must have been a boon to Joseph, for he was faithful and efficient in his duties as scribe. He wrote Joseph's letters and worked to get Joseph's history up to date. Coray was both scribe and friend. He took dictation during revelations and testified to the inspired manner of Joseph's leadership in defining the plans for the city of Nauvoo.

A New Baby for Emma—New Growth for the Church

On 13 June 1840, Emma gave birth to her seventh child, a son whom they named Don Carlos after Joseph's youngest brother. This baby brought immense comfort to Emma and to the whole family. Everyone delighted in watching him grow. Contrary to the popular pronunciation used for this name, the family pronounced the name "Don Carloss." In the case of Joseph's brother, the family sometimes abridged it to just "Carloss."

One year after they moved to Commerce, the city, now called Nauvoo, was granted its charter during the session of the Illinois legislature. A young representative from Springfield, Abraham Lincoln, went to the podium to publicly congratulate Bennett on the passage of the bill, which Joseph felt would protect the legal rights of the Saints in the future.[19]

With the adoption of this liberal charter,[20] Nauvoo was ready to grow; peace and harmony were in the air, hope and prosperity on the horizon. As missionaries went throughout the world preaching the message of the restored gospel of Jesus Christ, branches were built up throughout the United States, and converts flocked to the city from the British Isles, Europe, and Canada. There was a bustle of building all over the city. The European converts brought their architectural and building skills, their culture and their education.

Statesmen and politicians visited Nauvoo, curious to see what was going on at the bend of the Mississippi, on the outer edge of the country. One notable man, Stephen A. Douglas, called to see the Prophet. When their conversation turned to the future political ambitions of Douglas, Joseph told him the time would come when Douglas would aspire to the office of president of the United States. Joseph prophesied that if, when that time came, he should turn against the Saints, he would fail in his political desires. That time did come, and he did fail.

Joseph himself knew the secret of successful government. One time when he was asked how he governed so diverse a people, coming from so many different countries with their peculiar manners and customs, he responded, "I teach them the *truth* and they govern themselves."[21]

Inspired Translations

At last, surrounded by faithful friends and protected by the charter which provided for a local court system and a well trained and loyal militia, Joseph was able to pick up the threads of his prophetic calling. His ability to make a new start, without losing ground in his work, was largely due to Emma, who had preserved many of his important papers and manuscripts, as she fled from Missouri.

Now, with a peaceful society in which to work, the Prophet freely expressed himself in public addresses, and in counsel with the brethren who had been tried by fire along with him. In this atmosphere, the doctrines of the gospel began to distill upon the Church.

One of the ongoing projects he tackled at this time was translating the Book of Abraham from the scrolls he obtained with the Egyptian mummies. The text opened up new knowledge of God and his kingdom.

He was also expanding his understanding of the mission of the Savior, Jesus Christ; and in his study of the New Testament, he was discovering doctrines that had been lost or dropped from modern Christianity, which now were to be restored and made available. The plan of salvation was unfolding in wonderful ways.

Baptism for the Dead

One of the doctrines introduced was baptism for the dead. Joseph first taught the doctrine on 15 August 1840, during a funeral sermon for an old friend and associate, Seymor Brunson.

During the sermon he read from 1 Corinthians chapter 15, in which the Apostle Paul was teaching the principle of a literal resurrection to people who had long been practicing the rite of baptism for the dead, but who had not believed in resurrection, i.e., the literal reuniting of the spirit and the body, as Jesus was raised from the dead. Joseph reiterated that Jesus taught that man must be born of water and of the spirit in order to enter the kingdom of heaven. Since baptism is essential, there must be provision made for those who would die without having had the benefit of receiving this ordinance. Joseph taught that people could now act for their friends who had departed from this life, by being baptized in their behalf.

Shortly after delivering this sermon, Joseph wrote to Brigham Young, Heber C. Kimball, and the other apostles who were in England, informing them of the doctrine:

> I presume the doctrine of baptism for the dead has ere this reached your ears, and may have raised some inquiries in your minds. . . . It was certainly practiced by the ancient Churches; and St. Paul endeavors to prove the doctrine of the resurrection

> from the same, and says, "Else what shall they do which are baptized for the dead if the dead rise not at all, why then are they baptized for the dead?". . . You will undoubtedly see its consistency and reasonableness; and it presents the Gospel of Christ in probably a more enlarged scale than some have imagined it. . . .[22]

The people were so exuberant about being able to be baptized for their dead relatives, they rushed to the river and began to perform the baptisms.

Wilford Woodruff records that the brethren barely had time to eat or rest, since they were constantly in the river, baptizing people for their loved ones who had died. However, in their enthusiasm, they failed to get proper direction. Men were baptized for women and women for men. Due to the chaos that could result, Joseph was given direction to instruct them and clarify the procedure. He told them there must be a witness, and a record must be kept. The ordinance was to be performed by those who held the priesthood, and those being baptized could only do so for those of their own sex. [23]

Emma Baptized for Her Deceased Relatives

Emma was among those who were baptized at the first, before the clarification was given. She had received word that both her parents had died, so she was baptized for her father, uncle, mother, and sister as well as several aunts. Afterward, the baptisms for the men were performed again.[24]

Joseph taught, "Seeking after our dead is the most important responsibility we have to perform in this life." He insisted that "if we neglect it, it is at the peril of our own salvation."[25] Throughout the remainder of his life Joseph often touched on the subject of salvation for the dead, in sermons and in conversations.

Although there seems to be no direct statement by Emma concerning this doctrine, in later years, her son, Alexander, not only believed in the doctrine, but found consolation in it. When his brother Frederick died without having been baptized, Alexander, recognizing the scriptural insistence that baptism was essential, suffered agony of spirit concerning his brother's eternal fate. Alexander had studied the revelations given to his father, and he prayed about the problem. In his personal history, Alexander said that peace came to him and that he received a spiritual reassurance that the time would come "when baptism may be secured . . ." for Frederick.[26] His mother, having herself participated in the ordinance of baptism for the dead, could not have discouraged him in such a hope. However, Alexander did not live to see this work accomplished.[27]

Emma at the Building of Temples

During Joseph and Emma's life together, the Church dedicated at least five temple sites. Two temples were built and cornerstones were laid for two more. In Nauvoo, the temple site was dedicated on 6 April 1841.[28] The pomp and circumstance of uniform, rank, and file gave the event a distinctly military flavor. The following description of the militia's maneuvers is found in the *Times and Seasons* of 15 April 1841: "At half past 9 o'clock A.M. Lieutenant-General Smith with his guard, staff and field officers, arrived at the ground, and were presented with a beautiful silk national flag, by the Ladies of Nauvoo, which was respectfully received and hailed by the firing of cannon, and borne off by Colonel Robinson, the Cornet, to the appropriate position in the line; after which the Lieutenant-General with his suite passed the lines in review."[29]

We are not informed which ladies of Nauvoo carried the flag. Perhaps Emma was one of them. Artists who have painted representations of the scene portray Emma wearing a black riding dress and a feather-plumed hat, while riding on a white horse. Joseph III said his mother rode their black horse at parades and that she wore her veil thrown back. Jesse N. Smith recalled that Emma and Eliza R. Snow were among the "bevy of mounted ladies elegantly gowned and very attractive when they appeared upon the parade ground upon the parade day and were assigned places of honor."[30]

Building a New Temple, Building the Kingdom of God

At the Church conference held 2 October, Joseph declared that baptism for the dead was no longer to be performed in the river. A

temporary baptismal font was built in the basement area of the
temple site. Situated under the area for the main hall of the temple, it
was made of laminated pine. Under the font, there were twelve oxen
carved out of wood, on which the bowl of the font was placed. It took
eight months to complete. The water was supplied from a thirty-foot
well in the east end of the basement.[31]

One can visualize Emma and Joseph walking arm in arm in the
peaceful city. Did they watch the process of the artisans carving oxen
for the baptismal font and quietly talk about the skill of the workmen
and the time when it would be completed at last? As they strolled
around the temple lot, visiting with the workmen, did Emma touch
the cool stone face of the sunstone, smoothing the surface with her
hand, marveling, wondering what was coming in the future?
Imagining how it was for Emma and Joseph gives personal significance to such little sentences as "Rode to the temple grounds with
Emma," or "Today Emma and I walked out around the temple and
visited with the workmen."

A Time of Reconciliation

In June, Joseph received a letter from William W. Phelps, from
Dayton, Ohio. Phelps had come to the point that he felt he should
repent. "I am as the prodigal son," he wrote, "I never doubt or disbe-
lieve the fulness of the Gospel. . . . I have seen the folly of my way,
and I tremble at the gulf I have passed. . . . I will repent and live, and
ask my old friends to forgive me." This letter was accompanied by a
plea in Phelps' behalf, signed by Orson Hyde and John E. Page,
addressed to Hyrum, Joseph and Sidney.[32]

On 22 July 1840, Joseph replied. While making plain the depth
of pain Phelps had caused, he yet reopened the door for Phelps to
return. "When we read your letter, truly our hearts melted. . . . It is
true we have suffered much in consequence of your behavior. The cup
of gall, already full enough . . . was indeed filled to overflowing, when
you turned against us. . . . However, the cup has been drunk. The will
of the Father has been done, and we are yet alive, for which we thank
the Lord. . . . Believing your confession to be real and your repentance genuine, I shall be happy once again to give you the right hand

of fellowship and rejoice over the returning prodigal. . . . Come, dear brother, since the war is past. For friends at first are friends at last. Yours as ever, Joseph Sm. Jun."[33]

Phelps returned, was baptized, and thereafter, humbly and joyfully lent his energy and considerable talent to helping build up the Church.

Another prodigal, Frederick G. Williams, had found himself excommunicated when he arrived at Quincy in March 1839. He came before the conference and humbly acknowledged his errors. He was accepted back with a unanimous vote of the congregation, and was rebaptized.

Frederick and Rebecca had been living in Quincy, but frequently went to Nauvoo to visit the Prophet and his family. Finally they moved to Nauvoo and were once again neighbors to the Smiths. Frederick G. Williams died in 1842. Rebecca and her youngest son, Ezra lived for a time in the Mansion house. They eventually went to Utah and settled in Salt Lake City.

Death of Loved Ones

Father Smith, the Patriarch, died 14 September 1840 and was laid to rest in the yard by the Old Homestead.[34] This greatly beloved man was mourned by hundreds of men and women who had known him as a kind and gentle friend. Robert Thompson addressed the crowd who attended the funeral:

> A Father in Israel is gone. The man whom we have been accustomed to look up to as a Patriarch, a Father and a Counsellor. . . . If ever there was a man who had claims on the affections of [this] community, it was [Joseph Smith, Sr.,] . . . a man faithful to his God and to the Church in every situation, and under all circumstances . . . called like the Patriarchs of old, to leave the land of his nativity, to journey in strange lands, and become subject to all the trials and persecutions which have been heaped upon the Saints. . . . Like the apostle Paul he could exclaim (and his life and conduct have fully borne out the sentiment), None of these things move me, neither count I my life dear, so that I may finish my course with joy.

> . . . The life of our departed Father has indeed been an
> eventful one, having to take a conspicuous part in the great work
> of the last days; being designated by the ancient prophets, who
> once dwelt on this continent, as the Father of him, whom the Lord
> had promised to raise up in the last days; to lead his people. . . .

Thompson went on to recount the privations suffered due to persecution, recalling that at the time Joseph and Hyrum were taken prisoner at Far West, Father Smith's "constitution received a shock from which it never recovered . . . broken in constitution and in health, and since then he has labored under severe affliction and pain."

He praised his father's character and the unique privilege of being the father of the Lord's Prophet, called to bring forth the latter-day restoration, and being the father of a stalwart and loyal family. "Father Smith," he said, "by a uniform, consistent, and virtuous course, for a long series of years, has proved himself worthy of such a son, and such a family, by whom he had the happiness of being surrounded in his dying moments; most of whom had the satisfaction of receiving his dying benediction."[35]

Father Smith was attended at his death by his entire family, to whom he bid a tender farewell, and gave each a last blessing. These blessings are recorded by his mother in her book, *History of the Prophet Joseph Smith by His Mother.*[36] They are instructive to modern readers, giving an intimate perspective on the individual acts and personality of Joseph's brothers and sisters, as well as his father and mother.

Emma's association with this family places her in intimate contact with all the events related in Lucy's history. Emma's feelings must have been especially poignant in respect to Father Smith's passing, since after leaving Pennsylvania, Joseph's parents and brothers and sisters were as her own family.

Almost a year later, in August 1841, a twofold sorrow came to the family. On 7 August, Joseph's beloved brother, Don Carlos, died after what is believed to be a brief bout with pneumonia. Emma's feelings could not have been deeper if he had been her own brother. She had known him since he was nine years old, and he had lived with them from time to time over the years. His care over Emma and the children from the Kirtland exodus to Joseph's imprisonment and extended trip to Washington, D.C., had been constant. His death at age twenty-five left his widow, Agnes, and his two little girls, Sophronia and Josephine, to be watched over by Emma and Joseph. A baby daughter had preceded him in death.[37]

There was not time to properly mourn this brother's passing before they were stricken again. Joseph's history for Sunday, 15 August 1841, contains the heartbreaking statement: "My infant son, Don Carlos, died, aged 14 months, 2 days."[38]

A few days after the baby's death, another dear friend, Robert Thompson, who had served as Joseph's scribe as well as editor of *Times and Seasons*, also died. Robert's wife, Mercy, was the sister of Hyrum's wife, Mary. His death was as that of a brother to the entire family.

These deaths not only saddened them; their occurrence left a heavy burden upon Joseph. The *Times and Seasons* was without an editor. Sickness was a continual problem in Nauvoo. Many widows and orphans needed to be cared for.

Years later, Emma, speaking of the death of her baby, Don Carlos, said this was the hardest loss she sustained because she had had him longer than the other babies she had lost, and all the family had learned to love him so much.

The Nauvoo Legion

In spite of their great sorrow, the work of the kingdom of God was going forward on the earth. Joseph often preached to large numbers of people "on the green," a large grassy area down the hill from the temple site. A stand had been built from which speakers could be seen and heard by the vast crowds who gathered in the open air to receive instruction and counsel from their Prophet and other leaders in the Church.

The Legion marched in parade, trained, and drilled on the green. According to the Legion report, there were 1,490 men in the Nauvoo Legion in 1841.[39] After all Joseph had endured at the hands of unrighteous militia, he took great delight in the Nauvoo Legion. Such city militia units made up the nation's military in those days. Each city organized its own unit, under state commission. Nauvoo city officers had applied for and were granted a state commission. There was no military officer in the state who outranked Joseph. He held the rank of lieutenant-general. He took seriously the task of drilling and training the Legion, which lent him a sense of security he had not heretofore enjoyed.

Saints Abandon Kirtland

Some of the brethren who had sacrificed a great deal in order to build the temple in Kirtland wondered if they might return there now that things were more peaceful. Hyrum's response to this has proved to be prophetic. All the Saints dwelling in Kirtland and surrounding area were counseled to come to Nauvoo and build the temple. Said Hyrum, in due time the Lord "will send forth and build up Kirtland." He also promised that after many years, their children would "possess the land of Kirtland and build it up again."[40]

The command to abandon Kirtland now brought those faithful Saints who had remained there to Nauvoo. More than a hundred years would pass before Hyrum's prophecy would come true. It is literally coming to pass in our day as congregations of the Latter-day Saints have been reestablished in Kirtland.

The Foundation Increases

Almost over night, the mosquito-infested swamp town of Commerce, Illinois, had become a thriving city, worthy of its name, "Nauvoo," which as stated earlier, means "beautiful resting place." And it was a beautiful place. Under the protection of the hospitable Illinois government, the Saints prospered in business, in society, and in spirit. John C. Bennett was mayor of Nauvoo. William Marks was stake president. There were many bishops to care for the poor and administer the various wards, or congregations, in Nauvoo, and in the surrounding areas where the Saints had settled, both in Iowa and Illinois. The poor were cared for by providing everyone with a means for making a living.

There were fewer disputes than there had been in Far West. A humbled and eager people listened to the description of their duties and for a time at least, the work prospered without men seeking to aggrandize themselves or accuse each other as they had in Missouri.

The Council of the Twelve Apostles was once again complete, consisting of Brigham Young, Heber C. Kimball, Parley P. Pratt, Orson Hyde, William Smith, Orson Pratt, John E. Page, Willard Richards, Lyman Wight, Wilford Woodruff, John Taylor, and George A. Smith.

In the First Presidency, William Law and Sidney Rigdon were counselors, and Joseph and Hyrum were co-presidents of the Church.

On 24 January 1841, Hyrum was sustained as Patriarch to the Church to succeed his father, holding "the sealing blessings of [Christ's] Church, even the Holy Spirit of promise, whereby ye are sealed up unto the day of redemption."[41]

With the quorums of the Church finally functioning as they were intended, the Twelve were free to go abroad and preach the gospel of Jesus Christ. The Seventies, who were appointed as missionaries to the world, took up their duties. Joseph was unanimously elected Trustee-in-Trust of The Church of Jesus Christ of Latter-day Saints in January of 1841.[42]

In the fall of 1841, Orson Hyde went to the Holy Land, and on 24 October, he dedicated that land for the return of the Jews to their homeland. He wrote of his sacred experience of kneeling on the Mount of Olives to offer his prayer; his letter describing these things must have been read with great joy by Emma as well as Joseph and the brethren.[43]

Indeed, there was cause for great rejoicing; but as the year 1841 closed, it became apparent that political issues would once again be a trouble spot for the Saints. John Taylor wrote:

> There were always two parties, the Whigs and Democrats, and we could not vote for one without offending the other; and it not infrequently happened that candidates for office would place the issue of their election upon opposition to the "Mormons," in order to gain political influence from religious prejudice, in which case the "Mormons" were compelled, in self-defense to vote against them, which resulted almost invariably against our opponents.[44]

Joseph Duncan campaigned for the office of governor on the platform that if elected, he would exterminate or drive the Mormons from the state. Naturally, the Mormons voted en masse for Ford.

If only Emma's view of events passing at this time were available! It may be surmised that she was occupied in the usual pursuits of a wife and mother in an era prior to any modern conveniences. She may have worried about Joseph Duncan's campaign threats, or she and Joseph may have joked about them. The Prophet named his horse "Joe Duncan" for reasons known only to himself.

As the campaign rhetoric heated up, newspaper articles against the Latter-day Saints began to appear throughout the country. Thomas Sharp of the *Warsaw Signal* was especially hostile. Some of the brethren suggested they should buy him out, but Joseph said to let him alone because "the more lies he prints the sooner he will get through."[45]

Joseph's Letter to the Editor[46]

Not all the presses were anti-Mormon. John Wentworth, editor of the *Chicago Democrat,* wrote to Nauvoo requesting that the Prophet write a "sketch of the rise, progress, persecution and faith of the Latter-day Saints."

On 1 March, a concise history of Joseph's life, his vision, his calling to preach the gospel "in power, unto all nations that people might be prepared for the millennial reign [of Christ]" was printed. He said, "I was chosen to be an instrument in the hands of God to bring about His purposes in this glorious dispensation." He told of his bringing forth the Book of Mormon and recounted the persecutions they had suffered, at the same time putting them in perspective, and ended with thirteen statements of belief which would become known in future generations as "The Articles of Faith."

Quoted here is part of this letter:

> Persecution has not stopped the progress of the truth. . . . Elders of the Church [have] gone forth and planted the Gospel in almost every state of the Union, . . . England, Scotland and Wales, . . . Germany, Palestine, New Holland, the East Indies, and other places.
>
> The standard of truth has been erected: no unhallowed hand can stop the work from progressing, persecution may rage, mobs may combine, armies may assemble, calumny may defame, but

the truth of God will go forth boldly, nobly, and independently til it has penetrated every continent. . . .

We believe in God the Eternal Father, and in his son Jesus Christ, and in the Holy Ghost.

We believe that men will be punished for their own sins and not for Adam's transgression.

We believe that through the atonement of Christ all mankind may be saved by obedience to the laws and ordinances of the Gospel.

We believe that these ordinances are 1st, Faith in the Lord Jesus Christ; 2d, Repentance; 3d, Baptism by immersion for the remission of sins; 4th, Laying on of hands for the gift of the Holy Ghost.

We believe that a man must be called of God by prophesy, and by laying on of hands by those who are in authority to preach the gospel and administer in the ordinances thereof.

We believe in the same organization that existed in the primitive Church, viz: apostles, prophets, pastors, teachers, evangelists &c.

We believe in the gift of tongues, prophesy, revelations, visions, healing, interpretation of tongues &c.

We believe the Bible to be the word of God as far as it is translated correctly; we also believe the Book of Mormon to be the word of God.

We believe all that God has revealed, all that he does now reveal, and we believe that he will yet reveal many great and important things pertaining to the kingdom of God.

We believe in the literal gathering of Israel and in the restoration of the Ten Tribes. That Zion (the New Jerusalem) will be built on the American continent; that Christ will reign personally upon the earth, and that the earth will be renewed and receive its paradisaic glory.

We claim the privilege of worshiping Almighty God according to the dictates of our conscience, and allow all men the same privilege, let them worship how, where, or what they may.

We believe in being subject to kings, presidents, rulers, and magistrates, in obeying, honoring and sustaining the law.

We believe in being honest, true, chaste, benevolent, virtuous, and in doing good to all men; indeed we may say that we follow the admonition of Paul "we believe all things we hope all things," we have endured many things and hope to be able to endure all things. If there is anything virtuous, lovely, or of good report or praiseworthy we seek after these things. Respectfully &c.

JOSEPH SMITH

Notes

1. *HC,* 4:3-5, taken from Wilford Woodruff, *Leaves from My Journal,* chapter 19.

2. Ibid

3. *HC,* 3:353-55.

4. *HC,* 3:358-59.

5. Joseph Smith, Letter to Emma, 9 November 1839.

6. *HC,* 4:52, Hyrum Smith, Letter to Joseph.

7. *HC,* 4:2-24.

8. *HC,* 4:40

9. Ibid.

10. *HC,* 4:39-49.

11. Emma Smith letter to Joseph (printed in *Saints' Herald,* December 1879 p. 352). I am indebted to Richard L. Anderson for this information.

12. *HC,* 4:50-53.

13. *HC,* 4:78; Matthew S. Davis, Letter to wife, Mary, 6 February 1840.

14. Joseph Smith Letter, 26 February 1840; see *HC,* 4:88.

15. *HC,* 4:88.

16. *HC,* 4:89.

17. *HC,* 4:248-49. Some historians have given John C. Bennett credit for having drafted the Charter, and undoubtedly he did help. Bennett's skills were good, but his ethics were not. He apparently made private "deals" with men of both the Whig and Democrat parties, implying or even promising the Mormon vote if they passed the bill. Since they all thought they were going to receive this vote, the bill passed without investigation. Thus, when election time came and the Mormons voted, the losers felt betrayed.

18. *HC,* 4:133-35. Howard Coray and his wife Martha remained steadfast friends; later Martha helped Lucy Smith prepare the manuscript of her *History of the Prophet Joseph Smith.* She was assigned to this task by Brigham Young. It was also printed by the RLDS Church, under the title, *Joseph Smith and His Progenitors for Many Generations* in 1912 (Lamoni, Iowa) and reprinted by Herald Publishing House (Independence, Mo.) in 1969.

19. "Lincoln . . . had the magnanimity to vote for our act, and came forward, after the final vote, to the bar of the house, and cordially congratulated [Bennett] on its passage" *Times and Seasons,* 1 January, 1841, p. 267.

20. *HC,* 4:239-49.

21. In Hyrum L. Andrus and Helen Mae Andrus, *They Knew the Prophet* (Salt Lake City: Bookcraft, 1974), p.134.

22. Dean C. Jessee, *The Personal Writings of Joseph Smith* (Salt Lake City: Deseret Book, 1984), p. 486.

23. Wilford Woodruff, *History of His Life and Labors* (Salt Lake City: Bookcraft, 1964), p. 165.

24. Nauvoo Temple Records, LDS Archives.

25. Andrew Ehat and Lyndon Cook, *The Words of Joseph Smith* (Provo, Utah: Religious Studies Center Brigham Young University, 1980), pp. 106-107.

26. Inez Davis, "Alexander Hale Smith," unpublished family history, pp. 5-6. Typescript copy in author's possession. Original in RLDS Archives.

27. Ibid. The LDS Church performs this ordinance in the temples. Frederick was baptized by proxy in 1971 at the Cardston Temple, at the request of Gracia N. Jones.

28. *HC,* 4:326-31.

29. *Times and Seasons,* 15 April 1841.

30. See Jesse N. Smith, *Six Decades in the Early West: The Journal of Jesse Nathaniel Smith, 1834- 1906,* ed. by Oliver R. Smith (Provo, Utah: Jesse N. Smith Family Association, 1970), 3rd ed. Thanks to David Boone for this entry.

31. *HC,* 4:446-47.

32. *HC,* 4:141.

33. *HC,* 4:163-64.

34. Lucy Smith, *History of the Prophet Joseph Smith By His Mother,* ed. Preston Nibley (Salt Lake City: Bookcraft, 1958), p. 314 ftnt.

35. *Times and Seasons,* vol. 1:171, for funeral of Joseph Smith, Sr.

36. Lucy Mack Smith, *History of the Prophet Joseph Smith By His Mother,* pp. 308-14.

37. See Smith genealogy. Database in author's possession.

38. *HC,* 4:402.

39. *HC,* 4:415.

40. Pearson H. Corbett, *Hyrum Smith, Patriarch* (Salt Lake City: Deseret Book, 1963), p. 262; see also Doctrine & Covenants 124:83.

41. *HC,* 4:284; see also Doctrine & Covenants 124:91-96.

42. *HC,* 4:286. This confused the legal title of property and would be the source of financial difficulties for Emma, after Joseph was killed.

43. *HC,* 4:114; dedication prayer is found *HC,* 4:454-59.

44. *HC,* 4:481.

45. *HC,* 4:487.

46. Jessee, *Personal Writings of Joseph Smith,* pp. 218-20.

A

Book of Records

Containing
the proceedings
of
The Female Relief Society of Nauvoo.

The following appropriate frontispiece
was found lying on an open Bible, in the room
appropriated for the Society; at its first meeting
(Written on a scrap.)

"O, Lord! help our widows, and fatherless
children! So mote it be. Amen. With
the sword, and the word of truth, defend
thou them. So mote it be. Amen."

This Book
was politely presented to the Society by
Elder W. Richards;
on the 17th of March, A.D 1842

Photocopy of the title page of the original Nauvoo Relief Society minute book.
Courtesy of LDS Archives.

CHAPTER 12

The Time of Fulfillment

"[Emma] was a woman of great prominence among the people: Large and well proportioned, of splendid physique, dark complexion, with piercing eyes that seemingly looked through; noble in appearance and bearing and certainly favored of the Lord, who called upon her to prepare the first hymn book of the [Latter-day Saints], and by revelation styled her the 'Elect Lady.'" (Woman's Exponent, 1908 [vol. 36, no. 7])

Emma's immediate future might be described as the best of times and the worst of times, blended subtly together in what turned out to be the last three years she and Joseph would have together in this life.

Massive construction projects were planned for Nauvoo, including the temple, a hotel to be called the Nauvoo House, a mansion for the Prophet and his family, and a store building. This store, sometimes referred to as the Red Brick Store, was so called because its entire interior was painted a true brick-red color. The Prophet hoped the store would provide a decent living for his family. It was in the upstairs room over this store, that Emma's calling as an "elect lady" came to fruition; and it was the place wherein Joseph would administer sacred ordinances to the brethren.

A Stillborn Son

On 6 February 1842, Emma suffered another disappointment, giving birth to a stillborn son. We have no information concerning this event other than her record of it in their family Bible and a vague reference in family correspondence. There were other pressing events unfolding in which Emma would become actively involved.

Organization of the Women

Early in 1842 some of the women in Nauvoo recognized a need for the women of the Church to organize themselves. Sarah Kimball, wife of Hiram Kimball, was young, wealthy, and idealistic. She wanted to provide material for the sisters to make clothing for the men laboring on the temple. Women who could not afford the materials could give their time and sewing skills, so everyone would benefit. Several women urged this plan, and Eliza R. Snow was asked to write a set of by-laws to take to the Prophet and see if he approved.[1]

Eliza wrote the by-laws according to the agreement the sisters had outlined. When Joseph read them, he complimented the ladies, but said the Lord had something more in store for them. He asked them to meet with him in the room above his store.

On 17 March 1842, a group of eighteen ladies gathered for the meeting with Joseph. With him were Elders John Taylor and Willard Richards. Among the ladies present were Emma, Sarah M. Cleveland, Elizabeth Whitney, Sarah Kimball, Bathsheba Smith, Desdemona Fullmer, and Eliza R. Snow. They listened excitedly while Joseph outlined the Lord's plan for the women of the Church.

By way of introduction, the Prophet noted that women are naturally compassionate. They readily see the needs of people and are quick to extend comfort and assistance. He said the Lord had directed that the women should be organized for the purpose of giving them strength—one might interpret his meaning as *authority*—to express their benevolent natures and assist the priesthood in looking after the needs of the poor, the sick, or the lonely.

He suggested the women be organized after the order of the priesthood, with a president and counselors. He recommended they elect their president by vote and that the president should choose her counselors and a secretary. Then Joseph, John Taylor, and Willard Richards withdrew to let the women make their selection.[2]

Emma Chosen President of the Nauvoo Female Relief Society

After the women voted, the men returned and the Prophet acknowledged the sisters' choice of Emma as president. From the minutes of the first meeting, recorded by Willard Richards, we read:

> President J. Smith read the revelation to Emma Smith from the Book of Doctrine and Covenants; and stated that she was ordained at the time the revelation was given, to expound the scriptures to all; and to teach (the) female part of the community; and that not she alone, but others may attain to the same blessing.
>
> The 2nd Epistle of John 1st. verse was then read show[ing] that respect was there . . . and that was why she was called an elect lady because she was elected to preside."[3]

After a short discussion concerning a name for the organization, they decided to call it the Nauvoo Female Relief Society. Its primary objective was to render compassionate service and charity.

During his remarks at the first meeting, the Prophet made it clear that until the women were thus organized, the Church was not completely organized.

As president, Emma chose two counselors—Elizabeth Ann Whitney and Sarah M. Cleveland. These two women had taken her into their homes when she was homeless and destitute, rendering compassionate service to her. To receive the calling as counselors in this important organization was both an acknowledgment of Emma's trust in them and the Lord's acknowledgment of their capability to fulfill a sacred service to the women of His church. Eliza R. Snow was chosen as secretary.

John Taylor "laid his hands on the head of Mrs. Smith and blessed her and confirm'd upon her all the blessings which had been confer'd upon her that she might be a mother in Israel and look to the wants of the needy, and be a pattern of virtue; and possess all the qualifications necessary for her to stand, preside and dignify her office, to teach the females those principles requisite for their future usefulness."[4]

A mother in Israel! A pattern of virtue! These were more than titles; they foreshadowed things to come and served to accentuate Emma's motherly relationship to the daughters of Zion. Emma was to set an example and to prepare the women of her day for the blessings she and they were to receive, as daughters of God, and set the pattern for the women of the Church through future generations.

Emma took her commission seriously. Her words to the Relief Society reflect a magnificent command of language, a tender heart, and a clear understanding of eternal principles of virtue and right-eousness. Secretary Eliza R. Snow recorded the minutes of each meeting. From these minutes we learn that Emma focused on a three-fold theme: Unity, Purity, and Charity. In a future day (in 1913) the Relief Society would adopt as its motto "Charity Never Faileth."

In the context of 1842, Emma's messages stood out pointedly as a warning to the ladies of Nauvoo of the current dangers Emma saw manifesting themselves. Yet, the same statements could be presented with equal application to any congregation in our modern world. To be chaste, pure in word and actions, and loving to all—these objec-tives stand as truths which have universal application for all who hope to someday enter into the presence of their Father in Heaven.

Regarding unity, Emma urged the women not to tattle on one another in petty gossip. She urged them to keep a prudent outlook and "when they were privy to private things, to keep them to themselves."[5]

This admonition brought forth a question: Did it mean the Society was to be a secret society? Emma answered that it was not. She taught that any problems between members should be kept to themselves, not broadcast to the world at large. Good, she said, was to be shared openly. But she warned, "The tongue can sometimes be an unruly member and ought to be controlled."[6]

When speaking about purity, Emma urged caution, so as to avoid even the appearance of evil. She admonished the women to be watchful of all their actions and deeds and see to it they did nothing to bring reproach upon themselves or the society. She taught that by being virtuous they would obtain the blessings of the Lord and have His spirit to be their companion.

She invited the sisters to "throw a cloak of charity over faults that might be apparent. . . . Instead of criticizing, to forgive."[7] She instructed them in their duties to serve the poor and needy; to extend comfort to widows and orphans. In short, she urged, as did the Savior, to love and serve one another. These admonitions are as timely now as they were then.

Emma received official and public recognition as first lady in the Church, and first lady among the women. She was elected and chosen to preside, not for self-gratification, but called to set an example of virtue, "that others may attain the same blessing. . . ."[8]

By all evidence, Emma did set an example of virtue, in word and deed. All her days Emma's house was never empty, as widows and orphans, the hungry, the sick, the lame, and the weary from all walks of life found rest there. Emma nursed the sick, comforted the lonely, and even in her own poverty, she divided her meager resources with those who were in need. It was not a grim duty to her, but a matter of fact. Emma wore her calling as "first lady" with dignity. Years later a friend remembered, "Sister Emma was benevolent and hospitable; she drew around her a large circle of friends, who were like good comrades. She was motherly in her nature to young people, always had a houseful to entertain or be entertained."[9]

The Saints enjoyed cultural and social development, and there was a theater in which some of Nauvoo's leading citizens took leading roles in such dramatic presentations as "Damon and Pythias."[10]

Joseph and Emma's family enjoyed singing together, praying and playing together—they frequently rode out into the country to visit their friends, or to work on the farm. They ate together, danced, and socialized, as comfortably as people do today. Church history reveals how the serious and the pleasurable mingled in their daily lives.

The Book of Abraham

During the morning of 1 March, Joseph's history says, "I commenced publishing my translations of the Book of Abraham in the *Times and Seasons.*"[11] That evening when the Twelve and their wives went to Wilford Woodruff's house, Joseph and Emma were present as well. Emma must have enjoyed these social gatherings at which they invariably joked and relaxed. Joseph often taught them marvelous truths, sometimes regarding science and matters that were proven many years after his death.[12]

Glory and Shadows

In May 1842, Joseph gave several of the brethren special instructions in a room above his red brick store. Of these events it is recorded: "In this council was instituted the ancient order of things for the first time in these last days. And the communications I made to this council were of things spiritual, and to be received only by the spiritual minded: and there was nothing made known to these men but what will be made known to all the Saints of the last days, so soon as they are prepared to receive, and a proper place is prepared to communicate them."[13]

Joseph promised the Saints when the temple was finished—and in all temples which would later be built—the Saints would receive their blessings. The sacred principles to which he referred are mentioned in Malachi, pertaining to the turning of the hearts of the fathers to the children and the hearts of the children to the fathers, and in the New Testament, recalling those keys the Lord gave to his apostles: "And I will give unto thee the keys of the kingdom of heaven; and whatsoever thou shalt bind on earth shall be bound in heaven: and whatsoever thou shalt loose on earth shall be loosed in heaven."[14]

By administering the priesthood endowment to the apostles and a few other brethren, Joseph felt assured that if his life were taken, they had sufficient knowledge and keys of authority to finish anything he had left undone.

Satan must have understood better than the Saints themselves how important it was for Joseph to lay this foundation of heavenly authority, for it seems that Satan raged in the hearts of men from this time on, in an all-out effort to prevent the completion of Joseph's mission.

Although Nauvoo was thriving, the political climate in the country was boiling with controversy over issues such as slavery, taxation, and trade agreements. At first, many politicians in Illinois courted the Mormon vote, recognizing their potential power in the ballot box. On the other hand, there were some with opposing values, who sought to spread rumors against the Church, and against Joseph personally, in order to stir public opinion against the Saints.

The Exposure of a Plot to Destroy the Work

Early in 1842, it became apparent that John C. Bennett was not all he had pretended to be. While he had been brilliant in promoting the building up of Nauvoo, it came out that he had been teaching false doctrine; like Sampson Avard in Missouri, Bennett had been using Joseph's name to support his evil purposes. When Joseph challenged his behavior, he acted as though he were repentant, but thereafter secretly plotted Joseph's destruction.

Finally, Joseph became aware of plans to make an attempt on his life, which he blamed on Bennett. Bennett resigned his office as mayor. A hearing was held wherein Bennett admitted his own wrongdoing and publicly absolved Joseph from guilt, then he left town. On 19 May 1842, Joseph was elected mayor of Nauvoo, in Bennett's place. Unfortunately, this was not the end of Bennett's treachery.

Emma had never liked Dr. Bennett and had refused to accept medical treatment by him. She preferred to trust her own knowledge of herbs and nursing. She was probably not surprised when he turned out to be a scoundrel.

As soon as he was away from Nauvoo, Bennett began maneuvering in state politics and made a public attack upon Joseph. Joseph therefore explained to the press why Bennett had been removed as mayor. This inflamed Bennett, who raised a public outcry against the Mormons and claimed that he had only joined them in order to find out their "secrets" and expose them. He, like Philastus Hurlburt, wrote a book and lectured, with the express view of rousing political hatred against the Church. Although his hateful attacks on the Prophet and the Church did not further his own political career in Illinois, he was responsible for increased pressure upon Illinois officials to have Joseph Smith extradited to Missouri for a supposed attempt on the life of Governor Boggs. Of course, Joseph could not have made the attempt, even had he a mind to since he was far away from Missouri at the time of the incident. However, there was a price on Joseph's head in Missouri. His enemies hoped to get him back into that state; then they could rid the world of him for good. Using political maneuvers, they finally succeeded in their demand to have the matter investigated in the Illinois courts.[15]

Joseph was ordered to attend a hearing on the extradition. In this atmosphere of hostility, he did not expect a fair hearing; so during the summer of 1842, he went into hiding while his wife and friends tried to persuade Governor Carlin to deny the extradition request.[16]

Emma Visits Joseph

A deputy sheriff went to Nauvoo looking for Joseph on 10 August 1842, but he was not at home. Church history records that this deputy tried to frighten Emma and the brethren into revealing his location but they were not moved by his threats.[17]

Joseph went to his Uncle John Smith's at the nearby community of Zarahemla, across the river in Iowa, then sent word to Emma to come and visit him. After dark, Emma went with six men—Hyrum Smith, William Law, Newel K. Whitney, George Miller, William Clayton, and Dimick Huntington—in a skiff between the islands to visit him. Since it was considered unsafe for them to meet on shore, they met in the river mouth of the slough, between Zarahemla and Nauvoo. After visiting, Emma and the others went back to Nauvoo, and Joseph returned to his exile.[18]

The following day, William Law talked with the sheriff, who admitted that the course being taken against Joseph was illegal. William Clayton and John D. Parker took word to Joseph. On 13 August, Hyrum received a letter that stated, "Governor Carlin . . . said the proceedings were illegal and he should not pursue the subject any further."[19] This informant suggested that Joseph take the first boat down the river and start for home. This should have been good news, but the Prophet's friends thought it was a scheme to put him off guard so their enemies in Missouri could bring a force to kidnap the Prophet and take him back to Missouri.

Joseph again sent for Emma. He later wrote describing how Emma had to employ diversionary tactics to visit him: "To avoid suspicion, Emma walked to Sister Durphy's and waited the arrival of a carriage which passed off down the river with William Clayton and Loren Walker, with raised curtains, receiving Emma by the way, without any discovery. . . . About four miles down the river, the carriage turned on the prairie and passing around the city, turned into the timber opposite Wiggan's farm, when Emma alighted and walked to Brother Sayers', and the carriage returned. I was in good spirits, although somewhat afflicted in body, and was much rejoiced to meet my dear wife once more."[20]

Emma spent that night and the next day, Sunday, with him. They enjoyed "conversation . . . on various subjects, " and read his history together. They "both felt in good spirits and very cheerful." That evening they ate dinner together, then Emma, accompanied by Brothers Derby and William Clayton, left for Nauvoo.[21]

Emma brought letters from Joseph for Wilson Law, brother of William Law and major-general of the Nauvoo Legion, concerning the legal procedure necessary to get the case resolved. On Monday, the city was full of rumors that the Illinois militia was on its way to Nauvoo. Some felt this was true and others thought it was just a scheme to alarm the citizens.

Reflections

Joseph's reflections about this time are found in the *History of the Church:*

> . . . The names of the faithful are what I wish to record. . . . These I have met in prosperity, and they were my friends; and I now meet them in adversity, and they are still my warmer friends. These love the God that I serve; and they love the truths that I promulgate; they love those virtuous, and those holy doctrines that I cherish in my bosom with the warmest feelings of my heart, and with the zeal which cannot be denied. I love friendship and truth; I love virtue and law; I love the God of Abraham, of Isaac and of Jacob; and they are my brethren, and I shall live. . . .[22]

Joseph also recorded the names of many who had particularly ministered to his needs.[23] He particularly noted his brother Hyrum, and Emma:

Brother Hyrum, what a faithful heart you have got! Oh may the Eternal Jehovah crown eternal blessings upon your head, as a reward for the care you have had for my soul! Oh how many are the sorrows we have shared together; and again we find ourselves shackled with the unrelenting hand of oppression. Hyrum, thy name shall be written in the Book of the Law of the Lord, for those who come after thee to look upon, that they may pattern after thy works.[24]

Of Emma, Joseph later described his feelings when she came to see him while he was in hiding:

How glorious were my feelings when I met the faithful and friendly band, on the night of the eleventh, on Thursday, on the island at the mouth of the slough, between Zarahemla and Nauvoo; and what unspeakable delight and what transports of joy swelled my bosom, when I took by the hand, on that night, my beloved Emma—she that was my wife, even the wife of my youth, and the choice of my heart. Many were the reverberations of my mind when I contemplated for a moment the many scenes we had been called to pass through, the fatigues and the toils, the sorrows and sufferings, and joys and consolations, from time to time, which had strewed our path and crowned our board. Oh what a commingling of thought filled my mind for the moment, again she is here, even in the seventh trouble—undaunted, firm, and unwavering—unchangeable, affectionate Emma![25]

My Dear Emma

Joseph and Emma's correspondence during this time of exile gives a clear picture of what was happening:

My Dear Emma: I embrace this opportunity to express to you some of my feelings this morning. First of all, I take the liberty to tender you my sincere thanks for the two interesting and consoling visits that you have made me during my almost exiled situation. Tongue cannot express the gratitude of my heart, for the warm and true-hearted friendship you have manifested in these things towards me. The time has passed away, since you left me, very agreeably thus far; my mind being perfectly reconciled to my fate, let it be what it may. I have been kept from melancholy and dumps, by the kindheartedness of Brother Derby, and his interesting chit-chat from time to time, which has called my mind from the more strong contemplation of things and subjects that would have preyed more earnestly upon my feelings.

Last night Brothers Hyrum, Miller and Law and others came to see us. They seemed much agitated, and expressed some fears in consequence of some maneuverings and some flying reports which they had heard in relation to our safety; but, after relating what it was, I was able to comprehend the whole matter to my entire satisfaction, and did not feel at all alarmed or uneasy. They think, however, that the militia will be called out to search the city; and if this should be the case, I would be much safer for the time being at a little distance off, until Governor Carlin could get weary, and be made ashamed of his corrupt and unhallowed proceedings. I had supposed, however, that if there were any serious operations taken by the governor, that Judge Ralston, or Brother Hollister would have notified us; and cannot believe that anything very serious is to be apprehended, until we obtain information from a source that can be relied upon.

I have consulted whether it is best for you to go to Quincy and see the governor; but, on the whole, he is a fool; and the impressions that are suggested to my mind are, that it will be of no use; and the more we notice him, and flatter him, the more eager he will be for our destruction. You may write to him whatever you see proper, but to go and see him, I do not give my consent at present.

Brother Miller again suggested to me the propriety of my accompanying him to the Pine Woods, and then he [would] return and bring you and the children. My mind will eternally revolt at every suggestion of that kind, more especially since the dream and vision that was manifested to me on the last night. My safety is with you, if you want to have it so. Anything more or less than this cometh of evil. My feelings and counsel I think ought to be abided. If I go to the Pine country, you shall go along with me, and the children; and if you and the children go not with me, I don't go. I do not wish to exile myself for the sake of my own life, I would rather fight it out. It is for your sakes, therefore that I would do such a thing. I will go with you, then, in the same carriage, and on horseback from time to time as occasion may require; for I am not willing to trust you in the hands of those who cannot feel the same interest for you that I feel; to be subject to the caprice, temptations, or notions of anybody whatever. And I must say that I am prepossessed somewhat with the notion of going to the Pine country anyhow; for I am tired of the mean, low and unhallowed vulgarity of some portions of the society in which we live; and I think if I could have about six months with my family, it would be a savor of life unto life, with my house. Nevertheless, if it were possible, I would like to live here in peace and wind up my business; but if it should be ascertained to be a dead certainty that there is no other remedy, then we will round up our shoulders and cheerfully endure it; and this will be the plan: Let my horse, saddle, saddle-bags, and valise to put some shirts and clothing in, be sent to me. Let Brothers Derby and Miller take a horse and put it into my buggy, with a trunk containing my heavier clothes, shoes, boots, &c; and let Brother Taylor accompany us to his father's, and there we will tarry, taking every precaution to keep out of the hands of the enemy, until you can arrive with the children. Let Brother Hyrum bring you. Let Lorin Farr and Brother Clayton come along, and bring all the writings, and papers, books, and histories, for we shall want a scribe in order that we may pour upon the world the truth, like the lava from Mount Vesuvius. Then, let all the goods, household furniture, clothes, and store goods that can be procured be put on the boat, and let twenty or thirty of the best men that we can find be put on board to man it, and let them meet us at Prairie-du-Chien; and from thence we will wend our way like larks up the Mississippi until the towering mountains and rocks shall remind us of the places of our nativity, and shall look like safety and home; and then we will bid defiance to the world, to Carlin, Boggs, Bennett, and all the other . . . motley clan, that follow in their wake, Missouri not excepted, and until the damnation of hell rolls upon them, by the voice, and dread thunders, and trump of the eternal God. Then in that day will we not shout in the victory, and be crowned with eternal joys, for the battles we have fought having kept the faith and overcome the world?

Tell the children it is well with their father as yet; and that he remains in fervent prayer to Almighty God for the safety of himself, and for you and for them.

Tell mother Smith that it shall be well with her son, whether in life or in death; for thus saith the Lord God. Tell her that I remember her all the while, as well as Lucy [Joseph's youngest sister] and all the rest. They all must be of good cheer.

Tell Hyrum to be sure and not fail to carry out my instructions, but at the same time if the militia does not come, and we should get any favorable information, all may be well yet.

Yours in haste, your affectionate husband until death, through all eternity; forever. Joseph Smith.[26]

Dear Husband

When Emma received Joseph's letter, she answered promptly:

Dear Husband, I am ready to go with you if you are obliged to leave; and Hyrum says he will go with me. I shall make the best arrangements I can and be as well prepared as possible. But still I feel good confidence that you can be protected without leaving this country. There are more ways than one to take care of you, and I believe that you can still direct in your business concerns if we are all of us prudent in the matter. If it was pleasant weather I should contrive to see you this evening, but I dare not run too much of a risk, on account of so many going to see you.

General Adams sends the propositions concerning his land, two dollars an acre, payments as follows: assumption of mortgage, say about fourteen hundred, interest included. Taxes due, supposed about thirty dollars. Town property one thousand dollars. Balance, money payable in one, two, three or four years.

Brother Derby will tell you all the information we have on hand. I think we will have news from Quincy as soon as tomorrow.

Yours affectionately forever, Emma Smith.[27]

Wilson Law, one of Joseph's business associates, also sent a letter advising him: "On the whole, I think it would be better for you to absent yourself till the next governor takes the chair, for I do think if you are not here they will not attempt any violence on the city; and if they should, they will disgrace themselves in the eyes of the world, and the world will justify us in fighting for our rights, and then you can come out like a lion, and lead your people to victory and glory in the name of the Lord of hosts."[28]

Wilson Law wrote again the next day and suggested that there was every reason to expect that Joseph could be protected right there in the city. He advised Joseph not to go to the Pine Woods, but to remain, however long it might take, within the protection of the city and its laws. He commented that he believed Joseph could stay in safety within the city for weeks and months without being betrayed. The Prophet knew that this was true, for he had spent weeks on end in hiding.

The plan was to wait it out, until after the elections, and hope a new governor and new political scene would be more favorable.

Emma's Letter to the Governor

Although Emma did not personally go to see Governor Carlin, she did write to him, pleading the case of her husband and the people of Nauvoo. Written at night when she was alone, this rare document by Emma herself shows her intellectual gift of reasoning, her admirable command of language, and her unwavering loyalty to her husband and the Church.

Nauvoo, August 17, 1842
To his Excellency Governor Carlin:
Sir:—It is with feeling of no ordinary cast that I have retired, after the business of the day, and evening too, to address your honor. I am at a loss how to commence; my mind is crowded with subjects too numerous to be contained in one letter. I find myself almost destitute of that confidence, necessary to address a person holding the authority of your dignified and responsible office; and I would now offer, as an excuse for intruding upon your time and attention, the justice of my cause.

Was my cause the interest of an individual, or a number of individuals, then perhaps, I might be justified in remaining silent. But it is not. Nor is it the pecuniary interest of a whole community alone that prompts me again to appeal to your Excellency. But, dear Sir, it is for the peace and safety of hundreds, I may say, of this community, who are not guilty of any offense against the laws of the country; and also the life of my husband, who has not committed any crime whatever; neither has he transgressed any of the laws, or any part of the constitution of the United States; neither has he at any time infringed upon the rights of any man, or of any class of men, or community of any description. Need I say he is not guilty of the crime alleged against him by Governor Boggs? Indeed it does seem entirely superfluous for me, or any one of his friends in this place, to testify of his innocence of that crime, when so many of the citizens of your place, and of many other places in this state, as well as in the Territory, do know positively that the statement of Governor Boggs is without the least shadow of truth: and we know, and so many others, that the prosecution against him has been conducted in an illegal manner; and every act demonstrates the fact that all the design of the prosecution is to throw him into the power of his enemies without the least ray of hope that he would ever be allowed to obtain a fair trial; and that he would be inhumanly and ferociously murdered, no person, having a knowledge of the existing circumstances, has one remaining doubt: and your honor will recollect that you said to me that you would not advise Mr. Smith ever to trust himself in Missouri.

And, dear Sir, you cannot for one moment indulge unfriendly feelings towards him, if he abides by your counsel. Then, Sir, why is it that he should be thus cruelly pursued? Why not give him the privilege of the laws of this state? When I reflect upon the cruel and illegal operations of Lilburn W. Boggs, and the consequent suffering of myself and family, and the incalculable losses and sufferings of many hundreds who survived, and the many precious lives that were lost—all the effect of unjust prejudice and misguided ambition, produced by misrepresentation and calumny, my bosom heaves with unutterable anguish. And who, that is as well acquainted with the facts as the people at the city of Quincy, would censure me, if I should say that my heart burned with just indignation towards our calumniators as well as the perpetrators of those horrid crimes?

But happy would I now be to pour out my heart in gratitude to Governor Boggs, if he had rose up with the dignity and authority of the chief executive of the state, and put down every illegal transaction, and protected the peaceable citizens and enterprising immigrants from the violence of plundering outlaws, who have ever been a disgrace to the state, and always will, so long as they go unpunished. Yes, I say, how happy would I be to render him not only the gratitude of my own heart, but the cheering effusions and joyous souls of fathers and mothers, of brothers and sisters, widows and orphans, whom he might have saved, by such a course, from now dropping under the withering hand of adversity, brought upon them by the persecutions of wicked and corrupt men.

And now may I entreat your Excellency to lighten the hand of oppression and persecution which is laid upon me and my family, which materially affect the peace and welfare of this whole community; for let me assure you there are many whole families that are entirely dependent upon the prosecution and success of Mr. Smith's temporal business for their support; and, if he is prevented from attending to the common vocations of life, who will employ those innocent, industrious, poor people, and provide for their wants?

But, my dear Sir, when I recollect the interesting interview I and my friends had with you at your place, and the warm assurances you gave us of your friendship and legal protection, I cannot doubt for a moment your honorable sincerity; but do still expect you to consider our claims upon your protection from every encroachment upon our legal rights as loyal citizens, as we always have been, still are, and are determined always to be a law-abiding people; and I still assure myself that when you are fully acquainted with the illegal proceedings practiced against us in the suit of Governor Boggs, you will recall those writs which have been issued against Mr. Smith and Rockwell, as you must be aware that Mr. Smith was not in Missouri, and of course he could not have left there; with many other considerations, which, if duly considered, will justify Mr. Smith in the course he has taken (viz., going into hiding).

And now I appeal to your Excellency, as I would unto a father, who is not only able but willing to shield me and mine from every unjust persecution. I appeal to your sympathies, and beg you to spare me and my helpless children. I beg you to spare my innocent children the heart-rending sorrow of again seeing their father unjustly dragged to prison, or death. I appeal to your affections as a son, and beg you to spare our aged mother—the only surviving parent we have left—the insupportable affliction of seeing her son, whom she knows to be innocent of the crimes laid to his charge, thrown again into the hands of his enemies, who have so long sought for his life; in whose life and property she only looks for the few remaining comforts she can enjoy. I entreat of your Excellency to spare us these afflictions and many sufferings which cannot be uttered, and secure to yourself the pleasure of doing good, and vastly increasing human happiness—secure to yourself the benediction of the aged, and the gratitude of the young, and the blessings and the veneration of the rising generation.

Respectfully, your most obedient,

Emma Smith.

P. S. —Sir, I hope you will favor me with an answer. E. S.[29]

This letter was carried to Governor Carlin, at Quincy, by William Clayton. He gave it to him in the presence of Judge Ralston. It was reported to Emma later, that after reading the letter, the governor expressed astonishment at the judgment and talent manifest in the manner of Emma's address. He even gave the letter to Judge Ralston to read.

Notwithstanding this compliment to Emma, Clayton was not encouraged by the discussion he heard. He returned to Nauvoo with the opinion that Governor Carlin was not a friend upon whom they could rely.[30] Pressure was being brought to bear upon Governor Carlin to honor the extradition of Joseph to Missouri because of the slanderous claims being made in the press by John C. Bennett.

Carlin's answer to Emma, written on 24 August, confirmed Clayton's conclusion; the governor refused to extend any help to her whatsoever.[31] Even so, Emma did not let the matter drop. As president of the Relief Society, and with the help of Eliza R. Snow, she wrote another letter on 5 September. It rehearsed again that the claims against Joseph were false, and explained their source as being centered in lies put forth by John C. Bennett, who had at one time been prominent in Nauvoo and the Church, but had been discovered to be immoral and had been cast out of the Church and the community. The vicious efforts of Bennett to inflame public wrath against the Latter-day Saints were, according to this letter, prompted by the fact that Joseph had made public charge against Bennett, making it hard for him to attain the political power he wanted in the state of Illinois, hence the pressure to get Joseph extradited to Missouri.

The ladies of Nauvoo petitioned Governor Carlin to "not suffer [Joseph] to go into the state of Missouri (should he be demanded); for we know that if he should, it would be the delivering up the innocent to be murdered."[32] They also pleaded that he not allow the Saints to be delivered into the hands of mobs, but to afford them legal protection.

In his letter to Emma, Governor Carlin had avowed his inability to help her; if he helped the Mormons, he stood to lose support for his political ambitions.[33]

Joseph was not unwilling to have a hearing, but there was no safety for him, since the lawyers and judges were behind the effort to kill him. His friends continued to hide him, believing that if he complied with the governor's suggestion to give himself up, his life would be forfeited.

In his lonely hours, contemplating his friends who had stood by him through his perilous circumstances, Joseph reflected:

> I find my feelings . . . towards my friends revived, while I contemplate the virtues and the good qualities and characteristics of the faithful few, which I am now recording in the Book of the Law of the Lord,—of such as have stood by me in every hour of peril, for these fifteen long years past,—say, for instance, my aged and beloved brother, Joseph Knight, Sr., who was among the number of the first to administer to my necessities, while I was laboring in the commencement of the bringing forth of the work of the Lord, and of laying the foundation of the Church of Jesus Christ of Latter-day saints. For fifteen years he has been faithful and true, and even-handed and exemplary, and virtuous and kind, never deviating to the right hand or to the left. Behold he is a righteous man, may God Almighty lengthen out the old man's days; and may his trembling, tortured, and broken body be renewed, and in the vigor of health turn upon him, if it be Thy will, consistently, O God; and it shall be said of him, by the sons of Zion, while there is one of them remaining, that this man was a faithful man in Israel; therefore his name shall never be forgotten.
>
> There are his sons, Newel Knight and Joseph Knight, Jun., whose names I record in the Book of the Law of the Lord with unspeakable delight, for they are my friends.
>
> There is a numerous host of faithful souls, whose names I could wish to record in the Book of the Law of the Lord; but time and chance would fail. . . .[34]

As he poured out his memories of friends living and dead, and his appreciation for all who had in any way given him comfort, he prayed:

> Oh Thou, who seest and knowest the hearts of all men— Thou eternal, omnipotent, omniscient, and omnipresent Jehovah—God—Thou Eloheim, that sittest, as saith the Psalmist, "enthroned in heaven," look down upon Thy servant Joseph at this time; and let faith on the name of Thy Son Jesus Christ, to a greater degree than Thy servant ever yet has enjoyed, be conferred upon him, even the faith of Elijah; and let the lamp

of eternal life be lit up in his heart, never to be taken away; and
let the words of eternal life be poured upon the soul of Thy
servant, that he may know Thy will, Thy statutes, and Thy
commandments, and Thy judgments, to do them. . . .[35]

That evening, 22 August 1842, he received a note from Emma,
informing him it was her opinion he should return home as she
believed she could look out for his safety better there than elsewhere.
Under cover of darkness, he returned home and enjoyed a short time
with his family. He was unable to remain there, however; he spent
much of his time in hiding during the remainder of the year.

Blessings for the Children

During Joseph's absence, Emma and the children became very ill.
How she must have longed for Joseph's presence and comfort as she
cared for their sick children, herself weak and ill—perhaps from
worry as much as anything! On one occasion it is recorded that
Emma was re-baptized (which was common in those days) in the
river, for her health.

On 9 September, about midnight, Joseph sneaked into his home,
under cover of darkness, where he stopped for a few minutes to offer
a blessing upon the heads of his sleeping children.[36] That same night,
Joseph sent a letter to the brethren from a secret hiding place. In such
communications as this we see the indomitable spirit of confidence
Joseph felt concerning the work of the gospel of Jesus Christ, in spite
of his personal troubles:

> Now what do we hear in the gospel which we have received?
> A voice of gladness! A voice of mercy from heaven; and a voice of
> truth out of the earth; glad tidings for the dead; a voice of glad-
> ness for the living and the dead; glad tidings of great joy. . . .
> And again, what do we hear? Glad tidings from Cumorah!
> Moroni, an angel from heaven, declaring the fulfillment of the
> prophets—the book to be revealed. A voice of the Lord in the
> wilderness of Fayette, Seneca County, declaring the three
> witnesses to bear record of the book! The voice of Michael on the
> banks of the Susquehanna, detecting the devil when he appeared

as an angel of light! The voice of Peter, James, and John in the wilderness between Harmony, Susquehanna County, and Colesville, Broome County, on the Susquehanna River, declaring themselves as possessing the keys of the kingdom, and the dispensation of the fullness of times!

And again, the voice of God in the chamber of old Father Whitmer, in Fayette, Seneca County, and at sundry times and divers places through all the travels and tribulations of the Church of Jesus Christ of Latter-day Saints! And the voice of Michael, the archangel; the voice of Gabriel, and of Raphael, and of divers angels, from Michael or Adam down to the present time, all declaring their dispensation, their rights, their keys their honors, their majesty and glory, and the power of the priesthood; giving line upon line, precept upon precept; here a little, and there a little; giving us consolation by holding forth that which is to come, confirming our hope!

Brethren, shall we not go on in so great a cause? Go forward and not backward. Courage, brethren; and on, on to victory! Let your hearts rejoice and be exceedingly glad. Let the earth break forth into singing. Let the dead speak forth anthems of eternal praise to the King Immanuel, who hath ordained, before the world was, that which would enable us to redeem them out of their prison; for the prisoners shall go free. . . .

Behold, the great day of the Lord is at hand; and who can abide the day of his coming, and who can stand when he appeareth? For he is like a refiner's fire, and like fuller's soap; and he shall sit as a refiner and purifier of silver, and he shall purify the sons of Levi, and purge them as gold and silver, that they may offer unto the Lord an offering in righteousness. Let us, therefore, as a Church and a people, and as Latter-day Saints, offer unto the Lord an offering in righteousness; and let us present in his holy temple, when it is finished, a book containing the records of our dead, which shall be worthy of all acceptation.[37]

This splendid expression of faith shows that even in exile, buoyed up by his loyal friends and the unwavering support of his wife, the Prophet threw off depression and received the renewed faith for which he had prayed.

Due to the Nauvoo City Charter, and through the loyalty of his brethren, family, and influential friends, Joseph was able to avoid the ultimate disaster of being returned to Missouri until Governor Carlin was finally replaced. In the coming new year, Joseph would be cleared through court action of all charges, and freed from the dangers that had kept him and Emma in constant anxiety throughout the year of 1842.

With the end of Governor Carlin's term and the beginning of Governor Thomas Ford's, a new political climate prevailed. On 2 January 1843, Joseph was granted a hearing at Springfield, Illinois. Josiah Butterfield was his counselor and presented the case. It proceeded through 5 January. The following day, Joseph was released both by the order of the court at Springfield and an executive order of release from Governor Ford.[38]

On Tuesday, 10 January, they returned home to Nauvoo. Later that week, Joseph's appreciation was expressed in a letter to Josiah Butterfield, Esq.:

> I now sit down to inform you of our safe arrival home . . . after a cold and troublesome journey of four days. We found our families well and cheerful. The news of our arrival was soon generally known; and when it was understood that justice had once more triumphed over oppression, and the innocent had been rescued from the power of mobocracy, gladness filled the hearts of the citizens of Nauvoo, and gratitude to those who had so nobly and manfully defended justice and innocence was universally manifest; and of course I rejoiced with them, and felt like a free man at home. . . .[39]

The Jubilee

In thanksgiving for the Prophet's release and what was viewed as a universal saving of the people, 17 January was appointed by the Twelve Apostles, as "a day of fasting, praise, prayer and thanksgiving before the great Eloheim."[40] A public meeting was held at Joseph's house. The house was crowded to overflowing. There were meetings held in many other parts of the city as well, as there was great joy in the city that their prophet had been delivered from the threat of extradition to Missouri.

The following day, a party assembled at the Prophet's home. Beginning at ten in the morning, it was attended by all of the Twelve apostles and their wives: Brigham Young and Mary Ann; Heber C. Kimball and Vilate; Orson Hyde and Marinda; Parley P. Pratt and Mary Ann; William B. Smith and Caroline; Orson Pratt and Sarah; John E. Page and Mary; John Taylor and Lenora; Wilford Woodruff and Pheobe; George A. Smith and Bathsheba; Willard Richards and Jeanetta. Hyrum was there but his wife, Mary, was unable to attend because of illness.[41] Undoubtedly Lucy Mack Smith attended, as well as Joseph's counselor, William Law and his wife Jane. There were others, not named, as well as numerous children.

Joseph presented each guest with a card that was especially printed for the occasion. On these cards were the words of the Jubilee Song written by William Law and Willard Richards, as well as a second Jubilee Song by Eliza R. Snow. These songs were sung by the entire company, with great feeling. The *Times and Seasons* carried an article describing the event:

> The following beautiful verses were written and sung as will be seen from their reading on the occasion of Joseph Smith's release from the hands of his persecutors.
>
> Mr. Smith and his Lady made a feast and invited upwards of fifty of their friends to partake with them; which was indeed a day of conviviality and rejoicing, and might properly be called a day of jubilee or release.[42]

Jubilee Song by Eliza R. Snow

That deed—that time we celebrate,
So rife with liberty;
When the official pow'rs of State
Pronounc'd the Prophet free,

CHORUS:
When Foul oppression's hand was stay'd—
A feast of Liberty,
The Prophet and his Lady made,
To crown the jubilee.

'T'was once, no subject, theme of song,
For honest men to gain,
Those rights that legally belong
To every humble swain.
When foul opression's &c.

Some patriot feeling yet remains—
Such as our fathers felt,
When on Columbia's fertile plains
Their blood, they freely spilt.
When foul opression's &c.

Protection's wreath again will bloom,—
Reviv'd by Thomas Ford;
Which under Carlin had become
Like Jonah's wither'd gourd.
When foul opression's &c.

Like Freedom's true and genuine son,
Oppression to destroy,
His Excellency has begun
To govern Illinois.
When foul opression's &c.

His 'Mormon' subjects fondly trust,
The citizens will share,
A legislation wise and just,
While he retains the Chair.
While foul opression's &c.

Long, long, they'd felt injustice's weight,
And grappled with its yoke;
Ere the authorities of State
The Prophet's fetters broke.
When foul opression's &c.

The justice done a righteous cause
By those who stand in pow'r;

Does honor to our country's laws,
In this degen'rate hour.
When foul opression's &c.

And while we give our feelings scope
And gratitude award,
To Edwards, Butterfield and Pope,
We'll not forget the Lord.
When foul opression's &c.

The Lord who guides the Prophet's cause;
Inspir'd our rulers' minds,
To execute those equal laws,
And break the chain that binds.
When foul oppression's &c.

Elijah's God! We'll praise his name,
And own his mighty hand,
Who bring his Prophet's foes to shame
In this republic land.
When foul oppression's &c.

Tho' wicked men should rage and scoff—
Though earth and hell oppose,—
The Lord will bear his people off
Triumphant o'er their foes.
When foul opression's &c.

Now let the Prophet's soul rejoice—
His noble Lady's too;
While praise to God with heart and voice
Is heard throughout Nauvoo.

CHORUS:
When foul oppression's hand was stay'd,
A feast of Liberty;
The Prophet and his Lady made,
To crown the jubilee.—[43]

We have no idea what tune was used to sing this song. Obviously it was more boisterous than musical. For Relief Society birthday programs, the sisters in my ward have sung these words to the tune of "Yankee Doodle Dandy," and they fit without much adjustment.

Singing this song, and the others, undoubtedly refreshed these good friends of Joseph and Emma. The Jubilee lasted all day, with Joseph and Emma serving the food. The space was small so they had to eat in shifts: at the first table were twenty-one people, twenty at the second and eighteen at the third. Joseph and Emma ate at the third table. Fifteen sat at a fourth table, including children and household help. Joseph recorded in his history that this occasion was made even more special by the fact that it was the anniversary of his marriage to Emma. They had been married sixteen years.

Joseph Re-elected Mayor

Even as Emma and Joseph celebrated with their friends, private conversations between Joseph and the other Church leaders centered around the question of how long they could count on the apparent friendliness of politicians who had gained office in Illinois. John C. Bennett had left Nauvoo, but he had not forgotten his hostility against the Mormons. Even Governor Ford's dismissal of the charges in January was tempered by pointed advice for Joseph to "refrain from all political electioneering."[44]

On 23 January, Joseph published a statement in *The Wasp,* to the effect that he was revolted by the idea of having anything to do with politics and he wished to be left alone to attend to the spiritual affairs of the Church.[45]

Less than two weeks later, on 6 February, city elections were held in Nauvoo and Joseph was elected mayor by unanimous vote.[46] On 21 February, he addressed about 300 men gathered on the temple grounds. Referring to some of his former friends by name, he explained, "There is a great deal of murmuring in the Church about me. . . . They'll say . . . 'Brother Joseph, how I love you; can I do anything for you?' and they go away and secretly get up opposition, and sing out our names to strangers and scoundrels with an evil influence."[47]

He also answered the concern about his disregard for the governor's directive to refrain from politicizing.

> There is one thing more I wish to speak about, and that is political economy. It is our duty to concentrate all our influence to make popular that which is sound and good, and unpopular that which is unsound. 'Tis right, politically, for a man who has influence to use it, as well as for a man who has no influence to use his. From henceforth I will maintain all the influence I can get. In relation to politics, I will speak as a man; but in relation to religion I will speak in authority.[48]

On 3 March, a bill was introduced in the Illinois legislature, to limit the powers of the Nauvoo City Charter. The targeted item was Nauvoo's provision to allow the writ of habeas corpus, which serves as a protection for the accused and provides a way for the accused to obtain justice in the event of possible false charges being filed. There was a hot debate suggesting a "danger" that such a bill might cause the Mormons' vote to go with the Whigs, whereas they had previously supported the Democrats. Nevertheless, the bill passed, fifty-eight to thirty-three.

Joseph's brother William was in the legislature at the time, and fought to keep the bill from passing. Failing that, he called for an amendment, renaming the proposed bill and titling it, "A bill for an act to humbug the citizens of Nauvoo." This caused considerable sensation in the House, but did not change the fact that the bill had been passed. No action was taken in the senate, so the issue was not settled.[49]

Emma must have recognized that the loss of their power to issue habeas corpus could leave them vulnerable once again to a hostile community and court system.

Hastening the Work

Joseph seemed to sense that his time was short. On one occasion he said that he was not afraid to die so long as he was not hanged. On another he remarked that the world should not be troubled with him much longer. His people failed to comprehend these warnings at the time. There is no recorded indication of Emma's recognizing the impending doom. When Joseph told Emma he very much wanted to stay and complete his business, he was referring to the completion of laying the foundation of the kingdom of God. Having established the preliminary structure of the Church by 1842, he had but one essential labor yet to perform: the restoration of the fullness of the priesthood. While in hiding, the Prophet had spent his time writing and explaining the principles of the gospel to his associates, constantly refining the organization and doctrines of the Church.

One of the doctrines Joseph taught was that the relationship of marriage is an eternal one. In an April discourse, he gave a touching description of how familial relationships may be expected to continue after the resurrection.[50] On 16 July, he publicly said, "A man must enter into an everlasting covenant with his wife in this world or he will have no claim on her in the next."[51]

The Prophet urgently desired for the temple to be completed in order for the general membership of the Church to receive the fullness of blessings being manifest through him.

Joseph and Emma Sealed for Time and Eternity

For many years, Joseph and Emma seem to have had an eternal understanding, signing their letters with expressions of "forever" and "eternally yours," but they had never been sealed together by the ordinances of the priesthood. The Prophet's urgency to finish laying the foundation of the organization of the Church exceeded the speed with which the Saints could complete the temple. Therefore, Emma's home became the scene of sacred ordinance work.

On 28 May 1843, Emma was sealed to Joseph in the new and everlasting covenant. This took place in the upper room of the Old Homestead. Prior to this time, the Prophet had performed marriages uniting other couples for eternity; now, through the power vested in the priesthood, he had claim upon Emma throughout all the time here and the eternities hereafter.[52]

A Family Vacation

Early in June of 1843, the family took their first and only vacation. They traveled about 200 miles north, to Dixon, Illinois, where they visited Emma's sister, Elizabeth Wasson.[53] It must have been quite an exciting outing for the children—young Joseph, who was ten; Julia, eleven; Frederick, seven; and Alexander, who was five. Young Joseph recalled that they were going to visit Emma's relatives. Her brothers David and Alva had recently moved to Illinois as well as two of her sisters' families, Tryal and Michael Morse, and Elizabeth and Benjamin Wasson. Emma must have looked forward to this rare opportunity to be with her family. They had barely arrived at the Wassons', and the children had begun to play with their cousins, when Stephen Markham and William Clayton came with a warning that Governor Ford had signed a writ, being carried by two men from Missouri, who desired to arrest Joseph and take him to Missouri.[54] The order was illegal, issued on the old charge, for which Joseph had already been cleared in court. However, since Governor Ford had signed the writ, Joseph would need to seek legal assistance to keep from being taken to Missouri, where they knew he would be killed.

The Missourians arrived before Joseph had time to avoid them. They took him at gun-point, tied him up, and put him in a wagon. Stephen Markham tried to hold the team, giving time for Emma to bring Joseph's hat and coat. Leveling the gun point blank at Markham, the deputy from Missouri ordered him to let them go, which he did.

They went to the town of Dixon, where Joseph asked for counsel, but was refused. However, people in Dixon resented the highhanded manner of arresting a man and refusing him due legal process. In addition, Emma's brother-in-law, Benjamin Wasson, used his influence to help him. Soon Joseph had obtained a writ of habeas corpus and filed a countersuit against the Missourians. A deputy from Dixon took everybody into custody, and the entire group was supposed to find the closest judge who would hear the case and investigate the entire situation.

A message was sent to Nauvoo to let the brethren there know what was happening. It directed that members of the Legion be dispatched to make sure Joseph was not taken across the Mississippi, into Missouri.

Emma and her children were left at the Wassons; it was up to them to get themselves home. They left that very night. Church history suggests that her nephew, Lorenzo, drove them but Joseph III says it was Lorin Farr. Of course, it is entirely possible that both Lorenzo and Lorin were involved in helping them get to Nauvoo. On the trip home their buggy broke down, having one of the wheels burn through the axle. It took them four days to get home. Joseph III had his fingers crushed in the carriage door and suffered a painful wound, which Emma doctored with a mixture of whiskey and wormwood. The boy fainted from the shock and pain of it, and recalls his mother solicitously bathing his face.[55] How her patience must have been tried by these circumstances, yet she remained calm and in control. Once home, Emma had to wait some time before she received word about Joseph and the others. Young Joseph recalls the preparations for the crowd that would be coming to the hotel for a trial before the municipal court.

We rehearse these events in a few sentences. She lived them—anxious hour after anxious hour—coping with food preparations for guests and the pressing needs of her little children even as she worried and prayed for her husband. If her faith in their mission flagged, she never revealed it. To the contrary, many who saw her face her trials have said when things got tough, her cheerful manner buoyed up others.

The Saints Rescue Their Prophet

As soon as word reached Nauvoo that Joseph was a prisoner in the hands of deputies from Missouri, the Legion went into action. Groups of men went to the river crossings, intending to see to it that no one took the Prophet across. The Nauvoo Legion spread out over the entire area, which roused considerable excitement wherever they went. A posse from Nauvoo finally met up with Joseph and his captors, and escorted them to Nauvoo. In the Municipal Court of Nauvoo, the writ to take Joseph to Missouri was ruled illegal; the two Missourians were treated to dinner, served by Emma in the Prophet's home, and were sent back where they came from without having succeeded in taking Joseph.

While the city and Joseph's friends celebrated what appeared to be a triumph over evil, in reality, the fact that he was dismissed in a Nauvoo court, served to focus attention on the power granted the city under its charter. Although the court in Nauvoo had acted fully within the law, by overruling the writ signed by Governor Ford, they lighted the fuse to an already explosive political situation. The details of Joseph's arrest and release, including the desperate riders who covered sixty miles a day on horseback in their effort to prevent his being taken to Missouri, reveal to modern readers that life in Illinois, in 1843, was primitive beyond our comprehension. This was the frontier of America, and one cannot help but thrill at the heroic effort of Joseph's friends to free him from those who held him at gun-point during the tedious wagon trip from Dixon to Nauvoo.[56]

After her husband was home, Emma must have overheard the heated conversations of his friends around their supper table; she may have recalled the mounting troubles in Ohio and Missouri, and wondered what the outcome would be. Joseph was uncharacteristically moody. He would say to his friend, Isaac Allred, "Come, fiddle for me," and Isaac would play his fiddle, playing rousing tunes to cheer up the Prophet and make him smile, then he would play tender melodies such as "The Last Rose of Summer." He always ended these evenings playing the Prophet's favorite hymn, "A Poor Wayfaring Man."[57]

In the haven of safety provided them by faithful bodyguards and the loyal Nauvoo Legion, Emma must have looked at the thousands of loyal Saints gathered to listen to Joseph's speeches from the stand. No doubt she prayed that they would be protected from what seemed to be developing into another awful situation.

A Multitude of Problems

Political and social pressures mounted all during the summer of 1843. Old enemies got together with new ones to pool their efforts to destroy the Prophet. As mayor of one of the largest cities in Illinois, President of the Church, and latter-day prophet, acclaimed by thousands of faithful believers, he was seen as a nuisance—nothing short of a threat—to the men who aspired to political office for the purpose of selfish ambition.

For Emma, the political and ecclesiastical tumult was eclipsed by events of a more personal nature. Just as they were about to settle their family into the beautiful new home which was nearly completed, the Prophet recorded what is today known as Section 132 of the Doctrine and Covenants. This is undoubtedly the most controversial revelation given through the Prophet.[58]

With each step in the development of the Church organization, Joseph had wrestled with the burden of helping his people understand the full measure of the restoration of the gospel and of the kingdom of God. Each new phase of the Restoration had brought conflict, apostasy, and persecution. It was therefore inevitable that the revelation recorded 12 July, "relating to the new and everlasting covenant, including the eternity of the marriage covenant . . . also plurality of wives," would bring conflict.[59] Although it was recorded in 1843, it is evident from historical records that the doctrines and principles involved had been known by the Prophet since 1831.

In this revelation, the Abrahamic law was restored. Had the Prophet failed to restore this principle, by which ancient prophets had established numerous posterity under a sacred covenant, he would not have fulfilled the restoration of all things required in the dispensation of the fullness of times.

Coming as it did in an age of rising Victorian attitudes, among people steeped in Puritan ethics, and colliding with a frontier culture imbued with almost unprecedented political ambition, the doctrine could not fail to rouse contention.

Emma's ordeals in New York, Ohio, and Missouri must have seemed minuscule compared to the ordeal of having to support her husband in a principle that struck at the very heart of her expressed desire to see the Church accepted and respected in society.

When the revelation was shown to her, she was greatly upset. But in spite of her distress, she bore up publicly. We read that within a few days of this most traumatic experience of her life, she went with the Prophet and their family, with a large group of friends, on a pleasure cruise on a riverboat. Joseph had bought half interest in the *Maid of Iowa,* and had arranged for it to pick them up at the Nauvoo

House landing, just north of the city, about six in the evening and return at dusk.[60]

The Mississippi has many moods. There is an incredible beauty on the river with the sun setting in the western sky. A myriad of colors play over the water reflected from gold-rimmed clouds tinged with pinks, blues, and shimmering streaks that are almost mauve, over the horizon. Perhaps Emma drew apart from the group, leaned her arms on the railing, and watched the vivid evening light fade to dusk–not at peace within–not at peace without. Was she afraid?

The next Sunday, 16 July, Joseph preached in the grove west of the temple. People who heard him speak that day said he touched briefly on the subject of the everlasting covenant, showing that a man and his wife must enter into a covenant in this world, or he will have no claim on her in the next world. But, he said, "On account of the unbelief of the people, I cannot reveal the fullness of these things at present."[61] During this sermon, he observed, "The same spirit that crucified Jesus is in the breast of some who profess to be Saints in Nauvoo."[62]

The Prophet attended to his usual responsibilities, putting up hay on his farm and spending time at home. The conflict over doctrine must have weighed heavily upon them both. On 23 July, he said, "The burdens which roll upon me are very great. My persecutors allow me no rest, and I find that in the midst of business and care the spirit is willing, but the flesh is weak."[63] Undoubtedly, Emma was also feeling the strain; her health was very poor at this time.

When he addressed the people in the grove, Joseph had said, "The only principle upon which [my enemies] judge me is by comparing my acts with the foolish traditions of their fathers and nonsensical teachings of hireling priests, whose object and aim is to keep the people in ignorance for the sake of filthy lucre; or as the prophet says, to feed themselves and not the flock." He asked a rhetorical question, "Have the Presbyterians any truth? Yes. Have the Baptists, Methodists, etc., any truth? Yes. They all have a little truth mixed with error. We should gather all the good and true principles in the world and treasure them up, or we shall not come out true 'Mormons.'"[64]

How remarkable was this man, how beyond his time, and at times how frustrated in his effort to lay a secure foundation for the Lord's kingdom. In addition to facing endless persecution, he continually had to swim in a sea of doubt from his own beloved Emma. Without reconciliation with Emma, he could not function in the restoration of the fullness of the priesthood.

The Mansion House Completed

The new house at last completed, the family moved into it on 31 August 1843. For the first two weeks in her new home, Emma was deathly ill, overcome with the chills and fever so common to those who lived in that swampy area. More than likely she suffered from malaria. But she must have also been overworked and under extreme stress. She was the subject of special prayers in meetings of both the brethren and the Relief Society. On 10 September, Joseph's history reports that Emma was somewhat better.

One source of stress for her was the stream of guests coming to their home, to be fed and housed. At times it was a great strain to provide food for the company. During one discussion about how to deal with the expense and numbers of guests, William Phelps made the suggestion that Joseph should do as Napoleon—have a table only large enough for one. Emma's hearty response to this was that Joseph was a bigger man than Napoleon; he could never eat without his friends.[65]

The solution was supplied by Joseph: "I found myself unable to support so much company free of charge, which I have done from the foundation of the Church. My house has been a home and resting place for thousands, and my family many times obliged to do without food, after having fed all they had to visitors; and I could have continued the same liberal course, had it not been for the cruel and untiring persecution of my relentless enemies. I have been reduced to the necessity of opening 'The Mansion' as a hotel."[66]

Having kept an unofficial "inn" for many years, Emma must have agreed with Joseph's decision, for it would have made things much easier for her to cover the expense of entertaining so much company. She had entertained Indians, statesmen, would-be congressmen, and humble immigrants; contemporaries who mentioned her in later years usually described her as busy, pleasant, and cheerful.[67]

During this time, she also became reconciled with Joseph. How that was accomplished, we are not informed. It is a matter of record however, that in September 1843, she gave him the support he needed so he could move forward with the restoration of those sacred ordinances the Lord had promised would come.

Fullness of the Priesthood Conferred for the First Time

From the time the Saints had been forced to leave Kirtland, Joseph had been frustrated in his efforts to dispense the fullness of the priesthood ordinances to the Church. Partial ordinances were given throughout the years, but there were further ordinances and blessings yet to come forth. In each public sermon the Prophet included a plea to the Saints to finish the temple. The walls were rising; the beautiful building could be seen from miles around. Passengers on the riverboats craned their necks at it as they went by, and often, boatloads of people stopped to wander through the streets of Nauvoo and marvel at the quaint European design of the buildings and the incredible rock structure that would house the Saints in their worship of the Most High God. Nauvoo was becoming a beautiful place, and was the more notable because it was located at the westernmost edge of the United States.

Through consecration of all they possessed, the Saints had built the Kirtland Temple in only three years. In Nauvoo, they gave liberal donations to build a new temple. The sisters of the Relief Society throughout the Church, including those who lived abroad, were encouraged to pledge one cent a week. But even with this great sacrifice, the temple was far from finished.

In September, Joseph felt the need to proceed with the restoration of the fullness of priesthood ordinances; the fullness of the priesthood requires that women as well as men be endowed and sealed. Sometime on or before 28 September, the Prophet administered the ordinances of washing and anointing to Emma in the upstairs room of their newly completed Mansion House.[68] She was the first woman in this dispensation to receive these blessings. Up to this point, she had received earthly recognition and honor as an "elect lady." Now, having come up through affliction, she was qualified to fulfill the fullest purpose of her election.

In a most sacred meeting in the upper front room of the Mansion House, Emma was present with Joseph and a number of others, where, "for the first time in the history of the Church the fullness of the priesthood was conferred."[69]

This was the culminating event in the Restoration—the capstone of the foundation of the kingdom that had been spoken of by Daniel. Having been called to fulfill this vital work of salvation, Joseph had given the Apostles, and other brethren, as they were ready, sacred keys bestowed upon him by the ancient prophets in the Kirtland Temple. He alone comprehended the full measure of God's plan of perfecting and redeeming mankind. It was his constant desire to have the Nauvoo Temple finished so the Saints could receive these blessings. Apostasy and persecution had prevented his revealing the full import of those keys, except to a few trusted brethren; and even they, according to Benjamin F. Johnson, had no more understanding than the ABCs of the gospel.[70]

At a meeting held 28 September, the Prophet led the company in a special prayer. Then he gave instructions and dictated the words of the ordinance to Patriarch Hyrum Smith and Stake President William Marks. They anointed and blessed Joseph, sealing upon him his calling and election.[71] As he had been promised in his patriarchal blessing, he was blessed and sealed up to his eternal exaltation. After this, Emma was called up and anointed, and sealed to her eternal position by his side. Joseph taught that no more glorious blessing could be conferred in mortality than those which had just been administered to him and his wife, and that through this restoration, the *foundation* for the kingdom of God was complete. He explained that each Church member, when worthy, would receive the fullness of the priesthood blessings.[72] Emma's most vital contribution in the Restoration was to stand beside her husband in this final duty; and in it, her "election" was ratified. She became an Elect Lady indeed—the first of all women of this dispensation to be fully endowed.

By thus establishing this sacred ordinance, the Prophet and Emma opened the way for all people, both living and the dead throughout all time to eventually receive the blessings alluded to by the Apostle Peter. "Wherefore . . . brethren, give diligence to make your calling and election sure: for if ye do these things, ye shall never fall: For so an entrance shall be ministered unto you abundantly into the everlasting kingdom of our Lord and Saviour Jesus Christ."[73]

In the initial introduction of these blessings, those who participated had no more comprehension of the full significance, perhaps,
than an eight-year-old has when he or she is baptized. Those Latter-
day Saints who went on to obtain knowledge and understanding
would gain spiritual insight into the same things Joseph had been
shown. Those who put them in a worldly context considered it, at
best, ridiculous, and at the worst, blasphemous. Just as in Kirtland
and Missouri, some who partook of the most sacred of blessings, lost
faith—those who lost faith became enemies.

Emma's participation in the restoration of these ordinances was
not known for many years. Records that have come to light in recent
years make it clear that ordinances were performed in Emma's home
and in the room above the brick store, which was arranged to serve as
a temporary temple.[74] And in time, Emma's part would become
known from private journals of contemporaries.

Throughout the year of 1843 and into the early part of 1844,
Emma presided under Joseph's direction over the administration of
sacred ordinances for women. She probably administered the washing
and anointing to Mary Fielding Smith, and according to Heber C.
Kimball's journal, to his wife Vilate, and "meny other females."[75]

During the winter of 1843, Emma presided over the women's
portion of the ordinance work. Joseph's mother received her washing
and anointing and was administered her sealing ordinances. Bathsheba
W. Smith, wife of Joseph's cousin, George A., said, "I received the ordinance of anointing in a room in Sister Emma Smith's house in Nauvoo,
and the same day, in company with my husband, I received my endowment in the upper room over the Prophet Joseph Smith's store."[76]

When one understands that the principle of sealing is scriptural,
the Bible becomes a rich source of evidence that there is a fullness of
blessings reserved for those who love when others would hate, who
reach out when others would withdraw, and who bring their lives into
harmony with the divine precepts taught by the Savior. It also
supports the eternal promise that death will never separate those who
are thus joined by the power of the holy priesthood. This authority
has been restored upon the earth in the last days, and pertains to the
principle referred to by the Apostle Paul when he declared, "Neither
is the man without the woman; Neither is the woman without the

man in the Lord."[77] This blessing comes to the present generation through the united participation of Joseph and Emma and was one part of the Restoration Joseph could not have completed without her. True to the covenants she had made, Emma would never speak directly of these ordinances. They were sacred beyond all description.

Even viewed from a distance, this period of Emma's life takes on an aspect of a giant roller-coaster ride, as she faced a grim struggle with problems and challenges sandwiched between soaring heights of glorious blessings. Placed as it was, on the razor's edge between indescribable trials and the ultimate sorrow, this moment—which is Emma's highest moment of earthly glory—has been so eclipsed by her sacrifices and by bitter controversy and debate, that for more than one hundred years it has remained unknown by historians and biographers. Only now, in an age when contemporary documents have come to light to clear up the shadows, do we fully appreciate this sacred event in which Emma's glorious role in the restoration of the gospel of Jesus Christ was culminated. All women in this dispensation who obtain their holy endowments follow in the footsteps of this "Mother in Israel," Emma Hale Smith.

Notes

1. Susa Young Gates, ed., "A Record of the Organization and Proceedings of the Female Relief Society of Nauvoo, Illinois (March 1842-March 1844)." Willard Richards presented them with the first record book, which is now in the LDS Archives; hereafter cited as "Relief Society Minutes."

2. Relief Society Minutes.

3. Ibid.

4. Ibid.

5. Ibid.

6. Ibid.

7. Ibid.

8. Ibid.

9. *Woman's Exponent* (1908), 36:7.

10. *HC,* 6:350.

11. *HC,* 2:235-38, 289, 320; see also *HC,* 4:520 and *HC,* 2:350-51.

12. *HC,* 4:519.

13. *HC,* 5:2.

14. Matthew 16:19.

15. *HC,* 5:12-15.

16. *HC,* 5:90-119

17. *HC,* 5:89.

18. *HC,* 5:90.

19. *HC,* 5:91.

20. *HC,* 5:92.

21. *HC,* 5:93-96.

22. *HC,* 5:107.

23. *HC,* 5:108

24. *HC,* 5:107-108.

25. *HC,* 5:107.

26. *HC,* 5:103-104.

27. *HC,* 5:110.

28. *HC,* 5:110-12.

29. *HC,* 5:115-17.

30. *HC,* 5:118-19.

31. *HC,* 5:130-31.

32. *HC,* 5:147.

33. *HC,* 5:153-55.

34. *HC,* 5:124-25.

35. *HC,* 5:127-28.

36. *HC,* 5:128-29.

37. Doctrine & Covenants 128:19-24.

38. *HC,* 5:216-17.

39. *HC,* 5:250.

40. *HC,* 5:252. For further study on the Prophet's use of the word *Eloheim,* see Andrew Ehat and Lyndon Cook, *The Words of Joseph Smith* (Provo, Utah: Religious Studies Center, Brigham Young University, 1980), Index.

41. Ibid.

42. *Times and Seasons* (1 February 1843), 4:96.

43. Ibid. These verses fit perfectly when sung to the tune "Yankee Doodle."

44. *HC,* 5:232.

45. *HC,* 5:259.

46. *HC,* 5:264.

47. *HC,* 5:284-85.

48. *HC,* 5:286.

49. *HC,* 5:295.

50. Ehat and Cook, *Words of Joseph Smith,* pp.196-97; see also *HC,* 5:510.

51. Ibid., 233; see also p. 193 ftnt. 7.

52. Andrew F. Ehat, *Joseph Smith's Introduction of Temple Ordinances and the 1844 Mormon Succession Question,* Master's Thesis, Brigham Young University, Provo (December, 1982), pp. 63, 263; hereafter cited as Ehat thesis. Brigham Young's diary also confirms that this meeting took place in the Old Homestead.

53. In his *Memoirs,* Joseph III writes the name Wassen, but according to

Richard Anderson, the correct spelling is Wasson.

54. Mary Audentia Smith Anderson, ed., *Memoirs of President Joseph Smith III—1832-1914* (Independence, Mo.: Herald Publishing House, 1979), pp. 36-37.

55. Ibid; see also *HC*, 5:431-44. *HC*, 5:452 comments on Emma's return to Nauvoo.

56. *HC*, 5:461-65.

57. Isaac Allred history, obtained from Linda Isom, Las Vegas, Nevada.

58. Gracia N. Jones, "My Great-Great Grandmother Emma Hale Smith," *Ensign*, August 1992, pp. 30-39. While the issue of polygamy has been greatly overblown, we in the family must become reconciled to the indisputable fact that Joseph was instrumental in restoring a doctrine that embraced an eternal covenant of marriage and restored the Abrahamic Law under which patriarchs in the Old Testament married several wives. The fact that they did so, under the direction of the Lord, and that God blessed them and their posterity, is scriptural. The fact that the celestial covenant and the telestial reality were not a happy blend is well documented anciently, as well as in nineteenth-century Mormonism. Condemnation of immoral conduct is, and always has been, an ideal of the LDS Church. Those who equate plural marriage with adultery may never be reconciled to the Prophet's teachings. The fact is, God did not condemn the ancient prophets for having more than one wife, except in cases where they took them on their own, without the blessing of the living prophet. On the other hand, the scriptures are filled with admonitions to be morally pure. Generally speaking, the Lord has advocated one wife for one man, but has, in very rare instances in the scriptures, given directions through His living prophet, to do otherwise. See Book of Mormon, Jacob 3. The purpose given therein, is to "raise up seed unto me" (i.e., God). The restoration of all things in this, the last dispensation, was Joseph's assigned responsibility. That he did so is documented beyond doubt. That he restored this practice in the Victorian Era, explains, to some degree, why he was killed. Society would not accept any new dispensation of God's word, or doctrine. The doctrine was practiced because it was commanded; when the need was fulfilled, social pressure was allowed to bring the earthly practice to an end. In 1890, Wilford Woodruff, as prophet and President of the Church, was directed by the Lord to issue the Manifesto. (See Doctrine & Covenants Official Declaration, pp. 291-92).

59. Doctrine & Covenants 132.

60. *HC*, 5:510.

61. Ibid.

62. Ibid.

63. *HC*, 6:165-66.

64. *HC*, 5:516.

65. *HC*, 5:517.

66. *HC*, 6:33.

67. *HC*, 6:43. This gives an account of a pleasant dinner in the hotel, in which Emma expressed her thanks to their friends for their support.

68. Ehat thesis, p. 94. Documentary proof of this ordinance having been performed came to light in 1982, through the efforts of Andrew Ehat. Prior to this time, it was merely a matter of speculation, with some assuming it had never taken place.

69. Ehat thesis, p. 95.

70. Benjamine F. Johnson, Letter to then Church Historian, George S. Gibbs, 1903, LDS Church Archives, Salt Lake City, Utah.

71. Ehat thesis, p. 96.

72. Ibid.

73. 2 Peter 1:10-11

74. Ehat thesis, p. 96.

75. Stanley B. Kimball, ed. *On the Potter's Wheel: The Diaries of Heber C. Kimball* (Salt Lake City: Signature Books, 1987), p. 56. Research uncovered by Andrew Ehat in his thesis has abundantly verified that Emma is being referred to in Heber C. Kimball's diary. Copy in author's possession.

76. N. B. Lundwall, compiler, *Temples of the Most High* (Salt Lake City: Press of Zion's Printing & Publishing Co., 1941), p. 246. The date for Bathsheba's endowment is 23 December 1843. She received her anointings from Emma (Ehat thesis, p. 103). Mary Fielding Smith also received her anointings from Emma; she was proxy for Jerusha in her sealing to Hyrum, and was sealed to Hyrum. (See Ehat thesis, pp.102-103, for dates and other early ordinances performed.) After the temple was completed, before the Saints fled to the West, Don Carlos' widow, Agnes Coolbrith, received her endowment and sealing in the temple (Ehat thesis, pp. 102-103).

77. 1 Corinthians 11:11-12.

Joseph's last letter to Emma. The letter is written by his secretary at the time, Willard Richards, but Joseph's postscript is in his own hand.
Courtesy of RLDS Archives.

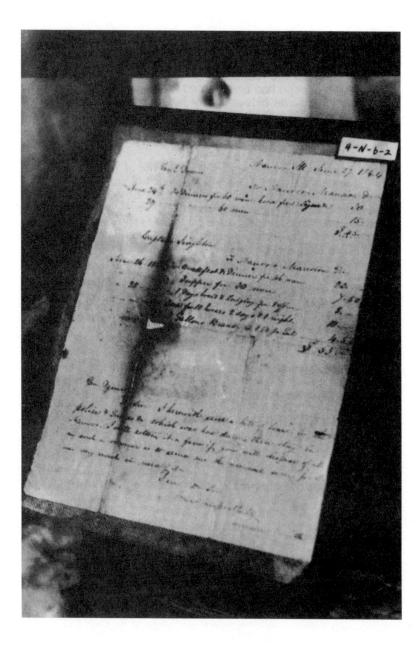

Governor Ford's bill from Emma.
Courtesy of Wilford Wood family, Bountiful, Utah.

CHAPTER 13

"My Husband Was My Crown"

"After he came back from across the river, I felt the worst I ever felt and after that I looked for him to be killed." (Emma Smith)

Emma must have watched the rising storm approaching as 1844, an election year, loomed on the horizon. Blended with the many successes they had enjoyed, they experienced a constant harassment by political and ecclesiastical enemies. Joseph and the brethren knew the political atmosphere of the state and country was of utmost importance to the safety of the Church. It was clear that if the political power swung against them, they could easily be outcast again.

An Interlude of Hope

In Nauvoo, Church leaders recognized the nobility of the principles being revealed concerning the eventual government of Christ upon the earth. They eagerly believed that the day had come when a prophet of the living God would at last wield righteous dominion in government. Like the Jews who saw in Jesus the hope of breaking the yoke of unrighteous government, Joseph's followers saw a hope that the time had come for righteousness to prevail at last. Both failed to perceive the essential timing, that God—not man—would establish the government that will someday, according to the Prophet Daniel, break into pieces all other governments upon the earth. Just as the Jews put Jesus on a donkey and paraded him through the streets of Jerusalem, in effect, the Saints put Joseph on a political donkey and paraded him before the public as a potential candidate for the United States presidency.

In March 1844, news leaked out that Joseph would probably be a candidate for president. Outsiders were quick to catch the implications of adulation by a numerous following. Rumors concerning the "kingdom of God," about which Joseph often preached, caused his political enemies to fear him. Bent as he was upon laying a foundation for the Lord's eternal plan of salvation, Joseph did nothing to dispel the implications. He was therefore erroneously identified by outsiders as a man who was grasping for power and dominion in the political arena of the world. The fact that the "kingdom" of which Joseph taught was not of this world any more than Christ's had been, was lost on a people who could not see beyond their own finite circumstances.

On 17 May, a state convention was held for the Central Committee of the National Reform Association, during which it was confirmed that, "Joseph Smith of Nauvoo is recognized respectfully as a candidate, declarative in the principles of Jeffersonianism, or Jefferson democracy, free trade, and sailors' rights, and the protection of person and property."[1]

Sidney Rigdon, who was in Pennsylvania, was nominated for vice-president.[2] The Honorable John S. Reid, who had defended Joseph in his 1829 trials in New York, attended, and strongly endorsed the Prophet. He later said, "Little did I think that I was defending a boy that would rise to eminence like this man. . . ."[3]

That evening there was a caucus, but Emma was ill, so Joseph could not attend. Later that night, hearing noises outside, he went outside. There he found a large group burning a barrel of tar in the street, giving toasts and generally celebrating his candidacy for the presidency. When he was noticed among them, they lifted him on their shoulders "twice round the fire, and escorted me to the Mansion by a band of music."[4]

What did Emma think of his running for president? After the discouraging experiences of the previous summer when he had been ready to resign from all but church-related business, it seems peculiar that he should have accepted the nomination. His own reasons were that he had ascertained the choice before the people was corruption or corruption; therefore, he actively advanced himself as a potential candidate.[5]

He authorized the brethren to spread throughout the country, preaching the gospel, and he approved their advocating his election. At the same time, correctly assessing the political temperament of the nation, he realized that unless there was a miracle, it was only a matter of time until the Church would be driven again.

During the early spring he appointed a committee of men to explore the West, to find a place to build a new city where the Saints could await the redemption of Zion. This would appear to indicate that his decision to run for president was more a personal statement than any expectation on his part that he might win.

The announcement of his candidacy attracted wide news coverage. Such a bold move could not fail to excite violent opposition. Just as Jesus' enemies in Jerusalem had jealously guarded their earthly dominion and put Him to death, the political enemies of Joseph in Illinois combined their forces to stop him. Even as Joseph's loyal friends hit the campaign trail in his behalf throughout the entire country, a meeting of local politicians from Warsaw and Carthage discussed reports that Joseph's platform was so popular and his reputation so far reaching, they were certain that if he did not succeed in this election, he surely would in the next.[6]

Plans to hold a national convention of the National Reform Association in Baltimore, on 13 July 1844, gave his enemies a time limit. One opponent reportedly said something to the effect that if Joseph lived two weeks, he wouldn't live two months.

In view of the danger, it is strange that Joseph made no effort to soften his stand. He said,

> I calculate to be one of the instruments of setting up the kingdom of Daniel by the word of the Lord, and I intend to lay a foundation that will revolutionize the whole world. . . . It will not be by sword or gun that this kingdom will roll on: the power of truth is such that all nations will be under the necessity of obeying the Gospel. The prediction is that army will be against army: it may be that the Saints will have to beat their ploughs into swords, for it will not do for men to sit down patiently and see their children destroyed. . . . God will always protect me until my mission is fulfilled.[7]

Eagerly, the Twelve and many of the brethren spread out across the nation to campaign for the man they believed was destined to become the next president of the United States. At the same time, an alliance was formed between the political committees of both the Whigs and Democrats of Hancock County. Some men within the city of Nauvoo joined in these meetings, which were specifically called to determine how to get rid of "Joe Smith." Among those who met were Joseph's one-time friends, Dr. Robert Foster; Francis and Chauncey Higbee, sons of his old friend Elias; and even his counselor in the First Presidency, William Law, who now declared Joseph a fallen prophet and proclaimed his own intention of leading a new church. Wilson Law, commander of the Nauvoo Legion, had also become estranged.

As in Kirtland and Missouri, the faithful and the unfaithful were sifted by a power struggle that was masked in political and doctrinal rhetoric. Thus, these men joined the conspiracy with his enemies at Carthage and Warsaw.

Vanishing Hopes

Joseph recognized the end as it approached. In April he spoke at a friend's funeral and publicly acknowledged that if it were not for some enemies in his own circle, he could live to be an old man. Poignantly he remarked, "You do not know me—you never knew me—no man knows my history. I cannot tell it. No man can. If I had not lived it myself, I would not believe it." He also commented that his enemies were calling him "a fallen prophet," but he said that he was not.[8]

Emma heard the words and saw the clouds of the gathering storm. She surely must have worried and struggled with her own crises—another baby coming, a hotel to run, and an increasing awareness that she and Joseph would never know peace on this earth. She was closer to him than anyone, but even she could not hear the meaning behind the words he spoke. Perhaps she had come to believe that he was impervious to danger. He was, after all, God's anointed prophet. Just as she had faith that no one could molest the golden plates, she must have believed that God would look after His own.

The political hoopla did not obscure Joseph's primary concern of building God's kingdom on earth. Huge crowds gathered to hear him preach. On 8 April, he spoke on the importance of finishing the temple. Thomas Bullock, Wilford Woodruff, Willard Richards, and William Clayton all kept notes of this sermon. Each has clearly outlined that the burden of his message was the issue of where Zion should stand. Rather than advocating that all Saints should gather to Nauvoo, he explained that the center stake of the Church would eventually be in Jackson County, Missouri, but that "the whole of North and South America is Zion." He said when the Nauvoo temple was ready, the Elders were to obtain their endowments there and go out and build up stakes "everywhere" so that the members of the Church could be prepared to go through the ordinances for themselves and then for their dead friends and relatives.[9]

Public tensions were rising, but privately, Joseph and Emma were closer than they had ever been. They often rode together, visiting their farm or riding over to the temple grounds. There among the workers and onlookers, they visited friends and watched the progress of the temple, which was now visible from a great distance. Curious passengers going upriver on the riverboats stopped frequently to look over the amazing community. These visitors were incredulous over the neat brick homes, wide streets, well-kept yards and gardens, and the happy, industrious people they met. Many took a meal at the Mansion House, hoping to meet the famed "American Prophet, Joe Smith," the would-be candidate for president of the United States.

Through all this, Emma was a gracious hostess and a good-natured participant in the conversations. Undoubtedly, she formed her own opinions of the political game, for in later years, Emma's grandchildren remembered that she made some special fried pastries, and when asked what they were called, she said that in an election year they were called "Candidates . . . all puffed up and full of [hot] air."[10]

Emma left Nauvoo on 20 April, going downriver on the boat as she had done several times to purchase supplies for the Mansion House. She must have been aware that she was leaving Joseph in the wake of a crisis, since on 18 April, William and Wilson Law had been excommunicated.[11]

On top of these wrenching sorrows, Emma had to contend with some snide newspaper coverage of her trip. The *St. Louis Republican* announced on 23 April that "the Mormon Prophet Joe Smith, has turned his wife out of doors for being in conversation with a gentleman of the sect which she hesitated or refused to disclose."[12] Although the *Boston Post* refuted this as false, saying that Emma only went to St. Louis on business,[13] the impression remained that they were separated. Their friends, however, knew differently.

Even so, they were not without domestic confrontations. A public hotel on the Mississippi River led to customers expecting the accustomed refreshments. Porter Rockwell had not yet finished the barbershop and bar that he was building across the street from the Mansion House, so in Emma's absence, Joseph let Porter put his bar in the Mansion House dining room.

Emma returned from her St. Louis trip on 24 April, and found the bar set up. Young Joseph, then only eleven, remembered long afterward, that his mother asked, "Joseph, what is the meaning of this? How does it look for a spiritual head of a religious body to be keeping a hotel in which a room is fitted out as a liquor-selling establishment?"

Joseph explained to her that all hotels had bars, and that he was only helping Rockwell out until his building was finished. Emma must have considered that a very poor excuse. She told him he could do as he liked about the bar, but if it remained in the Mansion House, she and the children were going to move into the Old Homestead. Young Joseph remembered that his father answered, "Very well, Emma. I will have it removed at once." And it was removed.[14]

Porter built his barbershop and bar across the street, and though Emma could prevent the sale of liquor in her house, she did not prevent its being served on the premises from time to time.

In May of 1844, Emma was in the third month of her eighth pregnancy. Most of the time she was too ill to go about her work and had to remain in bed. Joseph canceled his engagements and stayed with her as much as possible. No doubt they worried over the possibility of her losing this baby, as she had so many others.[15]

At this time, Joseph's enemies publicly declared him to be a fallen prophet. On 23 May, Hyrum went to the Mansion House to caution Joseph against speaking so freely about his enemies. Emma may have asked Hyrum to say something to him. Very likely she was concerned when he was so outspoken in public.

But Joseph refused to accept Hyrum's counsel on the matter. His stand had been made. His enemies were firmly committed to getting rid of him, and he was just as committed to exposing their falsehoods and proving their errors. Summoned to go before a grand jury on charges of immoral conduct, Joseph went to Carthage for the hearing on 27 May. The mob spirit was strongly apparent. To his disappointment, the indictment was deferred until the next term of the court, so he headed home. After a day spent in constant tension, with threats and warnings that his life was in danger and a round trip of about thirty miles on horseback, he "arrived home about 9 P.M., and found Emma sick."16

A few days later, his former-friends-turned-enemies issued a prospectus for a newspaper that would be published in Nauvoo, not just voicing their opinions, but calling for a rousing of the countryside to get rid of Joseph Smith.

The Nauvoo Expositor

The Nauvoo Expositor surfaced on 7 June 1844. It contained vile accusations against Joseph and called for "the unconditional repeal of the Nauvoo City Charter."17

As mayor of the city, Joseph took immediate action: "Monday, June 10, 1844,—I was in the City Council from 10 a.m., to 1:20 p.m., and from 2:20 p.m., to 6:30 p.m. investigating the merits of *The Nauvoo Expositor*, and also the conduct of the Laws, Higbees, Fosters, and others, who have formed a conspiracy for the purpose of destroying my life, and scattering the Saints or driving them from the state."18

In this meeting, Nauvoo's citizens expressed their fears that *The Expositor* would raise public enmity, such as they had encountered in Missouri. It was the general consensus of the city council that the paper must be stopped. Just as officials struggle today with the question of how far the first amendment to the Constitution goes in protecting scandalous publications, Nauvoo's mayor and council made a decision. It was not the calculated decision of a politician smoothing his own path to the White House. It was a united decision of men who had survived mob violence fanned by an unscrupulous press in Missouri, and who were now determined to remove evil from the temporary abode of Zion. Therefore, an ordinance was passed concerning libels, and *The Nauvoo Expositor* was declared a nuisance under this ordinance. The mayor was ordered by the council to "abate the said nuisance." Joseph ordered Marshal John P. Greene to destroy the press without delay, and Jonathan Dunham, acting major-general of the Nauvoo Legion, to assist, if called upon to do so.

About eight that evening, Greene reported that he had complied with the order. A crowd gathered in front of the Mansion, and Joseph addressed them saying that right had been done, that he would "never submit to have another libelous publication established in the city; that [he] did not care how many papers were printed in the city, if they would print the truth: but would submit to no libels or slanders from them." A loud "three-times-three" cheer followed from the crowd. Francis Higbee made threats to shoot Joseph "and all that pertains to him."[19]

Again, we must think of Emma—ill, pregnant, watching what to her must have seemed a replay of Missouri difficulties, yet her loyal heart recognizing that Joseph had done what he felt was the only thing he could to safeguard the people.

To understand these events, it is essential to view them in light of the times, and not superimpose present-day standards upon an era in which legal and social mores were frequently governed by prejudice, and violence against anything out of the mainstream was common. In 1844, the entire country was experiencing sporadic riots, with mobs driving, stoning, and burning homes of Catholics in Baltimore and Jews in New York City; robbers lurked in isolated roadways to stop carriages for whatever plunder they could get. The legal system of the outlying areas was not always efficient, and "law and order" were sometimes defined by numbers or guns. In those days, the press was especially powerful in swaying public attitude. In the extreme western part of the country, vigilante activity was apt to be employed if it appeared that due process might slight the popular goals of unscrupulous individuals. In Illinois, as in Missouri, many of the legal professionals were instigators of mob activities, as they aspired to political offices and saw the Prophet and the numerous Saints as a threat to their political ambitions.[20]

On 12 June, Joseph was served with a writ for causing a riot by destroying the property of William and Wilson Law *(The Nauvoo*

Expositor press). It was filed by Francis Higbee at Carthage, against Joseph, Hyrum, Samuel Bennett, John Taylor, C. Perry, Dimick B. Huntington, Jonathan Dunham, Stephen Markham, William W. Edwards, Jonathan Holmes, Jesse P. Harmon, John Lytle, Joseph W. Coolidge, David Harvey Redfield, Orrin P. Rockwell, and Levi Richards. They were ordered to appear in Carthage for a hearing on 23 June. Joseph had gone to Carthage in May, and he had observed the atmosphere. He knew that if he ever went there again, he would not return alive.[21] Therefore, he petitioned the Nauvoo court for a writ of habeas corpus.

On 13 June, he went before the Municipal Court of Nauvoo for a hearing. Testimony before this court brought out the particulars of the *Expositor* situation, and revealed the murderous spirit of his antagonists. The court decided that Joseph had "acted under proper authority in destroying the establishment of the Nauvoo Expositor," and that his "orders were executed in an orderly and judicious manner, without noise or tumult. . . ." Since no "riot" had taken place, this "was a malicious prosecution on the part of Francis M. Higbee; and that said Higbee pay the costs of suit, and that Joseph be honorably discharged."[22]

Naturally, this made the Higbees and their friends furious, and it gave outsiders the impression that doing away with the Nauvoo City Charter was essential, if they hoped to get rid of Joseph Smith.

Missionary Work Continues

In the midst of these problems, Joseph nevertheless tried to continue attending to the work of the Church. He received requests for missionaries to go to Arkansas and wrote promising that they would be sent. In June, all the Twelve Apostles except John Taylor and Willard Richards were traveling in the states, holding conferences and telling people of Joseph Smith's candidacy for the presidency. Meanwhile, the British mission was a great success. A newspaper was being published there, and another edition of the Book of Mormon was being issued.

In Nauvoo, a new edition of the hymnal, compiled by Emma, was off the press, and the brethren came and went from the Mansion

House as they took up their duties as missionaries for the Church. One could almost say the work of the kingdom was going forth without a hitch, in spite of the serious state of things in local, state, and national politics.

Emma struggled with her health, while continuing to run the hotel, and watch over her growing family—Julia, a lovely budding teen; young Joseph, eleven; Frederick, eight; and Alexander six. The family had a habit of holding an evening worship service, with prayer and singing. One visitor to the Prophet's home, early in the Nauvoo era, recalled, "I arrived at his house just as his family was singing, before the accustomed evening prayer. His wife, Emma, was leading the singing. I thought I had never heard such sweet heavenly music before."[23] Now, as troubles seemed to be surrounding them again, there was little opportunity for peace and singing with his family.

The Prophet had difficulty sleeping. Plagued with nightmares, he recognized his time was nearly up.

Mass Meeting at Warsaw

The atmosphere became even more tense as the resolutions published at a mass meeting in Warsaw included a call to force Joseph into court outside Nauvoo. They said:

> The time . . . has arrived, when the adherents to Smith, as a body, should be driven from the surrounding settlements into Nauvoo. That the Prophet and his miscreant adherents should then be demanded at their hands; and, if not surrendered, a war of extermination should be waged to the entire destruction, if necessary. . . . We hereby recommend this resolution to the consideration of the several townships, to the Mass Convention to be held at Carthage, hereby pledging ourselves to aid to the utmost the complete consummation of the object in view.[24]

Thomas Sharp, editor of the *Warsaw Signal,* lost no time in making the resolutions public. Soon outlying farms belonging to the Mormons were attacked. Some were set on fire, and the scattered families began to collect in Nauvoo for refuge. Joseph responded by writing a letter to the governor, informing him of the action that had taken place and asking him, if he was not satisfied with the action taken by the Nauvoo Court, that he "demand an investigation before Judge Pope [in Springfield] or any tribunal at the Capitol."[25]

Joseph's Last Sermon

Sunday, 16 June, with a rainstorm threatening, the Prophet preached his last sermon. He opened his text by reading from Revelations 1:6: "And hath made us kings and priests unto God and His Father: to Him be glory and dominion forever and ever. . . ."[26]

This was the last public testimony of a man who had completed what the Lord had required of him. He spoke of the nature of God, explaining many attributes of the Father, Son, and Holy Ghost, and man's relationship to them. He mentioned his difficulties, explained that he had done his best, as other Prophets before him had done, and as the Savior Himself had tried to do. He said, "They found fault with Jesus Christ because he said He was the Son of God, and made himself equal with God. They say of me, like they did of the apostles of old, that I must be put down." He challenged all to read the scriptures and believe them, not just in part, but in their entirety. He cited the revelations in the Doctrine and Covenants, the Book of Mormon, and the translations of the ancient prophets, Moses and Abraham, publicized in the Pearl of Great Price, and invited all people to study the word of God to learn the truth. He urged them to be open and willing to learn more and not assume that what they knew, or thought they knew, is all there is of truth.

When the record of his sermon ends, due to the rain, one is left bereft in the realization of lost information, recorded only in the hearts of those who were there to hear. It is unlikely that Emma, having been extremely ill for most of the weeks previous, braved the weather to hear what he said.

Thanks to Thomas Bullock, who was the Prophet's scribe at that time, and several others who wrote in their journals, a good portion of this sermon has been made available to us today.[27]

The Prophet's Last Public Speech

On 18 June, Joseph called the Legion together in the street near the Mansion House, and delivered the last public address he would make. Fearing trouble within the city, he had declared martial law in Nauvoo.

What must Emma have thought as the Legion formed up in orderly rows in the street about 2 p.m. The Prophet, dressed in full uniform, climbed on top of the frame building which was under construction. His speech was eloquent and emotional.

He called upon "God, angels, and all men to witness that we are innocent of the charges which are heralded forth by the public prints against us by our Enemies; and while they assemble together in unlawful mobs to take away our rights and destroy our lives they think to shield themselves under the refuge of lies which they have thus wickedly fabricated. . . ."

Joseph assigned the Legion to the duty of keeping peace within the city. He asked, "Will you die for me?" They answered, "Aye!" and he said, "I will die for you!" He drew his sword, pointed it toward heaven, and exclaimed, "I declare that this people shall have their rights, or my blood shall spill upon the ground!"[28]

He sent John Taylor to the governor with affidavits and a request that he allow the case to be moved to a different area than Carthage. The governor was already in company with Francis Higbee, Wilson and William Law, Foster, and others of the dissidents from Nauvoo. When Taylor arrived and tried to explain the situation Joseph was in, he was rudely interrupted and contradicted by the men there.

Governor Ford was not sympathetic. He replied that Joseph and the others must come to Carthage and stand trial and be cleared if they were innocent—or punished if guilty. Let the court decide. Apparently recognizing that the threat against Joseph's life was real, Governor Ford pledged his faith and the faith of the state of Illinois, that *he would guarantee their perfect safety.*[29]

Fateful Moments of Decision

In the afternoon of 22 June, Joseph had a consultation with his brother Hyrum, Dr. Richards, John Taylor, and John M. Bernhisel. It was determined that someone should go to Washington and lay the matter before President Tyler. Offering personal petitions to the president was a common practice at that time.

In the evening the Prophet asked Reynolds Cahoon and Alpheus Cutler to stand guard at the Mansion and not to admit any strangers. Soon after dusk, according to Abraham C. Hodge, who was present, a meeting was held in the upper room of Joseph's house. Hyrum, Willard Richards, John Taylor, William W. Phelps, A. C. Hodge, John L. Butler, Alpheus Cutler, William Marks, and some others were present. Joseph then presented the letter from Governor Ford and remarked, "There is no mercy here—no mercy here."

Hyrum said, "No, just as sure as we fall into their hands we are dead men."

Joseph asked, "What shall we do, Hyrum?" to which his brother replied, "I don't know."

All at once a brightness came upon Joseph's face. "The way is open," he said. "It is clear to my mind what to do. All they want is Hyrum and myself; then tell everybody to go about their business, and not to collect in groups, but to scatter about. There is no doubt they will search for us. Let them search; they will not harm you in person or property, and not even a hair of your head. We will cross the river tonight, and go away to the west."[30]

He then gave instructions to have the riverboat, the *Maid of Iowa,* brought to the landing and his and Hyrum's families to be put on board. At 9 p.m., Hyrum came out of the Mansion and shook hands with Reynolds Cahoon, saying, "A company of men are seeking to kill my brother Joseph, and the Lord has warned him to flee to the Rocky Mountains to save his life. Good-bye Brother Cahoon, we shall see you again." Joseph came out a few minutes later, having explained the situation to his family. He was in tears, holding a handkerchief to his face, and following his brother, he did not utter a word.

While waiting for the skiff to take them across the river, Joseph sent for William W. Phelps. He told him to take his and Hyrum's families to Cincinnati by the second steamboat, the next day. William Phelps was then to proceed to Washington and commence petitioning President Tyler and the Congress of the United States for redress of grievances, and for liberty and equal rights for the Church.

He told Phelps, "Go to our wives, and tell them what we have concluded to do and learn their feelings on the subject; and tell Emma you will be ready to start by the second steamboat, and she has sufficient money wherewith to pay the expenses. . . ."[31]

Emma's Ordeal Begins Anew

Once again Emma was called upon to prepare to flee and to await the outcome, while Joseph and Hyrum went into another dark night of exile. The men crossed the river in a leaky skiff rowed by Porter Rockwell. Willard Richards was with them.

In the morning, rumors flew thick and fast within the city. Emma was besieged with visitors and with questions she could not answer. A posse arrived to arrest Joseph. Not finding him, they indicated that "if Joseph and Hyrum were not given up, [the Governor] would send his troops and guard the city until they were found, if it took three years to do it."[32] Later that night the threat was strengthened by the statement that unless the mayor and city council of Nauvoo were in Carthage Monday, by 10 a.m., "Nauvoo would be destroyed and all the men, women and children in it."[33]

There was great fear among those people who had experienced similar troubles in Missouri. For others, it was a practical matter of land values and business, which would obviously be lost if Joseph abandoned Nauvoo. Some thought Joseph was a coward and was deserting the Church when it needed him most.

Emma sent Porter Rockwell to Joseph to entreat Joseph to come back. Reynolds Cahoon and Emma's nephew, Lorenzo D. Wasson, and Hyrum Kimball went with him. They brought a letter from Emma. Exactly what she wrote is not known. If she followed the same pattern she had in the past, she undoubtedly defined to Joseph what the situation was in the city, not shielding him from her feelings of anxiety, but offering him her support in any action he chose to take. Unless her letter is found, we should not presume to know what she actually did say.

Some of the men accused Joseph of cowardice, some comparing his act of running away to the fable of the wolves and sheep: when the wolves came, the shepherd ran from the flock and left the sheep to be devoured. Clearly the message received was that they had no faith in the safety of Nauvoo unless Joseph complied with the order to go to Carthage. To this he replied, "If my life is of no value to my friends, it is of none to myself."[34]

Joseph and Hyrum returned to Nauvoo. Mercy Thompson recorded seeing the skiff coming across the river, and watching as the men walked up to Hyrum's house. She said Joseph waited while Hyrum gathered his things and then the two of them went to the Mansion House.

In Emma's later years, she was asked about this time when Joseph came back across the river. She said, "I felt the worst I ever felt in my life, from that time I looked for him to be killed."[35]

A Last Farewell

We have no detailed account of Emma's last hours with Joseph. He was wakened early in the morning, and there are some journal accounts that report he left and then returned to his house three different times for words with his family. He wept openly as he rode away from his house to join Hyrum and the others who would accompany them to Carthage—John Taylor, Willard Richards, John P. Greene, Stephen Markham, Dan Jones, John S. Fullmer, Lorenzo Wasson (Emma's nephew), and a Dr. Southwick from Louisiana.[36]

On the hill beside the temple, he stopped and looked over the beautiful city—the neat brick homes, the wide, clean streets, the yards and gardens full of promise, the gray-white stones of the temple walls rising daily under the skilled hands of dedicated builders. Again he wept as he said, "This is the most beautiful place and the best people on earth. . . . Little do they know what awaits them."[37]

As he passed his farm, he stopped and gazed upon it for a long time. The others grew impatient and chided him. He answered, "If you had a farm like that and you knew you would never see it again . . . wouldn't you want to stop and look at it?"[38] His companions thought merely that Joseph was in a gloomy mood. They didn't believe this was the last time he would see his farm. How could they understand his depression? They were all in this together, and they had seen Joseph through bad times in the past—surely nothing really serious could happen to a man who would be in the protective custody of the governor of the state of Illinois? Surely nothing would happen to the Lord's prophet!

Along the way to Carthage they met the governor's militia, headed toward Nauvoo to confiscate the state arms which had been issued to the Nauvoo Legion after the Charter was granted, in 1840. Now the arms were being recalled. Retribution had begun.

The leaders of the militia asked Joseph to go with them back to Nauvoo to collect the arms. Before complying with this request, Joseph turned quietly to his friends and said, "I am going like a lamb to the slaughter, but I am calm as a summer's morning. I have a conscience void of offense toward God and towards all men. If they take my life I shall die an innocent man, and my blood shall cry from the ground for vengeance, and it shall be said of me, 'He was murdered in cold blood!'"[39]

After gathering up the state arms, Joseph went again to say farewell to his family. As they parted for the last time, he was overheard asking, "Emma, can you raise my sons to walk in their father's footsteps?"

"Oh, Joseph! You're coming back!" she said.

Again he asked the same question and again she responded with "You're coming back." When he asked a third time, Emma began crying. Joseph, too, wept as he embraced Julia, young Joseph, Freddie, and Alexander.[40] It has been said that he asked Emma to accompany him, but she refused. She was five months along in her pregnancy and her health was delicate. She was afraid of catching the chills and fever. It is possible that Joseph was making a wistful remark, desiring that Emma could go with him; but to all who realize his awareness of the danger waiting for him in Carthage, it seems unlikely he would have wanted to take her there. Still, parting from her was very painful. They were both in tears as they parted. Emma's grief at this farewell was witnessed by several people. All said she was beyond consolation.

There seemed to be no alternative for Joseph; either he must give himself up or the inhabitants of the city would be massacred with the sanction of the governor. Joseph had been assured by the Spirit of the Lord that all would be well with them if he went to the West; but without the faith of his people to sustain that assurance, he had no choice but to go to Carthage to what he knew would be certain death.

It was late when they reached Carthage. They went to the Hamilton House, which was a hotel. Due to malicious threats and taunting calls of mobs in the street under their window, they were unable to sleep. At the Hamilton House that night were also the Laws and some of the Higbees, as well as the governor's party. While the former Church members secretly plotted to destroy Joseph in court, one of their associates made it publicly known that they, too, thirsted for the blood of Joseph Smith. Realizing their danger, Joseph sent to the governor, requesting an immediate hearing.[41]

Joseph and Hyrum were escorted to an informal hearing, where the Carthage Greys, the local militia, made a great show of hostility, making it plain they intended to see Joseph and Hyrum dead. The governor sarcastically presented Lieutenant-General Joseph Smith and his brother, and mildly chided the militia for their disgraceful manners, saying that they should receive "satisfaction." If Joseph had ever hoped for justice and a fair hearing, his hope must have now vanished.

The charge against them was treason.[42] If witnesses could be heard before an unbiased judge, the charge could be proven false, but their enemies intended that the Prophet and his brother would have no opportunity for such a hearing.

Emma's Last Letter from Joseph

The last letter Emma received from Joseph was headed, "Carthage Jail, June 27, 1844, 20 past 8 o'clock." They were in protective custody in the jailhouse, in an upstairs bedroom. Joseph wrote most earnest instructions to her concerning what was to transpire in regard to the governor and his troops in Nauvoo. He asked her to convey to Brother Dunham that he was to "instruct the people to stay at home and attend to their own business." He also tried to allay fears by adding, "There is no danger of any exterminating order." But then he added a disquieting comment, "Should there be a mutiny among the troops (which we do not anticipate, excitement is abating), a part will remain loyal, and stand for the defense of the state and our rights."

He ended the formal portion of the letter, which was in Willard Richards' handwriting, by making an oblique reference to self-defense, which almost leads one to think he was trying to convey some kind of warning in an otherwise quite salutary letter. He wrote, "There is one principle which is eternal, it is the duty of all men to protect their lives and the lives of their household whenever necessity requires, and no power has a right to forbid it, should the last extreme arrive, but I anticipate no such extremity—but caution is the parent of safety. —Signed Joseph Smith."[43]

Obviously, he did not completely trust the governor nor the militia, and he wanted the leaders in Nauvoo to understand that if they were attacked, they would not be in the wrong to defend themselves. But he wanted to insure that the Saints would not be the aggressors. He added a postscript in his own hand which was certainly not much more personal, but perhaps was even more disquieting to her than his previous words:

"Dear Emma, I am very much resigned to my lot, knowing I am justified and have done the best that could be done. Give my love to the children and all my friends . . . and all who inquire after me; and as for treason, I know that I have not committed any, and they cannot prove one appearance of anything of the kind, so you need not have any fears that any harm can happen to us on that score. May God bless you all. Amen. Signed Joseph Smith."[44]

His second postscript was written by Richards. He indicated that they had just received word the governor was going to disband his troops, except a small guard to protect them at the jail, and the governor would go himself to Nauvoo and deliver a speech to the people there.[45]

When Joseph heard of this plan, he obtained an interview with Governor Ford at about 9:30. He asked that he be allowed to go along to Nauvoo. The governor promised he would take him along if he went. They discussed the danger. Governor Ford insisted Joseph and Hyrum would be perfectly safe in Carthage. He said he hoped Joseph would be acquitted, then added, "but I cannot interfere." He assured Joseph again that if he did go to Nauvoo, he certainly would take him along. With this lie upon his lips, he sent the Prophet back to the stone jailhouse. Then almost immediately, taking the militia under command of General Deming, he left the prisoners there—under "protection" of the Carthage Grays—men he well knew were avowed enemies of the Prophet and had plans to murder the Mormon leaders.[46]

No Time for a Blessing for Emma

Tradition says that just before Joseph returned to Carthage, Emma asked him for a blessing. The Prophet told her he didn't have time just then to give her a blessing, but for her to write the best blessing she could and he would sign it when he returned. A typescript copy of the blessing she wrote exists although the original has not been found. While it cannot be proven authentic, most scholars accept it as her work. The sentiments are drawn from the revelations, reflecting a great deal of consideration and heartfelt desire to draw upon words Joseph had used. Emma wrote:

> First of all that I would crave as the richest of heaven's blessings would be wisdom from my Heavenly Father bestowed daily, so that whatever I might do or say, I could not look back at the close of the day with regret, nor neglect the performance of any act that would bring a blessing. I desire the Spirit of God to know and understand myself, I desire a fruitful, active mind, that I may be able to comprehend the designs of God, when revealed through his servants without doubting. I desire the spirit of discernment, which is one of the promised blessings of the Holy Ghost. I particularly desire wisdom to bring up all the children that are, or may be committed to my charge, in such a manner that they will be useful ornaments in the Kingdom of God, and in a coming day arise up and call me blessed. I desire prudence that I may not through ambition abuse my body and cause it to become old and care-worn, but that I may wear a cheerful countenance, living to perform all the work that I covenanted to perform in the spirit-world and be a blessing to all who may need aught at my hands. I desire with all my heart to honor and respect my husband as my head, ever to live in his confidence and by acting in unison with him retain the place which God has given me by his side, and I ask my Heavenly Father, that through humility, I may be enabled to overcome that curse which was pronounced on the daughters of Eve. I desire to see my kindred and friends embrace the principles of Eternal Truth, that I may

rejoice with them in the blessings which God has in store for all who are willing to be obedient to his requirements. Finally, I desire that whatever may be my lot through life I may be enabled to acknowledge the hand of God in all things.

These desires of my heart were called forth by Joseph sending me word . . . that he had not time to write as he would like, but I could write out the best blessing I could think of and he would sign the same on his return.[47]

The Sacrifice

The day of 27 June passed slowly for the men waiting in the jail. The weather was humid; a thunder shower had passed through the area earlier in the day, so that when the sun came out, a stifling heat settled over the jail. The window was open. More thunderclouds were gathering.

Stephen Markham, Dan Jones, and Cyrus H. Wheelock (who had brought Joseph a pistol) left. After the governor left for Nauvoo, the temper of the guards changed, and they would not admit them a second time.

Joseph, Hyrum, Willard, and John were in the upstairs bedroom of the jailer's quarters. There was no lock on the door, nor bars on the windows. They all felt a terrible depression when they learned of the governor's departure. John Taylor attempted to relieve some of the depression by singing the hymn, "A Poor Wayfaring Man of Grief." When he finished, Hyrum asked him to sing it again. John protested that he didn't feel like singing, but Hyrum prevailed upon him, saying, "Never mind, just commence singing and the spirit will come."[48] John began to sing. His beautiful tenor voice carried the plaintive melody all the way through six verses. The words of the song were like a testimony, ending with:

"In pris'n I saw him next, condemned
To meet a traitor's doom at morn.
The tide of lying tongues I stemmed,
And honored him 'mid shame and scorn.
My friendship's utmost zeal to try,
He asked if I for him would die.

The flesh was weak; my blood ran chill,
But my free spirit cried, "I will!"

Then in a moment to my view
The stranger started from disguise.
The tokens in his hands I knew;
The Savior stood before mine eyes.
He spake, and my poor name he named,
"Of me thou hast not been ashamed.
These deeds shall thy memorial be;
Fear not, thou didst them unto me."[49]

As the closing strains settled upon a brooding silence inside the room, John Taylor glanced outside. He saw men with their faces painted black, coming toward the jail. Then a large party of men stormed the building.

The Carthage Greys made a poor show of defending the men in their care. Some said later that they fired over the heads of the mob; others said that their guns were loaded with blanks. In any case, it was all over in less than five minutes.

Hyrum fell first as he tried to hold the door. As he fell, he cried, "I am a dead man!" Joseph rushed to his brother's side, exclaiming, "Oh, my dear brother Hyrum!" He ran to the door and fired four times into the stairway. John Taylor, who had rushed to the window, was struck. The force of the bullet threw him back and he crawled under the bed, where he was shot several more times. Joseph ran to the window, while Willard Richards tried to parry the guns being fired in at the door, by hitting at them with his walking stick. He was pushed up against the wall behind the door, where he remained, unnoticed, which probably saved his life. As Joseph reached the window, he was struck from behind, and either jumped or fell out the window. Some have said he exclaimed loudly, "O Lord! My God!" before he fell to the ground beside the well. He was shot again after he was dead, in all taking four balls.

There have been many accounts made of the events that followed. Undoubtedly there was great delight on the part of the mob, who had succeeded in killing Joseph and Hyrum. There was also a great desire to keep their identity secret, and they feared the arrival of the Legion from Nauvoo. One account by an eyewitness states that someone yelled, "The Mormons are coming!" and a brilliant shaft of light burst across the area, frightening the mob, who swiftly ran away.[50] Whether it was a fear of supernatural retribution for the crime they had committed or terror that an armed force of Mormons might really be upon them, the effect on the mob was a hasty retreat out of town.

When all was quiet, Willard Richards went to the window and looked out. He could see Joseph lying quietly beside the well. Hyrum was dead on the floor. John Taylor, seriously wounded and lying in a pool of blood under the bed, called to him. Willard did what he could for him, but fearing the enemy would come back, the two men did not dare to stay where they were. Willard dragged his friend into the cells at the back of the building, covered him with a straw mattress, and waited for whatever would come. Both men expected to be killed at any moment. When all remained quiet, some people came up the stairs to see what had happened. They helped take John to where they could clean him up and attend to his wounds.[51]

In the wake of the slaying, nearly everyone in the town of Carthage had fled for fear of the Mormons coming to take revenge. The jailer and his wife and family had been in their kitchen down-stairs, in mortal danger. Bullets had barely missed the jailer's wife.

Documentation of Irony

Emma had been busy for the past three days with crowds of men coming and going between Nauvoo and Carthage. The governor and his troops had arrived in Nauvoo and went to the Mansion House, where they dined. Emma would surely have realized that they had left few, if any, trustworthy guards in Carthage. There in Joseph's own house, the governor sat in a meeting. A man rushed in and was over-heard saying to the governor, "Ere this time the deed is done."

Undoubtedly, the rumor that Joseph had been killed reached Emma's ears long before official word arrived. Ironically, at just about the same time her husband was being assassinated in Carthage, Emma was presenting the bill for lodging the men who should have been on duty protecting him. Signed by Emma, this bill lists the price of board and lodging for sixty men and their horses, for services rendered on 24-27 June. At the bottom she added a postscript asking that they pay promptly as she badly needed the money.[52]

At about 6 p.m., the governor addressed the people of Nauvoo, threatening and pacifying them, all in one breath. When he finished, the militiamen with him settled their account at the Mansion House before they rode back to Carthage.

Reports as to who brought Emma the news that her husband and brother-in-law were dead are inconclusive. In his memoirs, Joseph III quotes Wandell Mace, who indicates that word did not arrive until early on the morning of 28 June. Young Joseph III remembers a dusty rider coming with the news, but is not sure who he was. Throughout the city the news brought incredible sorrow. But in the homes of Joseph, Hyrum, and their relatives, there was a long wail of agony.

Alone Again

The bodies were brought home on 28 June, just one day short of the fourteenth anniversary of Emma's baptism.[53]

Once again Joseph had been forced to leave her, but this time he was not waiting in some hideaway for her to bring the children and come to him. Joseph was gone. Emma would be forty on her next birthday, and would bear her last son in five months. An eyewitness to Emma's grief recorded:

> When I entered the Mansion I found the wife of Joseph seated in a chair in the center of a small room, weeping and wailing bitterly, in a loud and unrestrained voice, her face covered with her hands. Rev. Mr. [John P.] Greene came in, and as the bitter cries of the weeping woman reached his ears, he burst forth in tones of manly grief, and trembling in every nerve, approached Mrs. Smith and exclaimed: "Oh Sister Emma, God bless you!" Then clasping her head in his hands, he uttered a long and fervent prayer for her peace, protection and resignation. The first words of the poor woman were: "Why, O God, am I thus afflicted? Why am I a widow? . . . Thou knowest I have always trusted in thy law." Mr. Greene rejoined to her that this affliction would be to her a crown of life. She answered quickly:

"My husband was my crown; for him and for my children I have suffered the loss of all things; and why, O God, am I thus deserted, and my bosom torn with this ten-fold anguish?"[54]

In that awful extremity, did Emma think of her father's parting words? "No good can ever come of it!"

Notes

1. *HC,* 6:386.

2. *HC,* 6:390.

3. *HC,* 6:396.

4. *HC,* 6:397.

5. See *HC,* 6:280-83 for documentation of his research concerning the political candidates and the results of his decision to become a candidate.

6. *HC,* 6:43 (introduction). Joseph made this comment: "When I get hold of the eastern papers and see how popular I am, I am afraid myself that I shall be elected; but if I should be, I would not say, 'Your cause is just, but I can do nothing for you'" (referring to President Van Buren's dismissal of his petition for redress for the Missouri persecutions).

7. *HC,* 6:365.

8. Andrew Ehat and Lyndon Cook, *The Words of Joseph Smith* (Provo, Utah: Religious Studies Center, Brigham Young University, 1980), p. 367.

9. Ibid., pp. 363-64.

10. Buddy Youngreen, *Reflections of Emma, Joseph Smith's Wife* (Orem, Utah: Grandin Book, 1982), pp. 103-104.

11. *HC,* 6:341.

12. *St. Louis Republican*, 23 April 1844. As cited in Linda Newell and Valeen Avery, *Mormon Enigma: Emma Hale Smith* (Garden City, New York: Doubleday & Company, Inc., 1984), p. 178.

13. *Boston Post* (1844), as cited in Newell and Avery, *Mormon Enigma: Emma Hale Smith*, p. 178.

14. Mary Audentia Smith Anderson, ed., *Joseph III and the Restoration* (Independence, Mo: Herald Publishing House, 1952), pp. 74-76.

15. Youngreen, *Reflections of Emma*, p. 35.

16. *HC,* 6:403-14.

17. *HC,* 6:443.

18. *HC,* 6:432.

19. *HC,* 6:457.

20. It was generally recognized by all parties, even at the time, that those who drove the Saints out of Illinois were no more concerned about the form of their religious worship than the Missourians were. Their real concern was the

Mormons' political influence, for these western areas of the country, in those early days, were inhabited by many renegade types who wanted to keep the country in their own control. A group such as the Latter-day Saints, who were unwilling to bribe or be bribed, or to participate in the schemes some of these men were running, for their own gain, could not be permitted to remain there. They must be driven out. It would have been no different had it been another faith, as long as the group was sufficiently influential and incorruptible. One major ambition of the enemies was to obtain all they could of the Mormons' property as cheaply as possible. The brethren were determined that they would hold out to sell, not just give it up.

21. *HC,* 6:543-46.

22. *HC,* 6:458.

23. In Hyrum L. Andrus and Helen Mae Andrus, *They Knew the Prophet* (Salt Lake City: Bookcraft, 1974), p. 147.

24. *HC,* 6:646.

25. *HC,* 6:466-67.

26. Revelation 3:6-12.

27. *HC,* 6:473-79.

28. *HC,* 6:498-500.

29. *HC,* 6:521-37; italics added

30. *HC,* 6:545-48.

31. Ibid.

32. *HC,* 6:549.

33. *HC,* 6:552.

34. *HC,* 6:552-58.

35. Emma Hale Smith Bidamon, *Emma Smith's Last Testimony*, February 1879, Reorganized Church of Jesus Christ of Latter Day Saints (RLDS) Archives, Independence, Mo.

36. See Ivan J. Barrett, *Joseph Smith and the Restoration* (Provo, Utah: Brigham Young University Press), 1967, p. 607. In the morning, Dan Jones, Stephen Markham, and Lorenzo Snow went together to request an interview with Governor Ford.

37. *HC,* 6:554

38. *HC,* 6:558.

39. *HC,* 6:555.

40. Linda King Newell and Valeen Tippets Avery, *Mormon Enigma: Emma Hale Smith* (Garden City, New York: Doubleday & Company, Inc., 1984), p. 190.

41. *HC,* 6:75-91.

42. *HC,* 6:561-65.

43. *HC,* 6:605.

44. Ibid.

45. Ibid.

46. Ibid.

47. LDS Church Archives; copy in possession of author. See also Buddy

Youngreen, "Joseph and Emma Slide Presentation," *BYU Studies* (Winter, 1974), p. 216, and LDS 1985 Relief Society Manual.

48. Henry A. Smith, *The Day They Martyred the Prophet* (Salt Lake City: Bookcraft, 1963), pp. 171- 73.

49. *Hymns of the Church of Jesus Christ of Latter-day Saints* (Salt Lake City: The Church of Jesus Christ of Latter-day Saints), no. 29.

50. Henry A. Smith, pp. 174-180; see also N. B. Lundwall, *Fate of the Persecutors of the Prophet Joseph Smith* (Salt Lake City: Bookcraft, 1952), pp. 167-233. There are many accounts of the martyrdom; these are but two of them.

51. *HC,* 6:612-15.

52. This document was preserved and came into the collection of Wilford Wood of Bountiful, Utah. It is used here by permission of his daughter, Lillian.

53. *HC,* 6:615-19.

54. E. Cecil McGavin, *Nauvoo the Beautiful* (Salt Lake City: Bookcraft, 1972), p. 144. Dr. B. W. Richmond was a bitter enemy of Joseph, but a guest in the Mansion House and a witness to Emma's grief.

Chapter 14

The Last Sacrifice

"*I have no friend but God and no place to go but home.*"
(Emma Smith)

With six precious infants buried, her husband dead, and the embryo of another son growing in her womb, Emma again found herself alone in a hostile world. In the past she had endured poverty, privations, and persecution with a remarkable degree of cheerfulness, knowing that Joseph would be there to reassure her and need her. Throughout their seventeen years together, Emma's chief concern was a simple triangle: Joseph, their children, the Church. With Joseph gone, Emma centered her concern upon her children and the need to protect and provide for them. In light of that duty, all other considerations would fade.

Viewing the Bodies

After the bodies of Joseph and Hyrum were carried into the Mansion House dining room on the afternoon of 28 June, the doors were immediately closed. A vast crowd had followed them to the house. Willard Richards addressed the bereaved Saints, admonishing them to keep the peace, stating that he had "pledged his honor, and his life for their good conduct."[1] Some other brethren spoke to them as well; the mourners were told to go home quietly and come back in the morning at eight o'clock, when they would be allowed to view the bodies.

Dimick and William Huntington, and William Marks "washed the bodies from head to foot." The wounds were filled with cotton soaked in camphor, and the bodies in "fine plain drawers and shirt, white neckerchiefs, white cotton stockings and white shrouds."[2] It was not a task for fainthearted men; it was performed by men who loved Joseph and Hyrum dearly.

When the bodies were presentable, the widows and their children were brought in. Dimick Huntington, the coroner, and John P. Greene, the marshal, were in attendance. There were others in the room, one of whom was Dr. Richmond, a guest in the hotel at the time. Dr. Richmond recorded: "As the door opened the Prophet's wife entered with two attendants. She advanced a few steps towards the body of Hyrum, swooned and fell to the floor. Her friends raised her up and gave her water, but she fainted again, and was carried out insensible. . . ." Emma made several other attempts to view the bodies, but each time she fainted and had to be carried out.

Hyrum's wife, Mary, entered, trembling at every step. Dr. Richmond recalled:

> [She] nearly fell, but reached her husband's body, kneeling down by him, clasped her arms around his head, turned his pale face toward her heaving bosom, and then a gushing, plaintive wail burst from her lips: "Oh! Hyrum. Hyrum! Have they shot you, my dear Hyrum—are you dead? Oh! speak to me, my dear husband. I cannot think you are dead, my dear Hyrum!" Her grief seemed to consume her, and she lost all power of utterance. . . . Her two daughters and two young children clung, some around her neck and some to her body, falling prostrate upon the corpse, and shrieking. . . . About ten minutes later Emma came back into the room, supported on either side. They led her toward Hyrum, one of the men shielding her view of Joseph. As she laid her hand upon Hyrum's brow, calmness came over her. Her eyes opened, and she said to her friends, "Now I can see him; I am strong now." She walked alone to her husband's bed, kneeling down, clasped him around his face, and sank upon his body. Suddenly her grief found vent; and sighs and groans and words and lamentations filled the room. "Joseph, Joseph," she said, "are you dead? Have the assassins shot you?" Her children, four in number, gathered around their weeping mother and the dead body . . . and grief that words cannot embody seemed to overwhelm the whole group. . . .[3]

Lucy recorded in her history:

> I had for a long time braced every nerve, roused every energy of my soul, and called upon God to strengthen me; but when I entered the room, and saw my murdered sons extended both at once before my eyes, and heard the sobs and moans of my family . . . it was too much, I sank back, crying to the Lord, in the agony of my soul, "My God, My God, why hast thou forsaken this family!" A voice replied, "I have taken them to myself, that they might have rest." Emma was carried back to her room. . . . Her oldest son approached the corpse, and dropped upon his knees, and lay his cheek against his father's and kissing him, exclaimed, "Oh, my father! My father!" As for myself, I was swallowed up in the depths of my afflictions; and though my soul was filled with horror past imagination, yet I was dumb, until I arose again to contemplate the spectacle before me. Oh! at that moment how my mind flew through every scene of sorrow and distress which we had passed, together, in which they had shown the innocence and sympathy which filled their guileless hearts. As I looked upon their peaceful, smiling countenances, I seemed almost to hear them say—"Mother, weep not for us, we have overcome the world by love; we carried to them the gospel, that their souls might be saved; they slew us for our testimony, and thus placed us beyond their power; their ascendency is for a moment, ours is an eternal triumph."[4]

From early morning to late in the afternoon on 29 June, the people of Nauvoo filed in one door and out another, pausing to look upon the Prophet and Patriarch, laid out in boxes lined with white cambric (a kind of tight weave white cloth, probably made of cotton). The boxes were covered with black velvet cloth which was held in place with brass nails.[5] There was a thick glass cover placed over each, through which the grieving Saints could view their faces for the last time. Despite the violent manner of their death, their countenances were peaceful in repose.

At five o'clock, the family asked that the Mansion be cleared so the relatives could have some time alone to bid farewell to their loved ones. There had been rumors that a reward of $1000 had been offered for Joseph's head, so they felt it was best to bury the bodies secretly. In order to accomplish this, the boxes holding the bodies were removed from the caskets and placed in another room. Then the caskets were filled with sandbags and fastened shut, to be taken to the tomb near the temple for public services and burial.[6]

The Funeral

The sun must have been getting low on the horizon by the time the hearse, carrying the sandbagged coffins, made its way slowly up Water Street and up Mulholland Street, to the temple lot where the tomb was prepared. Many thousands of Saints thronged the familiar gathering place near the temple, where Joseph had so often addressed them from a wooden stand built for this purpose. William W. Phelps delivered the eulogy. Thousands listened and mourned. Enemies watched, satisfied—but they could not have appreciated what this friend of Joseph said, in his lengthy address quoted here, in part:

> Be assured, brethren and sisters, this desperate "smite" of our foes to stop the onward course of Mormonism, will increase its spread and rapidity an hundred fold: The bodies of our brethren are marred, by physical force; because the flesh was weak; but the priesthood remains unharmed—that is eternal without beginning of days or end of years; and the "Twelve," (mostly now absent) are clothed with it, as well as others, and when they return, they will wear the "mantle" and step into the "shoes" of the "prophet," . . . and then with the same power, the same God, the same spirit that caused Joseph to move the cause of Zion with mighty power will qualify them to roll on the work until all Israel is gathered. . . . Anciently, as well as now, weak minded persons supposed that prophets and saints suffered death or trouble for their sins. . . . Not [Joseph]: The revelations he brought forth are everlasting witnesses that he, like the Savior, came not to "drink and be merry, for tomorrow we die," but to point out the way of life, and call upon all men, to repent and be saved.[7]

Where was Emma during this sermon? Nobody knows.

Secret Burial

At midnight, graves were dug in the ground inside the walls of the partially built walls of the Nauvoo House. A group of trusted men, including William and Dimick B. Huntington, Edward Hunter, William Marks, Jonathan H. Holmes, Gilbert Goldsmith, Alpheus Cutler, Philip B. Lewis, and Emma's nephew, Lorenzo D. Wasson, carried the two coffins out of the Mansion. This procession went through the garden, around by the pump, and across the street into the section of the Nauvoo House that had been ". . . built to the first joists of the basement."[8] They were preceded by James Emmett, on guard with his musket. After the burial was completed, they tramped the soil and covered the place with leaves, so it would not be suspected the ground had been disturbed. It seemed providential that a tremendous rainstorm struck shortly after they had finished, completely obliterating all evidence of the ground having been recently dug.

There may have been good cause to keep the burial place a secret. There was apparently some threat that implied someone might attempt to molest the graves.[9]

Later in the fall, at Emma's insistence, the bodies were moved to a place in the yard of the Homestead, under the dirt floor of the spring house. Dimick and William Huntington, Jonathan Holmes, and Gilbert Goldsmith assisted with this task. After a time the spring house was removed and the ground leveled. Emma planted lilacs in the vicinity, and the Prophet's son, who was born to Emma after the Martyrdom, David Hyrum, expressed in poetry and song, his thoughts and feelings regarding the place of his father's burial. The words of this song reveal a great deal about the feeling this young boy had absorbed concerning his hope of the resurrection, and his belief that his father was someone who would not be forgotten. He entitled his song "The Unknown Grave."

> There's an unknown grave in a green, lowly spot,
> The form that it covers will ne'er be forgot.
> Where haven trees spread and the wild locusts wave
> Their fragrant white blossoms o'er the unknown grave,—
> > O'er the unknown grave.

And nearby its side does the wild rabbit tread,
Or the bright sun shine, and the soft breezes blow;
Unheeding the heart, once responsive and brave,
Of the one who sleeps there in the unknown grave,—
    Low in an unknown grave.

The prophet whose life was destroyed by his foes
Sleeps now where no hand may disturb his respose
'Til the trumpets of God drown the notes of the wave
And we see him arise from his unknown grave,—
    God bless that unknown grave.

The love all-embracing that never can end,
In death, as in life, knew him well as a friend;
The power of Jesus, the mighty to save,
Will despoil of its treasure the unknown grave,—
    No more an unknown grave.[10]

Excited Communities Fear Mormon Retaliation

The same day as the funeral, a hue and cry went out to warn the
"citizens" that the Mormon leaders were dead, and to prepare for
battle. In this atmosphere, General H. Swazey, of Iowa Territory,
visited Nauvoo and offered assistance to the people there. The potential for civil war rising out of the incident was strong. Governor Ford
issued general orders to the state militia in the western counties to
"enroll as many men as can be armed in their respective regiments."
They were to investigate the mob activities at Warsaw. Willard
Richards assured the Governor and the public that the Mormons
were not going to attack anyone.[11]

In the aftermath of the murders, an uneasy quiet settled over the
country around Nauvoo, Carthage and Warsaw. The enemies of the
Church waited and watched to see what the Mormons would do.
Would they retaliate? Would they leave the country?

Within Nauvoo, horror and grief yielded to the practical demands
of daily life. Many who had apostatized, including William and

Wilson Law, Dr. Foster, and the Higbees, left the city to wait at a distance to see what would happen. Others, caught up in the general spirit of confusion, waited and watched for a chance to seize power, looking for an opportunity to draw a gathering after themselves.

Willard Richards sent a letter to Brigham Young, who was in Boston holding a conference on 29 and 30 June. By the time George Adams brought the letter, the brethren had scattered, and it would be more than a week before some of the Twelve would get the news; most of them learned of it through newspapers.[12] As soon as the Apostles learned of the disaster they returned to Nauvoo. All of them were burdened with sorrow, but they were also full of faith in the work which they were called to do—that of taking the restored gospel to the nations of the world.

Keys of Authority

Willard Richards sent letters to inform the traveling Apostles of the disaster. Each left his activities and started immediately for Nauvoo. It would be five weeks before Brigham Young arrived there on 5 August. By this time the flames of expectation had risen to a great height. Sidney Rigdon had arrived from Pittsburgh and was advocating that he become "guardian" of the Church. There was a meeting of the remaining members of the Twelve on 7 August, at the home of John Taylor, who was recuperating from his wounds. On 8 August, the showdown came; a large crowd gathered at the stand to hear what the brethren had to say.

Several of the brethren spoke, and then Brigham Young addressed the people. What happened then served to turn the hearts of the Saints toward Brigham Young as the one who should give them guidance and direction in Joseph's absence. It was an event that was spiritually discerned. Hundreds testified that it seemed as though Brigham was transfigured before them. While it was Brigham who spoke, it was Joseph's figure they saw and his voice they heard, saying, "the Quorum of the Twelve have the keys of the kingdom of God in the world. . . . You cannot fill the office of a prophet, seer and revelator: God must do this . . . ." He explained that in due time the Lord would show them who that would be, and it would be done by revelation. And as for the prophet, whoever he would be, "the Twelve must ordain him."13

There were those in Nauvoo who were saying that Joseph was killed because he was a "fallen prophet." But Brigham met this concept with the affirmation that "Joseph and Hyrum have given their lives for the Church."14 He observed that Joseph had laid a foundation, and "we will build thereon." He testified emphatically, "but few knew Joseph's character; he loved you unto death—you did not know it until after his death: [he] has now sealed his testimony with his blood. . . ."14

Brigham continued, "Joseph has finished his work, and all the devils in hell and all the mobbers on earth could not take his life until he had accomplished his work. . . . Let no man suppose the kingdom is rent from you; that it is not organized. If all the quorums of the Church were slain, except the high priests, they would rise up with the keys of the kingdom, and have the powers of the priesthood upon them, and build up the kingdom, and the devil cannot help himself."15

They would finish the temple, give the Saints their endowments, and carry the work they had been assigned. He called for a vote of the people to sustain the Twelve. The voting was unanimous in the affirmative.

On 15 August, Brigham and the rest of the Twelve published a letter in the *Times and Seasons* to reassure the Saints abroad that although they were called to mourn the loss of their beloved prophet and patriarch—

> You are not without apostles, who hold the keys of power to seal on earth that which shall be sealed in heaven, and to preside over all the affairs of the church in the world; being still under the same God, and being dictated by the same spirit, having the same manifestations of the Holy Ghost to dictate all the affairs of the church in all the world, to build up the kingdom upon the foundation that the Prophet Joseph has laid. . . . Joseph still holds the keys of this last dispensation, and will hold them to all eternity . . . ministering in heaven, on earth, or among the spirits of the departed dead, as seemeth good to him who sent him. . . .
>
> How vain are the imaginations of the children of men, to presume for a moment that the slaughter of one, two or a hundred

of the leaders of this church could destroy an organization, so perfect in itself and so harmoniously arranged that it will stand while one member of it is left alive upon the earth. . . . Let it be distinctly understood that the city of Nauvoo and the Temple of our Lord are to continue to be built up. . . . The Temple must be completed by a regular system of tithing, according to the commandments of the lord, which he has given as a law unto this church, by the mouth of his servant Joseph. . . .[16]

Such was Brigham's determination that they not abandon the objectives Joseph had set forth. The Saints were assured the work of the kingdom would continue to roll on—missionary work would continue—the temple would be built. They responded with industry and he gradually brought the city and the Church into a state of order.

Coping with Fear and More Disaster

The survivors of the Smith family not only had to cope with the anxiety of losing their loved ones and the senseless fear of the graves being desecrated; there was also fear that the enemies would not stop with ridding the world of Joseph and Hyrum, but they might extend their destruction to any and all members of the family.

Emma was sensitive to this danger and was especially watchful of her children during this time. Thirteen days after the tragedy, Emma had her fortieth birthday, on 10 July. Though still mourning Joseph's death, she saw her duty clearly before her. Her children's needs were obvious. Little Alexander, who had turned six on 2 June, and Freddie, who had turned eight on 20 June, could scarcely understand their loss. There had been no time or opportunity to arrange for Freddie to be baptized before the tragedy; now he never would have that experience. Julia was thirteen and Joseph would turn twelve in November. They all missed their father terribly, and everybody was suffering from the shock of what had happened to their family.

Emma was able to manage her household with the help of Sevilla Durfey, and she also retained Loren Walker, who had been employed by Joseph to attend to many and varied duties for him. Loren and his wife, Lovina (Hyrum's oldest daughter), and Lucy Mack Smith were all living in the Mansion House. Lorin and Lovina were a great help to Emma in taking care of the hotel, but as her pregnancy advanced, it must have been increasingly difficult to keep up with all that had to be done.

Before any of the family could begin to recover, another tragedy struck. Joseph and Hyrum's brother Samuel became the third martyr.

Samuel Dies

On the evening of the viewing of the bodies, Samuel went to his mother and quietly told her "Mother, I have had a dreadful distress in my side ever since I was chased by the mob, and I think I have received some injury which is going to make me sick."[17] Within a short time he had taken to his bed and he died 30 July. His mother attributed his death to a "bilous fever," brought on, it was believed, as a result of his desperate effort to outrun the mob and reach his brothers to defend them. However, nobody really knows what caused his death.

Widows and Orphans

Samuel's widow, Levira, whom he had married in 1841, had a two-year-old daughter, Levira, and was expecting another baby. They had lost another little girl, Lovisa, in 1843. Levira also had the care of Samuel's children from his first marriage to Mary Bailey, who had died with her baby Lucy in 1841. Samuel and Mary had had two daughters, Susanna, eight and a half, and Mary, seven, and a son, Harrison Bailey Smith. A month after Samuel's death, Levira's baby, Lucy, was born and died. Levira was too ill to take care of the children, so they spent most of the winter with Hyrum's widow, Mary.[18]

Mary Fielding Smith, like Levira, faced the formidable task of being both mother and father to her husband's orphaned children, as well as her own. The younger three of Hyrum and Jerusha's other children were left to her care. Ironically, she had never wanted to be a stepmother. Now she was the only parent her stepchildren had.

The children of the martyrs were close in age and had always been closely associated from their infancy. At eleven and a half, John was the same age as Joseph III, both having been born in Kirtland. Hyrum's daughters, Jerusha and Sarah, were close in age to Freddie; he turned eight the same month that Joseph and Hyrum were killed. Mary also had two little ones of her own: Joseph F., who was the same age as Alexander and little Samuel Harrison Bailey, all three having been born in Missouri in 1836, and were now six. Little Martha Ann was three. Mary proved herself a true saint as she put aside her own misery and lent her love and energy to Samuel's orphaned youngsters and tried to give encouragement and support to her sorrowing sisters-in-law.[19]

Don Carlos' wife, Agnes, had been alone since 1841. She had buried one little girl, but still had Agnes, eight and Josephine Donna, three. Counting the widows of Joseph's uncles, Lucy Mack Smith, Emma, Levira, Agnes, and Mary, there were seven Smith widows, and more than two dozen children left without fathers to protect them.

Emma and Mary (Hyrum's widow) took a trip to Quincy to see why no legal action was being taken against those who had killed their husbands. It was a newsworthy trip, the *Greensburg Pennsylvania Argus* reported when the martyrs' wives made this trip to see "what could be done to arrest the rascals who had killed their husbands."[20] Not surprisingly, they were not successful in achieving their objective. Mother Lucy, who was with Emma at this time, gave her sorrowing daughters-in-law all the comfort she could, commenting "I am convinced that no one but a widow can imagine the feelings of a widow."[21]

All the widows were grieving and struggling to make ends meet. But Emma had a unique problem. Her husband, the Prophet, was responsible not only for the family's business, but would be looked upon as responsible for all the debts of the Church. Within a short time, after it was known abroad that Joseph was dead, Emma began to receive bills that she feared would be claimed against his estate. In this crisis, as in others, Emma knew she had to rely upon herself and look to her security and that of her children. The ordeals of New York, Ohio, and Missouri had seasoned her, and that seasoning was bitter. She had come to feel, in the aftermath of the trials in Kirtland and Far West, that if Joseph was not there to protect her, she could trust no mortal. Not long after the burial of the martyrs, Emma went to Quincy where she took legal steps to protect all she felt belonged to her and the children.[22]

The Twelve Meet with Emma

Heber C. Kimball recorded that he visited Emma on 8 August, when he gave her some money, and "took up my receipt in presents of elder Willard Richards and Elder [William] Clayton."[23]

The twelve men who were sustained at general conference, in October 1844, were: Brigham Young, Heber C. Kimball, Orson Hyde, Parley P. Pratt, William B. Smith, Orson Pratt, John E. Page, Willard Richards, Wilford Woodruff, John Taylor, George A. Smith and Lyman Wight.[24]

On 4 October, the brethren made a personal visit to the widows. The visit was pleasant and Heber C. Kimball recorded in his journal that good feelings prevailed and it seemed like old times. Brigham Young sent a messenger to Emma asking her to give them the desk Joseph had been using, which belonged to the Church. Later Emma asked that some personal papers of the Prophet, which had been in the desk, be returned. She was refused these papers, which upset her. Brigham also wanted Emma to give them the manuscript of the inspired translation of the Bible. Because there was some dispute over what property belonged to the Church and what belonged to the Smiths, Brigham wanted Emma to turn everything over to the Church and let them take care of the debts, at the same time giving her and the children an allowance.[25] He told her he wanted to move Joseph and Hyrum's bodies to the temple grounds, where he believed Joseph had wanted to be buried. He also placed an armed guard at the door of their home.

Emma's reaction was not what he had expected from the grieving widow. She not only refused to give up the deeds or the manuscript of the Bible translation, she absolutely refused to allow the bodies to be moved to the tomb by the temple. Furthermore, she resented the armed guard at her door. Joseph III, in later years, wrote that it had probably been for their protection, but at the time, it had seemed like an attempt to keep the family under surveillance. From these fragmented memories, we begin to comprehend Emma's distrustful state of mind, which increased rather than diminished in the aftermath of her husband's death.

Emma Moves to the Homestead, Her Baby Is Born

In order to be relieved of the financial and physical drain the hotel caused her, Emma had rented the Mansion House Hotel to William Marks sometime in August. On 4 November, she moved her family back to the Homestead. Her baby was born there, about four in the morning on 17 November.

Before Joseph had left for Carthage, he had asked her, if the baby was a boy, to name him David. She fulfilled that request, giving him his second name in honor of his uncle, her dearly beloved brother-in-law, Hyrum. Eliza R. Snow penned a tender poem in recognition of little David Hyrum Smith, who had to come into the world fatherless.

> Sinless as celestial spirits—
> Lovely as a morning flow'r
> Comes a smiling infant stranger
> In an evil-omen'd hour
>
> In an hour of lamentation—
> In a time—a season when
> Zion's noblest sons are fallen,
> By the hand of wicked men.
>
> In an hour when peace and safety
> Have the civil banner fled—
> In a day when legal justice
> Covers its dishonor'd head.
>
> In an age when saints must suffer
> Without mercy or redress;
> Comes to meet a generation
> That has made it fatherless.

Not a share of father's fondness—
Not to know its father's worth—
By the arm of persecution
'Tis an orphan at its birth!

Smile sweet babe! thou art unconscious
Of thy great, untimely loss!
The broad stroke of thy bereavement,
Zion's pathway seem'd to cross!

Till in childhood thou had'st known him,
Had the age, thy father spar'd;
The endearment of remembrance,
Through thy life time thou had'st shar'd.

Thou may'st draw from love and kindness
All a mother can bestow;
But alas! on earth, a father
Thou art destin'd not to know.[26]

Emma graciously accepted the comforting visits of her friends who came to see her after her baby was born. Perhaps this was a time of healing—a rare, peaceful interlude.

Renewed Threats of Mobbing

The enemies of the Church observed the industry of the Saints going about their business of farming and trade and working on their temple. They determined to stir up trouble in hopes of forcing the "Mormons" to do something that would cause an uproar, so they would be justified in demanding their removal from the country. They used the unfriendly press at Warsaw to make threats and spread false rumors against the people who called themselves Latter-day Saints.

The brethren had been considering sending explorers to the West. They had even set up a committee in March 1845, to determine where the Church might expand. Before his death, Joseph had set up such a committee to investigate the West and the Rocky Mountains, even Oregon and Texas. It was hoped, however, that they would not have to abandon Nauvoo, though they were aware that that likelihood could manifest itself before long. Nevertheless, Joseph sent Wilford Woodruff to England, and others of the brethren resumed their labors. Regardless of what might happen in Nauvoo, the work of the Church was moving forward.

Trouble began in earnest in September, when the anti-Mormons had begun burning houses around Green Plains, Hancock County.[27] Brigham advised the people who were affected to take these assaults without retaliating. He suggested that if it became too difficult, they were to move in to Nauvoo, "closing and strengthening the body."[28] He presumed there would be no attack on the city itself.

There was a token effort to put down the riots, but it was rather ineffectual. Finally, when Sheriff J. B. Backenstos needed men to help him disperse the rioters, he called upon some men from Nauvoo to join the posse. They confronted the rioters and succeeded in stopping them, but in the process, the posse killed two men: Franklin A. Worrell, a lieutenant in the "Carthage Greys," and Samuel McBratney. Amazing as it may seem, but revealing as to the state of corruption in the area, Sheriff Backenstos and Orin Porter Rockwell were subsequently indicted for the murder of Worrell. Since it was obvious they had been stopping a crime when the deaths occurred, they were acquitted at the trial. But Governor Ford sent General Hardin with some militia to patrol, and Hardin sent out a directive for the people of the county "to keep the peace and obey the laws and constituted authorities."[29]

On 1 October, a convention had been held at Carthage where delegates from nine counties considered the "Mormon subject." They passed the following resolution: "It is the settled and deliberate conviction, that it is now too late to attempt the settlement of the difficulties in Hancock county upon any other basis than that of the removal of the Mormons from the state; and we therefore accept, and respectfully recommend to the people of the surrounding countries to accept the proposition made by the Mormons to remove from the State next spring, and to wait with patience the time for removal."[30]

This convention sent four commissioners to convey their demand that the Mormons leave the state, including General John J. Hardin,

W. B. Warren, and Senator Stephen A. Douglas, with whom Joseph had previously been friendly. Joseph had promised him that if he didn't turn his hand against the Church he would have success in his highest political ambitions, but if he did turn against them, he would ultimately be disappointed.

The demand to leave was not entirely unexpected. The state legislature had canceled the Nauvoo City Charter in February 1845. Appeals to the governor had done no good. The Church leaders had asked Governor Ford to bring action to assure the safety of the Mormon people, but he had replied in a letter headed Springfield, 8 April 1845, that he could not be responsible for defending them as public opinion was firmly determined to see them depart. He suggested that the only safe thing for them to do was to leave the county as soon as possible.[31] In March, the Church leaders appointed a committee to look into where the Church could move, toward the west. They responded to the governor that they were already making preparations to leave, and would, as soon as they could sell their property. Brigham made it clear he had no intention of just walking away and leaving everything, as they had done in Missouri.

Summer 1845 brought great effort on the part of all the people to complete the temple and to continue the missionary work in all the world. By June they sent word to the Saints that "the walls of our Temple are completed and the roof is nearly on."[32] Joseph's brother William Smith had returned in April. He was ordained Patriarch to the Church in May, and shortly thereafter, on 22 May, his wife, Caroline, died, leaving him with a loss that seems to have adversely affected his already precarious emotions. Apparently he demanded that he be given authority over the Church, claiming he should be the rightful head and stirring up a good deal of trouble in the family and in the Church. Finally, after all efforts to reason with him had failed, he was disciplined—by being excommunicated from the Church.

On 5 October 1845, the Church held general conference in the temple. Between four and five thousand people were in attendance. It was announced that the temple would be opening for the Saints to receive their endowments therein, and that preparations for removal were to be going on simultaneously with that effort.

Brigham Young and Willard Richards issued a statement in the *Times and Seasons,* on 1 November 1845, explaining that removal from the state would be the only option for them if they hoped to be able to live their religion in peace: "You all know and have doubtless felt for years the necessity of removal provided the Government should not be sufficiently protective to allow us to worship God according to the dictates of our own conscience."[33]

Instructions were given regarding the building of wagons in a style that would make them able to travel in the winter. That same issue of the *Times and Seasons* carried an official notice: "Elder William Smith having been cut off from the Quorum of the Twelve for apostasy, on the Sunday following, several letters and pamphlets having been read, showing he had turned away from the truth; on motion, it was unanimously resolved by the Church of Jesus Christ of Latter-day Saints, that the said William Smith be cut off from said church, and left in the hands of God. Signed W. Richards, Cl'k. November 12, 1845."[34]

Joseph's Uncle John Smith was ordained Patriarch to the Church in his stead.

William's excommunication left Lucy and Emma, and the other widows and orphans with the uncomfortable situation of either supporting the Church leaders, or the only remaining male member of Lucy's family. It was a heart-wrenching problem.

Lucy Mack Smith Pledges Loyalty to the Twelve

Lucy Mack Smith attended general conference where she addressed the Saints telling them that when they left for the West, she would go with them. She pled with them to promise that when she died they would bring her bones back to lie beside her husband in Nauvoo. They promised to do as she wished, and there was a general feeling of tenderness felt toward her, and between the Twelve and the Church membership. The Church showed a tender respect for this aging "Mother in Israel," whom they revered, not just because she was the mother of the Prophet and patriarch, but she was honored for her herself, having proven herself a leader, friend, and loyal Saint.

Undoubtedly, the Saints would have honored Emma in the same manner had she made herself available to them—but she had become closed and distant—distrustful and cold. It could not have helped Emma that William Marks, whom she had known and trusted for many years and depended on as president of the Nauvoo Stake, had a falling out with the brethren. When William and Rosanna Marks left the Church, perhaps Emma's already fragile belief in the future fulfillment of Joseph's expectations for the Church, simply withered within her soul.

Temple Endowments Given

Emma took no part in preparing the attic story of the temple, nor in preparing for the important ordinance work to be done there; that work was performed by others. The work went forward as soon as the building was sufficiently completed to be used. By 10 December 1845, the Saints were able to begin performing ordinances in the temple.[35] Three women to whom Emma had administered sacred ordinances in her home—Mary Ann Young, Vilate Kimball, and Elizabeth Ann Whitney—now began administering these ordinances in the temple to women. All those who had previously received these blessings had them reconfirmed upon them in the temple.[36] Lucy Mack Smith, Agnes Smith, Mary Fielding Smith, and Levira Smith all entered the temple and participated in these wonderful ordinances. Mercy Thompson, Eliza R. Snow,[37] and thousands of others rejoiced, realizing they were given extra spiritual strength and hope because of having received these ordinances.

Emma's absence from these meetings testifies to her state of depression and withdrawal from fellowship even with those to whom she had been closest for so many years.

Withdrawal of the Church from the United States

Early in 1846, it became evident to the Church leaders that unless they actually sent a vanguard of Saints out of Nauvoo, the agitators were going to stir up more and more trouble, perhaps even incite a massacre. In January and early February, the first wagons crossed the frozen Mississippi in their westward exodus.[38]

There was no expectation that Emma and Lucy would go in the winter camp. It was expected and hoped for that they would go at a later time. But Emma had already made up her mind she would not be going. When she heard of the deaths and suffering in the winter camps across the river in Iowa, Emma grimly remarked, "They might have known better than to have gone, and many of them did know better, for [I] told them better."[39]

In spite of the distress, and the pressure of their enemies to move out, many thousands of men and women received their endowments in the temple between 10 December 1845 and 7 February 1846. It was very hard for the Saints to leave their temple. Brigham announced the closure of the temple on 4 February, but the crowds thronged around unhappily, pleading to receive their endowments. Moved with compassion for them, he consented to continue for three more days. Six hundred endowments were given that last day.[40]

On 8 February, Brigham and the other apostles went to the temple and offered up a prayer: "I met with the Council of the Twelve in the southeast corner room of the attic of the Temple. We knelt around the altar, and dedicated the building to the Most High. We asked his blessing upon our intended move to the west; also asking him to enable us some day to finish the Temple, and dedicate it to him, and we would leave it in his hands to do as he pleased; and to preserve the building as a monument to Joseph Smith. We asked the Lord to accept the labors of his servants in this land. We then left the Temple."[41]

Some of the brethren had barely crossed the river, and others were in the process, on 9 February, when they saw smoke and flames coming from the temple roof. An overheated stovepipe had caught fire to some clothing hanging too close. The damage was extensive. Brigham and others fought the flames, which raged for about half an hour. It would be repaired and dedicated before summer.[42]

The same day the temple caught fire, another excommunication would take its toll upon the Council of the Twelve. John E. Page "yielded himself up to temptation, and he cannot resist the spirit of apostasy. . . . Therefore, your brethren in solemn council . . . have withdrawn the hand of fellowship from him until he comes to us and gives satisfaction for his dissension." This statement was signed by Brigham Young, Heber C. Kimball, Parley P. Pratt, George A. Smith, Orson Pratt, John Taylor, Willard Richards, with Orson Hyde, as clerk.[43] Eight of the Twelve had remained faithful, a majority.

With several thousand people camped or strung out across the winter prairie, the Church leaders wrote to the governor of Iowa Territory for permission to camp and raise crops to feed the stock that would be moving through.[44] They also asked permission to build temporary houses for the winter; permission was granted. Winter Quarters, on the banks of the Missouri River, on the Iowa-Nebraska border, became the major gathering place for the Saints until they found out where they would go. It was here that Brigham Young received a revelation that would strengthen him and his fellow laborers in the monumental task before them—taking the Camp of Israel into the western wilderness.

Although Emma and her family must have known about the commotion caused by the fire in the temple, they seem not to have made any comment about it, then or later. Several years later, when the building was destroyed by arson, they were most sorrowful.

Governor Ford's Observations

Governor Ford wrote of the exodus of the Mormons:

> During the winter of 1845-46 the Mormons made the most prodigious preparations for removal. All the houses in Nauvoo, and even the temple, were converted into workshops; and before spring, more than twelve thousand wagons were in readiness. The people from all parts of the country flocked to Navuoo to purchase houses and farms, which were sold extremely low, lower than the prices at a sheriff's sale, for money, wagons, horses, oxen, cattle, and other articles of personal property, which might be needed . . . in their exodus into the wilderness.
>
> By the middle of May it was estimated that sixteen thousand Mormons had crossed the Mississippi and taken up their line of march with their personal property, their wives and little ones, westward across the continent. . . .[45]

While Governor Ford's numbers are exaggerated somewhat, it does not exceed the number who eventually made the trek within the next few years.

Farewell to Friends

Who can fathom Emma's feelings as her old friends came to pay their respects before leaving for the West. The farewells, in some cases were tender and sad. Sometimes gifts were exchanged. The Woodruffs brought Emma some dishes they couldn't take with them. She gave several old friends walking sticks that had belonged to Joseph. She sold her cloak to Heber C. Kimball for Vilate, but she refused to sell Joseph's cloak.

Each act and word of Emma's, in these parting scenes, was remembered, sometimes recorded in diaries, but mostly held in reminiscence. Depending upon the atmosphere in which the reminiscence took place, the last poignant contact the Saints had with Emma took on either an aspect of compassionate sympathy or an air of criticism. It would be noted that she refused to give up the manuscript of the inspired translation of the Bible and other precious documents the Church wanted and needed. Emma felt she was guardian of these things, and at one time, when her house was set afire, but did not burn, she attributed the miracle of its being saved to her having the manuscript there. John Bernhisle made a copy of the inspired translation for the brethren,[46] but being unable to compare it to the original, the Twelve could not use it as one of the standard scriptures of the Church. Apparently Emma would not give her permission for them to use it. In the twentieth century, an exchange between the RLDS and LDS Churches of copies of these early documents, and a cooperative effort between scholars of both churches, have made it possible for the LDS Church to make available many important passages of the Joseph Smith Translation within the 1979 publication of the scriptures. Now this additional scripture has gone forth, in connection with the Bible, the Book of Mormon, and the Pearl of Great Price.

Temple Dedicated and Sold

On 3 May 1846, a formal dedication service was held in the temple. Wilford Woodruff had returned from England and officiated at the meeting. While thousands of Saints had left Nauvoo, there were still many in attendance at the dedication. When it was over, the leaders proposed to those present that the temple be sold and the proceeds used to aid the destitute Saints to get a new start. The voting in favor was unanimous. On 19 November 1848, one last vicious act of malevolent hatred was instigated to assure that they would never return: the temple was deliberately set on fire and burned beyond repair.[47] A few years later, a wind toppled the walls; the stones were taken to build other buildings. The time came when not one stone remained to tell where that magnificent structure had stood.

The enemies of the Church could not have understood the spiritual significance of the temple, nor the capacity for sacrifice within the hearts of the Latter-day Saints. Having fulfilled their promise to finish that sacred building, the Saints walked away, knowing that they were justified before the Lord. When it was destroyed, the Saints in the West felt the Lord had removed his temple.

Driving Out the Remnant

From February on, wagons rolled to the river, where they crossed on ice if it was firm, or flatboats, if it was flowing. This was a monumental exodus of wagons, teams, herds of cows, sheep and horses, and young and old, strong and weak. In spite of the fact that the Saints were leaving as rapidly as they were able, it was not happening fast enough for those who had demanded their removal. Many vicious acts were directed against any who were unfortunate enough to be in the way of the rioters. Bands of men blocked the roads, waylaid travelers, and harassed Mormons at any opportunity.[48]

With so much violence threatened, Emma, Lucy, Mary, and Agnes, with their many children, could not have felt any degree of security. As the wagons rolled across the river, the city was left with only about a thousand people, mostly those too old or too poor to manage the westward trek until some help could be provided for them. New citizens arrived, but most did not take sides with the Saints, and could not be relied upon, entirely.

In many ways, Nauvoo appeared to be almost a replay of the Missouri fiasco, wherein various bands of men, under leadership of state appointed officers, were supposed to control those who were against the Mormons, but in some cases, the troops themselves proved to have intentions of driving the Mormons out, even more quickly, if possible. In Illinois, these groups almost came to battle amongst themselves. Meanwhile, in Nauvoo, the few Latter-day Saint men remaining, less than 150, and about the same number of new citizens, were armed and willing to defend the town, at all costs.

The defenders of Nauvoo were under the leadership of Colonel Daniel H. Wells and William Cutler. These men and the little band with them "took up its position on the edge of a wood in the suburbs of Nauvoo, and less than a mile from the enemy's camp."[49]

Although the people had been promised another couple of months, the mobbers had no intention of allowing them to wait. On 7 September a demand was issued that Nauvoo's defenders surrender their arms, and that all the rest of the people had better cross the river—or be destroyed.

A Parting of the Ways

With the hot wind of persecution blowing, September 1846 still produced its harvest, though there were few left to gather the peaches, apples, and grain, standing heavy headed in the fields.

The Smith widows had held out against panic. They had stayed through the summer, hoping to harvest their crops in order to provide for their needs. Each had already chosen the course she was going to take. Soon these women who had sacrificed so much, who had been so much a part of each other, and who had stood together through unthinkable deprivation in Missouri, would be forced to a parting of the ways.

Did they know their parting would be for a lifetime?

Don Carlos' Widow Goes South to Forget

Agnes had written, in the spring, to her husband's cousin, George A. Smith, who had already started west: "If there was a Carlos or Joseph or Hyrum then how quickly I would be there." She assured him that she loved the Church and would love to be with her brethren, "but, alas," she wrote, "there is an aching void I seem never able to fill." With a tone of finality, she told him that she had "sold the old printing shop for seventy dollars and that she had removed her dead into Emma's garden."[50]

By fall, Agnes had become acquainted with William Pickett, from St. Louis. Formerly a lawyer in Mobile, Alabama, he was currently "foreman of the printing office of the Missouri Republican, later the St. Louis Republican." This was one of several Missouri newspapers that had castigated Governor Boggs for his infamous "extermination order."[51] We do not know whether he came to Nauvoo for news, but he was there at the end of the summer of 1846, and he was incensed by the wicked manner in which the Saints had been driven from their homes. William had come to know Agnes, and "this mutual affection ripened into love, and he persuaded her to marry him and come away with him to St. Louis, where he could give her and the two little girls a home in a civilized society."[52]

They left by river boat in September. As the boat moved slowly out to turn south, Agnes looked back. Nauvoo, "the beautiful," . . . was still lovely. It had not been destroyed, but it had been looted of all that was dear to her, physically and spiritually. The temple shining in the sun was like a gravestone, and the city, to her, a graveyard. She turned to her new husband as they walked slowly toward the prow of the boat, looking south to where their future lay. As they talked of the future, William extracted from his wife a promise that she was to keep as long as she lived, and her children after her. . . . The promise troubled her as she made it while still in the sight of Nauvoo. But as they neared St. Louis, and the city's skyline took shape ahead of them, her pledge seemed only natural and easy . . . that she was to enter this new life with William Pickett with her past forgotten and forever hidden. She agreed never to speak of her membership in the Church of the Saints, or of her marriage to a brother of the Prophet. This agreement was not made to bolster William's ego, but to ensure freedom forever from the kind of persecution that had followed the Mormons all their days. William had been as shocked by the rawness and the savagery running through the streets of Nauvoo as he had been at stories of rape and murder of Mormons in Missouri eight years before. He wished to make sure that no threat of this horror would ever touch his wife again.[53]

Agnes and her girls went with William Pickett to St. Louis, then on to California, where their identity would remain a secret for many years—little Josephine even changed her name to Ina, and took her mother's maiden name, Coolbrith. Don Carlos' daughter, Ina Coolbrith became a noted author and Poet Laureate of California.[54]

Hyrum's Widow Goes West to Raise a Prophet

For Mary, there was never a moment of doubt—she was going west. But she would not go empty-handed. She planned well, and when she heard of the oncoming trouble, early in September, she was ready to make her move. She and her children left on 8 September. Her farewell to Nauvoo is described by her daughter, Martha Ann (Harris) years later. Martha was then but five years old:

> We left our home, just as it was, all the furniture, in fact everything we owned. The fruit trees were loaded with rosy peaches and apples. We bid goodby to the loved home that reminded us of our beloved father. . . . We crossed the Mississippi River on a skiff in the dusk of evening. We bid good by to our dear old grandmother, Lucy Mack Smith. I can never forget the bitter tears she shed when she bid us goodby for the last time. She knew it would be the last time she would see her son's family again in this life. We did not realize this so much at the time as we have since. . . . I went with my mother every day for three weeks while she worked in the Nauvoo Temple. What joy that was to me.[55]

Little Martha did not realize at the time that Mary had arranged to have provisions, bedding, wagons, horses, and all the essentials and what household goods she could take with her moved across the river on a flat boat, to Montrose, Iowa.[56]

Emma had moved back into the Mansion House by this time, and Lucy Mack Smith was living there with her, when Mary Fielding Smith and her family went to say their good-byes.[57] Perhaps this is when Emma gave Mary a small pottery teapot, which Mary treasured and passed down to her daughter Martha Ann (Harris).[58] It was recalled that Lucy Mack Smith was so feeble, she used two canes when she tried to walk.

That evening they camped on Hyrum's farm; the next day they crossed over and camped on the Iowa side of the Mississippi. Mary's sister, Mercy and her family went with them. From that distance they "heard the cannonade" when they began firing on Navuoo. Her young son, Joseph F. Smith, a lad of six, absorbed his mother's deep faith in God, and honored her by a lifelong commitment to the priesthood. He became the sixth president of the Church, in Utah.

Samuel's Widow and Family

Samuel's son, Samuel Harrison Bailey Smith, had stayed most of the time, with his cousin, Elias Smith. In September, Levira's father, Gardner Clark, came and took the boy with him overland to Winter Quarters. Little Mary remained in Nauvoo at Emma's to help with the care of Lucy Mack Smith, as did Lovina and Lorin Walker. Susanna had been sent to live with her mother's sister in Wisconsin.

Levira must have gone with her parents, taking her little daughter Levira and spending the winter at Winter Quarters. Her father died there before spring, making it impossible for her to leave with the first company, and Samuel remained there with her. They went in the second company, arriving in the Salt Lake Valley in 1848. She married a man named Amey, a tinner, and later, she ran a boarding house in Salt Lake City.[59] Samuel H. B. Smith was also stalwart and faithful, a missionary all his days, and a worthy son of a worthy father.

Joseph's Widow, Mother, and Sisters

It must have been terrifying for Emma when she was warned by Dr. Bernhisle to take her family and leave. She almost waited too long. The riverboat captains had all been warned away, and the roads were barred by the posse, which was by now more than a thousand strong—with wagons, equipment, and every preparation for a campaign—approached Nauvoo and camped on the very same farm Mary and her family had just left. This posse was not going to Nauvoo to defend the remaining women, children, and old men still there, but to demand that those defending them give up their arms and surrender, and to force the remaining Mormons across the river.[60]

Lucy Mack Smith did not go west but lived in the home the Church deeded to her, often going for extended times to live with her daughters, Katharine Salisbury, Sophronia Stoddard McCleary, and Lucy Smith Millikin, who, with their husbands and families did not make the trek to the West.

Emma Leaves Nauvoo

We have no contemporary source to tell us what Emma thought or felt when it became obvious that the city was going to be invaded. Perhaps not believing anyone would actually invade the almost deserted city, she waited until the very last moment before accepting that she must abandon her home and get her family to safety. Before Emma left Nauvoo, she may have arranged for Lucy Mack Smith to go with her daughter Lucy Smith Millikin. There seems to be no record of where she went or what she did while the city was under bombardment. It must have been almost as bitter as death for this aged woman to part with her beloved daughters-in-law and her precious grandchildren, whom she would never see again in this life.

After being warned by Dr. John Bernhisle, Emma realized she must leave. She had rented the Mansion House and hotel to a new citizen of the town. Early in the morning on 12 September, she and the children went to the landing where a Mr. Grimes, the captain of the riverboat *Uncle Toby*, risked the ire of the mobs to pull into the landing. They hurried aboard with the household necessities she would need in Fulton. They were gone by seven o'clock; the battle of Nauvoo began that very day at ten o'clock. Emma could not have been far upriver before it began.[61]

They traveled upriver for eight days, arriving at Fulton, Illinois, on 18 September. Emma shared a rented house with two other families. It was crowded, as she had quite a group: her five children plus Savilla Durphee, Lucy and Lorin Walker, and two teenaged girls for whom she had taken responsibility. Joseph III remembers this as a pleasant time, with everyone helping one another; he enjoyed some social times with young people his own age.[62]

Emma remained in Fulton about six months. Because William and Rosanna Marks had gone to Fulton after they left the Church caused some to perceive Emma's retreat there as evidence that she, too, had apostatized.[63] For more than a decade, William Marks would ramble around in various religions before finally joining the Reorganization, formed by several men who had once been involved in the Church in Nauvoo. He was undoubtedly instrumental in helping persuade young Joseph III to join that group, in 1852. [64]

For Emma, those years in between the exodus of the Saints to the west and her son's establishment as the head of the Reorganized Church appear to have been years of silence on the subject of religion. We have no idea what discussions, if any, she had with the Marks family in Fulton. After she left there, she did not keep in touch with them. It is said by descendants of Hyrum's daughter, Lovina Smith Walker (who went with to Fulton with Emma and the children), that Emma spoke openly to her regarding the trials they had shared and the disappointments she had endured.

Home to Nauvoo

In January 1847, while the Saints were in Nebraska, at Winter Quarters, waiting for spring and preparing for the last leg of their journey west, Emma received a letter from Dr. Bernhisel telling her that the man who had been renting the Mansion House was planning to leave and take some of her property with him.[65] This news served to make Emma aware of her responsibility to her property and her future. The respite from tension she had enjoyed in Fulton was not to be permanent. She knew she must return to Nauvoo and look after the interests of herself and her children. It was time to return home and start life over. Emma is quoted as saying, "I have no friend but God and no place to go but home."[66]

With Lorin Walker driving the carriage, Emma and her children went back to Nauvoo as quickly as they could. She found her tenant preparing to leave, his wagon loaded high with her furniture. She confronted him and was able to retrieve her belongings.

At home in the Mansion House, she had hard work and loneliness to contend with—and memories. She bowed her back and plunged into the work. She tucked her memories away. The picture of herself in her riding dress and Joseph's picture, painted for the Nauvoo Map, were put away. The sight of his legion uniform upset her. According to family tradition, Emma felt that Joseph's political and military activities had caused his death.

She never mentioned those who had gone West. Eliza R. Snow would eventually succeed her as president of the Relief Society, and that organization would continue to the present. Emma's friend, Rebecca Williams, eventually went west under the protection of Heber C. Kimball. Sarah M. Cleveland moved back to Quincy. Sarah Cleveland's descendants came west, but it is not known when or where she died. Elizabeth Whitney, Caroline Crosby, Emily Partridge, and many other women must have regretted Emma's decision, yet none of her close friends appear to have made any statements blaming her for staying behind.

Although she seldom spoke about her friends of the early days, surely Emma felt twinges of nostalgia for them. Her hard life had often been made easier through their ministrations. The marvel and wonder of the Restoration, in which she was an active participant, is personified in their devoted and loyal friends, the Knight family: Father Knight and his sons, Joseph Jr. and Newell; Freeborn and Anna DeMille; and the gentle Polly and Sally, who had shared her baptismal day and died in Missouri. However, images of those who turned traitor cannot have always been kept at bay. The knowledge that not one of the men who caused the deaths in Carthage ever received so much as a fine would have been bitter. Perhaps she was silent because there was too much to say and she had lived in turmoil too long to trust anyone with her innermost thoughts.

Her children and grandchildren were her dearest associates, and they recalled that she was kind, but strict. In her last years she was slightly bent, but still held herself with great dignity. She was often asked impertinent questions, to which she replied, "That is personal," and withdrew.

She always wore a strand of gold beads, a cherished gift from Joseph, and she always wore an apron. She would turn up a corner of the apron with her fingers while chatting with a customer or friend in the hotel. The string of beads had broken and some were lost, but she threaded them again, filling out the string with amber. No doubt, golden beads and an apron seemed peculiar to those who didn't understand.

It is said that in the evening after work was done, Emma often climbed the stairs to sit alone in the dusk, gazing out the window at the river, tears streaming unheeded down her cheeks.

In retrospect, a great-granddaughter, Inez Davis, wrote:

> Back in that deserted city, near the water's edge, stood the Mansion House, not long since completed, home of a tall, dark-haired widow and her five children: an arrogant little beauty of fifteen, the adopted daughter, Julia; a solemn, brown-eyed boy of nearly fourteen, Joseph; Frederick, past ten, merry and sunny, with the brown eyes of his mother; a lad of blue eyes like his father, Alexander; and the little brother, baby David, loved and loving of them all, who was not quite two, for he was born after the cruel death of his father. Calmly, with a quiet courage, this woman, when nearly all had left, stayed on, except for a few months' refuge up the river at Fulton City, and raised her family in the deserted city. Her boys played and studied with the children of the new citizens. She baked cookies for them all. Time passed. Emma had no enemies in Nauvoo. She found herself and her children respected by all. She never spoke of religion, for although she still cherished the principles of the church her husband founded in her heart, she had come to the time when she had lost some of the illusions her friends still cherished, and had reluctantly bade them good-bye at the parting of the roads.[67]

The Relief Society in Utah, the Mansion House in Nauvoo

Eventually, among the Saints in the West, it would be remembered that Emma had opposed the idea of the Saints going across the river in the winter of 1846—that she chose not to go west with the Church. More than that, she kept her sons from going west once they were old enough to go; and she fostered in them a negative attitude toward Brigham Young.

With the passage of time, conflicting feelings gave rise to negative remarks elicited from Emma, or Brigham, by well-intentioned messengers, who kept each informed of what the other had said or done. Finally, years and miles apart—never having sat down face-to-face to talk out their differences, these two, Emma and Brigham, who loved Joseph best, became known for loving each other least. The media played a significant role in magnifying the conflicts. In time, the tradition that grew out of Emma's and Brigham's mutual antagonism created a foundation of prejudice that would blot out the tender, true feelings that once existed.

Among the women who had known Emma well, there was some disappointment, even some bitterness developed toward Emma for her refusal to go west. Yet, there remained in the hearts of true Saints a thread of sympathy, sadness, and regret, along with genuine appreciation for her sacrifices made during the founding years of the Church and a remembrance of her example as the first President of the Female Relief Society.

In Utah, the Relief Society would blossom and grow—eventually extending its mission of compassionate service to all the world.

In Nauvoo, there was the Mansion House—the scene of bitter struggles with inner conflicts and outward oppressions—and finally, the scene of the last public viewing of Joseph and Hyrum by thousands of grieving Saints. For Emma, there was the Mansion House—her home—a legacy for her children and a responsibility she would never relinquish.

Notes

1. *HC,* 6:626
2. *HC,* 6:627
3. E. Cecil McGavin, *Nauvoo the Beautiful* (Salt Lake City: Bookcraft, 1972), p.146.
4. Scot Facer Proctor and Maurine Jensen, *The Revised and Enhanced History of Joseph Smith by His Mother* (Salt Lake City: Bookcraft, 1996), p. 457.
5. *HC,* 6:627; see also McGavin, *Nauvoo the Beautiful,* p. 161.
6. Joseph Smith III said, in his *Memoirs,* "I do not know much about the cavalcade which formed, nor was I a witness to the depositing of the bodies, or the boxes supposed to contain the bodies of Father and uncle Hyrum in the temporary tomb, built in the hilside near the Temple. I remember some of the rumors passed around as to the place where the bodies were realy deposited, but I knew where they were subsequently buried, for I was present upon the occasion when, in the presence of two others, there was an opening of the place of deposit, and I saw the features of my father as they were exposed, and a lock of hair was cut from his head, a portion of which I have in my possession today, in a brooch which my mother used to wear." Mary Audentia Smith Anderson, ed., *Memoirs of President Joseph Smith III— 1832-1914* (Independence, Mo.: Herald Publishing House, 1979), p. 37; original spelling retained.)

7. Phelps, W. W. "The Joseph/Hyrum Smith Funeral Sermon," *BYU Studies* (Winter, 1983), pp. 11- 12; original document in LDS Archives.

8. *HC,* 6:628.

9. McGavin, *Nauvoo the Beautiful,* p. 162; see also Pearson H. Corbett, *Hyrum Smith, Patriarch* (Salt Lake City: Deseret Book, 1963), p. 431, which cites "security reasons" as the reason the bodies were buried secretly and location of the graves kept secret.

10. Ibid.

11. McGavin, *Nauvoo the Beautiful,* p. 165.

12. *HC,* 7:140.

13. *HC,* 7:240.

14. Ibid.

15. Ibid.

16. *HC,* 7:250.

17. Lucy Mack Smith, *History of the Prophet Joseph Smith by His Mother,* ed. Preston Nibley (Salt Lake City: Bookcraft, 1958), pp. 325-26.

18. Don C. Corbett, *Mary Fielding Smith: Daughter of Britain* (Salt Lake City: Deseret Book 1966), pp. 187-88.

One afternoon in August 1844, Levira told Susanna, Mary, and Samuel they could play out on the banks of the river, but she cautioned them not to go near the water. She was going to visit her parents, who lived some distance outside of Nauvoo. The children enjoyed themselves all afternoon, happy for a chance to play as much as they pleased. But then as the sun began to sink low, they hurried home, only to find nobody there and the door locked. They sat down on the doorstep and waited and waited. When nobody came, they finally fell asleep, huddled together on the step. After a long time, they were awakened and taken to their Aunt Mary's (Hyrum's widow) and given supper and put to bed. Mary looked after them for the rest of that winter. Their mother had not returned because she had become desperately ill. Her baby, Lucy, had been born, but did not live very long. Gentle, quiet Levira could not attend to her entire family.

These children were very sad and very lonely without their father or mother. They got along all right in the daytime, but each evening, they would go and sit on the doorstep of their own house. Their Aunt Mary sent the hired man to bring them home for supper. But the children were expecting Levira to be home, and when the hired man came to take them, they cried and sobbed so desperately, he sent word to Mary that they were very upset. Kindly, Mary sent word back for him not to force them against their will, but to let them stay. After they fell asleep, she had them brought back to her house, fed them, and put them to bed.

Finally, Susanna went to Wisconsin to live with her Aunt Hannah, sister to Mary Bailey. Mary went for a time to her grandmother, Lucy Mack Smith, and Samuel was sent to live with Samuel's Uncle Asahel's family.

19. Ibid. See also family genealogy records in possession of the author.

20. *Greensburg Pennsylvania Argus,* 23 August 1844, cited in Linda King

Newell and Valeen Tippets Avery, *Mormon Enigma: Emma Hale Smith* (Garden City, New York: Doubleday & Company, Inc., 1984), p. 207 ftnt. 41; p. 348.

21. Lucy Mack Smith, Preliminary Manuscript, LDS Archives.

22. Joseph Smith III, *Memoirs,* pp. 37-38.

23. Stanley B. Kimball, ed. *On the Potter's Wheel: The Diaries of Heber C. Kimball* (Salt Lake City: Signature Books, 1987), p. 79.

24. Reed Durham, Jr., and Stephen Heath, *Succession in the Church* (Salt Lake City: Bookcraft, 1970), p. 58.

25. Joseph III, *Memoirs,* p. 38. Joseph III's memories of the legal dispute over property reflects the antagonism which developed out of these disputes. While Emma managed to secure their home and farm, and some city lots, her action was looked upon by the brethren as presumptuous; As time went on, in order to keep any of her assets, she was forced into litigation to the end of her days.

26. For information on David Hyrum's birth, see the family genealogy records. See McGavin, *Nauvoo the Beautiful* (p. 171), for words by David Hyrum Smith.

27. *HC,* 7:488.

28. Ibid.

29. *HC,* 7:494; see also *The History of the Reorganized Church of Latter-Day Saints,* (Independence, Mo: Herald House, 1973) vol. 1:147; hereafter referred to as *RLDS History.*

30. *RLDS History,* p. 148, quoting *The Prophet of Palmyra,* p. 336.

31. *HC,* 7:396-398.

32. *HC,* 7:427.

33. *Times and Seasons,* vol. 6:1018-19.

34. Ibid. William Smith's behavior was so erratic at this time, the Church held a fast in his behalf. Even his mother, Lucy, was confused about William's rightful position, claiming she had a dream to the effect that he was to lead. It was only after the brethren talked to her in person, reasoning with her upon the revealed principles of leadership, that she was able to relinquish the hope that William would be placed as president of the Church. William was angered when he did not get his way, and dealt with his dismissal as he had in Kirtland when he had fought with Joseph. He became bitter against the brethren. We can perhaps understand how William was stressed beyond his ability to maintain himself; perhaps his losses were too overwhelming. His father had died in 1840, his brother Don Carlos in 1841, his three brothers, Joseph, Hyrum, and Samuel, in 1844, and his wife, in 1845—not to mention two sisters-in-law, and many nieces and nephews. He returned to Nauvoo in April 1845; in May, his wife, Caroline, died, leaving him with two young girls to take care of. The Twelve approved his call as Church Patriarch, but could not allow him to assume control over the whole church, as he seems to have presumed was his right. He became angry (as was often his nature when crossed) and made his disapproval very public. His bitterness served to oust him from the fellowship of the Twelve—and the Church.

35. *HC,* 7:543-48.

36. *HC,* 7:541.

37. Andrew F. Ehat, *Joseph Smith's Introduction of Temple Ordinances and the 1844 Mormon Succession Question,* Master's Thesis, Brigham Young University, Provo, Utah (December, 1982), pp. 102-103.

38. *HC,* 7:580

39. Valeen Avery, *Insanity and the Sweet Singer of Israel* (Ph.D. Dissertation, Northern Arizona University, 1984), p. 31.

40. *HC,* 7:580.

41. Ibid.

42. *HC,* 7:581.

43. *HC,* 7:582.

44. *HC,* 7:601.

45. *RLDS history,* 1:164.

46. *LDS Reference Encyclopedia,* written and comp. by Melvin R. Brooks (Salt Lake City: Utah, 1966), p. 196.

47. *HC,* 7:617. According to Joseph III, Joseph Agnew, a "river rat, a drunken lout, . . . confessed to the deed." Not long after this fire, which gutted the structure, "a fierce storm raged over the city and some parts of the south wall of the ruin fell. This so weakened the remaining portions of the temple on the north that before long they followed suit. The walls kept falling from time to time, bit by bit, until there remained standing only the south-west corner—one of the stairway towers near the main entrance. Finally the city council deemed it advisable, for the safety of the public, to raze this portion. This was done." So far as the existence of that particular building was concerned, "not one stone was left upon another," from the angel at the top of the spire with the brave trumpet in his hand, to the heavy foundation stones below.

"During the years which followed there was a gradual spoilation of the ruins of the Temple, to which I was witness. The place became a veritable quarry and provided the materials with which many homes, wine cellars, and saloons in the town were built. . . . The only stones left are those lining the well which was dug in the basement to supply water for the baptismal font" *(Memoirs of Joseph Smith III,* pp. 101-103).

In 1851, "the Temple grounds were purchased by the Icarian Society. . . ." They owned it until the Icarians group scattered, and the property "fell into the hands of some Germans," who built some buildings on the grounds.

Elder Loren C. Dunn has said, "Since 1937 some . . . descendants [of those who once built Nauvoo] have been buying back their ancestors' properties. Among these were Wilford Wood from Bountiful, Utah, and Dr. J. LeRoy Kimball, a Salt Lake City physician. Wood bought the first pieces of the temple site and several buildings on the Flat. . . ."

Elder Dunn continued, "The Church organized Nauvoo Restoration, Inc. in 1962, and J. LeRoy Kimball was named its first president. Since 1962 Nauvoo Restoration, Inc. has acquired about one thousand acres of land and restored or reconstructed seventeen buildings. Historical research and careful archaeological exploration precede each restoration, much of it contributed by volunteers." ("Introduction to Historic Nauvoo," *BYU Studies* [Winter 1992], p. 24.)

48. See Bancroft's *History of Utah* (pp. 226-33) as cited in *RLDS History*, 1:168-69. In August, Phineas H. Young, his son Brigham, and three others, who were found outside the city, were kidnapped by a mob, hurried into the thickets, passed from one gang to another . . . for several weeks they were under constant threat of death, and denied food and rest.

49. This is according to Bancroft's *History of the Mormons*, quoted in *RLDS History*, p. 170.

50. Josephine DeWitt Rhodehamel and Raymond Francis Wood, Ina Coolbrith: Librarian and Poet Laureate (Provo, Utah: BYU Press, 1973), p. 24.

51. Ibid., p. 25.

52. Ibid.

53. Ibid., pp. 25-26.

54. Ibid.

55. Pearson H. Corbett, *Hyrum Smith, Patriarch* (Salt Lake City: Deseret Book, 1963), pp. 442-43.

56. Ibid.

57. Ibid.

58. Teapot in author's possession.

59. Joseph III, *Memoirs*, pp. 223-33.

60. *RLDS History*, 1:170.

61. Mary Audentia Smith Anderson, ed., *Joseph III and the Restoration* (Independence, Mo: Herald Publishing House, 1952), p. 92. Joseph III said in his *Memoirs*, "We were quite a little company, for there went with us in this flight Jane and Nancy Carter, daughters of Jared Carter, William C. Clapp . . . and the families of Wesley Knight and Loren Walker. In the former family there were three children and in the latter one or two, our own consisted of my mother and her four boys (the youngest, David, had been born in November, five months after Father's death), her adopted daughter Julia, and Servilla Durfee [sic], long a helper in her household. This little group under the supervision of my mother went up river. . . . Loren Walker [sic] and Wesley Knight had been left to come overland with the horses, wagon, carriage, and household goods."

62. Ibid., p. 39

63. Ibid.

64. Ibid., p. 433.

66. From Vesta Crawford's notes, LDS Archives. Typescript copy in author's possession. See also Newell and Avery, *Mormon Enigma: Emma Hale Smith*, p. 243.

67. Vida E. Smith, quoting Inez Davis, "Alexander Hale Smith Biography" unpublished family history, pp. 5-6. Original in RLDS Archives. Typescript copy in author's possession.

Emma and baby David Hyrum, 1845. Family daguerreotype.
Copy in LDS Archives.

ℰPILOGUE

My Heart Turns to Emma

In the summer of 1985, I stood with my husband, Ivor, in the yard of the Homestead, on the east bank of the Mississippi. We looked across the road to where the Riverside Mansion stands silent in its place at the end of Water Street. Its red bricks, fired in Old Nauvoo, seemed to glow in the afternoon sun. Behind us, in the yard of the Old Homestead, descendants of the Smiths, in Nauvoo for the Joseph Smith, Sr., Family Reunion, milled around the family grave-yard. Reverently, they wandered in and out of the hewn log structure where Joseph and Emma lived when they first came to Commerce. Knowing that Emma had penned her letter to Governor Carlin, served countless meals, wept over her lost baby, hosted the Jubilee, and was sealed to Joseph in this old cabin, increased the depth of our experience in being there.

Here, in Nauvoo, Emma and the Prophet rode down the river road together on prancing horses. Here, they greeted converts from abroad. Here, a faithful father had to sneak into his own house, under cover of darkness, to bless his sick children.

Across the road stands the Mansion House—the place where the drama of Emma's life culminated—where she and Joseph received sacred ordinances. Not a shrine, just an old home, restored and inter-esting; visitors file through the lower rooms, some purchasing books and postcards in Emma's kitchen. Only a shallow hole remains where the hotel dining room, with guest bedrooms above, once stood, gutted by a fire. At the end of the street, beside the river, stands the Riverside Mansion, the third and last home, in Old Nauvoo, where Emma spent her last years after her family moved away.

A nephew, Jesse N. Smith, who lived with them before the
martyrdom and his going west, recalled, "I knew that queenly woman
. . . Emma Smith . . . I was greatly impressed with her personality. I
stood in awe of this lady."[1] He said Emma and the other ladies of
Nauvoo looked elegant as they rode in parades or watched Joseph as
he paraded on the Green with the Legion. I think of the Legion—
loyal and true—obeying Joseph's last request to "stay at home," even
when they could have taken terrible revenge upon his murderers. I
think of the many men who served as bodyguards through the years
and the men who went with Joseph and Hyrum to Carthage, yet were
all powerless to stop the sealing sacrifice.

In the dusky parlor of the Mansion House, Emma and Joseph
may have dreamed of his being elected to the presidency of the
United States—did they really hope to achieve that dream? When
Joseph left for the last time, there was no time for him to give his wife
a parting blessing, but he sent her word to write a blessing for herself.
In this home, she described the desires of her heart in this rare document—a true expression of Emma.

The dining hall is long since gone, where she fainted at the sight
of her beloved husband and brother-in-law, lying dead. Damaged by
fire, the dining room was torn down about 1890. But it stood in
Emma's day, where she served meals to the guests in her hotel, from
which she made a modest living. In this house, she wrestled with her
widow's decisions of how to provide for her little children after their
father was killed. Here she lived with her second husband, Lewis C.
Bidamon, whom she married on 23 December 1847, and with his
help, reared her five children.

According to Alexander, they were a "merry household," but in
the year that Joseph III accepted leadership in the Reorganized
Church, Emma worried about the outcome, and "the home circle was
much agitated."[2] Alexander was not religiously inclined nor was
Frederick, although young David Hyrum eagerly joined with his
brother Joseph. Emma seems not to have urged it, but reconciled
herself to the decision, finally gave her support, and prayed for her
sons' success.[3]

Emma's sons, and Julia, reached adulthood and married. From
time to time, each of their families lived in these houses. Joseph III

and his family, in the Old Homestead; Alexander's and David's families shared the Mansion House. Frederick and his wife had lived at the farm, but when Frederick became deathly ill, he was brought home to the Mansion House, where Emma nursed him until he died 13 April 1861. Julia's husband was killed in an explosion on a boat in Texas. She came back to Nauvoo, married again, and for a while, she and her husband ran the hotel for Emma. Lewis Bidamon tore down the old foundation, which was to have supported the grand hotel—the Nauvoo House—and used the brick to build a fine house for Emma, over the very spot where the martyrs were first buried in 1844. In this Riverside Mansion, Emma cared for her mother-in-law during Lucy Mack Smith's last four years, until her death on 14 May 1856.[4] Here, a few years before she died, she faced the sad realization that her youngest son, David Hyrum, was suffering such severe mental dysfunction it was necessary for him to be permanently hospitalized.[5] This tragedy she would refer to as her "living sorrow." For the last seven years of her life, the Riverside Mansion was her home. It was from this house that her dear family came and went, in 1875.

Alexander's daughter, Emma Belle, remembers:

> I knew Emma Smith Bidamon—
> I have heard people say, I wish I could have known Emma Smith, Joseph Smith's wife. I was only a little girl . . . so my memory is that of a little one. She was always neat with her hair nice and smooth. So brown. I . . . saw [her] sit in her low rocker, take down her hair and brush or comb it, part it in the middle and just back of her ears, then comb the back first, roll it and then comb each side carefully till all was smooth, then bring it down over her ears and roll it in with the back hair, then put her comb on each side. Her eyes were brown and sad. She would smile with her lips but to me, as small as I was I never saw the brown eyes smile. I ask[ed] my mother one day, why don't Grandma laugh with her eyes like you do and my mother said because she has a deep sorrow in her heart. When we left Nauvoo for Northern Missouri, we went by boat. And when on the boat we went by the Nauvoo House. There was Grandma at the window waving a tablecloth and as long as we could see her she waved to us a farewell. Mother said Watch children for we'll never see her again. Poor mother wept so she could not see it. To

Mother, that noble woman was all a mother could have been. As I grew older [I] remembered the many times I and my brother Don use to run down from the mansion house to eat breakfast with Grandma and go with her on a trip over the house to see that everything was okay. They are sweet dreams of childhood, as I never saw [her] again . . . .[6]

As promised in her patriarchal blessing, Emma lived to a good old age, and in many ways her last years were her best, for she was settled peacefully in a home at last, although her life was certainly not without sorrow.

In February 1879, seventy-four-year-old Emma was asked by Joseph III and Alexander to relate her early experiences. No one realized at the time that her answers would stand as the only formal record and her last earthly testimony pertaining to the work of the restoration of the Church. In this interview she affirmed, "I know Mormonism to be the truth; and believe the Church to have been established by divine direction."[7]

She died on the anniversary of the birth and death of her twins, 30 April 1879.

Her son, my great-grandfather, Alexander Hale Smith, told of his mother's death when he spoke to a group of students in Bottineau, North Dakota, in 1903. He related that he had been traveling and found himself on a train, within thirty miles of Nauvoo. Something whispered to him to go see his mother, so in a spontaneous moment of decision, he changed trains and made his way toward his old home. As he came in the door he was surprised at not finding his mother in the kitchen where he usually found her. Learning that she was sick, he hurried to her bedside. The moment he saw her, he knew she was not going to recover.

Heartsick, Alexander went immediately to find "Pa Bidamon," and asked if Joseph III had been sent for. Lewis answered that she was not seriously ill, but would soon be up and about. Knowing this was not the case, Alexander hastily sent a telegram to his brother. Then he went into the garden where he bowed down and wept bitterly. His anguished prayer to God was that his mother would not die.

After a while a consoling spirit came to him, informing him that he must let her go, that even if she got well, at best she would have just a few years, and those would be filled with pain and suffering. It was time to let her go. At last, he accepted the will of the Lord, trying to be comforted with the knowledge that she would be with his father, her beloved Joseph.

When Joseph III arrived, they and their adopted sister, Julia, who had come home to help, taking turns staying by their mother's side. At last, when the end was near, they gathered together in the room with their stepfather. Alexander was beside his mother, and Joseph III was across the room. Suddenly she raised up, stretched out her left hand and called, "Joseph! Joseph! Joseph!"

Alexander, thinking she was calling his brother, put his arm around her back and called, "Joseph, Mother wants you." But she fell back on his arm and was gone. With a great feeling of loneliness, Emma's three children comforted one another and wondered about her calling, "Joseph." Joseph III said he heard her say, "Joseph! I am coming!"

The nurse, Sister Revel, who had tended Emma all during her final illness, said, "Do you not know what that means?"

They said they did not. The nurse related that a few nights before, Emma had told her of a dream she had had. In the dream, Emma said Joseph had come to her. He told her to come with him, so she rose from her bed and put on her bonnet and shawl. Then he took her into a beautiful mansion and showed her through the many apartments. In one of the rooms she saw a babe in a cradle. She recognized her little Don Carlos, who had died when he was just over a year old. Snatching him up, she held him to her bosom and asked Joseph, "Where are the rest of my children?"

To this, Joseph had replied, "Be patient, Emma, and you shall have all of your children."

Emma had concluded by telling her nurse that "she saw a personage of light standing beside Joseph, even the Lord Jesus Christ."[8]

After relating this story in Bottineau, North Dakota, Alexander expressed his faith in the glorious day when he hoped that all the family would be reunited in a place where there would never be separation or tears or suffering; a place such as he had just described to the young people in terms he had learned from reading the revelations his father had received. He said:

The gospel of the Lord Jesus Christ is calculated to educate an individual and give him an understanding of the conditions of life and the conditions of death. . . . It is calculated to give the individual . . . understand[ing] that death is but the change from this condition or life, into another condition or life. And the gospel is that which reveals the fact that that part of man which dies, which is the body, passes into the tomb, lies its appointed time in the tomb, and then when the time God has set for it and the trump of God sounds, that body is quickened and brought forth from the tomb, and the spirit of man which never dies takes possession of the body and dwells in that body eternally, either in the heavens above or in the places designed as a punishment. I say that the gospel of the Lord Jesus Christ is the revealment of God relative to these conditions. . . . It is the revealment of God to the human family as to how they ought to live here in this mortal condition, so that when they pass from this mortal condition into the immortal condition they shall have been so educated that they can enter into the presence of, and commune with the holy beings who surround the throne of God.[9]

This son of the Prophet described the future city of Zion, and explained the process by which mortals perfect their lives, gaining self-discipline through daily toil and faith in the Lord Jesus Christ, who said, "In my father's house are many mansions . . . ."

Finally, Alexander concluded, "Do you wonder why, as a son of that mother, I plead for those who believe upon the Lord Jesus Christ and picture their beautiful home in the city of God, in the language that I do, when I realize that my mother occupies, or will occupy one of those beautiful mansions? It may be imagination; but it is grand; it fills me with a grand hope. It enables me to see in the inspiration of God the light and glory and joy and happiness in the city and home of our God, where will dwell the ransomed on this earth, when it shall have been redeemed."[10]

I Wonder, I Marvel

In Nauvoo, there is a kind of brooding peace over the places Emma called home. Standing beside the large granite monument that covers the graves of Emma, Joseph, and Hyrum, Ivor and I tried to sense some feeling of their spirit presence—but there was nothing, only a gentle breeze waving the lilacs and rustling the tall shade trees.

I asked myself, Do I believe? Do I really believe this story? Was my great-great-grandfather a Prophet, or a fool?

I asked myself if a man whose life was full of scandal, who was charged with treason, imprisoned, and killed in an obscure midwestern American town during the nineteenth century, could qualify as a prophet of God.

The scriptures answer: Isaiah was killed, Stephen was stoned to death, the Savior was crucified, and Paul was imprisoned. All were put to death for their testimony that they had personal acquaintance with God. All were killed with the sanction of corrupt leaders and by the people they tried to save. All were accused of treason and blasphemy, as was Joseph Smith. It would seem, then, that rather than being free from earthly scars, prophets must suffer in order to qualify. As the angel Moroni had told him, his name has become known for good and evil throughout the world.

I marvel that after all the injustice suffered by the Prophet and the Saints, they maintained their faith in the Constitution of the United States and in the ultimate triumph of good over evil. I wonder that as a besieged man in a frontier town, Joseph looked to the future and said: "Our name will be handed down to future ages. Our children will rise up and call us blessed and generations yet unborn will dwell with peculiar delight upon the scenes that we have passed through, the almost untiring zeal that we have manifested, the unsurmountable difficulties we have overcome in laying a foundation for a work that will bring about the glories and blessings that they will realize. . . ."[11]

What blessings, I wondered, do we realize? What glories? My mind turned to the testimony of the witnesses of the Book of Mormon. All three of those men broke with the Prophet during his lifetime, yet never denied their testimony of seeing the gold plates, shown to them by an angel, and hearing the voice of God. Two of those witnesses, Oilver Cowdery and Martin Harris, returned to the Church and were accepted back through baptism. David Whitmer never returned to the Church, but with his last breath declared that he had seen what he had seen, and would not deny it. The Book of Mormon, translated through the power of God by the Prophet chosen to set up the Kingdom in the last days, was published at a terrible cost in terms of personal sacrifice, printed in spite of opposition and hatred. Available today in more than eighty languages, it stands with the Bible as another testament to the divinity of our Savior, Jesus Christ.

The prophecies of Daniel are in the process of being fulfilled, and the world cannot perceive it any more than the Jews could recognize Jesus, when he walked among them. Even believers could not comprehend that God, not man, will determine when the Lord will come to reign over His kingdom. That He will come is sure. And in that day, all other kingdoms, governments, and powers shall yield up their power to Christ. In that millennial reign, the lamb and the lion will lie down together, and there will be peace amongst all men. That era could not come without a spiritual revolution. The revolution began in 1820, with a young man's prayer.

I thought about John Howland, who crossed the Atlantic on the *Mayflower* in 1620, and the miracle that saved him from a watery grave. He was an obscure young man and a member of a persecuted and hated people. Yet how much of this generation depends upon his having survived. Neither Joseph nor Emma would have existed, had he perished.

Joseph always maintained that he could not be killed until he had finished his work, which was to build the foundation upon which the kingdom of the last days would be established. Unwittingly, by killing Joseph and Hyrum, the mob set in motion a momentous power which would assure that building would go forward. All who had loved Joseph and Hyrum, and believed in the restoration of the gospel, would give that gospel a loyalty they might have withheld, had Joseph and Hyrum escaped martyrdom.

As the Saints trudged through the Mansion House past the bodies of their dead Prophet and Patriarch, a thousand missionaries were born in a day. Ten thousand mourners made a vow—someday they would build Zion. Until then, they would preach the word!

Led by the Twelve, the Saints went to the West with the clear intention to build upon the foundation Joseph had laid, raising the framework for a great work, which succeeding prophets have continued to define and extend. Today, the Church stands—a mighty fortress—an ensign to the world. It faces into the winds of social prejudice and holds up an unwavering standard of truth and virtue before a desperately wicked world. The Church extends hope in this life, and eternal life and exaltation hereafter, because it has the authority to bless mankind with the fullness of the priesthood ordinances, as well as continual revelation from on high.

Spires on the holy temples, symbols of eternal unity and peace, rise majestically in the Americas, in Asia, in the islands of the sea, and in Europe. With the announcement by President Gordon B. Hinckley of more to be built, soon they will be found in every land on earth. Persecution may rage, governments may rise and fall, and factions of various religious beliefs may ebb and flow, but The Church of Jesus Christ of Latter-day Saints will stand—not to control or infringe on the rights of men, but to bless them and invite them to come unto Jesus Christ. Eventually, faithful Saints, loyal citizens in every land, will worship in peace and rejoice as Joseph said, in all the glories and blessings of the gospel.

When Joseph died, there were about 20,000 members of the Church. Today, the membership is nearly eleven million. While still only a drop in the bucket compared to the mass of humanity, yet it is a vast leavening agent throughout the world.

Emma is honored as the first president of one of the oldest women's organizations in the world. The Relief Society, begun with eighteen women, now has 401,000 members in 160 countries.[12] This organization still has as its motto, "Charity never faileth." This motto, which was defined by a handful of women in Nauvoo in 1842, still continues its magnificent work. There are 73,500 women who are serving in leadership positions in LDS Relief Societies throughout the world. According to the Office of the General Relief Society, there are over 100,000 teaching classes, organizing activities, and coordinating service projects. In 1997, there were 400,000 hours given in the Humanitarian Center in Salt Lake City. During the political upheaval in many nations of the world, The Church of Jesus Christ of Latter-day Saints has provided an ongoing service to provide food and necessities as well as comfort to the needy, regardless of ethnic, political, or religious affiliation.

As Emma had hoped, when she spoke to the women of the Nauvoo Relief Society, this organization has risen to meet many emergencies and provided extraordinary service worldwide. And, as she also suggested, by living honorably, serving mankind, and keeping the commandments of God, the Latter-day Saint people have become respectable, "here and everywhere else."

Among the tributes of respect spoken at her funeral, it was said of Emma: "Was it not her loving hand, her consoling and comforting words, her unswerving integrity, fidelity, and devotion, her wise counsel, that assisted to make this latter-day work a success? If God raised up a Joseph as a prophet and a restorer of gospel truth, then did he also raise up an Emma as a helpmeet for him."[13]

Emma's glory—to be chosen to preside—to be the first among all women in this dispensation to receive the endowment—chosen to stand beside her husband, to be companion throughout eternity, to the Prophet who was chosen to open the dispensation of the fullness of times.

Joseph went to Carthage to die, knowing it before he went. He sealed his testimony with his own blood, for it is decreed, "The testimony of the testator is not in force until after the death of the testator."[14] Emma's sacrifice—to endure poverty and persecution for the sake of the gospel, yes—but most of all, the sacrament of widowhood, administered to her without her consent—yet, ultimately, the means through which her full measure of glory is assured. Theirs was a divine mission; together, they offered up a sacrifice–together they laid a foundation.

Standing in the shadow of the Old Homestead, Ivor and I speak of these things. The humidity and heat seem to wrap around us. I look up at the vacant, gleaming windows of the old Riverside Mansion, and I shiver in the August sunlight. For a moment Emma's image seems to hover in my mind's eye. I imagine her there at the window, waving to her beloved family. Yearning, I reach out to her. Although she is gone—and her sons, Joseph, Frederick,[15] Alexander, and David are gone—Julia too[16]—and Alexander's little wife, Lizzie,[17] whom Emma raised—and even the grandchildren are gone—and here am I, a fourth-generation granddaughter. My heart turns to Emma. I feel her reaching to me. I forget the span of years. I feel very, very close to them all.

Resume

Spanning the tenure of her mortal stay
Grim Life and Fate their outsize portions dealt;
Her mammoth need to succor keenly felt—
Her days an inspiration—or an anguished fray.
Love spurred her on—to taste both fire and ice.
No moan, nor cry—yet flame exacts its toll.
All heights and depths etched deeply on her soul
The blaze of glory, and the sacrifice.

Alice Lowe Corbett[18]

Notes

1. Jesse N. Smith, *Six Decades in the Early West: The Journal of Jesse Nathaniel Smith, 1834-1906,* ed. Oliver R. Smith, Jesse N. Smith Family Association, Provo, Utah, 1970. 3rd ed.

2. Inez Davis, *Story of Alexander Hale Smith, Journal History,* vol. 4, p. 4. Typescript copy in possession of author.

3. It is often asked, did Emma join the Reorganized Church? The answer is that the Reorganized Church recognized itself as "The Church"; therefore, by her baptism in 1830, Emma was a member already. Another question is asked, was Emma excommunicated by the Church leaders in Utah? The answer to this question is, she was not. By virtue of her having had her calling and election sealed upon her, during her lifetime, nothing short of deliberate shedding of innocent blood could separate her from the glories and blessings promised her, notwithstanding she had to suffer the buffetings of Satan. Who can say she did not?

Her letters reflect that she supported her sons in their efforts and she was proud of them, as they were upstanding men who sincerely tried to do right, as they saw it.

4. Lucy Mack Smith's death date has been found to be wrong in early publications: it is as stated in the text.

5. David Hyrum's mental breakdown was a severe hardship for the entire family. He had become mentally confused, and as Joseph III relates in his *Memoirs,* on 17 January 1877, he "had the unhappy responsibility of committing [his] brother David to the hospital at Elgin, Ill." (p. 174). The diagnosis was hopeless insanity. Examination of medical records shows that he died of diabetes, thirty years after he was committed. The symptoms of his illness have led modern doctors to speculate that he may have suffered from an uncontrolled case of hypoglycemia, which a careful diet might have alleviated. Emma had no consolation in such information, which comes only in modern days. Surely it would have broken Emma's heart to see her handsome son's brilliant mind and talent fade away into a living death in a hospital

for the insane. See Mary Audentia Smith Anderson, ed., *Memoirs of President Joseph Smith III—1832-1914*. (Independence, Mo.: Herald Publishing House, 1979).

6. Journal of Emma Belle Smith Kennedy, copy in author's possession; spelling and punctuation have been corrected. Emma Belle's journal is hand written. The daughter of Alexander Hale and Elizabeth Kendall Smith, she was about six years old when the family left Nauvoo in 1875. We might consider if the sorrow clouding Emma's eyes was uniquely due to the martyrdom of Joseph. According to family history, there was abundant reason for Emma's eyes to be sorrowful in 1874-75. Her sons were leaving Illinois, settling in Iowa, and Missouri. Joseph III had every intention of moving the headquarters of the church to Independence, Missouri, which he eventually did. This may also have been a worry, but the real problem was David Hyrum's illness.

7. Emma Hale Smith Bidamon, *Emma Smith's Last Testimony*, February 1879, Reorganized Church of Jesus Christ of Latter Day Saints (RLDS) Archives, Independence, Mo.

8. Alexander Hale Smith, "Sermon at Bottineau, N. D.," given on 1 July 1903; reprinted in *Zion's Ensign*, 31 December 1903.

9. Ibid.

10. Ibid.

11. Joseph Smith, Editorial, *Times and Seasons* (2 May 1842), 3:775-76.

12. LDS Church vital statistics report, *Ensign*, April 1995.

13. *Memoirs of President Joseph Smith III*, p. 186; see also "Emma's Funeral Service" preached by Mark H. Forscutt, RLDS Archives.

14. See Hebrews 9:16-18.

15. Frederick Granger Williams Smith died April 1862.

16. Buddy Youngreen, *Reflections of Emma, Joseph Smith's Wife* (Orem, Utah: Grandin Book, 1982), p. 80. Julia Murdock Smith was born to John and Julia Clapp Murdock, 1 May 1831. She remained with Emma until 1850 when she married Elisha Dixon. After Dixon's tragic death, Julia returned to live with Emma, until about 1857, when she married John Middleton. This marriage failed and Julia again returned to Nauvoo where she remained until Emma's death in 1879. Julia died a year and a half after Emma, of cancer.

17. Lizzie's full name was Elizabeth Agnes Kendall. Her parents joined the Church in England and were preparing to sail to America when her father, John Kendall, an Elder in the Church, was killed in an accident. Elizabeth's mother, Elizabeth Millikin Kendall, brought her three children, John, Isabelle, and Elizabeth, and sailed as planned, arriving in Nauvoo, about 1848. She made friends with Emma Smith Bidamon. She remarried and later died when Lizzie was about six. When the girl was ten years old, her stepfamily took her to Nauvoo and put her out on the street in front of a house, where a friend of her mother lived. This woman took her to Emma, who took her in and raised her as her own. She married Alexander Hale Smith.

18. Alice Lowe Corbett, author of this poem is a great-great-granddaughter of Joseph's uncle John Smith, through his son John Lyman Smith, who married Augusta Bowen, a daughter of Sarah M. Cleveland, Emma's friend in Quincy, and later counselor in the Relief Society in Nauvoo.

Author's Note

In historical research, one often deals with many disturbing factors. The first task is to find sources from which to learn about the events of the past. Then comes the task of evaluating the information that is found, a process that requires absolute consistency with what is already known as truth. The researcher must also evaluate any possible bias of the informant, weigh the value of the source, and come face to face with his or her own prejudice.

Much of the information in this book comes from Joseph Smith's history, *The History of the Church of Jesus Christ of Latter-day Saints (HC)*. The seven volumes, edited by B. H. Roberts, have served as my chief source although I have searched through and used many books. Concerning Joseph Smith's journal history, it is important to remember that his words were not necessarily in his own writing. It was often dictated, frequently recorded in the first person by his scribes, with whom he worked closely. Joseph often spent his evenings reviewing and revising his history—not to change facts, but to clarify the facts that had been recorded. The scribes were men he trusted, at the time, to faithfully record the important events and actions of his life.

In this book, as I have referred to Joseph's history, I have taken at face value those entries that indicate his opinions, feelings, and concerns, without attempting to distinguish when one of his scribes may have made the entry attributed to Joseph in the first person. In some entries, it is clear and has been noted in the text. For me, the published *History of the Church of Jesus Christ of Latter-day Saints* serves as a foundational document for studying Joseph's life. While there are those who debate and quibble over syntax or authorship, I feel confident, after years of examining some of the debated issues, that for the most part the scribes did a very good job.

I have had to confront the issue of how one's personal bias—one's ability to handle the discoveries, weigh them honestly, and use them in their correct context—has affected the writing of this book. After many years of working with the same material over and over, I am discovering answers to some questions that have eluded me for a long time. I admit that for years I turned a blind eye to some issues I just didn't want to deal with. Recently I had an experience that helped me understand Emma and her sons better than I ever did before. I will attempt to explain.

One of the most frequent statements I have found in LDS sources has to do with the apparently deliberate blindness of Emma's sons concerning some of Joseph's teachings during his lifetime: namely, that of the doctrine of eternal marriage, which included plural marriage, and also the "endowment," which was to be continued in the proper place, the temple. Although these teachings have been documented in contemporary sources, Joseph's sons did not teach the temple ordinances or other doctrines the Prophet had introduced, in spite of the fact that they became mighty preachers. To the contrary, they spent their lives contending that their father was never "guilty" of polygamy or anything like unto it.

The Church leaders in Utah told them to ask Emma, and they did finally ask her, just weeks before she died. According to *The History of the Reorganized Church of Latter-Day Saints,* Joseph Smith III, then president of the Reorganized Church, and Alexander Hale Smith, then Patriarch and Counselor in that church, visited Emma expressly for this purpose. Their visited lasted from 1 February to 10 February in 1879. At that time, the headquarters for the RLDS church was in Lamoni, Iowa. Emma was still living in Nauvoo.

Joseph III and Alexander went to see Emma with the particular intention of questioning her on the things they had avoided discussing with her for all those years—polygamy. They even prepared their questions beforehand. The printed version of this interview was published in the *Saints Herald* (as noted in footnotes on the text of this book, October 1879) after Emma died. Since this was the last interview they had with Emma, they considered it to be in the nature of a last testimony and gave it that title. It was not a sworn statement nor attested to by her as such; it only held that distinctive characterization in their eyes. It became thereafter, for her sons, and subsequently many of her posterity, as veritable truth.

The two men began by apologizing to their mother for bringing up painful subjects, then quizzed her on polygamy and asked if their father had been an adulterer. She said he was not an adulterer and indicated that he did not introduce polygamy. Her answers seem strange in light of what we know she knew at the time, and we are left to wonder if she had forgotten or deliberately chose to answer her sons questions falsely. It has been a point of contention ever since.

Her sons would not see her again until shortly before her death two and a half months later. They undoubtedly returned to their homes in Lamoni satisfied that they had done their duty by asking Emma the hard questions and obtaining from her the facts they felt they needed. With their interview behind them, it is doubtful they even considered bringing it back to her for her review. For them, her answers were sufficient to justify their continued opposition against any suggestion that their father had introduced polygamy, or the doctrines they believed were being taught in Utah, which they assumed to be based upon John C. Bennett's evil assertions. To them, this doctrine was synonymous with adultery, and once they had their mother's word that their father was not an adulterer, they were satisfied.

As I was completing this book, an article came into my hands which served to explain the mindset of Joseph III, Alexander, and possibly Emma, regarding these things. Richard Price, who heads an ultra-conservative faction of Restorationists and who has been excommunicated from the RLDS church, published an article in his magazine, *Vision* (published in Independence, Missouri), called "Joseph Smith Fought Polygamy?" The article quotes the scandalous statements made by Bennett in his flamboyant exposé of Mormonism. The text is disgusting, even sickening, as Bennett purports to reveal all the sacred ordinances performed in the temple. After quoting these fallacious statements, Price comments that Latter-day Saints in Utah will surely recognize the words of Bennett's description of the temple ceremonies.

However, the distortion is such that no temple-going Latter-day Saint would recognize anything whatsoever in the things described— but who is there to refute Price's absolute certainty that they are the same? Price has dedicated his life and energy to wage an all-out campaign continuing Joseph III's war, claiming that the prophet Joseph Smith would not and could not ever be guilty of such things.

After reading what Bennett published in his expose, I was finally able to understand that what Emma was denying, and what her sons were attempting to refute, were the evils published by Bennett, which he purported to be the truth. Although nothing could have been further from the truth, Emma's sons simply took Bennett's word that this was what the Mormons in Utah believed. Far across the country from Illinois, Brigham Young and the church leaders in Utah were faithfully building on the true principles Joseph had taught. They could not have understood the forces at play in the minds of the Prophet's sons.

When Joseph III and Alexander fought against what they believed to be the teachings of Brigham Young and the Church in Utah, it came from sincere hearts made indignant at the implications Bennett had imposed on the public mind against Joseph Smith and from misrepresentations filtered to them from apostates. When the Church leaders in Utah heard of Joseph III and Alexander's denunciation of what was to them a sacred and true doctrine, they naturally responded with anger at the apparent duplicity of Emma, whom they wrongfully blamed—in part due to this so-called "last testimony."

I had carefully read this "testimony" many times, and then one day as I was reading, I suddenly realized that this interview was not a sworn testimony at all, but merely an interview with an aged woman whose memory was not entirely clear. For example, when Emma was asked the question, "How many infants did you lose?" she answered that she had lost three. She mentions the firstborn son and the twins. She also mentions the adopted Murdock twins. But, I now saw, she did not mention her other lost infants. I can understand she might not recall the stillborn son she lost in early 1842. But how could she have forgotten little Don Carlos, who lived to be thirteen months old? She is quoted as having said it was the most painful loss because she had him longer. Wouldn't she have mentioned losing him as well as the others?

This lapse sent me on a search through Joseph Smith III's memoirs and the biography of Alexander Hale Smith. Neither makes any mention of this child; his name appears only within the text of Emma's obituary, which could easily have been added by the editor of the memoirs. What's going on here? I asked myself. It appeared that neither Joseph III nor Alexander remembered the little brother. One explanation is that they were only nine and three at the time, so it's not too surprising. Emma was in her seventies, so her lapse in memory is perhaps also understandable. They also went through much that they no doubt preferred to forget.

Shortly before Emma died, she told her nurse of a vision she had had. As I have studied her interview with her sons and the account of her vision, I realized that the vision did not spring out of a vacuum, but must have been the fruit of much pondering and remembering on her part. In the weeks after her sons left on 10 February, Emma was growing weary; she frequently had "bad spells" and took to her bed. Wouldn't many people, in failing health, begin to ponder the past? Did she consider the questions her sons had asked, and did thinking about those questions open the door to long-forgotten memories? Did she pray, asking whether the promises made to her and Joseph for time and eternity would come to pass?

I believe this could easily be the circumstances that led to her vision at the end of her life—the vision that dispels these conflicting issues. Emma saw her baby, Don Carlos (the one she did not mention in her interview). With joy, she took him up in her arms and asked the poignant question, "Joseph, where are the rest of my children?" She lost not three but five little babies (six counting little Joseph Murdock), and she wanted to know where they are.

Joseph's reply was, "Be patient Emma, and you shall have all of your children," a promise that, for me, dispels the implications left by the interview that there were no eternal covenants or ordinances made in the past. In fact, there *were* eternal promises made to Emma and Joseph, ordinances and endowments revealed through Joseph Smith, certainly not degrading and evil as those purported by John C. Bennett, but divine in nature—eternal in their scope for blessing not only Emma and Joseph, but all people.

I have concluded that if Joseph was a prophet, and I knew that he was, then the doctrines he revealed were true and that succeeding prophets have also been given authority according to their times. Hence, I knew that in 1890, Wilford Woodruff was inspired, as prophet, seer, and revelator, to issue the Manifesto ending the practice of plural marriage in the Church. (See D&C Official Declaration–1.)

Any time I discuss the doctrine of plural marriage, I want to include my strong testimony that Wilford Woodruff was equally called of God, as was Joseph, and had authority, if so directed by the Lord, to change the policy of the Church regarding the practice. I believe he was so directed. And I for one am heartily glad of it.

As to discussing more deeply what Emma's feelings were, we cannot possibly know what she felt. People have speculated and written and documented their point of view. But the fact is, we don't know what Emma felt. I personally can leave it at that.

It has always been a popular technique in the world to try to sensationalize various subjects in order to ridicule the Church, as if there were something shameful in the past for the Church to live down. Mostly this sensationalism is done using information from unenlightened sources with the intent to alienate people from believing, or even investigating the possibility, that God has in fact called prophets in these latter-days, as in ancient times.

From the time of Josephs death, a succession of men have held the office of President and prophet of the LDS Church. All have led the work with the gifts and talents they possessed, and with faith, humility, and honor; each has labored to build the kingdom of God, in order to establish a people committed to becoming pure in heart, or Zion.

The Church of Jesus Christ of Latter-day Saints is serving a mortal ministry designed to prepare its members for the Second Coming of the Lord Jesus Christ. If there are questions about this work, let them be asked of reliable spokespersons for The Church of Jesus Christ of Latter-day Saints. There are 60,000 missionaries in the world serving on their own time, unpaid representatives of this great work, taking the good news of the restoration of the gospel of Jesus Christ to every nation, kindred, tongue, and people. Theirs is the responsibility and calling to teach the truth to people throughout the world.

It is the desire of my heart that people will read the Book of Mormon and Pearl of Great Price, and study the modern revelations that came through the Prophet Joseph Smith. If they will do this and study the Bible, as well as the words that come through living prophets today, they will be enlightened with truth.

Standing as a testament to this truth are the remarkable lives of the Prophet Joseph and his wife, Emma Smith.

INDEX